Allies Divided

CSIA Studies in International Security

Michael E. Brown, Sean M. Lynn-Jones, and Steven E. Miller, series editors
Karen Motley, executive editor
Center for Science and International Affairs (CSIA)
John F. Kennedy School of Government, Harvard University

Published by The MIT Press:

Allison, Graham T., Owen R. Coté, Jr., Richard A. Falkenrath, and Steven E. Miller, *Avoiding Nuclear Anarchy: Containing the Threat of Loose Russian Nuclear Weapons and Fissile Material* (1996)

Allison, Graham T., and Kalypso Nicolaïdis, eds., *The Greek Paradox: Promise vs. Performance* (1996)

Brown, Michael E., ed., *The International Dimensions of Internal Conflict* (1996)

Elman, Miriam Fendius, ed., *Paths to Peace: Is Democracy the Answer?* (1997)

Falkenrath, Richard A., *Shaping Europe's Military Order: The Origins and Consequences of the CFE Treaty* (1994)

Feldman, Shai, *Nuclear Weapons and Arms Control in the Middle East* (1996)

Forsberg, Randall, ed., *The Arms Production Dilemma: Contraction and Restraint in the World Combat Aircraft Industry* (1994)

Shields, John M., and William C. Potter, eds., *Dismantling the Cold War: U.S. and NIS Perspectives on the Nunn-Lugar Cooperative Threat Reduction Program* (1997)

Published by Brassey's, Inc.:

Blackwill, Robert D., and Sergei A. Karaganov, eds., *Damage Limitation or Crisis? Russia and the Outside World* (1994)

Johnson, Teresa Pelton, and Steven E. Miller, eds., *Russian Security After the Cold War: Seven Views from Moscow* (1994)

Mussington, David, *Areas Unbound: The Globalization of Defense Production* (1994)

Published by CSIA:

Allison, Graham, Ashton B. Carter, Steven E. Miller, and Philip Zelikow, eds., *Cooperative Denuclearization: From Pledges to Deeds* (1993)

Campbell, Kurt M., Ashton B. Carter, Steven E. Miller, and Charles A. Zraket, *Soviet Nuclear Fission: Control of the Nuclear Arsenal in a Disintegrating Soviet Union* (1991)

Allies Divided
Transatlantic Policies for the Greater Middle East

Editors
Robert D. Blackwill
Michael Stürmer

CSIA Studies in International Security

The MIT Press
Cambridge, Massachusetts
London, England

© 1997 by the Center for Science and International Affairs
John F. Kennedy School of Government
Harvard University
Cambridge, Massachusetts 02138
(617) 495-1400

Library of Congress Cataloging-in-Publication Data

Allies divided: transatlantic policies for the Greater Middle East / Robert D. Blackwill
and Michael Stürmer, editors.
p.   cm.—(CSIA studies in international security)
Includes bibliographical references and index.
ISBN 0-262-52244-6 (pbk.: alk. paper)
1. Europe—Foreign relations—Middle East. 2. United States—Foreign relations—Middle
East. 3. Middle East—Foreign relations—Europe. 4. Middle East—Foreign relations—
United States. 5. International cooperation. I. Blackwill, Robert D. II. Stürmer, Michael.
III. Series.
D1065.M628A44   1997
327.56—dc21   97-21781
                                                                                    CIP

10 9 8 7 6 5 4 3 2 1
Printed in the United States of America

Contents

Acknowledgments

Over the past year, this book, co-sponsored by the Center for Science and International Affairs (CSIA) at Harvard University's John F. Kennedy School of Government and by Germany's Research Institute for International Affairs (Stiftung Wissenschaft und Politik, or SWP), has benefited from the assistance of many people. We are especially appreciative of the contribution made by Dr. Shai Feldman, Senior Research Associate at CSIA, who assisted in the planning stages of this project and read early drafts of each of the chapters. Both his insightful comments and those of German diplomat Detlof von Berg at Harvard's Center for International Affairs were useful in focusing each author's remarks and holding all to a prescriptive, rather than purely analytical, outlook. We would also like to thank Dr. Graham Fuller at RAND and Professor Rémy Leveau of the Centre Marc Bloch in Berlin for their presentations at the authors' conference on the subject of political Islam.

We gratefully acknowledge our staffs, who worked together over very long distances to collect contributions and ensure that this project remained on track. Our warm thanks go to Saskia Hieber of SWP, who managed all of the issues that arose on the European side, as well as to Kristin Archick of the Kennedy School of Government, who read drafts of chapters and assisted with our authors' conference. We are especially indebted to Lisa Slouffman, also of the Kennedy School, who has provided research and logistical support for every part of this project, from the preliminary research to the revisions of the final proofs. Karen Motley, Executive Editor of the CSIA Studies in International Security, has been helpful in guiding this manuscript through the latter stages of the publication process. Special thanks go to our editor, Teresa J. Lawson; without her invaluable advice and talent, this volume would surely not have been knitted together in the end.

Finally, we wish to express our gratitude to each of the authors whose contributions appear in this volume, for without their knowledge and their good nature in meeting our deadlines, this book would not have been completed.

Robert D. Blackwill
Center for Science and
International Affairs
Cambridge, Mass.

Michael Stürmer
Stiftung Wissenschaft
und Politik
Ebenhausen, Germany

April 1997

Allies Divided

Introduction

Robert D. Blackwill and
Michael Stürmer

The end of the Cold War has upset many of the old faultlines in the Middle East. It has removed Soviet military support for Arab regimes and has allowed massive Jewish immigration into Israel. Above all, it has shown again that neither the East-West divide nor the Arab-Israeli conflict are the sole sources of strife and upheaval.

The demise of the Soviet Union has also resulted in an expansion of "the Greater Middle East" itself, adding the Muslim lands of Central Asia to the region. Choosing a term with which to designate this entire area is not, in fact, a particularly easy task. In 1980, the *Washington Post* noted that "U.S. lack of experience and precision about the region is so great that there is continuing uncertainty about what to call it—the Middle East, Greater Middle East, Indian Ocean, Persian Gulf or Southwest Asia. All have been tried." In this volume we use the term "the Greater Middle East" for conceptual and strategic reasons. By this we mean the huge area from North Africa through Egypt, Israel and the Tigris-Euphrates valley, through the Persian Gulf region into Turkey and on to the Caspian basin.

We use this expansive geopolitical and territorial concept because we believe that parts of this area will increasingly influence other parts, and that Transatlantic policies should more and more take into account the growing web of interrelationships throughout the region.[1] A few of these inter-relationships are:

---

1. A word about Russia: the future of that enormously turbulent country will cast a shadow over much of what is discussed in this book. However, since this is a treatment of U.S.-European relations in the context of the Greater Middle East, we leave aside in this book the role Russia plays in this immense area. That is not to suggest that Russian influence in the region is intrinsically unimportant. To the contrary, in many of the substantive subjects of this volume, cooperation between

- a victory of Islamic extremism in Algeria would send shock waves all the way to Turkey and into Central Asia;
- a catastrophic breakdown in the Arab-Israeli peace process would weaken moderate governments throughout the Greater Middle East and complicate the West's interaction with most nations discussed here;
- the introduction into this area of additional weapons of mass destruction would dramatically change the strategic dynamic not only between Israel and its neighbors, but among the Islamic states themselves, and would also crucially affect U.S. power projection into the region;
- development of Caspian basin oil reserves will increasingly influence a variety of local and Western calculations regarding the future of energy supplies from the Persian Gulf.

Thus our aim in this book is to look at the sweep of trends from this entire area that will require policy responses from the United States and Europe.

Both Europe and the United States have vital national interests in the Greater Middle East. Throughout the history of the Occident, the Greater Middle East has played significant strategic, cultural, and religious roles as the gateway to trade in the East, the birthplace of Christianity and, more recently, as a primary energy supplier to the West. There is a certain irony in the fact that Europeans claim closer, longer, and more broadly based intimacy with Middle Eastern affairs, yet it is the Americans who now wield decisive influence in the region. However, no Western power has been safe without some measure of influence or control over the southern and eastern shores of the Mediterranean.

Ever since the Romans divided the vastness of their holdings between Rome and Constantinople, no power has managed complete control of the seas from the island of Aphrodite—today's divided Cyprus—to the pillars of Hercules at the Straits of Gibraltar. In the crusades of the High Middle Ages, knights and others who had been seduced by religious fervor attempted to recapture for Europe the birthplace of Christianity. Although ultimately they lost, 300 years of intermittent battle for the region profited the Europeans greatly in cultural and intellectual terms. During the Renaissance, the Europeans were slowly driven out of the eastern Mediterranean by

---

Russia and the Transatlantic community would make successful Western policies much more likely.

the Turkish fleet, but with the decline of the Ottoman Empire in the nineteenth century, European empires again turned their attention to this area. Britain and Russia began competing against each other in the "Great Game." Germany and Italy attempted to assert the ascendance of their newly unified nations by establishing colonies in the Middle East. From 1914 to 1943, when the last Axis troops were driven out of North Africa, the battle for power over the Mediterranean remained by and large undecided, except for the British protectorate over Egypt.

Although the U.S. Marine Corps anthem celebrates victory in the region, the United States was not substantially involved in its commerce, politics, or strategy until World War II drew it into the North African and Mediterranean theaters of war. V-Day in Europe, however, brought mounting suspicion, buttressed by archival evidence seized in occupied Germany, that the Soviets entertained expansionist designs on Turkey and the Dardanelles. After a conspicuous visit of the battleship USS *Missouri* in the Bosporus, President Harry S. Truman declared, in a message to both houses of Congress, that another totalitarian threat had emerged and that the United States would in the future have to play the protective role in the eastern Mediterranean that the depleted European nations were no longer able to fulfill.

For four decades, U.S. involvement in the region was defined by this threat, as well as by U.S. interests in the unencumbered flow of oil and in the security of the Jewish state. After the ill-fated British, French, and Israeli expedition into Suez in 1956 and the British withdrawal from the lands east of Suez in 1961, the United States took over the role of security guarantor in the region. The most beneficial result of U.S. policy in the Middle East has been relative overall stability in the region. In 1973, when Israel was forced into the Yom Kippur War, Israel's survival was assured by the United States as much as by Israel's triumph over the Arab forces. After this point, the United States assumed the role of peacemaker in the Middle East, becoming the third party to the peace negotiations; it acted not as an empire or as a peace enforcer with an agenda of its own, but as a catalyst interested in keeping the process on track. This relegated the Europeans, however, to a marginal role of providing economic aid for Middle Eastern governments and military support for the United States in the Gulf War.

The 1991 Gulf War was the high-water mark of U.S.-European cooperation in the Greater Middle East since Israel's establishment in 1948.

Transatlantic diplomacy led by the United States confronted Saddam Hussein with a unified Western front that uniformly insisted that Iraq withdraw from Kuwait or be forcibly expelled. Allied military forces joined American partners in their most extraordinary military success since the end of World War II. The result was a great Western victory that restored general stability to the Persian Gulf and ensured that Saddam Hussein was contained.

The U.S.-European harmony looks much different today. On virtually every issue that radiates from this vast area, the United States and the European Union (EU), led by France, hold different views on how best to protect Western interests and avoid emerging threats.[2] As Israel's closest ally, the United States tends to take a more sympathetic approach to Israeli concerns than do the Europeans. This is likely to produce ever more Transatlantic friction if negotiations between Israel and the Palestinians over final status issues move forward.[3] Washington's policy of "dual containment" of Iraq and Iran is not supported by the allies, who doubt that either of these approaches is sustainable over the period ahead, while the United States worries that European engagement will undermine Western deterrence of these two "rogue states" (a U.S. slogan that seems too simple-minded for many Europeans). In the Gulf, national economic stakes produced by energy dependence and commercial rivalries are so large on both sides of the Atlantic, and instability and violence in the area are so likely, that future discord between Washington on one hand and Brussels and European capitals on the other seems inevitable.[4]

Turkey and the Caspian basin are more probable bones of contention between Europe and the United States. In Washington, there is mounting frustration that the European Union seems unable to understand that the future of Turkey is a crucial geopolitical challenge for the West; instead EU negotiations with Ankara bog down in agricultural quotas, import duties, and alleged religious and cultural intolerance in Brussels. The EU has little sympathy for this U.S. perspective as it struggles with its simultaneous deepening and

---

2. For a broad treatment of U.S. and European approaches in the Greater Middle East, see Chapter 1 by Robert Satloff and Chapter 2 by Eberhard Rhein.

3. Richard N. Haass and Volker Perthes elaborate on U.S. and European policies toward the Arab-Israeli peace process in Chapters 3 and 4.

4. See Chapter 5 by Geoffrey Kemp and Chapter 6 by Johannes Reissner on the Persian Gulf.

widening, while shrinking from the daunting prospect of trying to bring Turkey into the European family (no Western government seems yet to have adopted policies that accurately reflect the growing strategic importance of Caspian basin energy resources and Central Asia).[5] With respect to preventing the introduction of weapons of mass destruction into the Greater Middle East, neither side of the Atlantic is doing nearly enough. However, with all their other preoccupations, the Europeans seem particularly myopic on this subject, which potentially represents the single most serious threat emanating from this area to Western vital interests.[6]

Finally, there is no Transatlantic consensus on the role of military force in coping with the problems of the Greater Middle East. The United States continues to develop increased military options through technological advances and enhanced force projection capabilities, options that allies worry may outrun American wisdom regarding when to use and when not to use force. At the same time, Europe falls further behind in military proficiency as it cuts defense budgets and develops a political culture that, within the EU, often appears to exclude a muscular approach and to conclude that the use of force is not a last resort, but no resort at all.[7]

How to manage these differences while at the same time pursuing constructive policies in the region is the subject of this book. We have gathered preeminent U.S. and European analysts to examine these issues together and to prescribe ways in which Transatlantic cooperation can reverse this troubling trend. This is not primarily a book about the Greater Middle East; rather, it is a book about Transatlantic relations regarding the Greater Middle East. We also wish to stress that policy prescription is the essence of this volume. Social science analytical techniques and regional expertise here serve the object of producing practical suggestions for policymakers. Not every policy idea in this book can or should be implemented; indeed some of them are mutually exclusive. But we do hope that we can help stimulate a more intense Transatlantic policy debate on how U.S.-European

---

5. Transatlantic policies toward Turkey and the Caspian basin are considered in Chapter 7 by F. Stephen Larrabee and Chapter 8 by Heinz Kramer and Friedemann Müller.

6. Chapter 9 by Richard A. Falkenrath and Chapter 10 by Joanna Spear discuss weapons of mass destruction in greater detail.

7. For further discussion of Transatlantic policies on military force projection in the Greater Middle East, see Chapter 11 by Richard L. Kugler and Chapter 12 by François Heisbourg.

cooperation regarding this crucial area can be heightened. A failure of cooperation would surely threaten vital and important national Western interests related to the Greater Middle East.

Chapter 1

America, Europe, and the Middle East in the 1990s: Interests and Policies

Robert Satloff

Differences of history, geography, economics, and demography set the framework for the U.S. and European relationships to the Middle East. Ironically, Europe—both as individual states and as a collective unit—can claim a longer, closer, and more organic connection with the Middle East than can America. However, while it has interests in the region that are more vital, immediate, and strategic, it is the distant power from across the Atlantic that has come to wield defining political influence and military power.

In the three decades since the Six Day War of 1967 and the British withdrawal from Aden four years later, Americans and Europeans have maintained an informal division of labor regarding the Middle East. According to this formula, the United States has been recognized as the leader of Western efforts on the two main regional projects: promoting Arab-Israeli peacemaking and maintaining Gulf security. The Europeans have generally limited their role to affirming, supporting, and financing U.S. initiatives; pursuing particularistic economic and political interests in various corners of the region; and sometimes summoning the strength to adopt positions that might set them apart from Washington in problematic but usually nonthreatening ways. While this secondary status may have rankled some Europeans given Europe's geographic proximity, historical connection, and organic economic and demographic links to the area, its logic was dictated by four key factors: Cold War competition with the Soviets, the legacy of

The author thanks Rachel Ingber, research assistant at The Washington Institute, for her invaluable assistance in preparing this paper.

European colonialism (especially in contrast with America's relatively untainted engagement with the Middle East), European weakness and divisions, and the ability of the United States to project power—political, military, and economic—into the region. This division of labor was on display most clearly in 1990–91, when Europeans dutifully joined the U.S.-led coalition to evict Saddam Hussein from Kuwait (after one particular European reportedly stiffened President Bush's resolve), and then just as dutifully sat with only observer status at the Arab-Israeli peace conference in Madrid.

As is so often the case, however, the best example of a trend may also have been the last. Events over the past decade have chipped away at the foundation of this U.S.-European understanding over the Middle East, leaving it fractured and vulnerable. The most important change was the demise of the Soviet Union. This seismic event had numerous implications for regional (let alone global) politics, including enlarging the very definition of the Middle East to include the Muslim republics of the former Soviet Union. In terms of the U.S.-European-Middle Eastern triangle, its main impact was twofold: to loosen the Cold War constraints that had previously restricted European activity, and to provoke a rethinking of European security that led many in Europe (especially in France, Italy, and Spain) to focus as much on the South (the Mediterranean) as on the East (Eastern and Central Europe). In contrast to the traditional military fear of the Soviets marching into Germany, the main concern of many southern Europeans was economic and social, namely, the impact of Islamic fundamentalism on the stability of North African states, with its potential to create a massive flow of Muslim refugees to Europe. This redirection and enlargement of European interests did not occur in a vacuum; on the contrary, it developed in the 1990s against the backdrop of a bloody civil war inside North Africa's largest state—Algeria—that brought the threat of the very tide of unwelcome migration Europeans feared most, and it was fed more recently by the coming to power of an Islamist prime minister in another country—Turkey—whose military power Europeans welcomed but whose cultural and social expansion Europeans kept at arm's length.

In addition to this southward tilt of European interests, a number of other critical developments have come together in the 1990s to help erode the quarter-century-old U.S.-European compact over the Middle East. These range across a spectrum of economic, political, and strategic interests. In commercial terms, this includes increased European chafing at the growth of U.S.-Middle Eastern (and especially

U.S.-Gulf) commerce at Europe's expense,[1] exacerbated first by U.S. ability to secure Gulf arms contracts in the aftermath of the Gulf War,[2] and then by UN sanctions on Iraq and U.S. efforts to isolate Iran, which tended to deny Europe access to important traditional markets. Thus, the United States enjoyed unprecedented commercial success in the Arab Gulf. In the diplomatic arena, the U.S.-European relationship has been vexed by the growing contrast between, on the one hand, U.S. dominance in "peace process" diplomacy and the deepening U.S. reluctance to provide supporting funds for the peace process (beyond the historic Camp David commitments to Egypt and Israel) and, on the other hand, the exclusion of Europe from a co-sponsor role in the diplomacy despite its provision of nearly 50 percent of all international support to Palestinian economic development and other regional support schemes.

More generally, a third factor in the decline of Transatlantic agreement is a sense of frustration combined with urgency among many Europeans that independent initiatives—on issues ranging from Mediterranean cooperation to the Arab-Israeli peace process—provide an opportunity to exert the common energies of the European Union (EU) in ways that would not only be useful and constructive but that might also right the perceived wrong of European bungling on Bosnia to the world Muslim community.[3] And fourth, the election in France of a neo-Gaullist president committed to asserting French influence in the Middle East via an activist, independent Middle East

---

1. The U.S. share of overall Middle East imports has grown from 11 percent in 1990 to 13.3 percent in 1995, with the European share decreasing from 45.5 percent in 1990 to 43.8 percent in 1995. Compiled from *Direction of Trade Statistics Yearbook* (Washington, D.C.: International Monetary Fund, 1996).

2. This helped raise the U.S. share of global arms exports from 33 percent in 1990 to 56 percent in 1994. In contrast, the Western European share has stayed constant over that time, at 26 percent of global exports, with Britain the largest European-arms exporter. See *World Military Expenditures and Arms Transfers* (Washington, D.C.: U.S. Arms Control and Disarmament Agency, 1995), pp. 16–19. For other details, see "U.S. Reduces the Influence of Europe—Special Report: Defence," *Middle East Economic Digest*, April 12, 1996.

3. French President Jacques Chirac explained the EU's decision to engage more heavily in the Middle East peace process in this way: "I believe it is legitimate for the EU to be included in these negotiations. . . . It is true that Europe displayed weakness, not to say its complete absence, at the time of the Bosnian crisis. Everybody is aware of it and we can but deplore it. Today we have taken a step in the right direction." France-Info Radio, October 6, 1996, cited in *Foreign Broadcast Information Service (FBIS)*, Near East–South Asia, FBIS-WEU-96-195 West Europe, October 8, 1996.

policy seemed explicitly designed, almost from its inception, to run counter to U.S. policy.

As a result of these developments, U.S. and European policies diverge to various degrees on a broad range of Middle Eastern issues, from the peace process to Gulf security to the very definition and scope of the two parties' political, strategic, and economic roles in the region. This chapter reviews each of the core U.S. and European interests in the Middle East and the chief policies that have been adopted to advance those interests. It closes with a series of observations and recommendations aimed at managing disagreement and restoring some measure of partnership to U.S.-European efforts in a region that both consider strategically vital.

Core Interests: The United States

Beyond the interests that accompany U.S. engagement in all regions of the world,[4] the United States has three main interests in the Middle East: Israel, energy, and regional stability.

PRESERVING THE SECURITY OF ISRAEL

The United States has a strong interest in supporting Israel's survival and security, based upon the two countries' shared democratic values; a unique historical relationship; close people-to-people bonds; religious and cultural ties; and overlapping (though not identical) threats, first from the Soviets and more recently from terrorism, religious radicalism, and the spread of weapons of mass destruction and missile delivery systems. This recipe of factors has made the U.S.-Israel relationship different from any other the United States has in the world. Though the two have often been at odds on core issues (as basic as the appropriate definition of Israel's borders), they are in many ways much closer allies than countries with which the United States has treaty obligations.

MAINTAINING THE UNHINDERED FLOW OF OIL AND GAS AT REASONABLE PRICES

The United States has a strong interest in maintaining access to the almost two-thirds of the world's proven oil reserves that are concentrated in the Gulf region. Significant oil disruptions, when they have

---

4. These include the protection of citizens, property, and assets; the promotion of commerce; defense of the freedom of the seas; and the advancement of basic human rights and humanitarian concerns.

occurred, have had a drastic effect on the U.S. economy. At the outset of the Gulf War, the loss of Iraqi and Kuwaiti oil from world markets initially doubled oil prices and aggravated recessionary trends in the United States. The oil shock of 1979–80 caused by the Iranian revolution and OPEC's success in raising prices contributed to a 3 percent loss of gross national product by the United States. The U.S. GNP lost 5 percent as a result of the recession aggravated by OPEC production cuts during and following the October 1973 Arab-Israeli War. For the sake of the U.S. economy and of the economies of America's European and Japanese allies, which are much more reliant on Gulf energy, preventing these types of disruptions is a top U.S. priority. There has been substantial change in the shape and nature of the oil market over the last quarter century, but a significant widening of sources of supply and the emergence of a more market-oriented system governing the supply, demand, and price of oil, the Middle East—and especially the Gulf—remains an area of acute concern. Here, key fears revolve around the stability of Saudi Arabia and its ability to maintain high levels of oil production, and around continued access to the Straits of Hormuz.

Complementing the U.S. interest in preventing disruption to existing sources of supply is the interest in expanding sources of supply. Currently the chief focus is on the Caspian basin, expected to be home to the next great "oil boom," and specifically on the political and strategic implications of the search for secure shipment routes for Caspian oil. This is an issue that cuts across bureaucratic agendas, touching on policy toward Russia, Turkey, Iran, the Gulf, and Europe.

ENSURING REGIONAL STABILITY

Separate from the interest in preventing disruptions in oil supply or price, the United States has a strong interest in preventing any single power—whether it be an extra-regional state (i.e., the Soviet Union, as was the preoccupation of U.S. efforts until 1990) or a potential regional hegemon—from controlling the Gulf or vital access routes to it, such as Egypt's Suez Canal. Here, the great danger of a regional hegemon is not only its ability to restrict the flow of oil and gas but also its ability to use those resources for sinister objectives, including funding aggressive programs of conventional rearmament and unconventional weapons development that would be used as tools of political and ideological expansionism and strategic challenge (as was the case with Iraq).

Core Policies: The United States

Over the past three decades, Washington has advocated a number of basic policies to advance its interests in the Middle East. These include promoting Arab-Israeli peace, developing strong bilateral relationships with regional partners, and actively deterring aggression in the Persian Gulf.

PROMOTION OF THE ARAB-ISRAELI PEACE PROCESS

The United States has sought to promote the Arab-Israeli peace process as a means to many ends: to build a community of interest among moderate states in the region in the pursuit of regional peace and stability; to help Israel achieve peace, security, and normal relations with its neighbors and the wider international community; to provide Arabs and Israelis with a peaceful format through which to seek redress for their grievances against each other; to permit regional allies to reduce military expenditures and focus instead on economic and social development; to isolate radical states and organizations while highlighting the benefits that would accrue to them from changed behavior; and to reduce the likelihood of war at a time when its potential costs have dramatically risen due to advances in technology and the spread of weapons of mass destruction and missile delivery systems. When the U.S.-Soviet competition defined international politics, the peace process had an additional (and dominant) rationale: to defuse tensions that could escalate into superpower confrontation. Along the way, it provided a diplomatic umbrella that would increase U.S. regional influence and the stature of U.S. allies while disadvantaging the Soviets and their regional allies. Though the stakes in the peace process have been lowered with the end of the Cold War, these stakes nevertheless remain high, and this has been reflected in America's continuing deep engagement in the peace process in the 1990s.

Since the Six Day War and especially the advent of Henry Kissinger's "shuttle diplomacy" following the 1973 Yom Kippur War, an emphasis on process has been a mantra of U.S. peacemaking initiatives. For Washington, the most just, effective, and lasting formula of Arab-Israeli peacemaking remains that which is embodied in the invitation to the 1991 Madrid peace conference: direct negotiations to create "real peace" based on United Nations Security Council (UNSC) Resolution 242.[5] However, it has long been U.S. policy that

---

5. See the text of the U.S.-Soviet invitation to Middle Eastern participants to attend the October 1991 Madrid peace conference.

the determination of the precise method to implement that purposely ambiguous resolution is a task for the parties to the dispute, not outside powers. While the United States has long had an opinion on some aspects of how UNSC 242 should be implemented—i.e., on each of Israel's borders—three core principles have evolved as to overall U.S. peacemaking efforts: first, the United States cannot and should not want peace more than the parties themselves; second, the United States cannot impose an agreement on the parties nor should the United States outline an "American plan" for resolution of the Arab-Israeli dispute; and third, enduring achievements are those made through direct negotiations, with America's principal contribution being to nurture an environment in which the parties themselves could reach accord.

Implementing this policy has four main components. These include working with core allies to achieve common objectives in the peace process; nurturing an environment in which progress is more likely; husbanding past achievements in the pursuit of future ones; and defending the process from its political and military adversaries.

First, the United States seeks to fulfill the responsibilities of an "honest broker" and "full partner" to the negotiations, offering to facilitate talks, ensure compliance with pre-arranged negotiating formats, transmit messages between parties, record hypothetical proposals, and periodically propose ideas that could bridge (or at least circumvent) obstacles. This is a policy that values persistence over showmanship, pursues incremental achievement over headline breakthroughs, and underscores commitment to a process rather than to any defined outcomes. At times, this near-religious attachment to "process" leads the parties to seek their own breakthroughs on a bilateral basis, and when they do so freely and without coercion, that is itself a success of the "process." In this regard, the United States rarely sets out markers based on some abstract sense of justice (e.g., "self-determination" for the Palestinians) because the United States has no interest in any particular outcome except one that terminates the conflict and redounds to the benefit of its allies—one of which the Palestine Liberation Organization (PLO) has never been.

Second, the United States works closely and, if possible, quietly, with Israel, coordinating tactics with the Israelis and helping to reduce the risks they face as they consider making tangible concessions of territory in exchange for the intangibles of peace and normality. Political coordination, economic assistance, and military aid are all components of a strategy that recognizes the basic inequality of the Arab-Israeli conflict, which is that for Israel, neither the extent nor the number of military victories can provide the strategic rewards it seeks—peace—while, for the Arab side, the alternative is not necessarily the case.

Third, the United States works to support, defend, and protect agreements and the peacemakers who made them, through both direct political, financial, and security assistance, and an active effort to forge an international donor coalition to do the same. Here, it is important to note the nature of the triangular relationship between the United States, the PLO, and Israel. U.S.-PLO relations are dependent on Israeli-PLO relations; U.S.-Israeli relations are independent of Israeli-PLO relations.

Fourth, the United States seeks to insulate the peace process from threats of rejectionist regimes and terrorist groups who seek to undermine it. Here, U.S. efforts to punish states that support international terrorism and to compel them to change their aggressive behavior through a policy of "containment" are a top U.S. priority. In addition, the United States has promoted an array of anti-terrorist tactics that alternate between being iconoclastic (such as the extraterritorial capture and arrest of terrorist suspects) and brimming with the spirit of international cooperation (such as the Sharm el-Sheikh anti-terrorism summit in March 1996). While there is some debate within U.S. policy circles on the best method of countering terrorism, U.S. policy has generally maintained a clear differentiation between fighting terrorist groups, movements, and their supporters, which focuses on police and security methods and has had pride of place in U.S. policy, and raising the socioeconomic conditions of Middle Eastern populations as a way to dry up the potential constituency to whom the terrorist option might have special appeal.[6]

In recent years, the terrorist challenge to U.S. interests has grown more acute by the direct targeting of garrisoned U.S. forces on friendly soil inside the Middle East, and especially by the use of terrorism by Middle Eastern radicals inside the United States itself. While the United States has never been immune from terrorism, these two developments—represented by the Riyadh and al-Khobar

---

6. In declaratory policy, U.S. officials have been fuzzy on the issue, but in practice, the policy is clear. On public diplomacy, see the speech by Anthony Lake, then National Security Adviser, to the Washington Institute's Soref Symposium, May 1994; and President Bill Clinton's address to the Jordanian parliament, November 1994.

bombings in Saudi Arabia and the World Trade Center bombing and related (though unconsummated) efforts in New York—are fundamentally different from previous episodes, such as the bombing of the Marine barracks in Beirut. The bombings in Saudi Arabia not only raise doubts about a regional ally whose stability has long been taken for granted, but also leave U.S. forces in the untenable situation of spending about as much time defending against terrorists from within the countries they are committed to protect as they do preparing to deter and, if necessary fight, the countries they are there to oppose. The New York bombing underscored how vulnerable the U.S. mainland itself is to terrorism and the frightening damage that could have been caused if the bomb had actually done what it was designed to do. Viewed in light of the Tokyo gas attack, the potential is truly terrifying. When added to the popular impact of the bombing of a federal building in Oklahoma City, the downing of a TWA airliner (which many perceive as an act of terrorism), and the series of Islamist radical suicide bombings in Israel, these terrorist acts have had the effect of making terrorism—preventing it, avoiding it, fearing it, punishing it—a national preoccupation and priority. What is particularly interesting, however, is that the recent episodes of Middle Eastern terrorism targeted against Americans have not been some group's response to U.S. support of Israel or U.S. peace process policy *per se*, but rather have been linked to other U.S. regional policies, such as support for the Mubarak government and the commitment to defend Saudi Arabia via the deployment of U.S. troops there.

DEVELOPMENT OF MUTUALLY SATISFACTORY RELATIONS WITH MODERATE ARAB STATES AND TURKEY

A second core U.S. policy has been to develop sound relations with moderate Arab states and Turkey. This is essential because of these states' role in ensuring regional stability, their importance for access to Gulf energy resources, and their role in the peace process. Since the fall of the Shah, the three pillars of U.S. Middle East policy have been Egypt, because of its pioneering role in peacemaking and its leadership position in the Arab world; Saudi Arabia, because of its influence among Gulf Arab states and its dominant role in control of regional energy sources; and Turkey, because of its geopolitical centrality, its relative military and economic power, and its roles as a Muslim democracy and as a bridge between the Muslim world and the West. (Since the fall of the Soviet Union and the creation of new independent Muslim countries in the Caucasus, the Caspian basin,

and Central Asia—the enlargement of the "Greater Middle East"—
Turkey's role has taken on a new and strategically critical dimension,
helping to win those new states over to the West and to help promote
secure access routes for Caspian Sea oil resources.[7]) While the United
States has significant policy differences with each of these states,
especially as regards their domestic human rights practices but also
on key regional political issues (e.g., with the Egyptians, on ties to
Libya and Sudan and their "counter-proliferation" policies; with the
Turks, on Cyprus and, more recently, on their relationship with Iran
and Iraq; with the Saudis, on their reluctance to actively support the
peace process), these problems are normally subordinated to larger
strategic interests.

STRATEGIC PARTNERSHIP WITH ISRAEL

A third core policy has been to build a strategic partnership with
Israel. Following the collapse of the French-Israeli strategic relationship and throughout the 1960s and 1970s, the military side of the U.S.-
Israeli relationship was essentially a one-way street in which the
United States committed itself (at first tacitly, then openly) to ensure
Israel's qualitative edge against any likely combination of Arab military power. Beginning in the Carter administration and then blossom-
ing in the Reagan administration, a complementary side of this
relationship took shape, known as "strategic cooperation." Premised
on the notion that Israel and the United States shared common
(though not identical) threats and that Israel had experience, know-
how, and expertise that could benefit America's ability to confront its
own threats, strategic cooperation sought to transform the donor-
recipient aspect of the military relationship into a partnership in which
Israel "gave" as well as "received." At first, the focus of strategic cooperation was Soviet activity in the Middle East; in the 1990s, this has
evolved into a series of joint efforts to address a range of regional
threats, including terrorism, radicalism, and the spread of weapons of
mass destruction and missile delivery systems. The expansion of
strategic cooperation has a derivative benefit to the peace process as
well, because the development of a U.S. strategic (as opposed to moral
or political) interest in Israel's well-being adds to Israel's deterrence,
diminishes the likelihood that Arab parties might resort to a military
option in their confrontation with Israel, and lessens the level of risk
Israel faces in offering compromises in peace negotiations.

---

7. See Chapter 7 by F. Stephen Larrabee and Chapter 8 by Heinz Kramer and
Friedemann Müller in this volume.

GULF SECURITY

The fourth key component of U.S. policy is to create security structures in the Gulf that protect against the emergence of any extra-regional or regional hegemon. Since the United States assumed primary responsibility for Gulf security in the early 1970s, there have been three main elements of this policy—reliance for regional stability on individual local powers, bolstered bilaterally with U.S. assistance; strengthened cooperation among local powers; and direct presence of U.S. forces. From 1972 to 1979, U.S. policy was to rely on the "twin pillars" of Iran and Saudi Arabia; this policy collapsed with the fall of the Shah. From 1980 to 1990, U.S. policy was to build up Saudi defenses, nurture incipient defense cooperation among the countries of the Gulf Cooperation Council (GCC) and, most important, adopt a balance-of-power approach toward the two other regional powers, Ba'athist Iraq and Islamic Iran. This policy collapsed with the Iraqi invasion of Kuwait, which underscored the fact that after unfortunate experiences with both Baghdad and Tehran, Washington realized that both countries advanced policies that were in fact fundamentally inimical to U.S. (and Western) interests. Since 1990, the United States has adopted a third approach, labeled "dual containment." This policy is founded on a clear recognition of the reality about Iraq and Iran, and seeks to contain and alter their aggressive policies through strict enforcement of UN sanctions (in the case of Iraq) and the imposition of an economic embargo (in the case of Iran). It aims to bolster inter-Arab cooperative security efforts and, most important, projects U.S. military force into the region in an unprecedented way as the counterbalance that preserves Gulf stability. Indeed, despite the relative decline in the importance of Gulf oil to the U.S. economy, the perception that the Gulf is central to U.S. interests and the willingness to expend U.S. military and financial resources to safeguard it are at least as strongly held today as ever before.[8]

At its core, dual containment is an interim strategy, designed to fill the vacuum left when the balance-of-power approach proved untenable; when either Iraq or Iran alters its policies (or when one undergoes a change of regime), dual containment is likely to be replaced with some form of renewed balance-of-power policy. The main difficulty with dual containment is that Iraq and Iran have proven fairly

---

8. See also Chapter 5 in this volume by Geoffrey Kemp and Chapter 6 by Johannes Reissner; and Chapter 11 by Richard L. Kugler and Chapter 12 by François Heisbourg.

impervious to change; the United States has encountered increasing difficulty in implementing these policies, thanks to the international community's fatigue in maintaining sanctions on Iraq, differing European tactics in dealing with Iran, and the emergence of terrorism against U.S. troops in the Gulf as a key factor in the thinking of both Washington and the host countries.

Viewed over time, it is important to note that U.S. Middle East policy has suffered from a fundamental strategic dilemma: to what extent are two of its main interests—"Israel" and "energy"—mutually exclusive? Until the late 1970s, many U.S. policymakers believed that there was a direct trade-off between the two and that U.S. policy was a delicate balancing act designed to separate as much as possible one from the other. Three events—one positive (the Egypt-Israel peace treaty, which capped a six-year process of weaning the most populous and powerful Arab state from the Soviet embrace and locking it firmly into Western orbit) and two negative (victories by Islamist radicals in overthrowing the Shah and in assassinating Anwar al-Sadat)—provoked a rethinking of this conventional wisdom. These events suggested that the real regional divide was less between Arabs and Israelis than between "moderates" and "radicals," implying that there is no necessary trade-off between U.S. support for Israel and U.S. efforts to ensure Gulf security by developing mutual satisfactory relations with key Arab states. Alexander Haig's strategic consensus initiative was the first to articulate this idea, but in the early 1980s the concept was not ripe and his preferred "common enemy" was the faraway Soviets. By the beginning of the 1990s, however, with the Soviets gone and Islamists fresh from victories in Afghanistan and Sudan and insurgent in Algeria, the idea had ripened. Ironically, in the end, it was the actions of a secular radical—Saddam Hussein—that confirmed this idea to many in the region. His invasion of Kuwait and his simultaneous firing of Scud missiles against Israel and Saudi Arabia provided visible evidence that common threats were shared by the Jewish state and the Custodian of the Two Holy Mosques and suggested that they also had common interests in regional stability. The Gulf War and the peace process launched in its wake had the effect of linking U.S. policies in the Arab-Israeli arena and U.S. policies in the Gulf in an unprecedented way, a trend that contrasts sharply with the historic U.S. approach to the two sub-regions.[9]

---

9. See the address to The Washington Institute's Soref Symposium by Martin Indyk, then Senior Director for Near East and South Asia, National Security Council, May 17, 1993.

Significantly, North Africa normally figures in U.S. Middle East policy to the extent that it directly affects these two main interests. Egypt, the region's most powerful and most populous state, is a great prize; its turn to the West was one of the great victories in the Cold War and its maintenance of peace with Israel and its supporting role in the Gulf War are crucial to U.S. regional objectives. Apart from Egypt, however, U.S. interests in North Africa are episodic, instrumental, or secondary. Libya was a chief concern when Muammar Qadhafi was an active exporter of terrorism, but since 1986, Washington's interest has turned elsewhere. Algeria received periodic attention, but not nearly as much as it would have if U.S. citizens or U.S. investments in Algeria's oil sector had been targeted in its civil war; inexplicably, they have not. Generally, U.S. interest in North Africa (apart from Egypt) is on standby, ready to engage in times of crisis (which could occur on short notice in numerous places and in numerous ways) but not otherwise a key component of U.S. regional activity.

Core Interests: Europe

For its part, Europe and its major constituent states have a set of strategic interests in the Greater Middle East that are often complementary to U.S. interests but sometimes diverge from them. Europe's three main regional interests are regional stability, especially in areas close to the European continent; energy; and migration.

PROMOTING STABILITY

The chief European interest in the Greater Middle East (especially North Africa, the Mediterranean basin, and Turkey) is to promote stability and prevent the spread of Middle Eastern conflicts—both inter-state and intra-state—to Europe. For Europe, the Greater Middle East matters because it is a next-door neighbor, a quarrelsome, nettlesome, exasperating, sometimes dangerous neighbor with whom it has a long, complex history of wars and conflicts; military domination (moving in both directions); and cultural, political, and economic challenge. Europe's proximity to the Middle East heightens its sensitivity about the potential for Middle Eastern problems to transform themselves into European problems. On occasion, this has been the case with various Middle Eastern problems, such as terrorism, Islamic fundamentalism, Arab-Israeli disputes, and revolutionary movements in individual countries. Insulating Europe from the spread of these problems is Europe's chief interest in the Middle East.

ENERGY

Europe has a strong interest in maintaining the unhindered flow of oil and gas at reasonable prices. In contrast to the United States, which imports less than 20 percent of its net usage of oil and gas from the Middle East (and just over half from all OPEC countries combined), Europe is much more dependent on the region for its energy, importing nearly half of its net oil and gas from the Middle East (and more than 85 percent from OPEC countries).[10] While the United States suffered from oil shocks and price rises in 1973 (as a result of the Arab boycott in the wake of the Yom Kippur War), 1978–79 (as a result of the Iranian revolution), and 1990 (as a result of the Iraqi invasion of Kuwait), the impact on the U.S. economy paled in comparison to the effect on the European economy. With that legacy in mind, and despite the changes in the oil market that decrease the significance of any single source of supply, Europe continues to maintain a keen interest in ensuring the unhindered flow of oil and gas at reasonable prices and in expanding sources of supply outside the Gulf (e.g., the Caspian).[11]

MIGRATION

A third key European interest *vis-à-vis* the Middle East revolves around the issue of migration. Given Europe's centuries-old engagement with the Middle East, this is a relatively new addition to the list of European regional interests; it would not have been on Europe's agenda thirty or forty years ago. However, the great burst of Muslim migration into Europe in the 1960s and 1970s—especially from North Africa to southern Europe, from Turkey to Germany, and from India and Pakistan to Britain—has provoked deep concern among many Europeans about the social, economic, and cultural implications of demographic change within societies that are far more homogenous than American society.[12] As Europeans wrestle with the implications of multiculturalism resulting from past waves of immigration, many are keen to ensure that further waves of migration—for example,

---

10. Compiled from the International Petroleum Statistics Report, December 1996, Energy Information Administration, U.S. Department of Energy.

11. See Chapters 7 and 8 in this volume (Larrabee; Kramer and Müller) on Turkey and the Caspian.

12. For demographic details, see Ceri Peace and Gunther Glebe, "Muslim Minorities in Western Europe," *Ethnic and Racial Studies*, Vol. 18, No. 1 (January 1995), pp. 26–45.

from strife-ridden Algeria—do not compound an already difficult and complex problem. Finding ways to deal with these twin challenges—absorbing past migration while preventing future unwanted migration—is becoming one of the most powerful rationales for European engagement in the Middle East.

In addition to these three primary interests, individual European states have their own special interests in the region and connections with individual Middle Eastern countries. These are largely shaped by history and geography, and in many places kept alive by commercial ties. Such is the case, for example, with the French connection to francophone North Africa and, in lesser ways, with relations between Italy and Libya. Traditional spheres of commercial interest play an important role in German-Iranian relations, French-Iraqi relations, and British-Gulf state relations. French ties with Lebanon enjoy the added factor of religion, which traditionally found Catholic France as the protector of the (Uniate) Maronite community of Mount Lebanon. Britain, along with France the dominant colonial power in the region, has some sentimental attachment to Saudi Arabia but not enough to count for much in strategic terms; in contrast to the French, for whom the Algerian experience was a searing moment in the nation's history, British strategists were almost always more modest in understanding the Middle East as a supply center and a way station on the road to India and the East.

Significantly, for none of these states is the security and survival of Israel considered nearly as central to their perceived strategic interests as it is for the United States. Two of them—France in the 1950s and 1960s and Britain in the late 1980s and 1990s—have developed what at times can be termed "strategic relationships," but, as the French case indicates, European-Israeli strategic ties tend to be instrumental and therefore inherently transitory. (London recently inaugurated what it calls "strategic cooperation" with Israel, but it was not long ago that a Conservative government imposed an arms embargo on Israel for more than a decade.) Historically, some European states (e.g., Holland) have maintained relations with Israel that are much warmer than the norm; others (e.g., Greece) have been cooler than the norm. The German case is *sui generis*, born of the Holocaust and shaped by the statesmanship of Konrad Adenauer and David Ben-Gurion. As a result, Germany has annually provided special economic development assistance to Israel, maintains extensive military-to-military relations, and has avoided offending Israeli political sensibilities by standing alone within the EU in refusing to endorse the concept of "self-determination" for the Palestinians in United Nations resolutions. However, in operational terms, it is unlikely that any of these states, even Germany, would veer too far from the European consensus should a regional crisis force them to choose between strategic interests and an emotional, historical, or political attachment.

Given this absence of fundamental strategic commitment to Israel, European policy has remained confined to the balancing of ties with Israel, based on historical, moral, and political factors, with what are perceived as Europe's more pressing strategic interests in the Arab world. Ironically, in recent years, the challenge of religious fundamentalism and its impact on regional stability has led some Europeans to view the region in moderate-radical, not Arab-Israeli terms, with a concomitant improvement in aspects of EU-Israeli relations (e.g., counterterrorism), but this has so far affected Europe's peace process policy in only marginal ways.

Core Policies: Europe

To advance the interests outlined above, European states and institutions have advocated policies that reflect their geographic proximity to the Middle East, their changing demography, and their judgment of the level of threat to access to the region's energy resources.

PROMOTING STABILITY

The central feature of European policy is a preventive effort against instability on Europe's periphery that could lead to European involvement in Middle Eastern crises, unwanted immigration into European societies, or upheaval in the process of political and social integration of Muslim minorities into their new host countries. The most ambitious initiative is the Euro-Mediterranean partnership—bringing together the European Union with the states of North Africa and the Levant in a broad political and economic dialogue, to create what French Foreign Minister Hervé de Charette called "the start of a new Mediterranean." Its basic goal is not dissimilar from one of the strongest rationales for the United States to seek Mexico's participation in a free-trade area: to tie Muslim states of the Mediterranean closer to Europe economically in order to keep them further away demographically. The cornerstone of "Euro-Med" is the creation of a free-trade zone in industrial goods and services among the EU and eleven Middle Eastern countries over a twelve-year transition period, based on a series of bilateral economic association agreements and trade accords. This process, to be lubricated by the injection of approximately $6 billion in additional European assistance to the region over the next four years (a far lower figure than originally proposed by European planners), is designed not only to create an expanded trading bloc but also to provide incentives for sound economic and financial decision-making by Middle Eastern participants, to create a framework for labor-intensive European-funded development projects,[13] and even to reduce intra–Middle Eastern conflicts by providing a non-threatening forum for participation across political divides.[14] As British Foreign Secretary Malcolm Rifkind said at Barcelona, Euro-Med had "two main themes: political stability . . . and economic growth. In reality these are actually only one subject."[15] So far, Euro-Med has had little discernible impact, but if free trade zones are indeed created on schedule, then the implications for political and economic change on both sides of the Mediterranean could be profound.

Euro-Med complements numerous EU and individual European relationships with Middle Eastern states. These are especially strong between Southern Europe and North Africa, with Paris, Rome, and Madrid profoundly concerned about the potential for political instability, especially at a time when they are investing so heavily in the region (in pipelines) as a cheaper and more direct source of energy than Gulf oil.[16] Another important example of this is the EU-Turkish customs union agreement, approved by the EU and Turkish parliaments in late 1995. (Compensatory funding to Turkey is being held up by the EU parliament out of human rights concerns in Turkey.)

---

13. EU initiatives can be effective in "persuading the young to stay in their countries by mounting projects which create jobs," argued one Euro-Med booster, Tunisian Foreign Minister Ben Yahya. *Middle East Economic Digest*, November 24, 1995.

14. Indeed, after boycotting the Casablanca and Amman Middle East/North Africa Economic Summits, Syria did participate, alongside Israel, in the inaugural Euro-Med Summit in Barcelona in 1995.

15. Malcolm Rifkind, address to Euro-Med Summit, Barcelona, Spain, November 28, 1995.

16. The share of natural gas in Europe's energy equation is expected to rise from one-fifth to one-quarter by 2010; half of it will be imported. European–Middle East gas pipelines either currently in use or under construction include the following: Algeria-Italy; Algeria-Morocco-Spain-Portugal; Algeria-France; Algeria-Belgium; Algeria-Turkey; and Libya-Italy. See "Putting a Price on Trans-Med Gas," *Middle East Economic Digest*, December 6, 1996.

In addition to economic and political initiatives like Euro-Med, European governments and institutions have also recently undertaken a number of security-related initiatives designed to promote stability in Middle Eastern states and deal with any sudden deterioration in the regional situation. The three most significant initiatives have been the creation of a Southern Europe–North Africa interior ministers' forum for discussion of terrorism and extremism (January 1995); the establishment, at European urging, of a North Atlantic Treaty Organization (NATO) dialogue with six regional states (February 1995);[17] and the formation by the Western European Union of EUROFOR, a 15,000-troop force of French, Italian, Spanish, and Portuguese units based in Florence, designed for peace-keeping and humanitarian missions in the Mediterranean; many Arab commentators have interpreted it as a "rapid deployment force" to North African regimes in trouble and to evacuate European nationals in emergencies.[18]

Two other components of Europe's efforts to keep Middle Eastern problems in the Middle East have been what one could call the "NIMBY" (not-in-my-back-yard) aspect of the anti-terrorism strategy adopted by some European countries and the general policy of "critical dialogue" with Iran, championed by Germany and France and supported to varying degrees by virtually all EU countries, at least until the April 1997 verdict in the "Mykonos" trial. The former refers to the stratagem of reaching tacit understandings with various terror-supporting states not to engage in terrorist activity within a country's boundaries or against its citizens abroad, in exchange for some political, economic, logistical, or other *quid pro quo*. While all states (the United States being no exception)[19] have entered into Faustian bargains at various junctures, several European countries—including Greece, Germany, and France—have at times raised this to a level of

---

17. These include Morocco, Tunisia, Algeria, Mauritania, Egypt and, interestingly, Israel. This dialogue followed the widely publicized statement of then–NATO Secretary General Willy Claes—later repudiated by NATO members—identifying Islamic fundamentalism as the most serious post–Cold War challenge facing the alliance.

18. See *al-Quds al-Arabi* and *al-Majalla*, January 2, 1997.

19. Algeria's Islamic terrorists have refrained from targeting U.S. citizens or assets in their otherwise ruthless campaign against the military-backed regime. Given overall U.S. policy toward Algeria—which is generally sympathetic to the Algerian government's predicament while urging Algiers to permit the participation of nonviolent Islamists in electoral politics—it is difficult to ascribe this apparent immunity from terrorism to any bargain with the Islamists.

policy. It is important to note that this European particularism on terrorism is not shared by all states and even has its limits among its
proponents, sometimes as a matter of principle (such as France's support for a tough stand on Libya, given Libya's role in the bombing of
a French civilian jetliner) and sometimes as a result of popular pressure (as is currently building inside Germany because of Iranian complicity in the Mykonos affair).[20]

This issue has been particularly perplexing in recent years for
France, which has sought to balance strategic interests in stability in
North Africa with the desire to insulate the home front from Middle
Eastern conflicts. On this issue, Paris has opted not to make a choice
but to pursue all policies simultaneously—sympathizing with and
supporting the Zeroual government in Algeria, taking harsh measures to prevent illegal immigration into France, reaffirming the
paramountcy of secularism in civil life against a rising tide of ethnic
and religious particularism, yet at the same time extending a welcoming hand to the Islamic world and criticizing others, including
the United States, for its "simplistic and outdated" approach to combating terrorism.[21] This "all-things-to-all-people" approach, however, has apparently not persuaded the Algerian Islamic terrorists,
who have made Paris a favorite target despite the French government's efforts.

In regions more distant from Europe, the Europeans adopt more
independent positions. Such is the case with Iran, where Europe has
a profound difference with the United States, born of drawing differing lessons from the Iranian revolution and differing individual
experiences with Iran since then. While both recognize Iran, with its
huge population, geostrategic location, and robust military and economic potential, as a major strategic prize, the United States believes
that, through its actions and behavior, the Islamic republic has earned
special status as the chief long-term threat to Western interests in the
region. To confront this threat, the United States has made Iran one of

---

20. The "Mykonos affair" refers to the trial in Germany of the accused murderers
of four Kurdish opponents of the Iranian regime at a Greek restaurant (called
Mykonos) in Berlin in September 1992. In March 1996, Germany's federal prose-
cutor issued an international arrest warrant for Iranian Minister of Intelligence Ali
Fallahiyan charging him with having ordered the killings. In a stunning verdict in
April 1997, a German court found that the highest levels of the Iranian government were directly complicit in the crime.

21. The words of French Interior Minister Jean-Louis Debre, Agence France
Presse, July 30, 1996, cited in FBIS.

the two targets of its assertive policy of "dual containment," designed to isolate Iran (as well as Iraq) in order to compel it to change its aggressive behavior and, in the meantime, to deny Iran the resources (including access to international trade and capital) to devote to its "rogue" activities. U.S. efforts to contain Iran have grown more comprehensive and sustained over the last two years. These efforts include the imposition of a full trade embargo on Iran, ending an anomalous situation in which the United States was one of Iran's leading trading partners despite its containment policy, and the unanimous approval by both houses of Congress of the Iran and Libya Sanctions Act.[22] These and other U.S. efforts emerged from America's long and bitter experience with the Islamic regime, when past initiatives to identify and strengthen "moderates" backfired, with disastrous results for U.S. interests. As for the "active containment" policy of recent years, evidence suggests that it has contributed to the economic weakness of the Iranian regime, which limits the resources available to Tehran for military modernization and other negative purposes. However, U.S. strategy has clearly not compelled Iran to alter its behavior, and it cannot be termed a success.

At the same time, these initiatives have provoked a harsh reaction among U.S. allies, who view the Iran and Libya Sanctions Act as an extraterritorial violation of international trade regulations. To varying degrees, virtually all U.S. allies share the U.S. perception of the current and potential threat from Iran—including Iran's pursuit of nuclear capability, its use of terrorism against the Arab-Israeli peace process and against regime dissidents abroad, its refusal to lift the *fatwa* against Salman Rushdie, its support of revolutionary and radical movements in numerous Muslim countries, and its aggressive military behavior in the Gulf—though some harbor doubts about specific charges of complicity in individual acts of terrorism. Changing Iranian behavior on these issues is the common objective of U.S. and European efforts (at least this is the public posture of both sides). However, despite this overall consensus, Europe (along with Japan) rejects any blanket effort to isolate Iran, which is the thrust of the U.S. approach. Instead, until Europe re-examined its approach in the wake of the Mykonos verdict, official European policy has been

---

22. This legislation, approved unanimously by Congress in 1996, authorizes a set of economic sanctions that the president must impose (except in case of national security) on countries and companies who invest $40 million or more in Iran's (or Libya's) energy industry.

to pursue a "critical dialogue" with Tehran that held out "carrots"—political contact and economic benefits, such as trade, trade credits, and debt rescheduling—designed to embolden and empower pragmatic elements in the Iranian regime and thereby encourage incremental changes in Iranian behavior. For some European countries, these carrots have even included political coordination (e.g., French-Iranian cooperation to achieve a cease-fire in Lebanon in spring 1996) and intelligence coordination (e.g., the high-level German-Iranian intelligence connection). Whether this policy is driven by a sincere belief in the wisdom of "engagement" as a means to affect Iranian behavior or merely as a cover for certain states to maintain trade links with Iran, to ensure access for Caspian oil pipelines transiting Iranian territory, or insulate themselves against Iranian-backed terrorism, is unclear. Few European officials ever boasted about the extent of positive change in Iranian behavior as a result of critical dialogue,[23] but despite numerous occasions when European officials threatened to terminate critical dialogue for lack of results,[24] the policy endured until even the most cynical European bureaucrat was forced to recognize that such dialogue politically was unthinkable. In its place, however, there is a policy vacuum; all that remains of the former European approach is European-Iranian trade ties, unfettered by any serious political dialogue. As a result, the gulf between Europe and the United States on Iran policy has survived the demise of critical dialogue, with Iran benefiting handsomely.

---

23. For example, "We have seen some small changes, but the results so far have been disappointing," commented British Foreign Secretary Malcolm Rifkind. *The Times* (London), November 5, 1996. Only France's de Charette is quoted as being "delighted" with the results of critical dialogue. *Le Figaro*, April 30, 1996, cited in FBIS-WEU-96-085, May 1, 1996.

24. For example, "Critical dialogue yes, but not at any price; we Europeans are agreed on this. We are close to the red line," said German Foreign Minister Klaus Kinkel. *Algemeen Dagblad* (Rotterdam), March 16, 1996, cited in FBIS-WEU-96-054, West Europe, March 20, 1996. Critical dialogue will now contain "more criticism and less dialogue," warned Italy's Foreign Minister Susanna Agnelli. *La Libre Belgique*, April 23, 1996, cited in FBIS-WEU-96-080, West Europe, April 25, 1996. An exchange with Malcolm Rifkind just before an EU trip to Iran, following the spring 1996 wave of Hamas–Islamic Jihad suicide bombings in Israel, is instructive: "*Question:* Is there the slightest chance of the troika mission to Iran actually changing minds in Tehran? *Rifkind:* I think one must be very doubtful. *Question:* Is it therefore worth it? *Rifkind:* The question is whether it would do any harm." Rifkind press conference, Palermo, March 10, 1996. Indeed, the express purpose of the troika visit, as outlined in an EU communiqué, was to seek Iran's condemnation of terrorism "once and for all." Reuters, March 10, 1996. (The "troika" refers to the current and next EU chairs and their immediate predecessor.)

While Iran is the clearest example of Washington and Brussels operating at cross-purposes, elsewhere in the Gulf a "political gulf" is emerging on policy toward Iraq. Technically, America and Europe share the same policy: commitment to the implementation of all UN Security Council resolutions on Iraq and maintenance of the full set of sanctions on Iraq until Baghdad complies completely and unquestionably with those resolutions. In practice, the United States and some European countries have contradictory approaches: France, for example, seems to want to find ways to relieve sanctions and reintegrate a chastened though rehabilitated Saddam Hussein back into the international community (denuded of weapons of mass destruction, of course), whereas Washington uses "compliance" as a way to avoid saying that its real intent is to use sanctions and other punitive measures to "tighten the box" around Saddam in the hope of a coup that might bring a new regime to power in Baghdad. For Washington (and London), Saddam is decidedly "irredeemable"[25] and UN resolutions allow them to avoid saying that awful truth; for Paris, Saddam is certainly "redeemable," with only sanctions (and periodic outrages by Saddam himself) standing in the way. In contrast to the Iran case, what lessens the impact of these divergent approaches is the fact that UN resolutions, drafted when the international consensus against Saddam was strong and almost universal, govern international action on Iraq. While the commitment to sanctions may erode, relieving sanctions (or modifying them) can only be accomplished through a positive decision of the Security Council. Similarly, in military terms, the United States has already been acting more or less unilaterally in the Gulf, with some limited (overt) British and (tacit) Arab support, for the past few years. This reflects, in part, differences of threat perception, with European states much more sanguine about the prospects for Gulf instability than the United States, despite having a greater *prima facie* interest in the region based on their energy requirements and sourcing.

However, over time, this American unilateralism is likely to be politically unsustainable even if legally appropriate and technically

---

25. On Saddam Hussein's irredeemability, see Indyk's Washington Institute speech, May 17, 1993; recently, Britain's Rifkind wrote: "I look forward to the day when Iraq is no longer ruled by a regime that ignores international obligations and brutalises its people. Such an Iraq would need international support but the country's isolation could then end"; this implies that the isolation would remain in place until the establishment of a new regime. *The Times* (London), November 5, 1996.

feasible. Four new factors—terrorism against U.S. forces in the Gulf, the rise of Arab Gulf states' fear of a resurgent Iran, the efforts of an Islamic nationalist government in Turkey to have the Northern Iraq vacuum filled (by Baghdad, if necessary), and the desire by many in the Arab world for the reintegration of Iraq to help bolster the Arab cause at a moment of tension and anxiety in the peace process—all contribute to the erosion of international vigor to maintain Iraqi sanctions until Baghdad's full compliance with UN resolutions. In this context, the actions of some European powers may hasten a political process that undermines the ability of the United States (and its dwindling list of coalition partners) to maintain a vigilant approach toward Iraq. As fate may have it, this process could "go critical" precisely at the moment when Saddam Hussein undertakes his next military adventure.

ADVOCACY OF THE ARAB-ISRAELI PEACE PROCESS

A second European policy is to advance an advocacy approach to the Arab-Israeli peace process. Here, Europe's historical approach has been to focus less on process than on outcome. To be sure, Europe shares with the United States an appreciation of the peace process as a means to an end, not just an end in itself; however, Europe has generally viewed the process as instrumental to advancing its other regional interests and has therefore viewed it as a means to a more-or-less specific end (that is, defusing Arab complaints about Western support for the creation of Israel, thereby removing a thorn in the development of European-Arab relations), and not merely to attain the rather selfless goal of termination of a conflict by an agreement that satisfies the concerns of all parties. As a result, Europe has preferred to offer its own views on key items on the bargaining table, regardless of their impact on Israel's negotiating posture, ostensibly in the expectation that this might propel the diplomacy forward. This includes recognizing the PLO as the "sole legitimate representative of the Palestinian people" as early as the mid-1970s (a designation that neither the United States nor Israel has yet made);[26] supporting Palestinian "self-determination" (which is generally recognized as support for independent, sovereign statehood);[27] and advocating

---

26. The Israel-PLO Declaration of Principles (the Oslo Accords) recognizes the PLO as the "legitimate representative of the Palestinian people," but not the "sole" one.

27. Sometimes European officials find support for these positions where none exists. "Great attention must be paid to the concerns of the Palestinians," said

Israel's "full withdrawal" from the Golan Heights as a legitimate condition for Syria's conclusion of a peace accord with Israel.[28] On balance, all this has been done within the context of European statements reaffirming Europe's commitment to Israel's "right to exist" in "secure and recognized boundaries" (as the language of UNSC 242 stipulates). Or, as French Foreign Minister de Charette said pithily, "France has chosen the camp of peace and it is attentive to both sides. France loves both sides."[29]

Curiously, Europe has steadfastly maintained this approach despite gaining little in tangible terms and seeming to have lost much. Specifically, the implication of Europe's adoption of these positions has been to earn it some political advantage with certain Arab states (but not a great deal) and to allow it to claim the moral high ground, but—most importantly—this policy has succeeded in precluding Europe from any effective role as honest broker or full sponsor of the negotiations themselves. Precisely because of the U.S. strategic interest in (and large-scale economic and military support of) Israel and its emphasis on process, not outcome, Arab parties understand that Washington is the address to which to turn in seeking results in the Middle East and that (as Sadat noted two decades ago) Washington holds "99 percent of the cards" in the region.[30] As a result, since 1973, progress in the peace process was achieved almost exclusively under U.S. auspices, with the Europeans playing a fairly marginal political and diplomatic role.

French Foreign Minister de Charette, "which were set out in UN Security Council resolutions and in the Oslo, Madrid and Taba accords, and which make provisions for, I recall, first of all the principle of land-for-peace and secondly the right of Palestinians to self-determination." In fact, neither "land-for-peace" nor "self-determination" is mentioned in any Israeli-Palestinian agreement. See de Charette's comments on Radio France International, October 27, 1996, cited in FBIS-WEU-96-209, West Europe, October 29, 1996.

28. U.S. policy recognizes, as a minimum, the need for "territorial compromise"—in President Bush's Madrid terminology—but does not mandate "full withdrawal" as a necessary precondition for Israeli-Syrian peace.

29. Hervé de Charette quoted on Radio France International, October 27, 1996, cited in FBIS.

30. When Washington did follow the European lead, in the 1977 Vance-Gromyko declaration in favor of an international peace conference, Anwar al-Sadat and Menachem Begin decided to go it alone. Conversely, the Oslo Accords—which brought together the PLO and Israel outside U.S. purview but with the assistance of a minor European power, once the PLO accepted Israeli conditions for recognition—in fact validates the wisdom of the U.S. approach of not articulating positions too far ahead of the Israelis but rather conditioning the environment so that the parties become ready to deal effectively with each other.

To compensate for their sideline status in the negotiations, Europe has effectively bought a seat at the peace table by "anteing up" in the coin of significant economic and development assistance to core peace process participants. The EU constitutes the largest donor to the Palestinian Authority, with the United States ranking only third, after Saudi Arabia.[31] In addition, the EU (and its member-states) have taken an active role in economic support of Jordan, Egypt, Syria, and Lebanon, and have carried the lion's share of responsibility on many aspects of the Multilateral Talks on Regional Issues.[32] And though not directly related to the peace process, Euro-Med does play an important supporting role. To some European leaders, like German Foreign Minister Klaus Kinkel, carving out a niche in economic matters is Europe's appropriate role in the peace process.[33] Others, however, reject the idea that adoption of partisan positions in the peace process precludes Europe from a status on par with the Americans and instead, as a result of their "footing the bill" for the process, contend that they deserve a larger role, proportionate to their financial contribution. Here, the critical factor is France, which dominates the U.S.-European approaches to the Middle East.

A Resurgent France

No single factor has altered the state of U.S.-European relations on specific Middle East matters more than the new, independent policy adopted by Jacques Chirac. The French president himself has

---

31. Since 1993, the EU has contributed $397 million to support the Palestinian Authority (PA) and other development and relief projects in the West Bank and Gaza; the largest individual donor is Germany. In December 1996, the EU and the PA initialed an agreement on full Palestinian participation in the Euro-Med economic arrangement.

32. The multilateral talks complement the bilateral negotiations among regional parties by bringing together Arabs, Israelis, and the European, American, Asian, and other global supporters of the peace process in working groups on five issues: economic development, environment, water resources, refugees, and arms control and regional security.

33. Speaking in Damascus, Kinkel said: "We do not aspire to a great political role in this regard; namely, the role of a broker, but we want to give advice on this and the other tracks. I tell you that we realize that the Arabs want us to play a more effective role in this regard, but I say that we should leave the political mediation to the Americans, and we, the Europeans, should concentrate further on the economic aid." Syrian Arab Television, July 6, 1995, cited in FBIS-NES-95-130, Near East/South Asia, July 7, 1995.

described his policy as a return to the "Arab policy" of Charles de Gaulle, and its reverberations are indeed being felt across the region. This was reflected in France's independent diplomacy in Lebanon following the Qana tragedy at the height of Israel's "Operation Grapes of Wrath" in spring 1996; French leadership of a tough EU statement on the peace process—the most critical of Israel in more than a decade—in October 1996, when Europe was not invited to the Washington Summit following the tunnel rioting episode; France's insistence on the appointment of an EU envoy to the Middle East peace process;[34] and France's tacit condoning of Saddam Hussein's invasion of Irbil in August 1996, its refusal to participate in the U.S.-U.K. expansion of the southern "no-fly zone" in September 1996, and its withdrawal from Operation Provide Comfort (the northern "no-fly zone" set up in 1992 at France's insistence) in December 1996. Under Chirac, France has diagnosed a "deficit of confidence" in the peace process—and, by implication, in the U.S. role—and has asserted Europe's claim to full "co-sponsorship" of the process[35] and, except when Iraqi provocations are too blatant even for Paris to ignore, to serve as Baghdad's advocate in the UN Security Council in the campaign to relieve Iraqi sanctions.

For the United States, two aspects of French policy are especially important to assess: how much practical impact will it have, and to what extent is the new policy defined by a new appraisal of French national interest as opposed to simply being a reaction to U.S. policy? The answer to the first question is that in some areas, it will have significant impact; elsewhere, little. It is highly unlikely that the French effort will win for Europe parity with the United States as sponsor and principal Arab-Israeli mediator, as Chirac has sought.[36] This is not because of U.S. efforts to keep Europe out; rather, this is because most

---

34. The day Europe approved the concept of a special envoy, de Charette said his role would not be to find a seat "at the negotiating table tomorrow morning. That will come about, no doubt, but all in good time." France-Inter Radio, October 28, 1996, cited in FBIS-WEU-96-210, West Europe, October 30, 1996.

35. On the deficit of confidence, see Chirac's statement to Lebanese students in Beirut, France-2 Television, October 25, 1996, cited in FBIS-NES-96-208, October 28, 1996.

36. Speaking in Damascus, Chirac said, "France and Europe must be present alongside the other parties as friends and as sources of proposals and not as mere partners for reconstruction. It is time for Europe to co-sponsor this process." However, Chirac has also said he does not want to "gate-crash the peace process." Radio France International, October 20, 1996, cited in FBIS-NES-96-205, October 23, 1996.

European leaders do not want the role,[37] and, more importantly, Europe's positions on key issues make it unattractive to Arabs—no less than to Israelis—given Europe's lack of influence with Jerusalem. However, along the way, France can cause substantial problems. For example, through its Lebanon intervention, France managed to inject Iran directly into the diplomacy,[38] giving the Islamic Republic unprecedented legitimacy at a moment when Iranian influence in the Levant was actually ebbing. So far, the monitoring mechanism that emerged from that episode has worked moderately well, but that has more to do with Israeli and Syrian interest for a variety of reasons in avoiding a renewal of conflict than with the adroitness of France's contribution. And France's activist advocacy of key Palestinian and Syrian demands cannot help but diminish the likelihood of eventual Palestinian and Syrian compromise in negotiations with the Israelis. Elsewhere in the region, French policy may even have more lasting repercussions. This is especially the case with Iraq. French actions over the second half of 1996 have diminished Western deterrence against Saddam Hussein on both Iraq's northern and southern borders. Seeing itself better off today *vis-à-vis* the international community than it was one or two years ago, Baghdad can believe that continued flouting of UN resolutions will improve its standing even more.

As to whether French policy is animated by a reaction to U.S. policy, there does seem to be a curious psychological subtext to France's new approach to the Middle East: that playing a role, especially one at odds with the United States, is beneficial for its own sake. If this is the case, remedying the problem is difficult to address in conventional bilateral consultations. Below are instructive interviews with Foreign Minister de Charette:

Aside from our participation from the Gulf War under U.S. command, we were absent from [the Middle East] scene. However I think irony was inappropriate. Those wielding it see France as a second-class power. And they are wrong. To be sure, we are not the most

---

37. "The EU wants to complement America's work, not to compete with it," wrote Britain's Rifkind. *The Times* (London), November 5, 1996. Italy's Agnelli said, when de Charette set off on his Lebanon mediation in competition with U.S. Secretary of State Warren Christopher, "When there are too many cooks, it is difficult to prepare the sauce." *La Libre Belgique*, April 23, 1996; cited in FBIS.

38. Paris acted as the *de facto* patron of Iranian Foreign Minister Velayati and facilitated his visit to Damascus as part of a round-robin of diplomacy precisely when U.S. Secretary of State Christopher was visiting Damascus to seek a post-Qana cease-fire.

important country in the world, but we do exist at our own station, which is high. On this mutating planet of ours, I meet many political leaders who would like France to be as active internationally as possible. Many of them are watching us. Provided it wants to, France can be a force to be reckoned with on the world stage.[39]

A few weeks later, he said:

France has made a remarkable comeback in [the Middle East]. For more than ten years, France had been passive and Europe had been totally absent from the zone. . . . We now play a full role in the Middle East. Our contribution to the collective efforts towards preventing the peace process from being jeopardized is now considered normal, natural and self-evident. All our partners accept French diplomacy's presence and I would even say the Arab nations call for it.[40]

This chest-beating sense of national self-esteem is especially strong when contrasted with his view of America's role in the Middle East. As de Charette noted caustically: "The United States has done a lot to build peace in the Middle East. But while the Americans are and remain our friends, it does not mean that we do not have anything to say in the matter. Is it not true that France is the nation with the best knowledge of the region?"[41] To France's chief diplomat, no answer would be diplomatic.

Managing Competition, Building Partnership

While America and Europe have different approaches to numerous Middle Eastern policy issues, the first conclusion to be drawn from an assessment of their respective Middle Eastern policy agendas is that nowhere are American and European strategic interests in fundamental conflict. While there will always be a certain level of competition, especially regarding commerce, this is not unnatural; nor should a certain level of political competition and divergence of views be cause for undue concern, especially given a history of often virulent U.S.-European disagreements over strategy and tactics when the stakes were far higher during the Cold War.

Often the perception of competition and conflict has been exacerbated by the injection of pettiness and pique into the policy process.

---

39. *Paris Match*, May 9, 1996, cited in FBIS-WEU-96-089, May 8, 1996.

40. *Le Figaro*, June 27, 1996, cited in FBIS-WEU-96-147, July 30, 1996.

41. *Paris Match*, May 9, 1996.

Such was the case with Europe's refusal to invite a U.S. observer to the Barcelona Summit (which irked the United States because of Barcelona's implications for the peace process, especially the Syria-Israel track), and with the lack of U.S.-EU consultation prior to the October 1996 Arafat-Netanyahu summit in Washington (in response to which the EU decided to name its own Middle East envoy and to approve the most scathingly anti-Israeli communiqué in sixteen years). While such pettiness may simply be a fact of life in the post–Cold War world, it can sometimes have unintended consequences that are inimical to the other party's core interests.

Moreover, to the extent that particular policies are a matter of national pride rather than strategic interest, engaging in public competition or criticism will only worsen the problem. To a certain extent, national pride is what drives French Middle East policy under Chirac. In contrast, while the United States has differences with both France and Germany on important regional issues, Germanic pride has never been a factor. While the United States need not play to Paris's vanity by conceding on key issues, Washington can take the high ground and avoid public rows that would only exacerbate the problem.

In general, therefore, a U.S. response to the time-honored call for greater consultation would help in smoothing the edges of U.S.-European conflict over the Middle East. This is not an innovative recommendation but it is a necessary one. It will not resolve differences but it will help to manage them.

As for specific items on the policy agenda, it is useful for the United States to recognize the organic European strategic interest in maintaining stability in North Africa and to permit the Europeans to take the lead in advancing policies toward that end. On a day-to-day basis, North Africa is an area of great strategic interest to Europe and relatively marginal interest to the United States. Therefore, it makes little sense for the United States to compete with Europe when the two parties' interests are complementary and America's stake is comparatively small. This is not a black-and-white recommendation; it is important for Europeans to understand the critical importance that the United States attaches to regime stability in Egypt and its connection with potential Islamic fundamentalist successes in francophone North Africa, and thus to recognize America's legitimate interest in Mediterranean developments (in addition to any impact on the peace process). In general, however, the Atlantic partnership would best be served if Washington permitted the Europeans to take the lead in issues in this area, especially since they are the only actors committed to investing significant political and financial capital to promote regional stability.

In the Arab-Israeli arena, however, it is difficult to imagine any party except the United States playing the pivotal broker or sponsor role in the peace process. This is a reality that Europeans need to accept; European pursuit of equality or parity with the United States only hurts the cause of peace and, in the process, injures the Atlantic partnership. By its actions and positions, Europe has disqualified itself from the broker/sponsor role—not just in the eyes of the United States and Israel but also in the eyes of those Arab leaders who understand what the United States (far more than Europe) brings to the table. Washington may no longer hold "99 percent of the cards," but what cards it has are still those the Arab parties want most: influence over Israel, strategic protection, and legitimacy. At a time when the international community discounts the peaceful protestations of a Likud government in Israel, the U.S. role is even more essential; precisely because the Europeans have staked out a condemnatory policy toward the Netanyahu government, their role is probably more marginal than usual. This does not mean that the EU and European powers cannot make important contributions, even beyond serving as the banker for Middle East development projects. However, the peace process cannot have more than one active sponsor, lest the sponsors become advocates for particular camps, not mediators. Europe's "contribution" to the process cannot be allowed to come at the expense of U.S. peace process efforts. An example of a positive contribution was the recent proposal by British Foreign Secretary Malcolm Rifkind for the eventual creation of an Organization for Cooperation in the Middle East. This forward-thinking idea expanded upon past proposals by Jordan's Crown Prince Hassan, Israel's current and former prime ministers, Benjamin Netanyahu and Shimon Peres, and Turkey's Foreign Minister Tansu Çiller, without contradicting or undermining any existing initiative. Another positive contribution was the agreement of some EU states to proposals by Israel and the Palestinian Authority to participate in an observer mission in Hebron following Israel's military redeployment. In contrast, a negative contribution was France's injection of Iran and Hezbollah into the diplomacy for a Lebanon cease-fire in May 1996. France has an important—even vital—role to play in helping to revive the concept of independent Lebanon, but to compensate for a lessening of Syrian control over Lebanon with an enhancement of Iran's role is too high a price to pay. The United States should welcome and encourage constructive political contributions to the peace process by Europe and its leading powers which complement their economic contributions. This will require closer U.S.-European coordination that expands areas of potential European contribution to the peace process without any derogation of the U.S. role as its principal political and diplomatic sponsor.

One issue on which the United States wishes Europe would display even greater leadership and foresight is Turkey. There are few more strategically important countries than Turkey, pivotal to key issues on three continents. With Turkey mired in a contest for its political soul between secular pro-Western forces and atavistic fundamentalist forces, now is the time for the West to extend a welcoming and encouraging hand to the former. While there is much the United States can do to assist the secular groups, especially in promoting closer military-to-military ties, the central question is EU membership: tying Turkey more closely to the West through the web of political, social, economic, and cultural links that are at the heart of the European Union. What pro-West Turks want is not immediate EU membership but only to be treated equally with all other EU applicants, hardly an outrageous demand for a faithful NATO ally. Turkey is Europe's to lose, and with it the West might lose the "Great Central Asia/Caucasus/Caspian Game" now underway with Russia and Iran.

On Iraq, the cold reality is that the direction of the West's policy toward Baghdad is essentially a U.S. policy issue; European actions have reduced the importance of Atlanticism in dealing with Iraq, though a reinvigorated European approach would surely be welcome. The key question is not how to revive U.S.-European coordination, but rather is an American decision about whether to escalate the confrontation with Iraq now or permit the erosion of "containment" to reach a point when Iraq's rehabilitation becomes a virtual inevitability. The fact that the United States virtually alone carries responsibility for deterring Saddam Hussein and maintaining a military force in the region adequate for confronting him, if necessary, makes this a peculiarly U.S. decision despite its global implications. With much of Europe having already signaled its accommodation with Saddam, U.S.-European consultations are important but are not—and should not—determine the shape and direction of U.S. policy.

Iran, not Iraq, should serve as the test of U.S.-European coordination. In strategic terms, the interests of the United States and Europe *vis-à-vis* Iran are complementary; however, they have adopted contradictory approaches toward dealing with Iran that have each failed to achieve their goals. Rather than adapt policies accordingly, each has the other to blame as a convenient scapegoat for these failures. As a result, the policies persist. Even if this leaves the United States on the moral high ground, it faces an Iran ever more capable of exerting its negative influence throughout the Middle East.

If there is shared concern among Americans and Europeans about the challenges posed by Iran to international peace and security— especially regarding Iran's support for international terrorism and its pursuit of weapons of mass destruction—then the tactical divide between the two can be bridged.[42] One way to do this would be for the United States to take advantage of the Mykonos verdict to call Europe's bluff on Iran.[43] This might entail an initiative along the following lines: The United States would propose to the EU a U.S.-European agreement on definitive criteria by which to judge the efficacy of any renewed form of critical dialogue. Criteria should focus on verifiable changes in Iranian behavior on defined issues, especially Iran's active support for terrorism against the Arab-Israeli peace process and its efforts to acquire or develop nuclear weapons. This agreement should be coupled with mutual commitments to amend each side's policy pending a review of critical dialogue following a twelve to eighteen month testing period. If such an accord is reached, then the United States should be willing to suspend implementation of the sanctions clauses of the Iran and Libya Sanctions Act until the close of the testing period and the U.S.-EU policy review. If the policy review indicates that Iran did indeed moderate its behavior based on the predetermined yardsticks, the United States would continue to suspend implementation of the Iran and Libya Sanctions Act, pending another eighteen-month review. If, however, there is no substantial change in Iranian behavior, then the Europeans would, by prior agreement, impose tighter restrictions on their own trade and financial links with Iran.

This approach contrasts with the proposal now making the policy rounds, that the United States should seek out its own engagement

---

42. Of course, this assumption may not be true: when Europeans complained in the early 1990s about the hypocrisy of U.S. containment policy at a time when the United States was Iran's largest importer of oil, the United States responded by ending all trade with Iran; however, this apparently did not impress the Europeans.

43. For further elucidation of this suggestion, see *Building for Security and Peace in the Middle East*, report of The Washington Institute's Presidential Study Group, Robert Satloff and Samuel Lewis, eds., Washington, D.C., March 1997.

with Iran, on terms less stiff than those that have been on the table for years, for an "authoritative dialogue" with Iranian official representatives. However, some European countries (e.g., Germany, Denmark) are themselves facing significant public pressure to stiffen their own policies toward Iran because of egregious Iranian behavior, and now is not the time for the United States to signal weakness to Tehran—or to Europe—by proposing a softening of the U.S. terms for engagement.

Finally, despite the differences that characterize U.S. and European approaches to the Gulf, now is the time to begin to discuss the "post–dual containment" era. At some point, the regime in Iraq or Iran (or even both) will either fall or undergo significant internal evolution. Until then, dual containment, with its commitment of U.S. ground, naval, and air forces in the Gulf (including Saudi Arabia), will continue to be the logical approach toward dealing with Gulf security; after that, however, a new strategy will be needed. If the Europeans are willing to commit the tangible resources to back up their desire for a greater role in the Gulf, fashioning a successor strategy to dual containment could be a joint U.S.-European effort. However, given Europe's equanimity with regard to Gulf security in recent years, despite its greater *prima facie* interest in the Gulf, this is a process into which the United States should proceed with prudence and caution.

Overall, the common agenda for America and Europe in the Middle East is broad. There are areas each considers vital—for Europe, North Africa; for America, Israel and the peace process— where one side should be given wide license. The open-ended questions for the Transatlantic alliance are Turkey, with its impact eastward, and the Gulf. From Washington's perspective, the key issue in both arenas will be whether Europe meets the challenge of acting more creatively and assertively than it has in the recent past to protect Western interests and preserve regional stability.

Chapter 2

Europe and the Greater Middle East

Eberhard Rhein

No other region in the world can compete with the Middle East[1] in terms of importance for the economic prosperity of the industrialized world. If the eight countries of the Gulf that hold some 40 percent of known global oil and some 25 percent of known global gas reserves[2] were to stop their exports to the rest of the world for just two months, the global system would nearly collapse: oil and gas prices would skyrocket because of severe energy scarcities; balance-of-payments difficulties would appear in several countries; there would be a frantic run on alternative energy sources like coal. But supply would not be able to adjust with the required speed.

Notwithstanding two major oil crises in 1973 and 1979, two costly military conflicts in the region (Iran-Iraq and Iraq-Kuwait), the setting up of an elaborate system of security stocks and monitoring under the International Energy Agency, the world behaves as if the oil and gas supply from the Middle East is as secure as the air we breathe.

The European Union (EU) has never, since its inception in 1958, attributed to the Middle East the priority in its external relations due to that region as the "nerve center of the world."[3] Three questions

---

1. The "Middle East" encompasses the Mashrak (Israel, Egypt, Palestine, Lebanon, Jordan, and Syria), the states of the Gulf Cooperation Council (GCC, comprising Bahrain, Kuwait, Oman, Qatar, Saudi Arabia, and the UAE), as well as Yemen, Iraq, Iran, and Turkey.

2. Unless important new finds are made in other parts of the world, which is rather improbable, the Gulf share of global reserves is bound to rise.

3. The term "European Union" (EU) is used throughout this chapter to cover the signatories of the Rome Treaties irrespective of the date of their accession, and even where other terms like EEC or EC would be more appropriate. The term Europe is used alternatively when no specific EU policies, or policy positions, are concerned.

therefore must be asked: what has been Europe's relationship with the Middle East in the past? What is the degree of cooperation or rivalry between the EU and the United States? How should the future relationship be shaped in order to respond to the challenges Europe will have to confront in the Middle East?

These are difficult but also necessary questions. There are no sweeping answers. But there is a need to put the Greater Middle East high on the agenda of the EU's foreign policy and provoke a productive debate in Europe, the Middle East, and the United States.

In comparing European and U.S. policies toward the Middle East, two important points stand out. The first concerns the convergence of their respective policy objectives. Both the United States and Europe have traditionally pursued one overriding objective in their overall relations with the Middle East: to secure the energy supply. They may, and they sometimes do, differ when it comes to the means to be applied in order to achieve that objective. Similarly, their historic links with individual countries in the region may dictate different priorities. The United States and individual European countries may find themselves at odds when it comes to selling civilian equipment and even more so with regard to selling military equipment to the region. Finally, differences in style or chemistry between U.S. and European actors may occasionally give rise to tensions. But whatever differences have surfaced and will do so in the future, they concern the detail of policy implementation rather than the basic policy approach. On this, there has always been consensus across the Atlantic. It is important that this consensus be preserved far into the next century, when the industrial world's energy supply will face challenges of unprecedented dimensions as the era of fossil fuel energy will progressively draw to an end.

Second, profound differences exist between the United States and the European foreign policy machineries, rendering any comparison between U.S. and European policies toward the Middle East a somewhat awkward exercise. There is, to begin with, no such thing as a common European Middle East policy. Europe and the EU lack a single responsible foreign policy actor comparable to the U.S. secretary of state or the U.S. president. The European Union equally lacks a clearly defined line of command between political authority and the bureaucratic machinery. Nor does it have any European policy think tanks undertaking analysis, intelligence, and forward planning for the EU as a whole. The Commission, the EU's executive branch, has been notoriously reluctant to develop any policy initiatives that go beyond matters of trade, economic cooperation, or development assistance. Indeed, it has neither the ambition nor the means (in terms of staff or material resources) to develop policy initiatives outside the economic sphere.

Policies are generated in the fifteen capitals of EU member countries. But by definition these bear essentially national marks. To be transformed into a "European policy project" they invariably have to pass the "consensual screening" of fifteen member states and the EU Commission. Not surprisingly, very little innovative coherent action has been generated in that process. European Middle East policy has so far been limited either to economic strategies conceived by the Commission, most conspicuously the concept of a comprehensive Euro-Mediterranean partnership,[4] or to declamatory reactions to events or policy decisions taken by other players (the United States, Israel, Syria, etc.).

The dilemma of Europe's Middle East policy, caught between lofty ambitions and good intentions on the one hand and incapacity to shape these into coherent policy approaches on the other hand, has probably never been brought home more clearly to Europe, the United States, and the region than during the Lebanon crisis in the spring of 1996, when the Italian foreign minister, in her capacity as acting EU president, toured the region without clearly defined objectives, while at the same time her French colleague also toured the region with the precise aim of brokering an armistice between Israel and Lebanon, parallel to a similar U.S. mission.

Still, twenty-five years of "European political cooperation" have left their mark on the overall EU approach to the Middle East: national assessments of countries and events tend to converge more and more, whatever the persisting differences of national interests. Most important, there is agreement among member states on three fundamental guidelines of the European Middle East policy: to create greater social and economic stability in the Mediterranean region; to establish peace and cooperation between Israel and the Arab world; and to secure Europe's long-term energy supply.

---

4. The concept of a Euro-Mediterranean Partnership was approved by the EU and twelve Mediterranean countries at the Barcelona Conference on November 27–28, 1995. It aims at the creation of a European-Mediterranean free trade area, substantially increased financial support of Mediterranean countries, the institution of political dialogue involving all the partners concerned, more internal democracy, and a more peaceful coexistence of all the countries of the region. These broad objectives were spelled out in the "Barcelona Declaration."

The rest of this chapter reviews this history and the convergence of U.S. and European policy. It outlines future challenges and policy prescriptions for the Transatlantic relationship.

Thirty Years of EU Relations with the Middle East: A Review

The EU's involvement with the Middle East has been rising over time, in particular since 1973, the outbreak of the first oil crisis. This section reviews the history of EU involvement with the Mashrak, the Gulf Cooperation Council (GCC) states, Turkey, and Iran.

THE MASHRAK

The Mashrak has been that part of the Middle East on which the EU has mainly focused its attention. It started with benign neglect. But Europe was harshly reminded in 1973, during the short but effective Arab oil boycott against the Netherlands, that its relationship with Israel was a vital element in Europe's overall relations with the Arab world.

Since 1973 the EU has been obsessed with the Israeli-Arab relationship. It carefully balanced its approach to Israel, on the one hand, and its Arab neighbors, on the other hand, in 1977–78, when it came to negotiate cooperation agreements with the whole Mashrak region.

Since 1995, the EU policy approach towards the Mashrak has become an integral part of the Euro-Mediterranean partnership initiative approved at the Barcelona Conference. The EU approach encompasses all the Mediterranean rim countries in the south and east.[5] Neither the GCC countries nor Iraq nor Iran are presently covered by this approach, which is dictated by the fact that the EU's concern about stability in the Mediterranean tends to outweigh its concern about security of the oil and gas supply.

The EU's overall strategic perspective toward the Middle East is therefore not quite the same as that of the United States. While both share the objective of secure energy supplies, on the EU side there has been a visible shift to overall socioeconomic stability in the region, particularly in the Mediterranean rim countries.

At the end of the twentieth century, so it seems, Europe is more apprehensive about sociopolitical upheaval at its doorsteps, both east and south, than about any disruption of oil flow from the Gulf. The

---

5. Libya is excluded; for political reasons it is at present not considered fit by the European side to qualify for membership in the "Euro-Med club."

EU wishes to see the Mediterranean progressively transformed into a zone of peace, stability, and prosperity. Its major instruments to that end are trade liberalization, cooperation, and policy dialogue. By creating a vast Euro-Med free trade area, comparable to the North American Free Trade Area (NAFTA), competitiveness, efficiency, and socioeconomic prosperity should be encouraged.

In parallel, both governments and civil societies of the twenty-seven partner countries are becoming involved in an intensive cooperation network, embracing subject matters as diverse and important as water management, transport, fisheries, energy, environmental policies, and even security.

The EU approach has an influence on the Middle East peace process. Indeed, the Barcelona framework is the only institutional set-up in which Israel and its Arab neighbors (with most of whom it does not have diplomatic, let alone contractual relations) freely discuss issues with a direct bearing on the political, economic, and cultural climate in the region. It is therefore remarkable that, so far, the crisis in the peace process following the Israeli elections in May 1996 was not followed by a standstill in intra-Mediterranean multilateral cooperation. But such a truce cannot last forever; should Israel persist in its hard-line attitude against its neighbors, incompatible with the basic principles on which the "Barcelona process" is based, its membership in the Mediterranean Club will sooner or later be jeopardized.

Another noteworthy EU contribution to the peace process has been through the Regional Economic Development Working Group (REDWG) set up in the wake of the 1991 Madrid Conference.[6] The EU has chaired this group with enthusiasm, and it can boast of having generated a sense of regional identity among the four core parties (Egypt, Israel, Jordan, and the Palestine Liberation Organization). More than one hundred technical meetings have been held, first in Europe but since 1995 almost exclusively in the region, to discuss issues of regional trade, transport, infrastructure, telecommunications, electricity, etc. Since the spring of 1996, a small secretariat functions in Amman in order to keep the process going.

THE GULF COOPERATION COUNCIL

EU relations with the GCC have so far not reached the same degree of intensity as EU relations with the GCC's Mediterranean neighbors. In 1989, both sides signed a cooperation agreement. EU and GCC foreign

---

6. The Spanish government hosted this historic conference in Madrid, during which the peace process between Israel and its Arab neighbors was re-launched.

ministers meet regularly, at least once a year, for a broad exchange of views on political and economic issues of common interest.

Security matters are largely excluded from this dialogue. The GCC States know that the EU is not the appropriate place to discuss security matters, except in the broadest political terms. The subject has therefore been taboo in EU-GCC relations. The GCC countries prefer to discuss such matters (including arms procurement) unilaterally with individual member states, essentially the United Kingdom and France, as they do with the United States.

EU-GCC relations have given rise to little or no controversy with the United States. Both sides consider the GCC a vital element of peace and stability in the Gulf and therefore of vital importance to global energy flows. Both have close political and business relations with GCC countries. The United States has never reproached Europe for not doing more to bolster the military capabilities of the GCC countries. The U.S. government fully realizes the constraints that impede the EU from taking any joint action, beyond what individual member states (the United Kingdom and France) pursue under their own responsibility, without any intra-EU coordination.

IRAQ

EU links with Iraq have never gone beyond the stage of formal diplomatic relations. There has never been a ministerial visit either from Iraq to Brussels or vice versa. The idea of formalizing relations has never even been explored, despite the weight and importance of Iraq in the Middle East context and in the Arab world. The explanation is simple (and similar to the EU-Libya non-relationship): the EU frowns upon entering into contractual relations with dictatorships or military regimes. Since the UN embargo against Iraq in 1990, relations have been practically frozen. Trade came to a grinding halt and has not recovered.

However, this situation is not going to last forever. Iraq will have to be re-integrated into the international community. The EU will have to re-establish channels of communication, and Iraq should be integrated into whatever system of regional security is established. It is too important a player, both politically and in the energy market, to be treated forever as a pariah state. But such changes are difficult to envisage without a change of the present leadership in Baghdad.

Iraq has not been a prominent object of EU-U.S. consultations, not even during the last six years since the start of the Kuwait crisis. Clearly, the EU has fully accepted and welcomed strong U.S. leadership on Iraq, and after the war Iraqi matters have essentially been relegated to the UN Security Council. There has been no perceptible pressure from the EU or individual member countries to soften, let alone to abolish, the UN mandatory embargo. European interests in Iraq are marginal compared to other countries in the region.

TURKEY

EU relations with Turkey have never been considered an integral part of European Middle East policy. This was invariably a "special case." Turkey has never been fully considered a European country, but neither is it considered fully Asian. It is at the crossroads between two continents, two cultures, and two destinies.

The EU-Turkey relationship is the oldest among all the countries of the region. Since 1964 Turkey has been associated with the EU; in 1996, the EU and Turkey completed their customs union after a transition period of more than thirty years.

Economically, Turkey constitutes the most important EU partner in the Middle East, more so than Israel or Saudi Arabia. Nonetheless, this has never been an easy relationship; it has always been fraught with crises. These have centered on internal political developments (democracy, human rights, censorship, torture, treatment of the Kurds, occupation of Northern Cyprus, etc.). As a full-fledged member of the Council of Europe, the Organization for Economic Cooperation and Development (OECD), the Organization for Security and Cooperation in Europe (OSCE) and the North Atlantic Treaty Organization (NATO), Turkey has always been judged—severely so—by the moral standards of European countries. Adding to the complexity are unresolved Greek-Turkish disputes.

However, Turkey, the EU, and the United States have over the past thirty years developed an intimate security relationship in which the EU has played the economic part of stabilizing Turkish society and the United States, bilaterally or via NATO, the more sensitive military part. Because of its geostrategic location and as the number one economic power in the Middle East, Turkey has to be seen as a pillar in any Western Middle East strategy. It is therefore of great importance to smooth whatever frictions arise between Turkey and both the EU and United States. This will only succeed if the EU and the United States proceed in close concert.

IRAN

The vicissitudes of the EU relationship with Iran over the past thirty-five years illustrate the way in which the EU responds to political changes on the side of potential partners. Up to the violent establishment of the "Islamic Revolution" in 1979, EU relations with Iran were normal and even quite close: thirty years ago Iran figured among the first countries with whom the EU concluded modest trade agreements. Up to the late 1970s, Iran was, together with Saudi Arabia, the EU's most important economic and trading partner in the Middle East, much more important than either Israel or Turkey.

By 1996, that relationship had substantially reduced in importance. As a trade partner Iran is hardly more important than Morocco. Politically, this partnership hinges on the tenuous thread of what is called the EU-Iran "critical dialogue," twice-a-year meetings, at an official level, between an EU and an Iranian delegation.[7]

During the past four years, this critical dialogue has at least allowed the two sides to keep basic lines of communication open. But it has done little to bridge the deep aversion and the gulf of mistrust created between the two sides since the establishment of the Islamist regime in Tehran in the late seventies. Sympathy in Europe has not grown over time, despite a more pragmatic approach within the Iranian regime. A combination of political and psychological factors have made it difficult for Europe to normalize its relationship with the biggest power in the Middle East, let alone to envisage a really close alliance. These include the hangover from the days of the Iranian Revolution; a certain respect for the radical U.S. condemnation of the Iranian regime; the continued anger at the Iranian *fatwa* against an EU citizen, Salman Rushdie; the revelations about state-supported terrorist actions on European soil; and apprehensions about Iranian long-term regional power plays. But this state of affairs cannot last forever, as it does not correspond to the vital interests of either side. Iran is bound to be a major regional power, thanks to its strategic position, its skilled population of approximately 125 million by 2025, its huge oil and gas reserves, its influential diaspora in Europe and the United States, and its great historical past. Nor can Iran ignore the fact that the EU will be, together with Russia and India, one of the key political players in its wider environment.

Iran has turned out to be the Middle East country on which EU and U.S. policies clashed intensely during 1996. The EU does not share the U.S. philosophy that Iran has to be totally cut off from the outside world in order to change the Iranian policy stance. The EU does not

---

7. The "critical dialogue" was set up in the early 1990s as a means of influencing Iranian policies in sensitive areas such as support of international terrorism, threats to European citizens, the Middle East peace process, etc.

believe in the virtue of unilateral trade and investment embargoes against Iran, which cannot be as strictly enforced as the international UN-monitored embargo against Iraq. It comes as no surprise that the EU has been deeply concerned by recent U.S. legislation with extra-territorial application (the Helms-Burton Act and Iran and Libya Sanctions Act) placing sanctions against new investments in Iran even on EU-based European as well as U.S. companies.

In April 1997, however, the EU moved much closer to the U.S. policy stance. It suspended the critical dialogue with Iran and called its ambassadors back from Tehran; this took place not so much because of U.S. pressure, but as a consequence of the decision of a German tribunal in Berlin in the Mykonos case which clearly indicated that Iranian high officials were responsible for the murder of Iranian dissidents in Berlin in 1992.

European and U.S. Interests in the Middle East: Convergence and Interaction

Comparing European and U.S. interests in the region, one arrives at the conclusion that they largely converge rather than diverge, at least as far as the core interests are concerned. Energy security has traditionally been the overriding concern in the region for both Europe and the United States. With the diversification of sources of supply to Central Asia, the normalization of relations with Russia, and the continuing stable yields of oil and gas from the North Sea, the interest in a secure oil and gas supply has temporarily diminished since the middle of the eighties. Europe's dependence on the Middle East nevertheless remains vital and is much greater than that of the United States, which imports only 20 percent of its total energy consumption, compared to 50–90 percent for European countries, with the exception of Norway and the United Kingdom.

Because of its higher dependence on outside sources, Europe seems more ready to pay a higher price for energy than the United States, and to accept a progressive increase of energy prices as a necessary incentive to energy savings and the introduction of alternative energies such as wind, solar, and nuclear power. In recent years, it has therefore no longer tried to influence the oil price strategy of its Arab partners. Oil prices have ceased to be an important subject of EU-Arab dialogue.

Regional stability has become a matter of increasing priority for Europe. It has replaced energy security as the number one concern of

European Middle East policy. This goes for the Mediterranean region, particularly for the Maghreb since the start of Algerian unrest in 1992.

Clearly, Europe is afraid that the impossibility that its Mediterranean neighbors can cope with their massive socioeconomic and political challenges may affect its own internal security through an inflow of illegal immigrants, the destabilization of its population of Maghreb nationality or descent (approximately four million people), or through a further rise of illegal drug smuggling from the region (Morocco, Turkey, Lebanon).

Thus the risk of internal destabilization, much more than that of regional military conflicts, has in recent years affected internal political stability in certain European countries, as the rise of xenophobic sentiment and the ascent of the extreme right in France testify.

For the United States, regional stability in the Middle East does not have the same quality of intensity. The region is too far away; the Algerian civil war is not at the doorstep; the phenomenon is understood rationally as a political problem, but not sensed as a threat to U.S. internal security, as similar unrest taking place near the American "soft underbelly"—Mexico, Central America, and the Caribbean—would be.

The protection of commercial and financial flows has never been seen as being of an importance equal to that of energy and regional stability, for both the EU and the United States. Europe has little foreign direct investment to protect in the Middle East, as the region has not yet been able to create an attractive investment climate. As for trade, Europe enjoys a normal proximity advantage, compared to the United States, in the region. It is this advantage, together with the wide range of its products, that helped make Europe the number one trading partner of the Middle East. At no point have export interests been a driving force behind the EU's Middle East policy. With a substantial annual export surplus of $15–30 billion (U.S.), this would have been unbecoming.

There is one major divergence between European and American interests in the Middle East: the security of Israel is not normally considered a core European interest.

Of course, Europe is committed to the existence of Israel as a legitimate state of the Middle East. But Europe no longer considers Israel's existence to be jeopardized by Arab military or political power. For Europe, the military, political, and economic power balance has changed dramatically in favor of Israel during the last thirty years. This is the basic reason for the more outspoken pro-Palestinian and pro-Arab stance by the EU, and certainly not in any economic stakes such as oil and gas security, or the importance of the Arab market to European exports. As an economic, political, scientific, or cultural partner, the EU has more in common with Israel than with any Arab country, but this does not and must not prevent the EU from taking a critical look at certain of Israel's policies which, as seen with European eyes, have not always been helpful, even under the auspicious sign of the peace process, in bringing about peace and cooperation between Israel and its Arab neighbors.

European interests in the Middle East are, however, not fully homogenous. They continue to be influenced by specific national preferences and shaped by geography, history, and economic links. Geographic proximity or distance certainly carries its weight within the European context: countries like Finland or Sweden do not feel the same intense interest in the Middle East as do France or Spain. They go along with whatever policies are being pursued within the EU; but they can hardly be expected to act as initiators.

Different European countries do not share the same focus when it comes to individual Middle East countries: Lebanon has a higher priority for France than it does for any other EU country; the same goes for Algeria, Tunisia, and Morocco, even if Spain and Italy compete with France for more economic and even political presence there. Similarly, Germany is traditionally considered as a "Turkish outpost" within the EU, so closely are the interests between the two countries interwoven, as a consequence of history and more recently, of Turkish migrants in Germany.

These "national components" of European Middle East policies constitute an obvious contrast to the United States. Wherever an individual state like France, the United Kingdom, or Germany has a particular interest in certain parts of the Middle East, it automatically assumes a "leader role." It can be expected to come up with initiatives; it is listened to; and it may even exercise a certain veto power, whenever the majority of member states would push the EU into policies of which the "lead country" might not approve.

Such national preferences have so far not been a major problem for establishing consensus within the EU, except as far as Turkey is concerned. In this case, the policy stance adopted by Greece has, indeed, obliged other EU members to discuss Turkey-related issues outside the EU institutional framework.

EU relations with Turkey would, however, remain complicated whatever the state of Greek-Turkish relations. The EU wishes to maintain very close economic and political ties with Turkey. But it is not, at least at this stage or in the foreseeable future, ready to envisage Turkey as a full EU member. On this point, there is an unspoken consensus among all EU members. The EU simply does not feel it can manage to absorb a big country like Turkey (with a population that is expected to reach 90 million people by 2025), which has severe internal divisions between the relatively developed west and the poor east, an unresolved Kurdish problem, and an equally unresolved conflict between secular and religious aspirations for society.

For the EU, Turkey's membership in NATO and in the EU are in no way linked to each other. From a European perspective, Turkey should therefore politely be told by both the United States and the EU that it would be inappropriate for it to drive a hard bargain over expansion of NATO towards Eastern Europe, the more so as such expansion would also serve Turkish strategic interests (Turkey having so long complained about its isolated forward position in the southeast).

From the European perspective, there is therefore no fear that the issue of Turkish NATO vs. EU membership might cause problems for the Transatlantic alliance. The Turkish threat of a veto to NATO enlargement is an understandable expression of Turkish frustrations with Europe, but is not a sustainable policy stance.

Considering the basic convergence of interests, it is normal that over time an increasingly close EU-U.S. interaction in Middle East affairs has developed. The EU has rarely pursued policies without taking into account U.S. interests or U.S. views, and more than once EU policy has been determined in Washington. This is not to say that the EU has not also occasionally competed with the United States or politely refused certain U.S. requests, but compared to the United States, the EU has been only a minor player.

The EU has been crippled in its capabilities through its own deficiencies: an efficient common foreign and security policy requires not only a strong notion of overriding common interest but also a clear vertical command structure, the ultimate power of decision and action being vested in a single source of authority. The EU could therefore not expect to be more than a second-class actor, and most of its "action" in the past has been of a verbal nature, messages "to whom it may concern" in the form of some one hundred declarations on Middle East events.

In the strategic field of security and defense, the EU continues to be a "non-actor." Without U.S. determination, Iraq might have occupied not only tiny Kuwait but the whole of the GCC. The EU would probably not have gone much beyond sending a reproachful telegram.

The same goes for the Arab-Israeli conflict. No one would seriously believe that the EU in its state of institutional weakness could have launched the peace process and brought the parties together in Madrid in the fall of 1991, as the United States managed to achieve after many months of difficult shuttle diplomacy.

Thus it was as a matter of course that the EU assumed the role of junior partner. This has not always been without problems; the EU has more than once tried to revolt against U.S. dominance in Middle East policies (the EU's vain efforts to put up a high profile at the Madrid Conference in 1991; at the signing of the Oslo Agreements in Washington in 1993; etc.). Grudgingly, the EU, and in particular some of its member states, France above all, always had to concede and accept the international "pecking order."

In spite of these deficiencies, the degree of consultation, coordination, and interaction between the two prominent actors, the United States and the EU, in the Middle East has increased enormously: a high degree of interaction and even intimacy exists today compared to twenty years ago.

This is in itself a clear demonstration of the EU's enhanced profile. It is being taken much more seriously; its positive role in the Middle East is clearly acknowledged; and the United States can no longer do without the political and, even more, the economic backing of the EU.

But the exchange of ideas, notes, intelligence, etc. between the United States and the EU continues to remain very much a "one-way street." This will only change slowly, depending on the EU's determination to develop a truly common foreign and security policy.

Challenges for the Future

Europe and the United States would be well advised to prepare themselves for more trouble in the Middle East and therefore to stand ready to intervene, to help, to mediate, and to smooth adjustment pains whenever and wherever necessary.

For Europe the three key challenges for the coming decades remain to:
• establish a greater degree of regional stability;
• secure the long-term supply of energy; and
• help bring about lasting peace and cooperation between Israel and its Arab neighbors.

Europe and its twelve partner countries in the south and east of the Mediterranean have jointly launched a comprehensive long-term strategy to bring about a higher level of prosperity, democracy, and peace in the Mediterranean. The "Barcelona Declaration" constitutes the blueprint for such a strategy.

Will it succeed in turning a region fraught with turmoil, poverty, lack of civil society, excess of government bureaucracy, absence of true democracy, widespread distrust between countries, and a host of troublesome socioeconomic problems into the zone of peace, stability, and prosperity that the twenty-seven foreign ministers have pleaded to create? Even after fifteen months of implementation efforts, it is still far too early to pass a balanced judgment. So far the signals are mixed.

Undoubtedly new determination and a mood of reform are taking root on the Mediterranean side. But it is also evident that skepticism remains strong. A lot of patient work will be required in order to turn the objectives of the Barcelona Declaration into political and economic reality by the target date of 2010. On the EU side, political priorities have, since the Barcelona conference, somewhat shifted away from the Middle East to other, even more urgent issues such as the European Monetary Union, constitutional reform, NATO's eastern enlargement, and, last but not least, unemployment. This shift of attention, if it were to last, would dim hopes of producing more prosperity and political stability in the region.

The EU will therefore have to invest much more of its political energy in the Middle East if it wants to avoid a painful reminder that instability on its southern flank may hurt its own stability and well-being. It must urgently proceed with the overdue ratification of the Association Agreements signed in 1995–96 with Israel, Tunisia, and Morocco, despite the inherent slowness of fifteen national parliamentary procedures.

These agreements constitute the implementation of the European-Mediterranean partnership initiative approved at the Barcelona Conference in November 1995. Other similar agreements with Jordan and the Palestinian Authority have been or will be signed in 1997, while negotiations with Egypt and Lebanon have almost been completed. Negotiation of an agreement with Algeria started in late 1996 and discussions with Syria may begin in 1998.

The EU must not delay any further the conclusion of the negotiations with Egypt and Lebanon on the grounds that certain rather marginal points relating to agricultural trade and the repatriation of illegal immigrants have not been solved to its full satisfaction.[8] It must continue to bolster the fledgling economies around the Mediterranean by very substantial financial support well beyond the turn of the century.

It seems unlikely that this central part of the EU's Middle East policy is fraught with possible EU-U.S. conflict. Both share an interest in regional stability, so the United States must wish as much as the EU that the Barcelona process will show tangible results—the sooner the better.

The United States must accept, in return, that the EU-Mediterranean free trade area that is to be progressively established until 2010 contains an element of discrimination against U.S. exports, just as the EU cannot but accept similar discrimination against its exports into the North American Free Trade Area countries.

Europe's long-term energy supply may be jeopardized by two different types of risks, one relating to a rise in energy prices, the other relating to an interruption of energy supply by a military conflict. The first risk is not likely to pose any major problems to Europe. The second one is an inevitable process that mankind will have to come to grips with. Western nations simply have to learn that the era of excessively cheap energy that has existed throughout the second half of the twentieth century will soon come to an end. The transitional period should be sufficiently long and the price increases sufficiently gradual, not by big jumps as in 1973 and 1979, that individual democracies can cope with the adjustment pains.

This does not mean that the EU and the United States should sit back until the day when oil and gas prices will have doubled or tripled sometime by the middle of the next century. Europeans are aware of the precariousness of the energy supply. They accept the need to prepare the post–fossil energy era, not only for reasons of energy policy: they are also more concerned than Americans about the negative environmental impact of burning huge and ever increasing quantities of oil, gas, or coal. That is why Europe seems more ready to embark upon an ambitious long-term program for the development of renewable energies. Such a program is presently being prepared by the EU Commission, which hopes that by 2010 the EU will be able to

---

8. The EU position on liberalization of agricultural trade with its Mediterranean partners remains extremely negative. It has rightly been criticized by its partners for not being in harmony with the overall objective of establishing Euro-Mediterranean free trade.

cover some 12 percent of overall energy needs by means of renewable energy, including hydropower. It should ideally involve the Mediterranean and Arab neighbors who might be interested and who possess the vast solar power potential needed to supply, in due time, the whole Euro-Mediterranean area with solar energy.

From the European perspective, it would certainly be welcome if the United States were to undertake similar steps to promote the use of renewable energies. Unlike Europe, the United States has the potential of producing substantial quantities of solar electricity on its own soil, particularly in the Southwest. Moreover, for more than a decade, it has successfully demonstrated that solar power can be produced at reasonable cost. But that potential will only be expanded if and when the United States decides to bring the level of gasoline and fuel taxation more in line with that prevailing in Europe.

The risk of another military conflagration in the Gulf region is more difficult to assess and to cope with. It is evident that the EU will not be capable, at least for another ten to fifteen years, of any preventive military action in the Gulf or anywhere else in the world. When it comes to securing energy supply by military power, the EU will not have any choice but to act in union with the United States, either by way of bilateral coordination, as in the Iraq war, or under NATO responsibility as in Bosnia.

Presently, the EU is not involved in any of the practical security arrangements that, following the Iraq war, have been put in place bilaterally between the United States, the United Kingdom, and France on the one hand, and Saudi Arabia, Kuwait, and the United Arab Emirates on the other hand (positioning of military hardware, presence of U.S. troops in the region, supply of equipment, training of Arab armies, regular visits of military vessels to the Gulf, supply of advance air reconnaissance, etc.).

For the time being, these arrangements, combined with the containment of renewed Iraqi and Iranian military buildup (through UN supervision and embargo upon the supply of sensitive military equipment to either country), should be a credible deterrent against aggression to member states of the Gulf Cooperation Council. In any event, there is hardly anything the EU might do to change the situation. It has neither the necessary political authority nor the military or financial means to become active on its own.

The question remains whether a purely defensive military posture is good enough to assure long-term security in the Gulf region. Would it not be appropriate, in addition, to strive for something like a multilateral "Charter of Peace and Stability" to which all countries of the region, including Iraq and Iran, as well as outside powers (the United States, Russia, the EU, Japan, China) would be invited to adhere? Such a contractual instrument would have to guarantee the territorial integrity of all the regional parties and oblige them to renounce the use of force in the settlement of any disputes. Moreover, they would have to commit themselves not to impede the free flow of oil and gas to the world. In return, the outside powers would, individually or collectively, play the part of guarantor states to such an agreement.

Such an ambitious deal would go a long way toward reducing tension and mistrust among the regional powers and consequently lessen the buildup of military power that, in the absence of confidence and trust in the Gulf, is bound to take place again sooner or later. It would also demonstrate to the world that its key powers are jointly determined to secure the energy supply from the Gulf.

Even a superficial political analysis of the interests of each of the players potentially involved in the building up of such a security structure demonstrates, however, that there is not the slightest chance of bringing them together, at least in the short run. The whole idea could be dismissed as either naive or unfeasible, but when the stakes for the industrial democracies are as high as they are in the Gulf, one must not be afraid of thinking the unthinkable.

It is therefore suggested that the EU launch a serious in-depth analysis of various risk scenarios arising in the Gulf and of appropriate political, economic, and, where necessary, military answers. This should become one of the priority assignments of the EU's future policy analysis unit. This analysis would in due course be shared with the United States and other appropriate partners.

Should that analysis lead to the conclusion that a comprehensive security structure, involving all regional and major outside powers, ought to be set up in the Gulf, the EU would have to explore modalities with the regional partners, starting with the GCC.

Finally, there will be no independent role for the EU when it comes to brokering the peace arrangements still to be negotiated between Israel on the one hand and Lebanon, the Palestinians, and Syria on the other hand. It is only through combined efforts of persuasion and, where necessary, gentle pressure alongside the United States that the peace negotiations will be successfully concluded.

However, when the EU feels that U.S. positions may not be sufficiently productive, it should try to influence them. This in turn requires that the EU follow much more closely the negotiation process in all its intricacies. The presence in the region, since the end of 1996, of an EU ambassador concerned with the peace process will help in that respect.

The EU should continue to play an overall balancing role between a strong, powerful Israel and its Arab neighbors. It is too often over-looked that Israel's national income is roughly equivalent to that of its five immediate neighbors combined (Egypt, Jordan, Lebanon, Palestine, and Syria). It will therefore remain essential for the EU's overall policy stance to strengthen the weaker Arab hand.

This goes in particular for Palestine. The EU and the international community at large have to see to it that the fledgling Palestinian entity can progressively be turned into a sustainable Palestinian state, whose extremely narrow land base must, under no circumstances, be further eroded by additional Israeli land claims for whatever reason.[9]

The EU should continue to "push" Israel and its neighbors into a more comprehensive network of regional cooperation. One conse-quence of the EU's new Mediterranean approach will be for Israel and its Arab neighbors to enter into free trade agreements similar to those with the EU. This would spur regional trade in a dramatic way. Both sides are, in principle, ready to embark on such a course. But as long as the political issues are not settled, that is, as long as the final status settlement has not been negotiated and successfully imple-mented, neither Jordan nor Egypt will, for internal political reasons, dare to enter into privileged relations with Israel.

Whatever these difficulties, the EU must not give up its efforts to help establish regional cooperation patterns as a means to create joint interests in peace and cooperation.

While the EU cannot do much to bring Syria and Israel back to the negotiating table, except to press Israel to return the Golan Heights (or most of it) in exchange for peace with Syria, it can help Syria in reforming its economic and, in a more distant future, even its politi-cal system by negotiating an association with the EU along the lines of agreements envisaged with all Maghreb and Mashrak countries. Initial talks started in 1996; they have shown that a lot of persuasion will be required in order to convince Syria that a full-fledged EU-Mediterranean partnership is in its long-term interest. Concluding

---

9. In 2020, both Israel and Palestine expect to have a population of eight million people each. But Palestine will at best administer one third of the land that Israel will own. Population density in Palestine will reach 1,800 people per square kilo-meter, more than four times as much as the Netherlands.

such an agreement with the EU would make Syria a much more reliable partner for everybody, including Israel. But this will require a lot of time, sensitivity, and patient talks.

Conclusions

From the late 1980s to the mid-1990s, the EU has undoubtedly become a more important international player in the Middle East. This is clearly visible in the economic sphere, where the EU, largely thanks to geographic proximity, constitutes the region's main partner when it comes to trade, tourism, foreign direct investment, and other financial flows, including aid.

However, the EU wishes, in addition, to play a bigger role in the political realm. It no longer wants to be confined to the role of "paymaster" for U.S.-inspired policies.

So far, however, experience has shown that due to its own institutional shortcomings, the EU is not yet up to its political ambition. Realistically, it has to be content with accompanying and complementing U.S.-led initiatives. The EU simply does not have anything comparable to the leverage of U.S. diplomacy, and even the power of the United States often proves ineffective to reach a settlement in the extremely complex political, historical, and psychological environment of the region.

The most reasonable approach for both the EU and the United States, at least in the medium term, will therefore be to pool, as much as possible, their respective resources, to join hands in diplomatic initiatives, and to share intelligence and political analysis. This is what is largely taking place, whatever the occasional outbursts of European diplomats' frustrations with their American colleagues or the feelings of hurt diplomatic pride.

The goal of effectiveness dictates close EU-U.S. cooperation in Middle East policies. Their core interests converge; where they differ, it has to do either with differences of the overall foreign policy approaches (world power vs. regional power) or with differences of judgment as to the best ways to handle specific situations (e.g., Iran, Libya, Israel).

From the European perspective, the allies are not *per se* divided on the Middle East, but rather constitute two forces acting in parallel toward the creation of a more peaceful and stable Middle East, both in their own interest and in that of the people of the region who deserve a better lot than wars, dictatorships, revolutions, and misery.

Chapter 3

The United States, Europe, and the Middle East Peace Process

Richard N. Haass

The fact that the Middle East is an intermittent source of friction between the United States and its friends and allies in Europe is a matter of import and curiosity alike. It is important because the stakes for everyone involved—the United States, the European Union (EU), European governments, and the peoples and governments of the region itself—are considerable. It is curious because, on the surface at least, American and European objectives—to promote peace and reconciliation between Israel and both the Palestinians and the Arab states—are the same. It is not obvious why the two should clash as often as they do, since they share many of the same goals. Particularly, both stand to benefit from diplomatic progress and suffer from renewed conflict.

What, then, accounts for the differences and the resulting Transatlantic friction? To a large extent—certainly more than most Europeans are prepared to admit—it is a consequence of a fundamental inequality in influence and roles. The United States is the dominant political and military force in the region—something that leaves many Europeans unhappy and frustrated because of disagreement with particular U.S. policies that they are powerless to change but that nonetheless affect European interests, because of resentment over U.S. primacy, or both. There is also a strong sense among European officials involved with this issue that U.S. policy is unduly influenced by domestic political considerations, something that leads to what they judge to be a U.S. approach that is too supportive of Israel.

The U.S. side is not much happier with the current state of U.S.-European relations regarding the Middle East peace process. U.S. officials tend to view European statements and actions affecting the peace process as "meddling" that only complicates the already difficult task of promoting political progress among the local parties. The result is mutual frustration and recrimination.

Is there danger in any of this? The short answer is "yes." European diplomacy that is perceived in the region as being "pro-Arab" or "pro-Palestinian" risks reinforcing Israeli tendencies to dig in and resist external pressures. This risk is particularly acute with the now-governing Likud Party, which lacks the historic ties to Europe associated with the Labor Party and its leadership. More significantly, there is the danger that European statements and actions will encourage Arab and Palestinian leaders to hold out. Independent and sympathetic European statements and diplomacy can fuel Palestinian and Arab desires to avoid compromise with Israel and avoid direct contact. Many in the Arab world retain the hope that the outside world will deliver something better than they can negotiate for themselves. Prospects for diplomatic progress in the Middle East are sufficiently modest without a European "bad cop" adding to the already immense difficulties confronting the United States.

A different kind of danger of U.S.-European differences over the Middle East is the potential impact on U.S.-European relations more generally. The end of the Cold War has ushered in a difficult period in Transatlantic relations. There is no longer a Soviet threat to coalesce around, even if the debates about how best to meet that threat were often a source of considerable friction. Moreover, the U.S.-European debate over the Middle East comes at a time when a number of other issues—what to do next in Bosnia, disagreements over Iraqi sanctions, NATO enlargement, the growth in American unilateralism, and the introduction of secondary sanctions to pressure Europeans and others not to deal with Cuba, Iran, and Libya—are already filling the agenda and buffeting the basic relationship. Differences over the Middle East are not likely to be the proverbial straw breaking the camel's back, but they are another burden that the camel could well do without.

This chapter attempts to do three things. First, it traces the origins of the rise in U.S. influence (and the concomitant decline in Europe's) in the Middle East and the peace process. Second, it assays the evolving situation in the Middle East in which the resulting Transatlantic frictions are played out. Last, the chapter puts forward some suggestions about what Americans and Europeans might do to better serve their common interests in the region and beyond.

A Shift in Power

The October 1996 visit to the Middle East by French President Jacques Chirac captured well how relations between Europeans and Americans had both changed and deteriorated. French frustration had apparently reached something of a new high in the wake of pronouncements and actions by the new and more conservative Israeli government. The French president made it clear that he was not satisfied that Europe be limited to a role of dispensing funds to buttress a peace process designed and implemented by Americans. Rather, he wanted Europe to be nothing less than a co-sponsor of the process itself. Chirac's personal style was reminiscent of Gaullism at its most assertive. Indeed, his trip to the region and Israel seemed at times designed deliberately to alienate the Israeli government, anger the Americans, and discomfit Chirac's European colleagues.

How did things get to this point? For a substantial part of this century—certainly from World War I until 1956—Europe (mostly Great Britain and France) was the principal political power in the Middle East. This position of influence was a reflection of European domination of world affairs and the more immediate result of colonial presence. As such, it was destined to fade with the demise of colonialism and the emergence of independent states in the area in the post–World War I period. The fact that the European powers were left largely depleted by World War II only contributed to this inevitability.

What happened, though, was both more abrupt and more dramatic than predicted. European influence in the region plummeted over Suez, when the United States pressured Israel, France, and Great Britain to desist in their collective attack on Nasser's Egypt. President Eisenhower was angry that this ill-conceived and poorly concealed enterprise distracted world attention from what Soviet tanks were doing in Hungary. Cold War requirements took precedence over imperial folly; never again would Washington allow European governments to threaten U.S. interests in a key arena of U.S.-Soviet competition. As the historian Albert Hourani noted in a seminal essay titled "A Moment of Change," "insofar as 'the West' still existed as a political entity in the Near East, it was the United States which was its representative."[1]

---

1. See Albert Hourani, "A Moment of Change: The Crisis of 1956," in Albert Hourani, *A Vision of History: Near Eastern & Other Essays* (Beirut: Khayats, 1961), p. 142.

In part as a result, European involvement in the Middle East over the past forty years came to be defined more by commercial than by diplomatic considerations. This has led to a distancing of European states, and France in particular, from Israel, and a parallel growth in European economic, military, and diplomatic ties with Arab states. The situation is not absolute or zero-sum—Europe remains Israel's largest trading partner, the source of approximately one-half of its imports and the recipient of one-third of its exports—but, to the extent that commercial concerns predominate, European governments tend to be more mindful of Arab interests than of Israeli interests.

A diplomatic evolution paralleled this commercial reorientation. Europe (both as individual governments and more recently as a collective acting through the European Union and related institutions) gradually became more sympathetic to the Arab and Palestinian positions in the peace process. There was a tendency, too, to voice criticisms of Israeli behavior ranging from the methods used to suppress the Palestinian *intifada* to the building of settlements. The dynamics this set in train tended to be self-reinforcing, improving European-Arab ties and pulling down those between Europe and Israel.

At the same time, the scale of the European diplomatic effort became increasingly modest and operated very much in the shadow of what the United States was doing.[2] Europe would send visitors to the region and issue pronouncements, but these carried little weight, especially in Israel, where the European embrace of the "Arab" interpretation of UN Security Council Resolution 242 was seen as unhelpful or even hostile.[3]

One can point to some exceptions to this trend of declining European importance, most recently and significantly the discussions leading up to the September 1993 Oslo accord. Europeans played an

2. For background on Europe's approach to the region, see François d'Alançon, "The EC Looks to a New Middle East," *Journal of Palestine Studies,* Vol. 23, No. 2 (Winter 1994), pp. 41–51.

3. Security Council Resolution 242 calls for a "just and lasting peace in the Middle East" to be brought about by Israel returning territory it captured in the 1967 war in exchange for acceptance. The resolution, the foundation of all subsequent diplomacy, does not specify how much of the territory Israel is to return. The traditional Arab position calls for the return of all the territory and the re-establishment of borders that existed prior to the 1967 war. The position of successive Israeli governments is that UN 242 does not require Israel to return all of the territory and that the amount of land to be handed over will reflect the quality of the peace and security arrangements. Most Israelis, including most "doves," reject a return to the 1967 borders.

important role in providing a venue for representatives of the Israeli government and the Palestine Liberation Organization (PLO) to meet privately and explore the potential to establish a new *modus vivendi*. The effort succeeded in bringing about direct PLO-Israeli contacts at the official level and in creating a framework for Israel's military withdrawal and the establishment of Palestinian self-rule in areas of the West Bank and Gaza occupied by Israel since 1967.

A number of factors merit mention, however. These events took place when a Labor government was in power in Israel and with a foreign minister, Shimon Peres, who had long and deep ties to European socialists. Such ties are notably absent in the Likud and are increasingly rare in the "Sabra" (home-grown) generation vying for power in the Israeli Labor Party. In addition, the European party at Oslo was Norway, not the EU. Nor was it France or Great Britain, the two European countries with the greatest direct regional experience and who tend to dominate EU policy deliberations on this part of the world. Moreover, the European role was limited; Europe acted more as a facilitator than as a partner or driving force, as the United States had been prior to and during the October 1991 Madrid peace conference that brought Israel and all of its immediate neighbors face-to-face for negotiations for the first time. Europe's reduced role was made stark by the desire of Palestinians and Israelis to sign the Oslo accord on the White House lawn. American blessing of the accord was deemed necessary even though the U.S. contribution to its negotiation was marginal.[4]

The corollary to what might be summarized as Europe's decline and tilt was an American rise and tilt. The year of 1956 was critical in that it marked the willingness and ability of the United States to act decisively in the region. Such U.S. power and influence were not again seen until the October 1973 war, when the Nixon administration acted to ensure that Israel would be secure but that its victory on the battlefield would (unlike 1967) be incomplete. U.S. influence stemmed from Israel's growing dependence on U.S. military supplies and from Israel's recognition that it could not afford to offend the United States, given Israeli vulnerability and the fact that its adversaries were backed by the Soviet Union.

---

4. See especially Jane Corbin, *The Norway Channel: The Secret Talks that Led to the Middle East Peace Accord* (New York: Atlantic Monthly Press, 1994); and David Makovsky, *Making Peace with the PLO: The Rabin Government's Road to the Oslo Accord* (Boulder, Colo.: Westview, 1996).

The end to the 1973 war and the agreements that separated Israeli forces from those of Syria and Egypt after the end of the fighting heralded the arrival of the U.S. era of Middle East peacemaking. Although the crucial initiatives and decisions were undertaken by Anwar Sadat and Menachem Begin, the United States was the important and active third party to the negotiations that resulted in the Camp David Accords and peace between Israel and Egypt. More than a decade later—after the United States as the senior partner and Europe very much the junior achieved victory over Iraq in the Gulf War and the Soviet Union in the Cold War—the United States convened the October 1991 peace conference in Madrid. The European Community was invited to the conference but had no role other than cheerleader for what was essentially a U.S.-created *fait accompli*.

The United States became Israel's critical external security partner in the late 1960s and has remained so ever since. Israel is the largest recipient of U.S. security assistance and is on a par with America's closest allies when it comes to eligibility for military hardware that exploits the most advanced technologies. The pro-Israel orientation of U.S. foreign policy is demonstrated by a tradition of close consultation over both strategic challenges and diplomacy. This U.S. bond with Israel was certainly strengthened by the Cold War, as the Soviet Union armed and provided diplomatic support to Arab confrontation states. But it is no less important to note that U.S. sympathy and support for Israel predated the Cold War, the result of the political influence of American Jewry and widespread support throughout the United States for Israel the underdog, and it has survived the Cold War's demise, again for domestic political reasons and a sense of moral and historical commitment.

Why is the European diplomatic role in the Middle East not greater, more like what many European (and certainly French) officials appear to desire? Resentment of the United States could lead one to believe that it is all a result of American machinations to freeze Europe out. There is something to this, to the extent that U.S. officials have been known to view their European counterparts as nuisances who have little to contribute but criticism.

But the modesty of Europe's role is more a reflection of European weakness than American jealousy. Some of this relative weakness is structural. The EU must act on a basis of consensus and it is often difficult for its members to agree. France's views are not universally shared; Dick Spring, Ireland's foreign minister in the latter half of 1996 when Ireland held the rotating EU presidency, made it clear that he did not support French President Chirac's ambitions.[5] And for years Germany has been wary of appearing to pressure Israel. Even more fundamental is the reality that Europe cannot bring to bear the same level of resources available to the United States. Being a super-power has its advantages, just as not being one brings limits.

Europe's weak hand is mostly a result of Europe's own choices, however. Earlier it was suggested that Europe has tended to tilt toward the Arab position and the United States toward Israel. This is a simplification but not one without truth. One result is that Europe has aligned itself with what is clearly the weaker side in the conflict and has alienated itself from the side that is stronger. (Israel enjoys the upper hand militarily and possesses what is tangible and sought by the other party, namely, territory.) This alignment is manifested in many ways, from regular diplomatic pronouncements calling for full Israeli withdrawal from the occupied territories and the establishment of a Palestinian state to the decision in late 1994 to scrap an eight-year-old embargo and resume arms sales to Syria. Europe has forfeited much of its ability to influence Israel but has gained little in so doing; indeed, there is not a lot of evidence to suggest that Europe has been able to elicit much flexibility from the Arab states and Palestinians.

Interestingly, U.S. closeness to Israel has not diminished U.S. influence with the Arab parties, as is sometimes suggested. (There is thus good reason to dispute Volker Perthes's judgment in Chapter 4 of this volume that "there is a general feeling on the Arab side that America's pro-Israeli bias makes it impossible to trust, and to rely on, the United States.") Even before the Cold War had ended, there were signs of Arab disaffection with Moscow. Sadat asked his Soviet advisers to leave, realizing that he could wage neither war nor peace successfully so long as they stayed. The result was Camp David and the emergence of a close U.S.-Egyptian economic and military relationship. Egypt is not alone, however. With the Cold War's demise there is no rival superpower to turn to; not surprisingly, Arab willingness to work with Washington has increased. This was and remains a factor in the calculations of both Syria and the PLO, both of whom were long dependent on the Soviet Union for backing. Moreover, there is the hope that the United States, because of its close ties to Israel, can influence or even compel it to be more accommodating.

---

5. See Judy Dempsey and Alexandra Capelle, "Israel: Chirac Calls for European Involvement in Peace Plans," *Financial Times*, October 24, 1996.

The Deteriorating Context

There is more than a little irony in the fact that the mounting signs of European frustration and desire to be allowed back into the peace process come at a time when the prospects for ambitious diplomacy are decidedly poor. Israel's new government and the PLO were scheduled to begin final status talks in the spring of 1997. (Final status talks were held for a short time before Israel's June 1996 election but made no headway.) The goal is to complete these talks and sign a treaty in three years, by May 1999. This goal will not be met. The issues of final status are the most difficult: Jerusalem; Palestinian control of territory and desire for statehood; the fate of Jewish settlements; the "right" of millions of Palestinian refugees to return "home"; and access to water. These issues would be difficult and perhaps impossible to negotiate even if the will to do so existed on all sides.

As a result of these difficulties, neither the will nor the ability exists to conclude an Israeli-Palestinian final status agreement formalizing the terms for peace. The PLO leadership fears losing support and, in the end, legitimacy, if it is seen to compromise important political goals. There is the additional fear that Hamas and other Islamic radicals would gain at the PLO's expense if anything were done to weaken the claim to Jerusalem. It is often safer to espouse dreams that are whole than accept realities that are inevitably incomplete. The PLO is not immune to this truism.

For its part, the Likud government of Benjamin Netanyahu campaigned on a series of positions, subsequently enshrined in government guidelines, that oppose a Palestinian state, the right of Palestinian refugees to return, and any dilution of exclusive Israeli sovereignty over a united Jerusalem. For Israelis, too, it is politically less risky to live with an imperfect status quo than to contemplate controversial alternatives. It thus strains credulity to imagine a ceremony on the south lawn of the White House in the second Clinton administration in which the current government of Israel agrees to give up far more than it has ever promised and Palestinians agree to accept much less than they have ever demanded.

Prospects are no better and are arguably worse for a treaty between Syria and Israel. The new Israeli government has been explicit in its intention to maintain sovereignty over the Golan Heights and in its refusal to return all of the territory gained in the 1967 conflict. The notion of minor agreements in exchange for some normalization and peace appears unrealistic. There is no evidence that Syrian President Hafez al-Assad was prepared to accept part of a loaf when he rejected the Rabin government's offer of the entire Golan Heights in exchange for peace, security arrangements, and a degree of normalization.

One can only speculate on why President Assad acted this way. Assad, known to be a tough bargainer, may have been holding out to get a better deal after an election that he expected would be won by Shimon Peres. He may simply have run out of time owing to Labor's decision to hold elections that spring rather than later in 1996.[6] There may have been a lack of negotiating pressure or incentives from the United States. Assad's priorities may have been elsewhere. He wants to keep power for himself and the minority Alawite sect that runs Syria. Maintaining Israel as an adversary and not opening Syria up to the outside world serves these ends better than peace. It is understandable that President Assad would prefer dominating what there is of Syria over enlarging its territory only to weaken his hold. But whatever the explanation, the result is the same: the prospects for an Israeli-Syrian treaty are bleak, especially so long as Syria insists that Israel commit itself in advance to full withdrawal from the Golan Heights.

Similarly, there is no chance of an agreement between Israel and Lebanon. Lebanon is not an independent actor. Syria, which continues to maintain thousands of forces there and would be in a position to intimidate the Lebanese even if it did not, will not permit a separate peace between Lebanon and Israel. No amount of Israeli inducement, not even a unilateral withdrawal from the narrow strip of territory it holds in southern Lebanon, would be enough to bring this about.

One significant exception to this pattern of deteriorating regional peace prospects was the January 1997 protocol (brokered by the United States) in which Israel agreed not only to undertake its promised withdrawal from Hebron (the last of the West Bank cities it pledged to leave in the Oslo accord) but also committed itself to implementing the remaining parts of the Oslo arrangements, including withdrawal from other occupied lands and resumption of final status talks. In so doing, Likud and Prime Minister Netanyahu tied themselves to the Oslo process and increased the odds that a meaningful Palestinian political and territorial entity would result.

---

6. Walid al-Mouallem, Syria's ambassador to the United States and head of its delegation that met to negotiate peace with Israel, argues that an agreement would have been completed but for the sooner-than-expected Israeli election and its result. The interview with al-Mouallem is printed in the *Journal of Palestine Studies*, Vol. 26, No. 2 (Fall 1996).

There were, however, negative developments both before and after the Hebron accord that raise the question of whether it did in fact constitute a breakthrough. Economic conditions in the Palestinian areas have worsened in part because of long-lasting closures that preclude the movement of goods and people to or through Israel. Petty and not-so-petty harassment of Palestinians has grown more frequent. The decision by Israeli authorities in September 1996 to open a tunnel running alongside Muslim holy places in the heart of Jerusalem triggered a violent reaction in which elements of the Palestinian security forces turned their guns on Israeli citizens. In December 1996, the Netanyahu government declared that it would resume financial incentives for Israelis choosing to live in settlements. And in February 1997, the Netanyahu government announced its plans to proceed with a new settlement at Har Homa in East Jerusalem, a decision seen by Palestinians and many others as both unwise (by focusing attention on the highly sensitive issues of settlements and Jerusalem) and inconsistent with the spirit and letter of the Madrid and Oslo processes. This announcement, together with the forced closure of several official PLO offices in Jerusalem and the decision to withdraw from only nine percent more land (most of which was already under Palestinian political control) as the first step in implementing the Hebron accord, combined with an increase in Palestinian terrorism against Israeli targets to undermine any sense of positive momentum.

There is an obvious danger in all of the above. It is frequently said that the Middle East is like a bicycle: one either moves forward or risks falling over. The current situation in the Middle East—armed deterrence between Israel and Syria together with a patchwork quilt of Palestinian population centers, Jewish settlements, and Israeli-controlled land—is neither sustainable nor stable. Autonomy in particular must continue to grow in both breadth and depth or Israeli-Palestinian relations (and the current *modus vivendi*) will collapse.

Collapse of the current situation would be costly for both Israelis and Palestinians. Palestinians would face a loss of self-government, increased economic hardship, and a future of open-ended occupation with all that entails. But it would be no better for Israelis who, in addition to the expense of occupation and increased terror, would forfeit a chance to gain economic access to the region. Fewer resources would be available to focus on the emerging and ultimately more worrisome threats to Israel's security posed by Iran and Iraq. A radicalization of Palestinian and Israeli politics alike would result; any chance for peace would be postponed if not destroyed.

A collapse could be just as bad for the Israeli-Syrian relationship. Another war between these two antagonists could well involve weapons of mass destruction. Urban areas could become battlefields, civilians could become combatants. And even if this nightmare did not materialize, a conventional war would still involve staggering human and financial costs on both sides.

Re-calibrating Diplomacy

What, then, should be done? Washington remains the critical outside actor in the region. Russian co-sponsorship of the Madrid peace process is mostly a gesture. Europe's contribution should at most (and at best) be complementary and supportive. The correct approach for one and all is not to press ahead and try to substitute for what the local protagonists must do for and with one another, but rather to discourage them from taking steps that would be counter-productive and to assist them in implementing policies that would contribute to stability.

In so doing, the United States needs to change its approach to the Middle East. It would be futile to carry on as if nothing has changed. Moreover, to do so would bring with it a considerable opportunity cost. There is only so much time and energy for the president and his top aides to devote to foreign policy, and it is impossible to argue that two dozen additional visits to Syria would be more useful to U.S. national security than time spent consulting with leaders in Japan, China, Russia, Germany, and India. Even in the Middle East, other issues, including dealing with Iraq and Iran and helping states contend with internal political and economic challenges, deserve more attention from senior U.S. officials than the traditional peace process.

Some observers disagree with this advice. Frustrated with the slow pace suggested by Camp David and laid out in considerable detail by Madrid and Oslo, they urge that the parties move immediately to final status talks.[7] This desire to "leapfrog" the Oslo process and accelerate final status talks was advocated in the spring of 1997 by the Israeli prime minister. But how parties who found it so difficult to agree on Hebron are to agree on Jerusalem is baffling. The same could be said

---

7. See, for example, Henry Kissinger, "The Mideast Deal," *Washington Post,* November 27, 1996, p. A19; Charles Krauthammer, "Arafat Killed Oslo," *Washington Post,* April 4, 1997, p. A21; and Stephen P. Cohen, "Give Peace a Push," *New York Times,* April 7, 1997, p. A23.

for the other major final status issues, including rights to water, settlements, refugees, and the political, military, and economic character of any Palestinian entity. The logic of gradualism—to tackle the less difficult issues and build trust—still makes sense. As a result, any time devoted to the peace process should focus on limited but potentially feasible efforts. This is not a moment for drama.

Palestinians currently control daily life in Gaza and the principal West Bank cities. Israel and the Palestinians jointly have responsibility for the roughly 450 villages and towns that constitute one-fourth of the occupied territories. And Israel still has sole control of the remaining two thirds, an area that includes the bulk of its settlements, military installations, and so-called state lands. The second (October 1995) Oslo agreement called for further Israeli withdrawals at regular intervals from this last territorial zone. The most important priority, reiterated in the January 1997 Hebron accord, is to do so. Similarly, Israel could transfer greater authority to the Palestinians for control of towns and villages. The goal should be a series of *de facto* Oslo IIIs, a form of rolling autonomy. These efforts could be buttressed by increased contacts and exchanges in the business and academic worlds.

Just as important would be Israeli effort on behalf of the Palestinian economy. One thing that would help is easing the travel restrictions and closures that limit the opportunity for Palestinians to travel to and through Israel to work. It is not clear that this tactic does much to bolster security, but it clearly hurts the Palestinian standard of living, thereby creating more misery and adding to the propensity for violence. It would also help if Israel dropped its tariff and non-tariff barriers that have made it difficult for Palestinian agricultural and other goods to reach Israeli markets. Tax reform would help, too, so that Palestinians could pay any taxes to their own authority directly.

For its part, the Palestinian leadership must be seen to be doing everything possible to deal with the security threat. No one can expect 100 percent success—Prime Minister Netanyahu is incorrect when he suggests that "peace means the absence of violence"—but Israel has every right to expect 100 percent effort, something clearly lacking in the spring of 1997 when Palestinian leaders may well have encouraged violence by speaking of its possible outbreak and by releasing from prison individuals associated with violence. Palestinian leaders should resist calls for a new *intifada* and criticize those who do. Here, Israel can help its own case. It is far more likely to get what it wants in the way of cooperation against terrorism in the context of increasing autonomy than of its contraction. Such a context would make it far easier for the Palestinian Authority to sustain popular support for tough measures and make it easier to diminish the appeal of radicals and the tendency of the public to support them. Progress against terrorism is more likely to be the complement of a robust peace process than its substitute.

Settlements are another potential flashpoint. Palestinians see them as a unilateral act by Israel that prejudices final status and renders negotiations meaningless. It is one thing to allow for modest growth in existing settlements and quite another to accelerate growth dramatically or start new ones. A decision to do the latter would almost certainly lead to a breakdown of all talks and to renewed violence, particularly if it occurs in the absence of any good faith effort to achieve progress toward peace. It is for this reason that the building of new houses in the East Jerusalem area of Har Homa is so explosive.

Prime Minister Netanyahu suggested during his October 1996 White House press conference with President Clinton that his government could not be expected to do less to increase population in the settlements than the Labor government he replaced. This may be so, but no less true is it that Palestinians and the U.S. government were prepared to look the other way at what Labor was doing only because they had confidence in its commitment to a peace they judged as fair. Strong Palestinian and world reaction to the Israeli government's December 1996 announcement that incentives for existing settlements would be restored underscores just this.

Lebanon could well be an opportunity for unilateralism. The Israeli military presence in the south of Lebanon has failed to deter threats against northern Israel. Moreover, Israeli forces are increasingly a target of Hezbollah attack. Israel could simply pull its forces out. Such unilateralism makes sense. Israel's aims in Lebanon are security-related, not territorial. No mention of Lebanon *per se* is to be found in the government guidelines, suggesting the potential for Israeli flexibility. Withdrawal from Lebanon would reduce the vulnerability of Israeli forces—the costs of the presence were tragically and dramatically underscored by a crash of two helicopters ferrying troops to Lebanon in February 1997—and provide Israel a major diplomatic accomplishment. It would place pressure on Syria and Iran to halt their interference in Lebanon's internal affairs and to stop arming—or, better yet, to disarm—Hezbollah.

With or without such a unilateral step, Israel should make clear to Syria that it will hold Syria accountable for Hezbollah's actions in

Lebanon. Such a position is far from unreasonable. Syria is the dominant force in Lebanon, and Hezbollah's forces continue to operate in Lebanon thanks not only to Syrian tolerance but to its active enabling. Arms regularly transit Syria from Iran for Lebanon and Hezbollah.

What Israel should not do is repeat the error of the Peres government, which was to respond to Hezbollah attacks on northern Israel by attacking the Lebanese people and creating refugees. Instead, in addition to retaliating against any Hezbollah target that can be reached, Israel ought to communicate to Damascus that it is prepared to attack Syrian forces in Lebanon and interrupt Syrian support for Hezbollah. This risks widening the conflict, but the choice facing Israel is either to do so or to accept what have been mounting attacks on Israelis from Lebanese territory.

Similarly, Israel should signal Syria regarding any red lines involving water resources. There is no need to try to negotiate a specific accord with Syria, which would be impossible given President Assad's refusal to entertain any such normalization. But Israel can communicate its expectations and the consequences if Syria were to act otherwise.

The approach to diplomacy advocated here has its advantages. It is realistic and does not waste time seeking the impossible. There is little need for intense negotiations. It avoids the requirement of having to submit controversial agreements to uncertain and often critical political processes. This is not meant to diminish the value of treaties or other agreements. To the contrary, they are highly useful in locking in progress. The Egyptian-Israeli peace, however cold, is far more robust (and immune to the passions of the day) than would be informal understandings.

What is more, the day may come when it is again possible to negotiate agreements. There could, for example, be political evolution in Israel, in the form of a National Unity Government (in which Prime Minister Netanyahu would cast off many of his current associates and bring into government more moderate Labor Party leaders) or a successor Labor government. There could be a change of leadership in Syria. The Palestinians could become more democratic and more able to compromise. If such developments should come about, then diplomacy would have to be reoriented. An ambitious, high-profile initiative might be called for. Until then, however, the United States and Europe will need to content themselves with something more modest, if only to avert something far worse. In the new Middle East, the best is not only the enemy of the good, it is the enemy of peace.

Managing European-American Differences

There is no fix, easy or otherwise, to the problem of U.S.-European diplomacy toward the Middle East. Europeans understandably chafe at being left out of diplomacy or relegated to the role of paymaster for the Palestinians. Americans are obviously wary of others coming in and complicating (much less upsetting) all that is going on.

To be sure, as Volker Perthes correctly notes, Europeans are right to be concerned about the Middle East, given all that they have at stake. European dependence on the region's energy supplies is considerably higher than that of the United States. Also greater is their proximity to the region and vulnerability to refugee flows.

But to acknowledge a major European stake in the area is not to advocate a major European diplomatic role. It is far from clear that the Europeans bring to the table any comparative advantage; to the contrary, their participation carries with it some risk of complicating diplomatic efforts if it is not closely coordinated with U.S. efforts. French complaints notwithstanding, Europeans have failed to make a persuasive case for their inclusion. Indeed, there is something of a wistful quality to French calls for co-sponsorship, as if they could regain great power status simply by being granted such a role.

Still, the current situation in which Americans and Europeans work at cross-purposes or snipe at one another is less than ideal. It is good for neither U.S.-European relations nor the peace process.

What might be done? To begin with, Europeans should jettison the demand of France to be a co-sponsor of the process. It is neither necessary nor desirable.

European governments and the EU should forswear independent diplomatic initiatives unless asked by all the local parties directly involved, as was the case with Oslo. Should this circumstance arise, they should try to keep the United States informed to an extent agreed upon by the parties. Otherwise, Europe would be wise to content itself with what it can usefully do, including providing resources to buttress peacemaking, assuming a leading role in the multilateral negotiations established at Madrid, and continuing the process of European-Mediterranean dialogue begun at Barcelona in 1995 that brings the reality of political contacts and the hope of economic ones.

To do more, Europe will need to balance its policy. At a minimum, the EU should recant its call for self-determination by the Palestinians. The last thing the Middle East needs is more unilateralism. Any satisfaction of Palestinian nationalism will decidedly not come from PLO declarations but from negotiations involving Israel. The Europeans would also be seen differently by the United States and Israel if they were to drop their emphasis on Israeli-Syrian final status, especially since Europe's views (endorsed by Volker Perthes in Chapter 4) tend to mirror those of Damascus in calling for full Israeli withdrawal.

It would also be helpful if the Europeans proved to be as demanding of the Palestinians as they are of Israel. Too often EU pronouncements resemble Palestinians' wish lists. What is needed are clear and unconditional calls against all acts of violence and unilateral actions on both sides. EU pressure on the PLO to fully revise the organization's charter would be welcome. So, too, would be pressure on Syria to honor Lebanese sovereignty and on both Syria and Iran to disarm Hezbollah.

Change of this sort would require a response from Washington. The United States cannot simply criticize European involvement and hope it will go away. History suggests that Europe will be more active if the peace process founders or if the United States is seen as acting irresponsibly. In such circumstances, Europeans will worry about their interests and seek to fill a vacuum, no matter how futile or counterproductive the United States and Israel might judge such action to be.

This, then, becomes another argument for the United States not to compromise its basic beliefs. It is one thing to adapt tactics to changed circumstances, quite another to adapt principles. The U.S. government should speak out forcefully when it disagrees with what local parties are doing or saying; better yet, it should do all that it can to discourage them from taking such steps in the first place. The Clinton administration fell short on both counts in dealing with the Netanyahu government over the Har Homa settlement plan and Israel's implementation of its "unilateral" right to determine how much land to hand over to the Palestinian National Authority pursuant to the Oslo and Hebron accords. The United States retains considerable moral authority, something that must be used if it is not to be squandered. It should oppose increased settlement activity; this is not a question of legality but of practicality.

In addition, the United States should not walk away from its historic commitment to the notion of territory for peace. The reason is not to engage in an endless round of theological debates—the phrase is shorthand for a series of trade-offs that must include security for Israel—but to hold out hope and buttress a process that will survive as much on perceived potential as it will on results. There is no other basis for negotiations between Israel and Syria, if and when they are resumed. And there must be a territorial basis for Palestinian nationalism, but one that is consistent with Israeli security. This will probably mean something that is more than autonomy but less than a full-fledged state. Israel will come to accept this if it wants to be predominantly Jewish, truly democratic, and relatively secure. Prime Minister Netanyahu says it is his goal to make Israel more normal, to focus on economic issues as is the case with his counterparts in other countries. This will happen only if Israel continues to support a legitimate process of co-existence.

The United States and Europe also need to work harder with one another. Better consultations are needed, including regular meetings between whomever is handling the negotiations for the United States and his European counterparts. Only by being informed can the Europeans be expected to play a helpful, supportive role. It is similarly essential that there is close coordination about any move to consider the Middle East in the United Nations. The UN Security Council tends to move to the fore when things in the region are at their most volatile; as a result, there is a premium on avoiding surprises or actions that would isolate the United States or place it under greater pressure than it would already face. The sort of Security Council resolution supported by the French and British in March 1997, one that criticized Israeli plans for Har Homa and raised issues of both legality and final status, thereby ensuring a controversial U.S. veto, is an example of what should be avoided.

None of this is meant to portray consultations as a panacea. The truth is that both Europeans and Americans need to better understand the interests of the other and, more important, their common limits. Only the local parties—Israelis, Palestinians, Syrians—can make peace. What Europeans and Americans can best do is use their powers of persuasion, make good offices available when desired, reward peacemakers, and penalize those who block peace. If Europeans accept the modesty of their role, and if Americans do more to listen to and inform Europeans, they can probably do some good, if not for the Middle East, where it will be difficult to accomplish good, then at least for themselves, so that they are in a better position to tackle those issues—trade, Bosnia, Russia, Cyprus, and the Aegean—where U.S. and European cooperation will not only be desirable but decisive.

Chapter 4

Europe, the United States, and the Middle East Peace Process

Volker Perthes

While there is wide agreement that Europe—and the European Union in particular—should somehow be involved in the Middle East and the Arab-Israeli peace process, decision-makers and observers on both sides of the Atlantic have different views about what kind of role Europe actually should play, and to what extent it would thereby trespass on the turf of the United States. This article first gives a brief analysis of the Middle East peace process, where it stands at the time of writing and of its mid-term prospects; it then examines the debate about a European role in this process; analyzes the differences between European and U.S. policy approaches towards the region; and, finally, asks where and how Europe and the United States should cooperate.[1]

The Middle East after Israel's 1996 Elections

Israel's 1996 elections and the policies of the Netanyahu government in the first six months after its installation reveal two central features of Middle East politics. First, Israel's elections have shown how much that country, in terms of political culture, is actually part of its regional, Middle Eastern environment. The election results are very similar

---

1. "Europe," throughout this article, is used as shorthand for the member states of the European Union (EU). This is not to ignore that there are other European states that have a role to play in the region. Where I refer to the Middle East as a whole, I am speaking of the so-called MENA (Middle East and North Africa) region; the World Bank also uses this term. This region extends from the Maghreb in the west to Iran in the east.

to what we would expect to happen in Jordan, Egypt, or Syria, if free elections in any of these countries offered the choice between one leader promising peace with concessions, and a rival one claiming that he would make peace without any concessions to the other side. The majority of Israelis would prefer "peace" with only cosmetic withdrawals from occupied Palestinian and Syrian territories, as much as the majority of the Jordanians, Syrians, and others would prefer a "peace" that would regain their territory but limit political, economic, and social interaction with Israel as far as possible. For the time being, therefore, it is not the peoples in the Middle East that can make peace with each other, but, at best, some enlightened political leaders.

Second, Israel's elections and Middle East politics thereafter have shown that the agreements between Israel and the Palestinians, the Israeli-Jordanian peace treaty, and various bilateral and multilateral negotiations and summits have not yet yielded a new and harmonious Middle East. Rather, the peace process has to be understood as part of regional politics, that is, as an element of the Arab-Israeli conflict, rather than its replacement. It is a process through which regional actors try to improve their positions relative to each other. These actors are always willing to involve external powers—the United States, the European Union (EU), Russia—not to promote these powers' agendas, but to strengthen their own position in their struggle for power and resources.

Therefore, Israel's elections and the policies of the Netanyahu government constitute a setback, but they are not the end of the peace process. The Arab states made that very clear. Their reactions, as clearly shown at the Cairo Arab summit of June 1996, expressed concern, but no nervousness. The message of the Arab leaders to Tel Aviv as well as to Washington and Brussels was simple: we are concerned about the change from Shimon Peres to Benjamin Netanyahu; however, we consider the Israeli elections an internal affair, and we expect the new Israeli government to honor the agreements that its predecessors signed. Doubts regarding the seriousness of Israel's peaceful intentions had been around even before Netanyahu's victory, particularly after the sixteen-day war Israel wrought on Lebanon in April 1996 ("Operation Grapes of Wrath"). In fact, the Middle East peace process, slowly proceeding since the Geneva Conference following the October War of 1973, has had to encounter more than a few setbacks and obstacles in the past, some of them probably more severe than "Grapes of Wrath" and Netanyahu. Instead of speaking of the agony of the peace process, it might therefore be helpful to ask what actually has been achieved and what prospects for progress there are for the mid-term future of Arab-Israeli relations.

THE PEACE PROCESS: A DIFFICULT EXERCISE OF LEARNING

The peace process entered into a new stage with the Madrid Conference of 1991, which brought together, for the first time, representatives of all major parties in the Arab-Israeli conflict. A return to pre-Madrid politics seems all but impossible. Most important, Israel's right to exist is no longer in question, particularly since the Palestine Liberation Organization (PLO) has decided to remove from its national charter all passages that deny that right. In Israel, even some Likud politicians have realized and spelled out that peace between Israel and its neighbors will not be obtained, and that Israel's existence as a democratic state cannot be secured, without the application of the "land-for-peace" principle on all fronts and the achievement of some form of Palestinian sovereignty. Knowing that, however, does not necessarily compel Israel's leaders to act accordingly; a peaceful neighborhood, after all, is not the only option.

Therefore, despite the readiness of the Arab side to deal with Netanyahu and despite Netanyahu's repeatedly expressed interest in a continuation of negotiations with all Arab parties, we should not expect any substantial progress, particularly between Israel and Syria or between Israel and Lebanon, in the near future. On the Palestinian track, Israel's Likud government has been forced to learn. Most important, by signing the January 1997 protocol on Hebron, Netanyahu has explicitly endorsed the Oslo agreements that he initially rejected.[2] The Israeli government can still drag its feet and make life hard for the Palestinian population and leadership, but it will not be able to turn history back to before "Oslo." The Palestinian Authority (PA) exists on the ground today (if with limited sovereignty); it is internationally acknowledged; and an Israeli attempt to reoccupy the West Bank towns now under Palestinian authority would have to reckon with a well-trained Palestinian police force of 30,000. The events of September 1996 demonstrated that an Israeli attempt to disarm or dismantle the PA would not succeed without terrible losses.

---

2. These are the Israeli-Palestinian Declaration of Principles of September 1993 ("Oslo I") and the Oslo II or Taba agreement of September 1995. They provide, among other things, for the establishment of the Palestinian Authority (PA) in the West Bank and Gaza Strip, the gradual transfer of power to the PA in major parts of the Occupied Territories, and further negotiations about a final status.

As long as Netanyahu maintains, however, that there will be no Palestinian state and no compromise on Jerusalem, and even insists on building new settlements, we need not expect that the final status negotiations will reach a solution by 1999, as originally planned.

Israel's relations with the neighboring Arab states are likely to remain frosty, even if negotiations of sorts take place. Egypt has maintained a stable "cold peace" with Israel since 1979. From an Egyptian national-interest perspective, President Hosni Mubarak has little reason to warm up his country's relations with Israel. Rather, by getting tougher—in words, rather than deeds—on Israel and its government, he can increase his domestic support and, more important perhaps, stabilize Egypt's leadership position in the Arab world. Jordan, having concluded a peace treaty with Israel in 1994, was eager to establish a warm and multilayered relationship that would bring the country into a privileged position regarding the expected economic dividends of peace as well as political influence in the Palestinian territories. Developments so far have been disappointing, and the Jordanian leadership has found it wise to fall into line with Egypt and slow down its opening towards Israel.

On the Syrian-Israeli and Lebanese-Israeli tracks, negotiations became serious at the beginning of 1994. By 1996, before the Israeli elections, agreement had been reached, in principle, on the territorial component of a peace treaty, i.e., on the principle of full Israeli withdrawal. What remained to be discussed were border lines and the other components of peace: security arrangements, water, and "normalization." Syrian policymakers had finally come to the conclusion that peace with all its implications—full neighborly relations including political as well as economic interaction—had to be faced, and that a treaty could and would be negotiated with Shimon Peres after his expected reelection. Substantial fears remained regarding the challenges of peace and normalization to the Syrian economy as well as to Syria's regional position and to its domestic political structures. What apparently helped the Syrian leadership to decide that they should proceed to an agreement with the Israelis were the prospects for Syria of the new Mediterranean policy of the EU. In March 1996, Syrian-European talks about a partnership agreement began. Damascus obviously has a strong interest in European financial aid. Above that, and more important in the long run, European assistance to reform the Syrian economy and prepare it for competition in a Euro-Mediterranean economic area will also make it easier for Syria to face the challenges of a new regional division of labor in a more open Middle Eastern economic and social space that would include Israel as a full and normal member.

After the Israeli elections, however, Israeli-Syrian negotiations were not resumed. The hard-line approach of the Netanyahu government again strengthened those skeptics in the Syrian political class who have cautioned against any quick settlement of the conflict. One might argue that Damascus missed a chance by not doing much to speed up negotiations with the Rabin and Peres governments. Today, however, the ball is back in Israel's court.

While Syria can live with the stalemate, Lebanon urgently needs regional peace. Lebanon will only regain its sovereignty—gain an Israeli withdrawal from the south and end or at least reduce Syria's tutelage—once Damascus and Tel Aviv have agreed on a settlement of their conflict. Lebanon also needs peace to accomplish its reconstruction program and keep the confidence of investors. Beirut has good reason to expect that in a new, peaceful Middle East it could regain some of its former position as a regional center of finance and services. Any deterioration of Syrian-Israeli relations, however, and war in particular, would affect Lebanon more than any other country. A "Lebanon-first" solution, proposed by Israel's prime minister in the summer of 1996, would therefore be to the liking of not a few Lebanese politicians, but it is hardly realistic. Netanyahu himself obviously did not take his proposal seriously, and Damascus will continue to insist that the Lebanese issue be settled as part of the Syrian-Israeli agenda. For the time being, therefore, Lebanon can at best hope to limit the extent of the struggle over the Israeli-occupied "security zone" in the south. The five-nation Israel-Lebanon Monitoring Group,[3] set up after "Operation Grapes of Wrath" to contain the military conflict between Israel and Hezbollah, has so far worked quite successfully and could help to build some confidence even in the shadow of continued limited warfare.

Netanyahu will have to learn that Israel cannot in the long run ignore Syria and its legitimate demand to regain its territory for peace. The "no war–no peace" situation that has been maintained at the Golan front since 1974 can probably be prolonged for another couple of years, and there are political forces on either side who would favor its indefinite continuation. The costs must be under-

---

3. The ILMG consists of military officers from Israel, Lebanon, Syria, France, and the United States.

stood, however. As long as Netanyahu, or any other Israeli premier, maintains his refusal to speak about and eventually commit his country to full withdrawal from the Golan, he will not only fail to establish peace with Syria, but will also be unable to normalize relations with those more distant Arab states that have established cautious political as well as commercial contacts with Israel. The idea that Israel could bypass Damascus—or Gaza, for that matter—and start real business with Dubai, Riyadh, or Rabat will prove to be an illusion. Despite all the inter-Arab conflicts, the systemic links that tie the Arab world together are still too strong to allow the Arab states in the Gulf or the Maghreb to ignore the fate of Palestine, the Golan, and South Lebanon. Even the states of the Gulf Cooperation Council (GCC), as well as Tunisia and Morocco, whose interest in regional peace is not in doubt, have linked any further normalization with Israel to progress on the Palestinian-Israeli and Syrian-Israeli tracks. Also, a revitalization of the multilateral talks, particularly of the talks on Arms Control and Regional Security (ACRS), which started after the 1991 Madrid Conference and had made tangible progress, is unlikely as long as the bilateral Palestinian-Israeli and Syrian-Israeli tracks are blocked.

In spite of the irreversibility of central aspects of the peace process, therefore, the old Middle East has by no means vanished. As long as this process remains frozen, politics in the Middle East are likely to preserve their *realpolitik* or power-politics character. Regional foreign policies will most likely continue to reflect a zero-sum understanding of security and international relations, based on the assumption that whatever my neighbor gains in terms of security will necessarily be at the expense of mine, rather than cooperative approaches. The majority of the region's political elites still regard military power as a legitimate means of regional politics, not simply of defense. Limited war between Israel and Lebanon, and even between Israel and Syria, can therefore not be excluded. The Israeli leadership even more than the Syrian can be expected to engage in acts of brinkmanship at times. Repeated low-level or middle-level violence will certainly remain a feature of Israeli-Palestinian relations. Early hopes for a regional peace dividend (through reduced arms spending, increased intra-regional economic cooperation, and higher in-flows of international investment capital) have proven to be unrealistic. We cannot know today whether Israel's prime minister will make a pragmatic turn in the years to come, whether he will eventually give up his unrealistic electoral promises of achieving security and peace without the necessary territorial and political compromises and rid himself of his more extremist coalition partners, or whether it will take another Israeli election to bring back substance to the peace process. The first scenario cannot be ruled out, but the second seems more likely.

Calling on Europe

Meanwhile, calls for an increased European role in the Middle East and the peace process can be heard from both sides of the Atlantic. The issue is not so much whether Europe, and the EU in particular, should become more active, but rather what kind of role it should play, and whether and how European activities would conflict with U.S. policies. Calls for a European role are based on quite different theoretical as well as practical arguments. Three main lines of reasoning can be distinguished.

First, a realist world view holds that after the end of bipolarity the international system will be characterized by multipolar competition. This implies that there is room for more actors, even in regions that, in times of bipolarity, were theaters of superpower contest. The Middle East was a key region for U.S.-Soviet strategic rivalry between 1956, when the United States helped to oust Britain and France from the region after their Suez adventure, and 1989 and the end of the Cold War. Now instead of remaining but a junior partner of the United States, Europe should seek to further its own geopolitical and economic interests in the region. This line of reasoning is subscribed to by many political realists from the region itself. They clearly expect or hope that U.S. power and influence in the region will be balanced by major European states or the EU, which ought to evolve as a new global power and to some degree take the place once occupied by the Soviet balancer. Some Europeans who, for the sake of simplification, can be labeled "neo-Gaullist," also think in this vein, but they rarely spell it out.

Second, there is the burden-sharing argument: while U.S. leadership is still needed, globally as much as in the Middle East, Europe as well as Japan should bear some of the burden of Western hegemony. With regard to the Middle East, there are actually two variants to this argument. The first one centers on the economic burden, stressing that Europe should not be allowed a free ride while the United States bears all the responsibility for the peace process as well as the material costs of guaranteeing Western strategic interests in the region. Europe should therefore increase its economic aid and even take a

lead in such matters as the multilateral talks on regional development. The second variant goes one step farther, calling also for some
political division of labor: Washington, according to this view, would
maintain its leadership function, but it would adopt a lower profile
and involve the Europeans to reduce some of the practical problems
that form an obstacle to the peace process.[4] Both variants spring from
the feeling, in some form or other, that the United States is over-
stretched, and that the "high-water mark of U.S. involvement in the
Middle East lies in the past."[5] This line of reasoning is, quite naturally, mainly an American one. There is little disagreement that Europe
should somehow share the burden of Western policies towards the
Middle East. What is in dispute is how much of such burden-sharing
one should actually call for if it leads to European demands for a part
in political decision-making, that is, if Europe accepts "taxation" only
in exchange for representation. Thus, U.S. "globalists" would rather
limit the European role in the Middle East to its economic dimension,
whereas area specialists and policymakers with a better knowledge
of the region are more likely to accept, or even demand, stronger
European political involvement. More often than not, this position
springs from a self-critique of U.S. policies toward the region. "It is
useful to remember," writes William Pfaff, "that there would be no
peace process had it been left to the United States."[6]

The third line of reasoning focuses on the interdependence
between the EU and the states immediately involved in the peace
process, which are seen as part of a broader Mediterranean–Middle
Eastern region. As interdependencies grow, Europe has to deepen its
commitment towards the region. This line of reasoning has an ideal-
ist variant emphasizing Europe's interest in furthering peace, democracy, and development among its neighbors, and a more realist variant stressing that Europe's security and economic interests demand
both socioeconomic development and political progress in North
Africa and the Middle East, especially the peaceful resolution of the
Arab-Israeli conflict. European commitment, therefore, cannot be

---

4. See Michael C. Hudson, "To Play the Hegemon: Fifty Years of U.S. Policy
Towards the Middle East," *Middle East Journal*, Vol. 50, No. 3 (1996), pp. 329–343.

5. William Quandt, "Shrinking U.S. Agenda in Middle East Affairs" (interview),
International Herald Tribune, September 9, 1996.

6. William Pfaff, "EU Should Weigh In on Mideast Peace Process," *International
Herald Tribune*, October 26, 1996.

restricted to economic aid; rather, it has to include a political and probably also a security dimension. This line reflects very much the thinking behind the Mediterranean initiative and current Middle Eastern policies of the EU;[7] and it generally finds support from international financial institutions as well as from within the region. EU states disagree about how active and independent Europe's political role in the Middle East ought to be, with France and the other Southern European states pressing for more assertiveness, and Germany, the Netherlands, and Britain cautioning against it. But there also is a widely accepted common denominator of European policies towards the region. This common approach has been demonstrated by various policy declarations on the Middle East, most prominently the Venice Declaration of 1980, which became famous (and was scorned, at that time, by Israel and the United States) for its early demand that the PLO be a partner to negotiations, as well as more recent activities such as the Mediterranean initiative, Europe's material support of the PA, and the appointment, in 1996, of a high-ranking diplomat (but not of a minister or prominent elder statesman, as some European governments would have liked) as the EU's special envoy for the peace process.

Whether calls for an increased European role in the Middle East are driven by worries and uneasiness regarding developments in the region, particularly the lack of progress in the peace process, or instead by more self-centered American or European concerns, none advocates any form of U.S.-European rivalry. The aim is, instead, to find the grounds for some form of partnership or division of labor, and to develop common perspectives for a new Middle East policy. Even France's Foreign Minister Hervé de Charette, while stating somewhat boldly in the summer of 1996 that his country had to be considered a major player in the Middle East, has made it clear that France wants "full coordination" of U.S. and European policies.[8]

---

7. On the Mediterranean initiative, which was officially launched with the Barcelona conference of November 1995 and aims at establishing a Euro-Mediterranean free zone and "area of peace and stability," see Chapter 1 by Robert Satloff and Chapter 2 by Eberhard Rhein in this volume.

8. *Le Monde*, July 25, 1996. Calls for a Transatlantic partnership on Middle Eastern issues originate from both sides of the Atlantic. See, among others, Kenneth W. Stein, "Transatlantische Partnerschaft im Nahen Osten? Europa und die USA müssen aktiver werden," *Internationale Politik*, Vol. 51, No. 9 (1996), pp. 33–39; Martin Winter, "Nahostpolitik ohne Konzept," *Frankfurter Rundschau*,

We may assume however, that a "concentric and coherent" Transatlantic policy toward the Middle East would practically only be brought about if regional stability or the access to the Middle Eastern oil resources—strategic interests of Europe and of the United States, that is—were actually threatened.[9] Any close policy coordination with respect to the region would only occur under conditions that both sides want to prevent. In normal times, interests seem to be too far apart, approaches too different, and risk perceptions are, evidently, not the same.

Different Priorities, Different Approaches

The more Europe increases its activities towards the region and the peace process, the more differences between European and U.S. perceptions and approaches will become evident. Europe has tended to focus on the region as such, while U.S. policymakers have generally viewed it from a global perspective. Europe gives more importance to structural political and socioeconomic developments and to the establishment of multilateral, regional, or subregional structures, while the United States attaches more importance to military risks, to high-level diplomacy and, if need be, to military power as policy instruments. And whereas the United States is definitely an outside actor, Europe is a close neighbor of the region (if not, as some would claim, part of it), which necessarily entails a different kind of relationship with regional actors.

A common European approach to the Middle East and the Arab-Israeli conflict began to emerge from the early 1970s. Perhaps because of geographic proximity, Europe has paid more attention to regional dynamics and links, while the United States has tended to view the region as a strategic area with two main flashpoints, namely the immediate Arab-Israeli conflict theater and the Persian Gulf. As a result, in the judgment of U.S. Ambassador Robert Hunter, Europe has generally had a better understanding of the linkage between the "two ends" of the region.[10] Not surprisingly, the United States and

---

September 4, 1996; Pfaff, "EU Should Weigh In on Mideast Peace Process"; and Britain's Foreign Secretary Malcolm Rifkind, "Blueprint for a Region at Peace," *The Times* (London), November 5, 1996.

9. Stein, "Transatlantische Partnerschaft im Nahen Osten?" p. 38.

10. Robert E. Hunter, "Western Europe and the Middle East Since the Lebanon

Europe also have different understandings of what their interests in the region are, and what is threatening those interests. It seems evident that vital or strategic interests of Europe and the United States with respect to the region are not as such in conflict, whereas commercial interests are no doubt competitive. There are, however, obvious differences of priorities and concerns.

In both Europe and the United States, interests and concerns are usually defined with respect to the wider Middle East rather than just Israel and its neighbors. U.S. interests in the region, often clearly stated by policymakers, basically comprise the free flow of oil at reasonable prices, the security and well-being of Israel, plus Arab-Israeli peace, the stability of friendly regimes, and, more recently, the nonproliferation of weapons of mass destruction.[11] European policymakers do not deny the importance of any of those U.S. interests. They have their own lists of priorities and specific concerns, however, which can be gathered, implicitly rather than explicitly, from various European policy statements such as the Barcelona declaration as well as from the policy debate within individual EU countries.

Highest on the EU's priority list is regional stability. While this concept is conspicuously absent from the U.S. list of priorities, it is central to European thinking about the future of the region.[12] The following issues also rank prominently: the Arab-Israeli conflict; migration; the spread of radical political Islam; terrorism and the export of regional conflicts to Europe; and the socioeconomic development of the region

---

War," in Robert O. Freedman, ed., *The Middle East after the Israeli Invasion of Lebanon* (Syracuse, N.Y.: Syracuse University Press, 1986), p. 106.

11. See, among others, Anthony Lake, "Mideast Remains of Vital Interest to the U.S.," address to the Washington Institute, May 17, 1994, U.S. Policy & Texts, May 20, 1994, pp. 14-17; and Robert Pelletreau, "Remarks on U.S. Middle East Policy before the House International Relations Committee," September 25, 1996, documented in USIA: Daily Washington File, Internet Edition, September 25, 1996. The proliferation issue was not part of Lake's list of U.S. vital interests in the region. Other issues mentioned by Pelletreau but not by Lake include combating terrorism, the promotion of democracy, and the enhancement of U.S. business opportunities.

12. Note the naming of European regional initiatives: the Euro-Mediterranean Zone of Peace and Stability; the stability pact, etc. The same tendency is evident from a look at European policy documents. See, for example, Commission of the European Communities, *Future Relations and Cooperation between the Community and the Middle East*, Communication from the European Commission (93) 375, September 8, 1993. In this key document, there is only one explicit reference to European interests, namely the "security and stability of the region" (p. 1).

(which in turn is supposed to limit mass migration and political radicalism and to support stability). There is a stated interest, too, in furthering democracy and human rights. No clear position, however, has so far emerged regarding potential conflicts between "democracy" and "stability." In practice, where a choice must be made between the two, European policymakers (and Americans likewise) will probably continue to give priority to the latter.

Oil and weapons proliferation are not very much an issue in the European discourse, unlike that of the Americans. This is the case irrespective of Europe's dependence on Middle Eastern oil, which is still higher than that of the United States. Europe being not only the main consumer of Middle Eastern oil but also the main supplier of goods to the Middle East, European policymakers would find it hard to imagine that any Middle Eastern producer, let alone Middle Eastern producers collectively, would try to cut off Europe from its oil supply. Arms proliferation, particularly the proliferation of ballistic missiles capable of reaching Europe, is being discussed, but the issue is not a major concern of policymakers. Rather, there is a European consensus of sorts that a military threat from the region does not exist, whereas risks emanating from economic imbalances between Europe and its Mediterranean neighbors as well as from social crises and political instability in those countries have to be taken seriously.[13] Migration plays a major role: not so much as a security threat posed by today's or tomorrow's prospective migrants, but as a phenomenon contributing to the rise of xenophobic movements in European states, thereby endangering internal stability. Finally, there is no clear or uniform European position on political Islam and on how to deal with radical Islamic movements both in the Middle East and at home. But there is, throughout much of Europe, an obsession with the potential threats of political Islam, not shared in the United States. This may partly be due to the fact that, in case of a takeover by Islamist forces in any country of the region, Europe would most likely face a large influx of refugees, and partly due to fears that violent conflicts between incumbent regimes in the region and their Islamist challengers could spill over to Europe via this migration. But it is also

---

13. See, among others, Roberto Aliboni, *Change and Continuity in Western Policies toward the Middle East*, Documenti IAI, No. 9513 (Rome: Institute of International Affairs, 1995); and Assembly of the Western European Union, Forty-second Session, November 4, 1996, *Security in the Mediterranean Region*, report submitted on behalf of the Political Committee by Mr. de Lipkowski, Rapporteur (Document 1543).

because Europeans, in general, find it more difficult than Americans to accept cultural diversity.[14]

There is no disagreement between Europe and the United States that a peaceful settlement of the Arab-Israeli conflict represents a major Western interest. Washington and Europe also agree on the legal principles that should be the basis of a settlement, namely UN Security Council Resolutions 242 and 338, the land-for-peace principle. A remarkable difference remains, however, between the American and the European positions: whereas the security and well-being of Israel feature as a prime U.S. interest, separate from but no doubt consistent with the interest in Arab-Israeli peace, European policy statements stress that security and peace for *all* states in the region, as well as safeguarding the legitimate rights of the Palestinians, must be the overall objective. Such differences are more than linguistic. They reflect different leanings due to domestic policy equations, geography, and economic interests.

Whereas some U.S. observers regard European policy as "pro-Palestinian,"[15] many others would agree that Europe simply does not share the pro-Israeli bias of U.S. Middle East policies. This bias has often been in conflict with other U.S. interests in the region, particularly with respect to the Gulf Arab oil-producing states, but there is hardly any doubt that, as Michael Hudson put it, America's Israel lobby has been more powerful than the oil lobby.[16] Strong emotional ties bind several European countries, particularly Germany and the Netherlands, to Israel. But in no European country is Israel, and the support for Israel, as powerful an issue of domestic politics as in the United States.

Moreover, geography is a major factor in determining Europe's relations to the Middle East in general, and to Israel and the Mediterranean Arab states in particular. European states and the EU can entertain special relationships with Israel and probably always will, but they cannot afford to rely on just one strategic partner in the region, as does the United States, or favor one party too much over the

---

14. See Ghassan Salamé, "Torn between the Atlantic and the Mediterranean: Europe and the Middle East in the Post–Cold War Era," *Middle East Journal*, Vol. 48, No. 2 (1994), pp. 226–249.

15. See Chapter 1 by Robert Satloff and Chapter 3 by Richard Haass in this volume.

16. See Hudson, "To Play the Hegemon."

others. Europe cannot ignore the fact that all southern and eastern Mediterranean countries are its neighbors. Regional destabilization hurts European interests even if it does not affect the security of Israel or the flow of Gulf Arab oil. Strong interdependence exists between Europe and the entire Middle East, in terms of security as much as of social and economic relations. European commercial interests in the region are much more diversified than those of the United States. Israel and its neighbors conduct 42 percent of their foreign trade with EU states, compared to only 16 percent with the United States. The picture becomes even clearer when the Maghreb states are included: they conduct about 65 percent of their foreign trade with the EU, but less than 6 percent with the United States.[17]

As a result, Europeans have generally been more open to Arab demands and positions. It has never been as easy for Europe as it has been for the United States to accept or even endorse Israel's use of military force against its neighbors. Thus, whereas Washington showed open support for Israel's war against Lebanon in April 1996,[18] even the most pro-Israeli European capitals voiced some criticism. And it is highly unlikely that one would find a prominent European analyst suggesting, as does Richard Haass, that Israel should threaten to hit Syrian targets in Lebanon, even at the risk of widening the conflict. Europeans have also always stressed the importance of comprehensive solutions to the Middle East conflict.[19] Europe was anything but enthusiastic about the Egyptian-Israeli peace treaty of 1979, probably underrating the exemplary function this treaty would have, and overrating the ability and willingness of the Arab world to ostracize Egypt for the separate deal with Israel. U.S. policy, in contrast, seems to neglect, more often than not, that the call for a comprehensive settlement is not only a normative demand but also a practical one. The U.S.-engineered Israeli-Lebanese agreement of 1983 was doomed to fail, mainly because it did not take the interests of other regional players, particularly Syria, into consideration. Europe's Venice declaration of 1980,

---

17. International Monetary Fund (IMF), *Directions of Trade Statistics Yearbook* (Washington, D.C.: IMF, 1996).

18. On U.S. policy towards that war, see Richard W. Murphy, "The Costs of Wrath: An American Perspective," in Rosemary Hollis and Nadim Shehadi, eds., *Lebanon on Hold: Implications for Middle East Peace* (London: Royal Institute for International Affairs, 1996), pp. 7–10.

19. See Chapter 3 by Richard Haass in this volume.

demanding that the PLO be part of negotiations—at a time when the United States still saw the PLO as a terrorist organization unacceptable as a partner in the peace process—was based on the realization that without the PLO, peace efforts could never be successful. Even after the Madrid conference, which underlined the need to have all parties on board, U.S. mediators seemed at times inclined to accept a less-than-comprehensive solution. Why otherwise, observers asked, would the U.S. secretary of state, in contrast to all speakers from the region, omit reference to Syria as a future partner for peace with Israel during the May 1994 signing ceremony of the Cairo agreement between Israel and the PLO?[20]

Finally, analysts and policymakers in the West should not forget that there are other actors around in the Middle East besides Europe and the United States. Regional actors have their own agenda, and they can display considerable creativity, force, and endurance when they feel that their vital interests are threatened. Failure to understand the agenda of regional actors, and their legitimacy, often entails the failure of policies towards the region.

Europe and the Peace Process: More than the Economy

Because of Europe's different leanings toward regional actors as well as for supposedly practical reasons, U.S. policymakers have generally doubted that Europe could play a positive political role in the peace process. Instead, it has been suggested that the EU and individual European states should devote themselves to the economic side of the process, disbursing financial aid and supporting the establishment of cooperative economic structures. Europe, indeed, is the most important financial contributor to the peace process in general, and to the PA in particular: some 45 percent of all international aid to the PA comes from European sources. In terms of total financial support to Israel and its neighbors, U.S. disbursements surpass those of Europe; more than 60 percent of U.S. aid to the region, however, goes to Israel only.

With U.S. consent, the EU has chaired the multilateral working group on regional economic development set up after the Madrid conference. Beyond that, however, most U.S. policymakers seem to

---

20. See Moshe Ma'oz, *Syria and Israel: From War to Peacemaking* (Oxford: Oxford University Press, 1995), p. 248.

agree that Europe should not try to mess around in the peace process.[21] Instead, the United States has been and ought to remain the only external player in this game; no other nation "is in a position to deal with the key parties to the conflict on the basis of trust and reliability," to quote former President Ronald Reagan.[22] The Clinton administration seems equally self-confident, claiming, in the words of the Ambassador to Tel Aviv Martin Indyk, that the United States is "uniquely capable of influencing the course of events."[23] It is worth noting that Arab intellectuals still embedded in yesterday's thinking share the perception of the United States as the only player in the region. Writes Majid Kiyali: "Through . . . its direct control of the region, America has become the decision-maker in all fields of the Arab-Israeli conflict; it has enforced the Madrid conference and the conditions of participation, and it also supervises the negotiation game."[24]

Both assumptions—that "trust" is the quality that makes the United States the key player in the region and that the United States alone can effectively influence the peace process—are to be doubted. While not all Arab policymakers would openly share the bold judgment of Syria's late chief negotiator, Muwaffaq al-'Allaf, that "America is an employee of Israel,"[25] there is certainly a general feeling on the Arab side that Washington's pro-Israeli bias makes it impossible to trust, and to rely on, the United States. It is true that no European state enjoys the standing, trust, and leverage which Washington has in, or over, Israel; however, no European country is as much influenced as the United States by pro-Israeli domestic lobbying.

Europe is far from enacting a common foreign and security policy in the Middle East or elsewhere. The EU, however, and individual European states have already proven that they can do more than

---

21. Chapter 3 by Richard Haass in this volume reflects this attitude well.

22. Quoted in Barry Rubin, "The United States and the Middle East," in Freedman, *The Middle East after the Israeli Invasion of Lebanon*, p. 71.

23. Quoted in Aharon Kliemann, *Approaching the Finish Line: The United States in Post-Oslo Peace Making* (Ramat Gan: The Begin-Sadat Center for Strategic Studies, Bar-Ilan University, Security and Policy Studies No. 22, 1995), p. 11.

24. Majid Kiyali, "al-sira' al-'arabi-al-isra'ili fi bi'a initqaliyya" [The Arab-Israeli conflict in an environment of transition], *Shu'un al-awsat*, No. 53 (July 1993), pp. 15–26.

25. Muwaffaq al-'Allaf in a roundtable discussion organized by and documented in the journal *al-Mustaqbal al-'arabi*, Vol. 19, No. 210 (August 1996), p. 95.

stand on the sidelines. The Israeli-Palestinian Declaration of Principles would not have been negotiated without the initiative and good offices of Norway (which, for the record, is not an EU member). The story of "Oslo" and the astonishment and disbelief of U.S. policymakers that anything of importance was happening in so small a European capital,[26] has underlined the ideological character of the opinion that no one except the United States can mediate in the Middle East. Also, the so-called April understanding and the Israel-Lebanon Monitoring Group established after "Operation Grapes of Wrath" would most likely not have come into being without the persistence of France's foreign minister. The U.S. secretary of state was certainly irritated by the presence of his French colleague in the region. It should not be forgotten, however, that the secretary came to the region days after the French minister, demonstrating thereby that, before the Qana bombing, the United States had not been interested in bringing the war to an end. France, arguably, played a substantial role, and delivered Syrian consent to the agreement because of the relations of trust it enjoys with all parties. European leverage may be limited, but trust is a hard currency in the Middle East.

Finally, one should not underestimate the importance for the peace process of the EU's Mediterranean initiative, the Barcelona process. Within the Barcelona framework, several working groups have been established to follow up on the initiative. While Syria and Lebanon have so far refrained from participating in the multilateral track of the Madrid process, Barcelona has made it practically possible for Israel, Syria, Lebanon, and the Palestinians to take part, together with others, in a structured multilateral high-level dialogue that includes economic, cultural, and security issues. This cannot make up for bilateral and multilateral peace talks, but it may help to revitalize them. Also, as noted, the European offer to extend substantial aid to regional states to make them fit for an eventual Euro-Mediterranean free trade zone may have encouraged Syria to overcome some of its fears related to the economic prospects of peace with Israel. And Europe could use the strong interest Israel has in its trade relationship with the EU, for instance, by conditioning Israel's privileged access to European markets on its respect of obligations towards the Palestinians. In practice, however, Europe's decision-makers have been as cautious as Americans in putting pressure on Tel Aviv.

---

26. See David Makovsky, *Making Peace with the PLO: The Rabin Government's Road to the Oslo Accord* (Boulder, Colo.: Westview, 1996).

Neither the EU nor any European state can replace the United States in its central role in the peace process. Europe has been supportive of the Madrid process and will remain so, in spite of hard feelings on the European side regarding the bystander role that Washington assigned to the EU at Madrid and after. But European policymakers have no interest in having regional actors make use of the policy differences between Washington and Brussels, Paris, or Bonn. Nor would Europe like to be considered the pro-Palestinian flag bearer balancing the pro-Israeli Americans. Europeans also know—and if they did not know before, they learned the lesson in the former Yugoslavia—that without the United States they cannot pursue any regional policy that might need the stick (or the threat of the stick) as well as the carrot. Less prone than Washington to use military force, particularly in its own neighborhood, Europe will therefore not challenge the United States in its role as the dominant external power in the region. However, as much as Europe is prepared to accept the United States as the main power broker and to support U.S. peace efforts, it also still is "anxious to help shape the direction" of the peace process.[27] If U.S. policymakers are interested in the success of this process, they should learn to engage Europe's strong interest in the region, accept that it plays a political and not just a financial role, and be ready to find some form of division of labor.

Comparative Advantages and Constructive Competition

Europe's acceptance that the United States will remain the chief regional power broker cannot mean that Europe blindly follows the U.S. lead. First, U.S. policy in the region has always been forceful, but not always successful, and there is no need to follow a partner all through its blunders. Second, Europe has its own concerns in the region, not necessarily shared by the United States. European policies have to be more even-handed and focus on a broader spectrum of regional partners, and the European approach to regional problems differs from the American. Instead of having one party follow the other, therefore, the comparative advantage of either side's approach and policy instruments should be put into the service of the peace process in what we may call a constructive competition of ideas and instruments. Thus, unilateral high-level diplomacy involving a certain amount of pressure is among the instruments with which the U.S.

---

27. Hunter, "Western Europe and the Middle East Since the Lebanon War," p. 105.

administration is certainly better equipped than the EU or individual European states. No European troika would have been able to make the Madrid conference possible. Nor would Jacques Chirac or any other European leader have been able to force Netanyahu to meet with Yasser Arafat and King Hussein under his supervision, as did Bill Clinton in October 1996, however limited the success of that meeting eventually was.

At the same time, European policymakers and bureaucrats seem to be more competent than their American colleagues in initiating and supporting the building of regional structures; to encourage, by their own example, regional integration and economic cooperation; and generally to give lessons—if anyone can—in multilateralism. It is unlikely that the U.S. State Department would have endeavored, or succeeded, in establishing a Barcelona-type dialogue structure accepted, in principle, by all regional players. Europe's strong interdependence and overall trustful relationships with most parties in the region is a real advantage that can be used not only to engage contending parties in multilateral dialogues but also for more singular diplomatic initiatives such as German mediation between Israel on the one hand and Iran, Syria, and Hezbollah on the other, or France's contribution to ending the April 1996 war in Lebanon. With their more diversified relations to states and societies in the region, Europeans also seem to have an advantage in promoting people-to-people diplomacy. This was demonstrated in February 1997, when some forty intellectuals from Israel, Jordan, Egypt, and Palestine, including partisans of Israel's Likud-led coalition as well as of Hamas, met under the auspices of the Danish government to sign a common appeal (the "Copenhagen Declaration") and establish a popular alliance for peace in the Middle East. The United States and Europe should give open and full encouragement to each other's initiatives that are supportive of the peace process. Until now this has not been the preponderant mode. Neither the U.S. reaction to Barcelona, which can, at best, be characterized as benign neglect, nor French laments about not being invited to the Washington meeting with Netanyahu and Arafat have been helpful.

To avoid misgivings and potential clashes of initiatives in the Middle East, it is advisable that the United States and Europe institutionalize the exchange of advance information and the discussion of policy initiatives, which need not necessarily then be followed up together, and coordinate policies, where possible. There are, of course, international organizations and institutions such as the North Atlantic

Treaty Organization (NATO), the World Bank, and the G-7 where policies pertaining to the Middle East are discussed among highest-level European and American officials. The more day-to-day coordination of European and U.S. policies in the peace process and debate on approaches towards the region may need a different format, though. Two variants could make sense.

First, it should be made mandatory for the U.S. and the EU special envoys to the peace process (Dennis Ross and Miguel Moratinos at the time of writing) to have regular, informal meetings. Such a format, smacking of equality, might not be too much to the liking of the U.S. administration, but it seems preferable to uncoordinated meddling by both sides in regional affairs with little knowledge of, or concern for, the other side's perceptions, plans, or programs. Second, it might be wise to set up a Transatlantic Forum on Middle East Policy to bring together Middle East experts with policymakers from both sides of the Atlantic for an annual policy-oriented workshop. Differences of view are not as such detrimental, but it could be harmful to ignore the theoretical and practical assumptions that are behind them on either side.

There is certainly no lack of issues for debate and coordination and also, perhaps less frequently, for common initiatives. To start with, Europeans and Americans share a body of experience regarding confidence-building and cooperative security that should be used to promote the development and implementation of security and confidence-building measures in the Middle East. A revitalization of the multilateral working group on Arms Control and Regional Security (ACRS) would be helpful, but it cannot be taken for granted. Europeans and Americans could nevertheless cooperatively organize seminars and workshops with regional parties; and they should both offer their good offices in case regional parties expect them to contribute more than just know-how. In the Egyptian-Israeli case, both Americans and Europeans have been participating in the Multinational Forces and Observers (MFO) in the Sinai since its establishment in 1981. The MFO could well serve as an example for an international force operating on the Golan after an Israeli withdrawal. Both the United States and the European states should be prepared to support such a solution with manpower and material resources.

NATO, as the main Transatlantic organization, can have only a limited role in the peace process. In 1994, NATO started a dialogue with Israel, Jordan, Egypt, Morocco, and Tunisia. This venture raised suspicions, especially in those regional countries that were not invited to the dialogue. With regard to the peace process, therefore, this dialogue should be extended to include all parties immediately concerned, including Lebanon, Syria, and the PA. Opening a dialogue channel between NATO and Syria, in particular, would have the advantage of demonstrating that the whole undertaking is indeed, as claimed, of a purely exploratory nature, and not in any way an attempt to build an alliance with some Middle Eastern actors against others. It might also help to get all regional parties, including their military elites, more used to the language and logic of cooperation. In the same spirit, observers from Israel and its neighbors could be invited to NATO maneuvers. Staff academies in both the United States and the EU states should offer stipends for officers from all those states.

As regards economic support for the peace process, some coordination of policies and programs is actually taking place between a large group of Western states and institutions, and additional U.S.-EU coordination does not actually seem necessary. Thus, under the sponsorship of the World Bank, the Advisory Committee for the PA has been established to coordinate between the Palestinians and international donors. While it might be useful to have the United States and the EU coordinate their policies regarding the international debts of individual states that play a role in the Arab-Israeli conflict and the peace process, it is highly unlikely that this could be achieved. Until now, national interest considerations, both political and commercial, dominate the approach of most European states as well as that of the United States to this question, particularly where relations with more powerful and economically important regional states are concerned, namely with Israel, Egypt, and Syria. As Europeans have failed, among each other, to implement a common policy on this issue, we cannot expect the United States and Europe to find a common approach which, moreover, would in some way link the question of aid to the peace process. Bilateralism will most probably prevail.

The same applies generally to the political and economic relations of the United States and Europe with most Middle Eastern states: mutual information is needed, but a common policy is unlikely to evolve. The EU has started to negotiate and conclude partnership agreements with Israel, Egypt, Jordan, Lebanon, Syria, and the PA. While these agreements may help to stabilize the integration of these states into a wider European economic space, they will not by themselves affect their relations with Washington. For instance, Europe will never have as privileged a relationship with Israel as the United States does, regardless of how preferential the conditions of Israel's partnership with the EU might eventually be.

There is one state among the immediate participants in the peace process where U.S. and European opinions are at considerable variance. This is Syria. The difference is not only of degree. Rather, U.S. and European policymakers seem to have different perceptions of the character of Syria and its regime. U.S. officials are often torn between categorizing Syria as another "rogue" state, and wooing Syria for practical reasons, namely Syria's participation in the peace process. Europe, in general, tends to view Syria as a difficult but rather normal Middle East actor that can be as much a partner for Europe and the West as other states around the Mediterranean. For the peace process to succeed, it would be helpful if the United States and Europe, despite conceptual differences, could agree that, first, Syria ought to play an important regional role after an eventual settlement of the Arab-Israeli conflict and, second, Syria must receive help to reform its economy and improve its social and educational infrastructure so it can face the challenges of peace and regional economic competition.

Finally, differences of opinion and approach are likely to evolve between European and U.S. policymakers with regard to those political groups in the region that in principle are opposed to the peace process in its actual form, particularly radical Islamists. As a matter of fact, neither the European nor the U.S. approach toward political Islam is very principled: whereas the general American attitude toward Islamic groups is more relaxed than the European, this is much less so regarding those particular Islamist groups, such as Hamas and Hezbollah, that play an active role in the Arab-Israeli conflict. Here, in contrast to a more diverse range of opinions among European officials, U.S. policymakers tend to subscribe to the Israeli doctrine according to which these groups are terrorist organizations that can only be dealt with by force. Such conceptual differences might be narrowed in a Transatlantic dialogue. Regarding policies, U.S. and European policymakers should find a common denominator to the effect that under no circumstances is it their business to fight political Islam or Islamist groupings. It would be in the common interest of Europe, the United States, and the Middle East if the energy and the mobilization capabilities of the Islamists could eventually be put to the service of reconstruction and development in Palestine, Lebanon, and other places in the region. This is unlikely to happen, however, as long as the basic questions of the peace process—territorial occupation and Palestinian sovereignty—remain unsolved.

Chapter 5

The United States, Europe, and the Persian Gulf

Geoffrey Kemp

The United States and Europe share mutual interests in the security of the Persian Gulf. It is the world's most important source of oil. Unfortunately, it is also a region plagued by conflict and instability. Loss of access to Persian Gulf oil, a precipitate increase in its price, or the massive transfer of oil revenues to anti-Western regimes would have profound consequences for the economic well-being and security of the Western allies. They also share interests in trade with this region. The increasing demand for consumer goods and various infrastructure projects in the richer Gulf countries are sources of revenue for both European and American companies. Over the long run, a stable and prosperous Gulf could be a very important source of business for Western companies. There are major opportunities to develop the energy resources of the region, particularly natural gas. If Iran and Iraq are rehabilitated as a result of political change, they both have huge potential for Western investment.

Nevertheless, despite these obvious common interests, the United States and Europe do not always see eye-to-eye on the management of Gulf affairs, even as the region lurches from one crisis to another. The high point in recent cooperation was the Gulf War, when the coalition put together by George Bush operated with great unanimity; even the Soviet Union was on board. It was unrealistic to believe that this coalition could survive the uniqueness of the 1990–91 crisis. Furthermore, Britain, France, Germany, Italy, and other Europeans have all pursued their own different interests and objectives in the region, and take different stands on various components of European Union (EU) Gulf policy.

Many questions arise in considering U.S.-European policy toward the Gulf: will U.S.-European interests diverge or converge as demand for energy changes and as Asia consumes and competes for more Persian Gulf oil? What will be the future of the U.S. military posture in the region? If there is U.S.-European consensus that the U.S. presence is beneficial, should Europe play a more active military role? What are the linkages between the U.S. Gulf strategy and the U.S.-European positions on the Arab-Israeli peace process? Since neither the U.S. policy of "dual containment" of Iraq and Iran nor the European support for "critical dialogue" with Iran have been successful, what should be done to improve U.S.-European cooperation?

To address these questions and to highlight the urgency of the problem, it is necessary to review the energy issue and the political conditions within the Gulf Cooperation Council (GCC) countries, Iran, and Iraq, as well as some of the more fundamental factors that lead to instability, including territorial disputes, economic asymmetries, and ethnic divergence. The chapter then reviews U.S.-European policy options concerning Gulf security and the problems of dealing with Iraq and Iran. It closes by recommending a more united and assertive U.S.-European approach to the region and arguing that a common policy is possible if it is better coordinated.

The Continuing Importance of Persian Gulf Energy

The countries of the Persian Gulf and Arabian peninsula—Iraq, Iran, Yemen, and the six GCC states (Bahrain, Kuwait, Oman, Qatar, Saudi Arabia, and the United Arab Emirates)—and their off-shore economic zones contain close to two-thirds of the world's proven petroleum reserves.[1] Over the next fifteen years, world demand for energy will reach unprecedented levels. It is expected to increase by 34–46 percent between 1993 and 2010.[2] The increased demand will be met primarily

---

1. "Worldwide Look at Reserves and Production," *Oil and Gas Journal*, Vol. 92, No. 52 (December 26, 1994). The *International Petroleum Encyclopedia* also offers a figure of 66 percent, cited by the Department of Defense, Office of International Security Affairs, "United States Security Strategy for the Middle East," (Washington, D.C.: U.S. Department of Defense, 1995). However, *World Oil* cites a figure approaching 54 percent in "Estimated Proven World Reserves, 1994 Versus 1993," *World Oil*, August 1995, p. 30.

2. These are figures prepared by the International Energy Agency in its *World Energy Outlook 1996* edition.

by oil, natural gas, and coal. The energy needs of the newly industrializing countries could more than double by the year 2010. At this point, Organization for Economic Cooperation and Development (OECD) consumption could represent less than half of world energy demand. The key players responsible for this dramatic growth are the booming economies of East Asia and South Asia.

World demand for oil will grow in parallel with these expectations. It is projected to increase from 70 million barrels per day (mbd) in 1995 to 92–97 mbd by 2010.[3] Based on current patterns—and assuming no catastrophic upheaval in the world economy—it is possible to suggest the general trend lines for the next fifteen years. Furthermore, there is enough oil in the ground and under the seabed in the Middle East, Russia, Asia, and the Americas to meet global demands into the indefinite future. The problem is getting the oil out of the ground and guaranteeing its distribution to the market place at an acceptable price. The primary obstacles to increased access to this oil are political, economic, ecological, and logistical rather than geological. They are tied into questions of sovereignty and regional stability. Thus, while the world is awash in oil (and coal and natural gas), the most promising sources for further production are located in two of the most politically unstable regions on earth, the Persian Gulf and the Caspian basin. Of these two regions, the Persian Gulf remains by far the most important.

Based on numbers generated by the International Energy Agency and other established sources, Persian Gulf oil suppliers may be called upon to provide 40–45 million barrels of oil per day in the year 2010, which would be a little under half of the world's requirements. The precise amount of oil needed will be dependent on the rate of world economic growth, the availability of alternative sources, capacity constraints on further production, and the price of oil. Low-price oil and high-growth economies with little efficiency will lead to increased demands on Persian Gulf oil because, at the margin, low prices make Persian Gulf supplies more cost-effective than oil that is more expensive to produce from other regions.

Whatever the final numbers, there is no doubt that two dramatic points stand out in all the authoritative projections. First, access to these resources will remain vital for the industrial world, giving the

---

3. Ibid., p. 3.

region great strategic importance and assuring that several of the region's countries will be extremely rich. Second, based on import trends, Europe is more dependent upon Gulf oil than is the United States, which gets increasing amounts of foreign oil from the Western hemisphere and Africa. However, given the fungibility of oil as a market commodity and U.S. concerns about oil prices and the danger of oil revenues in the hands of pariah states, these discrepancies in import numbers are unlikely to alter the common interest shared by the United States and Europe in securing Gulf oil. Nevertheless, the issue could become contentious if in the next century most Gulf oil goes to Europe and Asia, while the United States remains the only major country willing and able to defend the region with military force. The problem could be accelerated if the United States suffers serious casualties from more terrorist attacks in the region, and U.S. politicians begin to question the wisdom of a forward military presence absent strong European and Asian backing.

HOW STABLE ARE THE GCC COUNTRIES?

The Persian Gulf is one of the most highly armed regions in the world, and its infrastructure is extremely vulnerable. Political leaders run the gamut from brutal totalitarian dictators (Iraq) to corrupt mullahs (Iran) to enlightened monarchs (Oman). Both the United States and Europe have good relations with the GCC states. Alliance disagreements over how to manage this relationship primarily concern competition for arms sales.

The most challenging issues facing the GCC countries concern their relationships with Iran and Iraq and the internal social and economic problems facing each regime. Externally, with the exception of Saudi Arabia's air force, none of the GCC states can come close to matching Iranian and Iraqi military power, so the GCC countries rely primarily on the United States for protection. Internally, the dilemma for the Gulf countries is that while most have great riches, their societies are very conservative and the distribution of income, while certainly beneficial to many citizens, does not trickle down equitably to many lower-class residents and the work force of foreign expatriates. Discontent is evident in many of the states, especially Bahrain and Saudi Arabia, and the economic systems are permeated by corruption at the highest levels. (These social welfare issues are developed in more detail in Chapter 6 by Johannes Reissner.)

Six years after the Gulf War, the region is facing severe economic difficulties. In comparison to their relative affluence before 1990, the Arab

Gulf states are now experiencing significant shortfalls of revenues due to the costs of the war and sluggish oil prices. This is compounded by a growing population that is well aware of the revenues generated by oil and the enormous wealth that flows to the leadership. Weak economic growth creates a potent and potentially dangerous mixture when coupled with population growth. Throughout the Middle East, both rich and poor countries continue to face the daunting prospect of tens of millions of new people in need of employment and basic sustenance. Since much of the legitimacy of the Gulf monarchies depends on their capacity to distribute resources to their population and sustain the extensive services they provide, a shortage of revenues could seriously endanger internal stability and impair the military capabilities of the Gulf countries.[4]

The Gulf economies are extraordinarily dependent on the fluctuating price of oil in the world market, and they suffer when prices are low. In response to low prices, the Gulf countries must either expand their production or reduce production in an attempt to increase the price. Past attempts to control or reduce output have been a significant source of tension among OPEC members in the Gulf and, indeed, contributed to Iraq's invasion of Kuwait in 1990.

Another debilitating characteristic of the economies of the Gulf states is the dominant position of central governments. Governments own the national oil companies, collect oil revenues, redistribute the capital through the budget, and determine who will profit through spending and regulatory policies. Overall, in the Persian Gulf economies, government policies and spending are critically important even for the development of the private sector. Government spending, for example, is the engine of the construction industry in the private sector. The role of government in sectors like banking and finance, which are open to private capital, is also significant.[5] This intrusive role complicates the economic reform that most specialists believe is necessary to increase government revenue. However, privatization, reduction of government spending, and the imposition of new taxes carry a high political price for governments today.

---

4. James Bruce, "Land of Crisis and Upheaval," *Jane's Defence Weekly*, July 30, 1994, pp. 23–35.

5. The analysis of the major characteristics of the Gulf economies is based on F. Gregory Gause III, *Oil Monarchies: Domestic and Security Challenges in the Arab Gulf States* (New York: Council on Foreign Relations, 1994), pp. 44–58.

Strategically, the GCC states face a real dilemma. At the same time that their domestic political environment is becoming more fragile, they need U.S. protection even more and have been encouraged to spend more resources on arms, the bulk of which are American. However, the enhanced power and visibility of closer U.S.-GCC ties can exacerbate domestic tensions and provide a catalyst for political unrest. Anti-American rhetoric is used by both radicals and conservatives who disapprove of regime behavior. Many have suggested that this is the case in Saudi Arabia, with the recent bombing attacks against U.S. targets. Yet this is a risk that the GCC must take because the most extreme threat to their security is the military power of Iraq and Iran. This threat can only be offset by the U.S. security commitment.

The Islamic Republic of Iran

While Europe and the United States worry about Iran's support for terrorism, its rejection of Israel, its interests in weapons of mass destruction, and its bad human rights record, the mullahs have other troubles. The Iranian mullahs came to power in 1979 and established a new model of government where revolutionary Islam was to play the central role. It has not worked out as planned; not only has the Iranian model had extremely limited success outside Iran, but Iran now finds itself needing to defend the Ayatollah Khomeini's legacy among its own people. The regime has become very defensive and is widely disliked by many ordinary Iranians.

The underlying fear of the regime is that the West seeks to overthrow the Islamic Republic. It has good cause to be wary. In 1993, the Clinton administration announced a policy of "dual containment" of both Iran and Iraq. It was derived from an assessment that the current Iraqi and Iranian regimes are both hostile to U.S. interests in the region. President Clinton's policy was distinguished from previous ones that consigned American interests in the Middle East to a local balance of power between the key regional countries. America's interests in the Gulf were now thought to be too important to be left to the regional powers to manage. Dual containment entails an enhanced U.S. military commitment to the Gulf with closer military ties to such key powers as Saudi Arabia and Turkey.[6]

---

6. Geoffrey Kemp, *Forever Enemies? American Policy and the Islamic Republic of Iran* (Washington, D.C.: Carnegie Endowment for International Peace, 1994), p. 7.

Thus, U.S. military power poses a direct military challenge to Iran and dilutes potential Iranian influence in the Gulf. With Israel as its ally, U.S. military hegemony is a key manifestation of alien (foreign) intervention in the region. The U.S. naval vessels in the Gulf, Defense Cooperation Agreements and pre-positioned equipment in Arab Gulf states, and allied aircraft enforcing the no-fly zones over Iraq are a disconcerting presence. The Iranian leadership remembers past U.S. military actions against Iran during the Iran-Iraq war, the U.S.-led campaign to block arms from reaching Iran, and U.S. willingness to discriminate against Iran. Then, after being defeated by Iraq, Iran had to watch with humiliation as the United States and its allies trounced Iraq in Operation Desert Storm. Desert Storm reminded Tehran of its extreme vulnerability in the face of American military power. Furthermore, it takes note of Israel's strategic reach, including long-range aircraft, ballistic missiles, and nuclear weapons. Iran is also humbled by the global American campaign to stop any nuclear cooperation or sales to Iran while at the same time the United States vetoes efforts to curb Israel's nuclear program.

The mullahs' obsession with the United States—matched, it must be said, by a parallel U.S. preoccupation with the "pariah" state—obscures other security issues that would be of concern to any Iranian regime. Iran faces a number of potential security threats, many of which have little to do with the United States or the West. Coupled with Iran's economic difficulties, these issues help foster long-term insecurities in Iran.

Located in a zone of conflict and unrest, Iran faces strategic threats on all sides, with the most obvious, significant threat—aside from the United States—emanating from Iraq. The two countries fought an eight-year war that cost at least 200,000 Iranian lives and did significant damage to infrastructure and to the Iranian regime's standing. Fear of Iraq and a desire for revenge co-exist for the Iranians, most of whom were affected by the war. The War of the Cities, the heavy casualties, the POWs, the Iraqi use of chemical weapons, and the brutal fighting on the frontlines all took their toll.

Gulf relations are a second area of concern, and Iran has pursued a seemingly contradictory policy. On the one hand, the mullahs would like to lessen Iran's isolation and build stronger ties with its Arab Gulf neighbors. On the other hand, Iran's assertive, hegemonic tendencies appear especially strong while Iraq is contained. These undermine efforts to strengthen relations with the Gulf Arab states. This has led to mixed results; relations are better with some states, such as Oman and Qatar, than others. The Saudis were the key host of U.S. military forces during the 1990–91 Gulf crisis, and Saudi influence in OPEC and ability to keep Iran out of Gulf security talks frustrates Iranian policymakers. The Islamic rivalry between the two pits Iran's Shi'ites against Saudi Arabia's Wahabbis. Iran has differed with the United Arab Emirates over the control and sovereignty of the islands of Abu Musa and Greater and Lesser Tunbs; it has occupied them and refuses to submit the dispute to international arbitration. The Arab Gulf countries see Iran's tactics on the islands issue as evidence of its hegemonic aspirations. On their own, the Gulf Arab states pose no military threat to Iran, but their agreements with the United States create a problem for Iran. With the United States in their court, the Gulf states are able to act more brazenly toward Iran.

In several neighboring states, Iran is also threatened by unrest and civil war that tie into Iran's internal situation. Iraq is fragmented, and until recently Iraqi Kurds operated in an autonomous safe haven in northern Iraq. The Caucasus is a hotbed of civil strife, with the Armenian-Azerbaijani war, Georgian violence, and the Chechnya crisis. Afghanistan has been torn apart by a seemingly endless civil war. Further to the east, Iran has become embroiled in the chaos and fighting in Tajikistan, the one Central Asian country whose population is predominantly Persian-speaking and of Shi'ite faith.

The economic realm provides little comfort. Although Iran has been trying to attract investment to its new free trade zones by offering long-term exemptions from taxes, import fees, and customs duties, foreign investment is shrinking. The only success story was the rescheduling of the payments on Iran's huge debt to its European and Japanese lenders. Nevertheless, Iran continues to face serious problems making payments to regional and other creditors, such as Japanese trading houses.

Earnings from oil exports provide 90 percent of Iran's export revenues.[7] Iran needs to rebuild its deteriorating oil fields, which suffer from serious production and maintenance problems.[8] Attempts to be part of deals in the Caspian Sea and large claims to Qatar's adjacent

---

7. "Iran: Economic Structure," The Economist Intelligence Unit (EIU) Country Reports, November 23, 1995.

8. Elaine Sciolino, "Iran's Difficulties Lead Some in U.S. to Doubt Threat," *New York Times,* July 5, 1994, p. A1.

Persian Gulf offshore North Field gas reserves can be seen as part of Iran's effort to get a larger share of the resource pie. Yet natural gas development requires huge amounts of up-front capital investment and secure, long-term contracts with consumers. In this regard, the U.S. policy of trying to limit international investment in the Iranian energy sector has been partially successful and therefore costly for the regime.

The dilemma facing both the United States and Europe is that while the Iranian Republic faces a huge list of internal and external problems, many of its own making, the regime is in no imminent likelihood of collapse. The Iranian leadership is not monolithic; different factions openly and fiercely compete with each other for public support. While there is near-universal consensus that Saddam Hussein runs a tyranny in Iraq, there are more mixed reviews of the Iranian mullahs, with some observers arguing that the regime, though thoroughly repressive, has become less brutal and totalitarian since the death of Ayatollah Khomeini in 1989. Even the United States has refrained from calling for the overthrow of the Iranian regime; what is required is that the regime change specific policies. The U.S.-European debate concerns the most appropriate ways to bring about these changes.

Iraq

As long as Iraqi President Saddam Hussein remains in power, his hopes of ending Iraqi isolation, exporting oil, and rebuilding the military will be stymied. They are blocked by the UN sanctions regime imposed in 1990 after the Iraqi invasion of Kuwait, the Western military presence in the Gulf, and the determination of successive U.S. administrations to seek his ouster.

Inside Iraq, the sanctions have led to widespread poverty and the degradation of infrastructure and facilities. The Iraqi people are suffering food and medical shortages, and only an elite circle of Saddam Hussein's supporters are protected from the scarcity of goods. Iraq's oil reserves, the source of its potential wealth, are bottled up by sanctions, leaving the regime with limited financial resources.

In 1989 Iraq was pumping 2.8 mbd when its quota was 3.1 mbd. Some observers predict that once Iraq is permitted to sell its oil, its output could eventually rise from a theoretical maximum of 3 mbd to about 6.5 mbd, primarily because of the new exploration done by

Russian, French, and Italian companies.[9] Iraq's oil minister, Safa Hadi Jawad, has said that once the embargo is lifted, his country will start pumping oil at full capacity until it reaches the production levels of Iran. Most Western observers consider such predictions premature. Iraq currently has a provisional quota of 550,000 barrels per day, and Iran has 3.6 mbd.[10] Even if Iraq is permitted to export all of its oil, it will not be able to recover its full production ability right away due to poor maintenance of the fields and pipelines.

The first significant break in Iraq's bleak economic picture came in May 1996 with an Iraqi-UN agreement on a food-for-oil deal, as allowed under UN Security Council Resolution 986. Under the plan, Iraq is permitted to sell $2 billion of oil for six months—about 700,000 barrels per day. Although some of the funds are used by the Iraqi government for the purchase of food and medicine, hundreds of millions of dollars also go toward the Gulf War reparations fund, UN costs for the disarmament program in Iraq, and Kurdish needs in autonomous northern Iraq.

Meanwhile, the internal leadership struggle leaves the Iraqi president on constant guard, never sure of the direction of the next challenge. Reports of coup attempts periodically emanate from Baghdad. The August 1995 defection of Hussein Kamal Hassan al-Majid and another son-in-law with Saddam Hussein's two daughters demonstrated a deep split in the ruling family. Saddam Hussein's son and putative heir, Uday, has been criticized from many quarters and was the object of an assassination attempt in 1996.

Iraq is primarily composed of Sunnis (32–37 percent; roughly half Arabs and half Kurds) and Shi'ite Arabs (60–65 percent).[11] Iraqi Shi'ites, numbering some ten or eleven million people, constitute a majority in Iraq. These ethnic and religious splits are a significant issue for Saddam Hussein's Sunni Arab regime. Over the years, the regime has been in conflict with both Kurds and Shi'ites.

Like several other groups in Iraq, the Shi'ites are oppressed; their leaders have been arrested and executed by the hundreds. In March 1991, their uprising against Saddam Hussein was brutally crushed.

---

9. Hobart Rowen, "Over the Barrel," Washington Post, October 13, 1994, p. A19.

10. Philip Shenon, "OPEC Seeking to Raise Prices by Output Freeze," New York Times, November 22, 1994.

11. CIA, The World Factbook 1995 (Washington, D.C.: CIA, 1995).

The Iraqi government continues to target the Shi'ites by draining and shelling the southern Iraqi marshlands, but the Shi'ites in Iraq have received little international support. Many countries, including Saudi Arabia, fear the fragmentation of Iraq and the possibility of an Iranian-dominated Shi'ite entity in southern Iraq.

In the north, the Kurdish enclave raises similar fears for the Turks who would not like to see the formation of an independent Kurdish state on their borders. Until August 1996, the Iraqi Kurds operated an autonomous safe haven in northern Iraq, established just after the conclusion of the Gulf War in 1991. The safe haven has been battered by an Iraqi blockade, Kurdish in-fighting, and Turkish and, in 1996, Iraqi military incursions.

Relations with Iran, Kuwait, and Turkey form a central component of Iraq's external concerns. While Iran and Turkey have large armed forces, the key issues revolve around oil and water. Much of the tension between Iraq and Iran is linked to the ongoing Iraqi quest to secure access to the Gulf. Iraq's coastline, at only 36 miles (58 km), is shorter than the coast of Iran or any GCC state; even the tiny island state of Bahrain has a coast of 100 miles (162 km).[12] Iraqi leaders are obsessed with protecting, and in some cases expanding, their water access and port facilities. The Shatt al-Arab river has been the focus of major disputes and conflicts. Iraq's concern over this geographic inequity is unlikely to change even if the current regime is displaced.

Iraq has long coveted Kuwait. Within a week of Kuwaiti independence in 1961, the Iraqi president asserted that Kuwait constituted "an integral part of Iraq."[13] Since then, Iraq has maintained its claim to the tiny Gulf state, and Saddam Hussein's invasion of Kuwait temporarily fulfilled Iraqi hopes for absorption of the so-called "nineteenth Iraqi province." Control of Kuwait gave Iraq far greater sea access and full control of naval and port facilities at Umm-Qasr, where post-war border decisions have adversely affected Iraqi naval assets. Iraq's forced expulsion from Kuwait actually placed Iraq in a weaker position than it had before the war. The UN border demarcation commission results were highly favorable for Kuwait.

With regard to Iraq's policies toward Turkey, the Kurds and water access are key issues. Iraq is dependent on the Tigris and Euphrates

12. Ibid., p. 191.

13. Robert Litwak, *Security in the Persian Gulf 2: Sources of Inter-State Conflict* (Montclair, N.J.: Allanheld, Osmun, 1981), p. 25.

rivers. Sitting downstream from Turkey and Syria leaves Iraq in a vulnerable position. Both rivers originate in Turkey, and they combine in southern Iraq to form the Shatt al-Arab. Turkey's Grand Anatolia Project, designed to increase hydroelectricity and agricultural irrigation, has generated deep concern in Syria and Iraq.[14] Both countries fear that the Turkish project will reduce their share of the river and give Turkey the power to shut off the flow altogether during a conflict or crisis.

Thus the situation in Iraq is very different from that in Iran. In Iraq, the removal of one man, Saddam Hussein, could radically change the political environment and either usher a new, more cooperative relationship with the rest of the world or lead to a serious breakdown in the structure of the Iraqi state and a period of civil war and further chaos.

U.S. and European Policies toward the Persian Gulf

The United States and the European countries regard access to Persian Gulf oil at reasonable prices to be essential for the economic well-being of the industrial world; they agree that there are underlying sources of conflict and tension throughout the region that are promoted, in part, by radical states that have agendas inimical to Western interests. Both are fearful that the spread of weapons of mass destruction and a more intensified conventional arms race will raise the risks of confrontation, and both appreciate that the underlying sociological and demographic factors in many of the countries compound an already fragile political process. In sum, on the overall checklist of strategic, economic, and political items of concern in the Middle East, the United States and the Europeans usually talk with one voice.

There is also consensus that the United States is the only country that has the military and political clout to play a truly decisive role in Gulf security. There is little opposition in Europe to the major U.S. military commitment to security of the Gulf Cooperation Council countries in the Persian Gulf. In fact, there are small European contributions, notably from Britain and France, assisting in this process; they are underwritten, in the case of Iraq, by UN Security Council

---

14. Historically there have been other incidents, including a 1974 Iraqi-Syrian controversy over Syria's al-Thawra dam. Peter H. Gleick, "Water and Conflict," *International Security*, Vol. 18, No. 1 (Summer 1993), pp. 88–89.

resolutions stemming from Iraq's invasion of Kuwait in 1990. It is unlikely that the European military presence in the Gulf will be augmented unless there is another major crisis.

Within the United States, there has been very little controversy about the wisdom of maintaining such a large and expensive military contingency. This consensus could change if more Americans are subject to terrorist attacks in Saudi Arabia and if it becomes more difficult to get allied support for limited military operations against Iraq in times of crisis. Such a change in attitudes could have far-reaching repercussions for the stability of the region.

THE GULF COUNTRIES AND THE ARAB-ISRAELI PEACE PROCESS
The United States and Europe both recognize the linkage between the Arab-Israeli peace process and Gulf stability. A stable and secure Persian Gulf bolsters the prospects for Arab-Israeli peace. A successful conclusion of an Arab-Israeli peace has great relevance for the stability of the Arabian peninsula. The Arab-Israeli frontline states and Persian Gulf states are not operating in isolation from each other. Since 1993, the GCC role in Arab-Israeli normalization has become particularly important.

There are a number of areas where Gulf issues connect with the peace process. Like the GCC states, Egypt, Israel, and Jordan benefit from a successful U.S.-led containment of Iraq and a lessening of the Iranian threat. As the wealthiest Arab states, the GCC countries also have the opportunity, along with the United States, Japan, and the EU, to provide financial backing for Arab frontline states that make peace with Israel. On the negative side, conflict in the Gulf can spill over into the Arab-Israeli arena, as Iraq's attacks on Israel during the Gulf War demonstrated. Likewise, the spread of weapons of mass destruction affects all states in the region. Not only military problems link the Middle East's sub-regions: water scarcity, demographic growth, and economic dependence in the form of aid and remittances ensure that the people and countries of the region have relationships that provide the ingredients for both cooperation and conflict.

A successful resolution to the Arab-Israeli conflict would have positive benefits for the GCC, especially in dealing with the Iranian and Iraqi threats. Arab-Israeli peace would remove many of the irritants that have harmed U.S. cooperation with the GCC in the past. A setback in the peace process could once more put the United States in the awkward position of trying to work with Israel on the one hand

and the key Arab states on the other hand. In the past this was a divisive, time-consuming exercise which no U.S. administration would want to repeat. Since U.S. support is crucial for GCC external security, better U.S.-GCC ties would strengthen the overall security environment by weakening the power and outreach of Iran and Iraq. It would also weaken the opposition by Islamist and nationalist elements to the U.S. military presence in the Gulf. Furthermore, since the preconditions for a comprehensive Arab-Israeli peace assume that Syria and Israel have signed a peace treaty, Iran and other rejectionist countries would be further isolated. Iran's ability to create trouble in Lebanon and Israel would be significantly curtailed without Syrian acquiescence. If Iran's wings were clipped, the stability of the Gulf could be enhanced.

Since the signing of the Declaration of Principles between Israel and the Palestinians in September 1993 (Oslo I), some of the GCC states and Israel have proceeded with the normalization of relations. Several GCC countries have been participating in the Arab-Israeli multilateral talks that began in 1992. These relations become especially relevant at a time when some in the Arab world have suggested that Arab-Israeli normalization could be a casualty of intransigent Israeli policies. The Arab summit in Cairo in June 1996 did not directly threaten Israel, but did link continued progress on normalization with advances in the peace process. Should it come to pass that the key Arab states call for halting or reversing normalization with Israel, the Gulf states would be further intimidated and reluctant to make further gestures to Israel. This, in turn, would have negative implications for U.S. Gulf policy.

While the EU supports the Oslo peace process, some European leaders, especially in France, have begun to adopt a more critical attitude toward the current peace process and to voice complaints against Israel's new prime minister, Benjamin Netanyahu, and his Likud coalition. For some Americans, this behavior harks back to the early 1980s when the European Economic Community (EEC) made its own "Venice Declaration," distancing itself from the prevailing Camp David process that had begun in the late 1970s.

It is possible that U.S.-European disagreement over the peace process will worsen if the Oslo process stops or is reversed. This would affect U.S.-European relations in the Gulf and coalition policies toward Iran and Iraq. If the U.S. administration, Congress, and the influential pro-Israel institutions in the United States believe that

Europeans (or individual European countries) are unfairly taking sides against Israel in the peace process, the pressures to tighten sanctions against European companies who do business with Iran— viewed as one of Israel's most bitter enemies—will grow. Since the United States and Europe have much to gain by closer cooperation on Iraq and Iran, a public confrontation over Israel would be bad for all sides. The best policy is for Europe to work closely with the United States to assure that the peace process continues and that the dangerous situation in the Gulf be faced from a common perspective. (For more on U.S.-European relations and the peace process, see Chapter 3 by Richard Haass.)

DEALING WITH IRAQ AND IRAN

The two most contentious issues in U.S.-European relations are how to deal with Iraq and Iran. It is complicated because the Europeans have adopted common positions at the EU on Iran, but in practice they each have different approaches to the region dependent upon the issue and their interests.

IRAQ.   Concerning Iraq, the United States and Europe are bound by UN Security Council resolutions imposed on Iraq in 1990 following its invasion of Kuwait. Major disagreements have emerged, especially between the United States and France, over the use of force against Saddam Hussein and whether sanctions should be lifted if Iraq is certified to be rid of weapons of mass destruction. Britain and the United States have had more compatible policies concerning the military option, but only the United States has been able to exercise it in a major way. Most Europeans accept that the U.S. military deterrent remains an essential component to prevent any resurgence of Saddam Hussein, but there is skepticism that military power can be used to overthrow him. To the contrary, Europeans (and some Americans) argue that the limited use of military power can make matters worse, as was the case in the summer of 1996 when President Clinton launched a cruise missile attack on Iraqi air defenses following Iraqi troop movements in the Kurdish enclave in the north of the country. So long as Saddam Hussein remains in power, Iraq will pose a threat to the Gulf, which will require a U.S. security umbrella. This will become increasingly costly, burdensome, and dangerous for both the Gulf allies and the United States. Therefore, merely continuing to "contain" Saddam or "keep him in his box" is not a wise idea.

The United States' hard line policy towards Iraq was reaffirmed clearly and concisely by Secretary of State Madeleine Albright on

March 26, 1997:

We do not agree with the nations who argue that if Iraq complies with its obligations concerning weapons of mass destruction, sanctions should be lifted. Our view, which is unshakable, is that Iraq must *prove* its peaceful intentions. It can only do that by complying with *all* of the Security Council Resolutions to which it is subject. Is it possible to conceive of such a government under Saddam Hussein? . . . the evidence is overwhelming that Saddam Hussein's intentions will never be peaceful. The United States looks forward, nevertheless, to the day when Iraq rejoins the family of nations as a responsible and law-abiding member. This is in our interests and in the interests of our allies and partners within the region. Clearly, a change in Iraq's government could lead to a change in U.S. policy.[15]

This policy could face a European challenge if the head of the United Nations Special Commission (UNSCOM) finally provides positive certification that Iraq is now in full compliance with UN Security Council Resolution 687, which calls for the dismantling of all Iraq's weapons of mass destruction. Under these circumstances, a split among the Europeans and with the United States is possible since the United States, and probably Britain, will insist that all UN resolutions pertaining to Iraq be adhered to. Since this would require Saddam Hussein to conform to international human rights standards, there is near-universal consensus that he could not do this and remain in power. An equally serious U.S.-European confrontation is likely to occur concerning the future use of U.S. military power against Iraq if Saddam Hussein once more violates cease-fire agreements or makes menacing movements toward Kuwait or the Kurdish enclave in the north.

While most Europeans would also like to get rid of Saddam Hussein, there is a debate about what happens to Iraq after he goes. Some fear that the country will break apart and that a civil war drawing in Turkey, Iran, and possibly Saudi Arabia and Syria will result. Germany, in particular, has great concerns about the Kurdish problem in view of its own domestic relations with Turkey and the Kurdish Workers' Party (PKK) terrorism on its own soil. Nevertheless, there is broad agreement between the United States and Europe that the ouster of Saddam Hussein would pose

---

15. Remarks by Secretary of State Madeleine K. Albright at Georgetown University, "Preserving Principle and Safeguarding Stability: United States Policy Toward Iraq" (Washington, D.C.: U.S. Department of State, March 26, 1997).

major problems for the mullahs of Iran. The mullahs would either be drawn into an open-ended conflict, from which they are unlikely to emerge victorious, or alternatively, they could be faced with a new Iraqi regime that is pro-Western and which would eventually be able to pump more oil onto the market, thereby lowering overall oil prices.

The challenge for the United States and Europe is to prevent a serious alliance schism so long as Saddam Hussein remains in power, while seeking a more coherent policy on how to remove him and what to do once he has gone. This will not be easy but it can be no excuse for procrastination. The longer the alliance obfuscates and delays addressing these issues, the greater the probability that the next major Gulf crisis will divide rather than unite the Western powers.

IRAN.   Concerning Iran, the differences between the United States and Europe are over the implementation of policy. The U.S. dual containment policy toward Iran has been supplemented in 1995 by the imposition of a unilateral trade embargo, essentially ending all U.S. commercial relations with Iran. Then, in 1996, legislation was signed giving the U.S. president authority to impose a range of penalties on foreign companies who do business in excess of $40 million with Iran's energy industry. This could include denial of access to the huge U.S. market. The Iran and Libya Sanctions Act was initiated by New York Senator Alfonse D'Amato and has been greeted with extreme hostility by the European Union. The EU has threatened to retaliate against U.S. companies doing business in Europe if the new law is ever enforced. So long as this does not happen, the damage caused by the rhetoric and recriminations can be contained, but if European companies are penalized, a much more serious confrontation will be unavoidable. Since such a polarization would play into the hands of Tehran, a major diplomatic effort is needed to prevent it from happening. This will require compromise by both sides of the Atlantic.

Despite quarrels over the Iran and Libya Sanctions Act, the European countries agree with the United States that Iran's behavior has to change. The EU policy of engaging Iran in a "critical dialogue" was initiated at Edinburgh in December 1992. There were five areas where the EU wanted Iran to change its behavior: the Arab-Israeli peace process, terrorism, weapons of mass destruction, human rights, and international law. (For more details on Iran and Iraq's weapons of mass destruction, see Chapter 9 by Richard Falkenrath, and Chapter 10 by Joanna Spear.) The purpose of the critical dialogue was to keep channels open and influence the moderates in Tehran.

Americans are skeptical that this dialogue has achieved any meaningful results. However, the Europeans cite two occasions when European intervention in Iran has been beneficial to the United States and Israel. First, during Israel's "Grapes of Wrath" offensive in Lebanon in 1996, the United States asked France to tell Iran not to block a cease-fire. Second, Israel requested that the EU tell Iran not to use terror during the May 1996 Israeli elections. Each European country has a different spin on the definition of "critical dialogue," and although this term is now increasingly criticized in Europe—it is said to be neither critical, nor a dialogue—they do not accept the U.S. argument that economic sanctions will change Iranian behavior in the five designated areas.

The decision of the Berlin Appellate Court on April 10, 1997, which found the Iranian leadership ultimately culpable for the murders of Iranian Kurdish dissidents at the Mykonos restaurant in Berlin in 1992, led the the EU to suspend its critical dialogue with Iran and withdraw its ambassadors from Tehran. On April 29, the EU Court of Foreign Ministers agreed on the following:

- confirmation that under the present circumstances there is no basis for the continuation of the critical dialogue between the European Union and Iran;
- the suspension of official bilateral ministerial visits to or from Iran;
- confirmation of the established policy of European Union member states not to supply arms to Iran;
- cooperation to ensure that visas are not granted to Iranians with intelligence and security functions; and
- concertation in excluding Iranian intelligence personnel from European Union member states.[16]

It is important that Europeans and the United States use the Mykonos case to try to resolve their differences on Iran in order to avoid an escalation of rhetoric and mutual trade sanctions over Iran. What is required is a high-profile initiative by the United States and Europe to reach an agreed agenda on steps that Iran should take—and that it is believed to be capable of taking—in exchange for an eventual ending of the U.S. isolation of Iran. All Europeans agree that what the Iranians ultimately want is better relations with the United States.

---

16. The European Union Press Releases, "European Declaration on Iran," No. 26/27, April 29, 1997.

One way to set the agenda and benchmarks for Iranian behavior is to use the "good cop–bad cop" method. The essence of the good cop–bad cop technique is that both cops have similar objectives of enforcing the law. The good cop nurtures the subject, seeking his or her friendship. He relies on pleasantries and small but kind gestures, while warning the subject that it is much better to cooperate or else he or she will be turned over to the bad cop. The bad cop, on the other hand, uses threats and intimidation and unpleasantness to achieve cooperation. However, both cops understand the limits of their respective approaches: in the last resort, the good cop, too, must enforce the law and must be prepared to draw his gun. Likewise, the bad cop must also respect the constitutional rights of the subject and behave within the law. In other words, the good cop–bad cop policy involves a mixture of carrots and sticks.

How would this approach work in the case of a U.S.-European initiative on Iran? Clearly the roles are preordained: the Europeans would play the good cop, and the United States the bad cop. Europe would use its access and influence with Iran to make the argument, persistently and firmly, that unless Iran complies with certain standards and changes its behavior on specific issues, Europe will not be able or willing to act contrary to the policies advocated by the bad cop. This means that Europe would be prepared to consider tougher measures—the sticks—against Iran more in line with those proposed by the United States if, after a specific period of time, Iran refused to comply.

In return, if Iran does comply, the United States would be prepared to offer carrots and to soften its hard-line policy towards Iran. This could include loosening its economic sanctions and opposition to Iranian attempts to raise funds on the international capital markets.

Such an approach could include high-level initiatives by senior U.S. and European diplomats to formulate and agree upon a common action policy, including better coordination and interpretation of intelligence data on sensitive issues. The agenda would focus on the five areas of Iranian behavior on which the United States and Europe agree need to be changed—the peace process, terrorism, weapons of mass destruction, human rights, and international law. The approach should also establish benchmarks based on expectations of what changes in policy the Iranian regime is realistically likely to consider. The benchmarks are listed in Table 1.

Table 1. Benchmarks for Changes in Iranian Policy.

	Ideal	Possible
Peace Process	Recognition of Israel	Publicly accept Oslo process and accept Yasser Arafat and PLO as interlocutors for Palestinians
	Participate in regional multilateral talks, especially in Arms Control and Regional Security (ACRS)	Accept principle that peace between Israel and Arabs is beneficial for region, including Iran
	End all support for Hezbollah, Hamas, and Islamic Jihad	
Terrorism	End all support for third party radicals (Sudan)	Stop arms shipments to Hezbollah (to be coordinated with Syria)
	End terror and assassination programs against foreigners and Iranian opposition	Reduce funding for Hamas and Islamic Jihad; end all cooperation with dissidents in Arab Gulf
Weapons of Mass Destruction	Abandon all nuclear power and research programs	Accept open-ended International Atomic Energy Agency (IAEA) challenge inspections and enhanced IAEA monitoring
	Cancel chemical weapons/ biological weapons programs	Ratify Chemical Weapons Convention
	Limit surface-to-surface missiles to 150 kms	Cancel Nodong missile agreement with N. Korea
		Cancel remaining nuclear reactor deals
		Abandon attempts to acquire nuclear enrichment reprocessing capabilities
Human Rights and International Law	Abide by all international norms on human rights	Remove *fatwa* on Salman Rushdie
	Apologize for taking U.S. hostages in 1979	Permit Baha'is more freedom
		Release nonviolent political prisoners

A time frame for Iranian compliance would be agreed upon, as well as a methodology for assessing compliance. The Iranian government should be given a deadline to change unacceptable behavior or have *all* contacts reduced through a united U.S.-European policy.

Finally, a list of sticks and carrots (see Table 2) should be jointly considered in response to Iranian behavior. (It is more likely that

Europeans will agree to reduce diplomatic contacts and psychologically isolate the Iranian regime rather than resort to economic isolation. Nevertheless, this could have a significant impact on the Iranian leadership, since one of the issues Iran is most concerned with is its isolation.)

Table 2. Sticks and Carrots.

Sticks	Carrots
U.S. and EU priority effort to forge common G-7 position, including joint economic sanctions	U.S. to amend Iran and Libya Sanctions Act
U.S. to link North Korea negotiation to termination of Iran–North Korea Nodong program	U.S. to lift many unilateral sanctions
Bring Rushdie case before UN and World Court	U.S. to cease opposition to Iranian borrowing rights in concessionary financial markets
Intensify use of Voice of America and outlets to broadcast to Iran	U.S. to permit U.S. companies to conclude energy agreements in Iran
Preparations for political, economic, and military reprisals against Iran if Iranian regime proven to be directly implicated in terrorism against U.S. and citizens	

While the steps listed in Table 2 will not by themselves mollify the most severe critics of Iran, they would certainly represent great progress. Within the structure of this list, the components of a deal could be made. However, everything will come to naught if it is clearly demonstrated that the Iranian government has been behind recent terrorist incidents, especially the Khobar Towers bombings of Americans in Saudi Arabia. If there is overwhelming proof of Iranian involvement at the official level, then the United States and its European allies will have to take very tough measures together to avoid pressures on the U.S. president to act unilaterally. Most people agree that such unilateral action would be counterproductive unless carried to an extreme level for which very few have a taste.

Conclusion

An agreement on the Gulf between Europe and the United States—indeed all the G-7 countries—should spell out the conditions to be encouraged in the region. It should stress the huge opportunity costs both Iraq and Iran are incurring by continuing with, in the case of Iraq, Saddam Hussein's rule and, in the case of Iran, unacceptable behavior on the peace process, terrorism, weapons of mass destruction, human rights, and international law. A more coordinated U.S.-European initiative would have great clout with Japan and could not be ignored by either Russia or China. The alternative—U.S.-European competition and conflict over Gulf policy—is a recipe for a disaster that will benefit no one except the extremists.

Chapter 6

Europe, the United States, and the Persian Gulf

Johannes Reissner

The free flow of oil at reasonable prices is a shared interest of the United States and Europe in the Persian Gulf region. But regarding policies to secure this interest, the situation becomes blurred. Whereas the United States as a superpower is in a position to formulate interests and policies in a straightforward way, the Europeans have to look in two directions: to the Gulf and to the superpower. This is the main reason why it is difficult to find a comprehensive and coherent formulation of European interests and policies in the Persian Gulf beyond the basic interest in the free flow of oil, and regional stability as its prerequisite.

This chapter argues that the Europeans should formulate their interests, views of the Gulf region, and policies more explicitly. By observing the political behavior toward the Middle East of Europe, as a community as well as individual states, one is puzzled by the following question: Do they agree in principle with U.S. policies toward the Persian Gulf, with the dispute over whether sanctions or critical dialogue is the best way to treat Iran being just the exception to the rule? Or is that dispute, along with occasional complaints that the United States should consult its European partner more and should treat the countries of the area more sensibly, to be seen as a sign of greater differences underneath the surface?

The diplomatic-political interest in not letting such a difference come too much into the open is understandable. But European positions should not be left vague because both the Americans and the Europeans are confronted with a security dilemma in the Gulf.

This dilemma might be called "external security versus internal instability." No imminent change of this situation is likely, and the Europeans are already confronted with requests for a higher contribution to Gulf security; the debate over "burden-sharing" is open (see Chapter 11 by Richard L. Kugler in this volume).

This chapter first describes how the policy of "dual containment" introduced a new conflict perception into the Persian Gulf region, a conceptualization which, by dividing the area into "good guys" and "bad guys," bears witness to old Cold War thinking. Second, the destabilizing effects of relying purely on foreigners for security is explained by the fact that all the states of the region are rentier states. The history of the Gulf region provides ample evidence that efforts for external security often contribute to internal instability. The bomb attack against U.S. military installations in Dhahran, Saudi Arabia, in June 1996 is only the latest example.

Third, it is argued that despite the fact that Iraq is considered by the United States, Europe, and the countries of the Gulf as an enduring threat, the massive deployment of primarily U.S. forces to counter this threat is counterproductive. Fourth, the dangers posed by Iran are viewed in light of Tehran's change in foreign policy orientation from revolutionary to status quo. The fifth part of this chapter describes the links of the Persian Gulf region: the first, to the Middle East and the peace process, is most important, but I argue that Israel's legitimate security interests should not exclusively determine American and European views of Gulf affairs. The second link goes to the north, where Russia's chances to extend its influence were enhanced to no small degree thanks to the "dual containment" policy, and where a new rivalry between the United States and Russia is taking shape. Part six of the chapter discusses the future of the alliance, discussing the structural constraints of the alliance and the thorny debate over sanctions versus critical dialogue. I argue that in order to reach a common strategy, the United States should give up sanctions, to facilitate a purposeful and effectively coordinated policy using both "carrots and sticks."

I conclude that the growing conviction among the countries of the Persian Gulf—that a future security arrangement needs to include all the countries of the Gulf—should not be dismissed out of hand but encouraged.

The Dilemma: External Security Versus Internal Instability

With the British withdrawal from east of Suez in December 1971, a new chapter regarding oil security in the Persian Gulf was opened. Only four months later, the Soviet Union signed the "treaty of friendship and cooperation" with Iraq on April 9, 1972, and one month after that, Richard Nixon and Henry Kissinger went to Tehran to give the shah a promise for almost unlimited conventional arms deliveries. Despite its "two pillar" policy, based on Iran and Saudi Arabia, the United States bolstered the Iranian position, at least in military terms, as "guardian of the Gulf," fomenting ancient Arab fears of Persian hegemony. The Soviet invasion of Afghanistan in December 1979, just a year after the Iranian revolution, was followed by the Carter Doctrine, according to which any attempt by an outside power at controlling the Persian Gulf region would be considered an attack on the vital interests of the United States.

With the Iran-Iraq war triggered on September 23, 1980, by Saddam Hussein's aggression, all parties inside and outside the region were confronted with a new reality: aggression from within. The Reagan administration, despite its focus on "Soviet expansionism," considered neither Saddam Hussein nor the Ayatollah Khomeini to be "proxies" of the Soviet Union.[1] Even before Mikhail Gorbachev, tacit understanding and limited cooperation shaped the behavior of the superpowers in the Gulf. When Iraq attacked Iranian civilian vessels in February 1984, the dangers of a "tanker war" affecting the free flow of oil became evident. Washington's decision in March 1987 to protect Kuwaiti tankers against Iranian attack was a major step toward internationalizing the Iran-Iraq war. As several Western European allies joined the U.S. ships in their escort duties, it became a test of the alliance's ability to cooperate on out-of-area problems. Conflict containment was effective, but efforts at a more ambitious common strategy failed.[2]

Saddam Hussein's next aggression, when he sent his troops into Kuwait in August 1990, led to warfare between a regional power and the Western alliance, led by the United States. Despite the new

---

1. Helmut Hubel, "The Soviet Union and the Iran-Iraq War," in Hanns W. Maull and Otto Pick, eds., *The Gulf War: Regional and International Dimensions* (London: Pinter, 1989), p. 147.

2. Hanns W. Maull, "Alliance Cooperation and Conflict in the Middle East: The Gulf Experience," in ibid., p. 165.

dimensions of warfare in that area, the aftermath of the Gulf War turned out to be more important than the war itself for future security and policy strategies.

When in spring 1993, Iraq and Iran were declared by the U.S. administration to be inimical states and therefore objects of a "dual containment," that is, political isolation, a new political dimension was introduced in the Gulf region. Until then, Saddam Hussein, despite the harsh vocabulary used to condemn his aggression, was fundamentally considered by others in the region, in terms of the long history of regional rivalry and power play, as a leader who had simply transgressed the unwritten rules of the region and miscalculated international reactions. But with the proclamation of "dual containment," a touch of Cold War ideology was introduced, dividing the Gulf into "good guys" and "bad guys." Iraq and Iran represented the former "evil empire," and this perception was strengthened in the West by the ideology of the "clash of civilizations," which predicts a world in conflict along lines of civilizations, cultures, or religions. Despite repeated clarifications by the U.S. administration that it does not consider civilizations to be fault lines and will not at all make fundamentalism its prime concern, in average Western public opinion "dual containment" was blurred by the "clash of civilizations" ideology, and Western policies toward the whole of the Islamic world came to be seen that way.

This development, accompanied by huge arms sales, served the interests of Israel well, as it viewed Iraq and Iran as the main threats in its second circle of security. But the ideological split of peoples and governments of the Persian Gulf into irreconcilable enemies does not serve Western interests. The states of the Gulf Cooperation Council (GCC) see the necessity of military protection from outside, but also its adverse repercussions to their own stability. They refuse to demonize Iraq and Iran as enemies forever as the United States does, and the Europeans, more and more, share their attitude.

Internal Stability of Rentier States

The bombing of the housing complex of U.S. military personnel at Dhahran, Saudi Arabia, in June 1996 only highlighted the structural security problem of all of the GCC states. After the discovery of oil, they developed into rentier states.[3] For such states, allocation of oil

---

3. For the theory of rentier states, see Hussein Mahdavi, "Patterns and Problems of Economic Development in Rentier States: The Case of Iran," in M.A. Cook, ed.,

income—the oil rent—constitutes the most important relationship between ruler and ruled, and is the basis of the ruler's legitimacy. It does not matter whether the countries are governed by ruler, sheikhs, royal families, dictators, or members of a state class; the loyalty of the citizens is primarily dependent on the allocations and patronage provided. To foster loyalty to the ruler or government, interpretations of Islam (or secular, nationalistic ideologies as in the case of Iraq) may also be used. But Islam has no genuine intrinsic relation to the economic-political system, and it generally transcends the relationship between ruler and ruled as well as the territorial limits of the state.

The foreign policies of rentier states consist primarily of creating an environment that helps to secure the ruler's own position within the society. Thus a hegemonic aspect is inherent. It should not be forgotten that the Saudis, since their conquest of Mecca in 1924, have spent billions of dollars on outside fundamentalist Islamic movements, in order to create an environment positive to Saudi rule over the holy cities of Islam, Mecca and Medina. A change of mind seems to have occurred only since the middle of the 1980s, when it became apparent that Islamic fundamentalism could turn even against the self-proclaimed "guardian of the holy cities" (as King Fahd called himself).

Today Saudi Arabia is in a situation in which the rent from oil no longer suffices to accommodate the country's population, growing at an estimated 3.6 percent per year. In the view of ordinary people, the oil rent is instead being eaten up by huge military expenditures. The Saudi dissident Usamah bin Ladin, discussing the attacks against U.S. installations in summer 1996, said, "Cab drivers say their sons are unemployed because the budget is spent on U.S. forces and weapons."[4]

The many signs of internal instability in the GCC countries have to be seen in the light of the structural deficits inherent in the relationship between ruler and ruled in rentier states.[5] Efforts to introduce

---

Studies in the Economic History of the Middle East: From the Rise of Islam to the Present Day (Oxford: Oxford University Press, 1970), pp. 428-467; Hazem Beblawi and Giacomo Luciani, eds., *The Rentier State* (London: Croom Helm, 1987); and Peter Pawelka, *Der Vordere Orient und die Internationale Politik* (Stuttgart: Kohlhammer, 1993).

4. BBC, *Summary of World Broadcasts*, ME/2782 MED/15-19, November 29, 1996.

5. A comprehensive overview of internal instabilities is provided by Clive Jones, "The Security of Arab Gulf States and the End of the Cold War: External Security versus Internal Stability," in Jane M. Davis, ed., *Security Issues in the Post–Cold War World* (Cheltenham: Elgar, 1996), pp. 73–98.

democracy into the GCC states after the Gulf War did not work even to camouflage these deficits. Neither the United States nor the Europeans can change this state of affairs.

Iraq: Enduring Threat?

Europeans and Americans share the view with the states of the Arab peninsula that Saddam Hussein's Iraq still constitutes a threat to the region. They also agree that the territorial integrity of Iraq should be preserved and that UN sanctions (basically the prohibition of oil exports) should not be lifted until Saddam Hussein has met all UN requirements. These consist mainly of the eradication of all weapons of mass destruction (WMD) and their production and research sites; the destruction of ballistic missiles (those having over 150 km reach); and full access for UN inspection teams. U.S. containment and UN sanctions have brought enormous economic and political pressure to bear on Iraq but have not forced Saddam Hussein out. He is likely to stay in power. The UN "oil-for-food" program, giving Iraq the opportunity to sell $2 billion worth of oil to purchase food and medicine under U.S. supervision, will not diminish his power, nor will it bring much relief to the Iraqi people. Part of the sum is already allocated for other purposes.[6]

In regard to the UN sanctions, the principal agreement between the United States and Europe is safe. France, as a member of the UN Security Council along with Russia and China, favors a relaxation of the sanctions. However, Paris is bound by the European Union (EU) commitment, "that full Iraqi implementation of SC [Security Council] resolutions remain a prerequisite for the establishment of peace and stability in the Gulf region." This statement was reiterated during the EU–GCC meeting in April 1996, together with a commitment to the "unity, territorial integrity and sovereignty of Iraq."[7]

U.S.-European relations were strained by U.S. military raids against

---

6. Iraq is allowed to sell $2 billion worth of oil over six months. Of that, $600 million will be paid into the UN reparations fund, and a further $60–100 million will go toward the cost of UN operations in the country. About $260–300 million will be distributed by the UN in the three Kurdish governorates in the north of the country. *Middle East Economic Digest* (MEED), December 13, 1996, p. 5. An additional part of the $2 billion will go to Turkey for the maintenance of Kirkuk-Yumurtali pipeline. *Le Monde*, November 30, 1996, p. 3.

7. *Europe* (Brussels: Agence internationale d'information pour la presse), No. 6715 (April 25, 1996), p. 9.

Iraq in 1993 and 1996. They led to uneasiness on the European side about the adverse affects of American unilateral behavior and actions. Fears that Saddam Hussein could gain some sympathy from "moderate" Arabs were expressed in the European Parliament (EP) after June 1993, when the United States raided Baghdad with twenty-one missiles in retaliation for an attempt on the life of former president George Bush. The EP adopted a resolution (122 yes, 88 no, 8 abstentions) criticizing the United States for ordering the raid without prior consultation with the Security Council.[8] The missile attacks on southern Iraq in September 1996, as an answer to Saddam's intervention in the northern Kurdish area, provoked clear irritation over U.S. superpower unilateralism. Europe deplored the absence of consultation, and expressed sympathy for Arab feelings of humiliation. The impression gained ground that the United States had begun to feel free to do in the Gulf region whatever it wanted to do. In the GCC countries, the basic understanding is that, while U.S. presence in the Gulf is limited, they will have to live with their neighbors Iraq and Iran forever. This perspective is sometimes mixed with a general tendency to see in Europe, after the demise of the Soviet Union, a factor balancing U.S. predominance. But this does not imply Arab expectations of a substantially different policy from the Europeans.

Disputes between the United States and Europe will rise the moment the sanctions are lifted and Saddam Hussein is still in power. For the United States, it is definite that Iraq will not be part of a new Middle East until Saddam Hussein has been removed, as Geoffrey Kemp argues in Chapter 5 of this volume. For Europe, no such clear statement is to be found, but France has made it clear that it will deal with Iraq, and Germany tends in the same direction. One reason for France's interest in doing business even with Saddam Hussein is that Iraq is highly in debt for French weapons bought during the Iran-Iraq war.

Regarding the question of the extent to which Iraq could become a major threat again once the sanctions are lifted, Europeans seem to be more relaxed. Public opinion, at least in Germany, tends to regard excessively intense portrayals of Iraq as a threat as just a means to sell more weapons. It should be kept in mind that Iraq's intentions are first of all directed against Kuwait, and that in a realistic threat assessment for today or the near future, it is Kuwait that might come under threat from Iraq. The UN delimitation of the Iraqi-Kuwaiti border was accepted by Iraq only tacitly and for the moment. For all kinds of

8. *Europe*, No. 6023 (July 16, 1993), p. 5.

reasons, including history, Iraq views the agreement as humiliating. Nationalistic feelings are involved here, and any kind of action by Saddam Hussein that gives satisfaction to these feelings could find popular support among Iraqis. Therefore, a renewed threat against Kuwait can be imagined, but given the military buildup in the Gulf, it would be suicidal.

In the Gulf, the U.S. military presence consists of the U.S. Fifth Fleet and air power operating out of Kuwait and Dhahran, Saudi Arabia. U.S. military personnel in Saudi Arabia were increased to about 4,000 after the Dhahran bombing in June 1996,[9] and army and marine forces are training local armies and maintaining the logistical lines necessary should U.S. forces have to intervene again. In addition to this military presence, the United States has defense cooperation agreements with all the GCC states except Saudi Arabia. On the European side, Great Britain has defense agreements with Kuwait and the UAE (United Arab Emirates); France has defense agreements with Kuwait (1992), Qatar (1994), and the UAE (1995). These commitments should be seen in light of the fact that deterrence does not always require matching the enemy's capabilities, but can be effected by simply raising the price of aggression. Deterrence cannot, however, work as a substitute for politics. There are also adverse effects of the military buildup on the internal stability of the GCC states; thus, the reduction of forces, in particular on Saudi soil, is worth consideration.

Is Iran a Threat?

Iran is officially seen by the United States as a rogue nation and a threat to U.S. interests in the Persian Gulf and beyond. The European governments do not share this harsh verdict, but concede that Iran poses potential dangers. Their rejection of the U.S. sanctions does not mean that they do not believe in the threat of terrorism or the danger of Iranian production of biological and chemical weapons. Of Iran's suspected nuclear arms program, they are nearly as convinced as the United States. That final proofs are missing is not the reason that Europe does not follow the sanctions; instead, the reasons are to be found in Europe's economic interests and to a high degree in Iran's political and economic importance within the region, i.e., not only the Persian Gulf but the northern areas from

---

9. *Jane's Defence Weekly*, August 21, 1996, p. 15.

Turkey and the countries of the Transcaucasus and Central Asia to Afghanistan and Pakistan. That the U.S. isolationist policies against Iran hamper its interests in these regions is an important point of critique within the United States, too.[10] More generally, it is interesting to see that many analysts in American academia are reluctant to overlook Iran's regional importance and tend to understand Iran more as a collection of potential dangers than as a single threat to the region.[11]

Much depends on the calculation of Iran's hegemonic interests. As with the other rentier states, certain hegemonic aspects are structurally inherent in the foreign policy of rentier states. From this point of view, Iran is not less nor more hegemonic than Saudi Arabia. To depict Iran as hegemonic "by nature" is not just a recent point of view, developed among the Arab countries during the period when the shah posed as "guardian of the Gulf." Some scholars consider Iran's policy as being driven by hegemonic interests throughout history. However, after the revolution, because of the ideology of the "export of revolution" and Iranian claims against Bahrain, "hegemonic" became principally understood as "aggressive."

However, after the war with Iraq and the death of Khomeini, and, in particular, after the opening of the northern borders of the former Soviet Union, Iran felt compelled to adopt a pragmatic and regionally focused foreign policy. Especially in its policies toward the north, which include mediation efforts in the Nagorno-Karabakh conflict and the Tajik civil war, it became evident that after the revolutionary turmoil, Iran had again become basically a regional status quo power. Its first foreign policy goal is the preservation of the ter-

---

10. Bruce Laingen, "For U.S. and Iran, 17 Years of No Dialogue is Too Long," *Christian Science Monitor,* February 18, 1997, p. 19. For the spectrum of views in academia and politicians, see MEED, December 6, 1992, p. 12.

11. Graham Fuller, "Middle East," in Zalmay Khalilzad, ed., *Strategic Appraisal 1996* (Santa Monica, Calif.: RAND, 1996), p. 239; Fuller just gives the headline: "Iranian Threats?" See also Jerrold D. Green, "Political Reform and Regime Stability in the Post-War Gulf," in *Studies in Conflict and Terrorism,* Vol. 16, No. 1 (January–March 1993), p. 16: "Efforts to portray Iran and Iraq as equal threats to regional stability are belied by the recent historical record." Against this view an enumeration of threats posed by Iran is to be found in Geoffrey Kemp, *Forever Enemies? American Policy and the Islamic Republic of Iran* (Washington, D.C.: Carnegie Endowment for International Peace, 1994), pp. 51–68. For a detailed discussion of the military aspects of the Iranian threat, see Anthony Cordesman, *Iran and Iraq: The Threat from the Northern Gulf* (Boulder, Colo.: Westview, 1994), chaps. 2–10.

ritorial integrity of all countries of the region.[12] And in that Iran shares the main goal of all of its neighbors to the south as well as to the north.

In its relations with the Arab countries of the Persian Gulf, Iran had a kind of "honeymoon" from the end of the war with Iraq until its so-called "occupation" of the Abu Musa island in summer 1992. Not only were diplomatic ties restored together with trade—with the lesser sheikhdoms it had been kept alive even throughout the war with Iraq—but substantial cooperation was envisaged.[13] Thanks to its neutral stand and actions during the Persian Gulf War, Iran gained some credit as a responsible neighbor; it was even admitted as an observer to the annual summits of the GCC.[14]

But when, in August 1992, Iranian authorities prevented 104 passengers from the United Arab Emirates from entering Abu Musa island without valid UAE visas (the British, on their departure in 1971, divided administration of the island between Iran and Sharja, which is now a member of the UAE), this developed into a serious setback for Iran's efforts for regional cooperation. Arab reactions were slow in the beginning, but then developed into accusations against Iran's aggressiveness. On September 24, 1992, Iran declared its full sovereignty over Abu Musa and the Greater and Lesser Tunb islands. Iran made a massive deployment of troops, missiles, and heavy artillery, especially during the first months of 1995; the Iranian military buildup is now considered a threat not only to shipping in the Gulf, but also toward the smaller Arab Gulf countries in general.[15]

However, on the political level, the "island question" was successfully shelved. The GCC countries have demanded to bring the case

---

12. Johannes Reissner, "Zwischen Persischem Golf und Zentralasien: Neuorientierung der regionalen Außenpolitik Irans," in Albrecht Zunker, ed., *Weltordnung oder Chaos? Beiträge zur internationalen Politik* (Baden-Baden: Nomos, 1993), p. 361; and Henner Fürtig, *Liberalisierung als Herausforderung: Wie stabil ist die Islamische Republik Iran?* (Berlin: Zentrum Moderner Orient, 1996), pp. 54ff.

13. Figures for the Iran-GCC trade for the decade from 1983 to 1993 are given by Asghar Ja'far Valdani, "Iran and the Persian Gulf Countries: Prospects for Cooperation," in *Iranian Journal of International Affairs*, Vol. 8, No. 3 (Fall 1996), p. 600, Table I, "The Value of Trade Exchange between Iran and Member Countries of the PGCC."

14. Jerrold D. Green, "Iran's Foreign Policy: Between Enmity and Conciliation," *Current History*, Vol. 92, No. 570 (January 1993), p. 14.

15. For the amount of weapons, see Dan Caldwell, "Flashpoints in the Gulf: Abu Musa and the Tunb Islands," *Middle East Policy*, Vol. 6, No. 3 (March 1996), pp. 50–57.

before the international court in The Hague, but Iran refuses. The EU supports the idea only in general, calling for a peaceful solution of the conflict without mentioning the Hague solution.[16]

Because of Abu Musa, the GCC countries may not perceive Iran as a regional status quo power, but they treat Iran as if it were one. They see and treat Iran as part of the regional system, not as an outcast or a "rogue nation." In this, the GCC states follow the traditional ways of foreign policy among rentier states. Despite ongoing rivalry, each side is eager to keep the rivals appeased enough to avoid having differences explode, thus endangering the positions of the leaders of each. The basic difference between the GCC states and Iran is related to the Western, predominantly American military presence in the Gulf. Whereas the GCC sees it as its basic security guarantee, Iran views it as a threat. Nevertheless, trade relations, bilateral diplomatic interaction, and efforts at cooperation between GCC states and Iran are growing and deepening. That the Abu Musa case does not affect the relations with Iran more strongly than it does may also be explained to a certain degree by the rivalries among the United Arab Emirates on the island question despite its consolidated official stand.[17] History has its impact, too: the countries concerned have lived with the uncertain status of the islands since 1971, when the British left Abu Musa with its sovereignty partitioned.

Saudi Arabia and Iran are the most important rivals in the region. Beyond their differences in security policies for the Gulf, geopolitical and structural limits to Iranian-Saudi cooperation exist which even a regime change would not overcome.[18] Notwithstanding these barriers, the need for a better political climate is felt on both sides. One important sign in that direction was sent out by the Saudi Interior Minister Prince Naif last winter: he said that the Dhahran bombing of June 1996 is to be investigated by Saudi Arabia only, trying to quiet

---

16. The European Parliament reacted less even-handedly in the Abu Musa case by condemning Iran in a resolution of March 1993; see Reissner, "Zwischen Persischem Golf und Zentralasien," p. 361.

17. The problem of the three islands is complicated by the fact that they fall under the jurisdiction of different emirates of the UAE. Therefore, in November 1992, Iran and Sharja may have agreed to abide by the 1971 agreement concerning Abu Musa. Iran and Ras al-Khaymah however, did not reach any agreement on the Tunb islands. Caldwell, "Flashpoints in the Gulf," p. 54.

18. Shahram Chubin and Charles Tripp, *Iran–Saudi Arabia: Relation and Regional Order,* Adelphi Paper No. 304 (London: International Institute for Strategic Studies [IISS], 1996), p. 53.

U.S. suspicion of any Iranian involvement.[19] This statement, directed against rumors of a possible U.S. strike against Iran (including contingency plans to knock out its main oil terminal on Kharg Island),[20] was, of course, welcomed by Iran.

One of the reasons for Riyadh's interest in a better political climate with Iran is to be found in its fears for its own position of dominance within the GCC. Tehran's efforts to establish good bilateral relations with individual GCC countries, for example the beginning of negotiations between Kuwait and Tehran over their common border in the Persian Gulf shelf, are followed by Riyadh with suspicion.[21] With its own Islamist opposition challenging the religious legitimacy of the "House of Saud" by accusing it of "American Islam," a phrase coined by Khomeini, it is important for the Saudis to be called again, at least in official Iranian language, "brothers in Islam."

Regional and Issue Links

The Persian Gulf region is linked to the Middle East in many ways. Stability in the Gulf and the peace process are considered interdependent to a high degree by the United States, Europe, and the Gulf countries. President Clinton, after the missile strike against Iraq in September 1996, declared U.S. intentions "to build support for a comprehensive Middle East peace" as part of "America's vital interests in the Persian Gulf region."[22] Britain's Foreign Minister Malcolm Rifkind went even further in linking Gulf security to the peace process when he proposed the establishment of an Organization for Cooperation in the Middle East (OCME). It was welcomed by Israel's Premier Benjamin Netanyahu, who also indicated the possibility of including Iran.[23] But the Iranian media protested and, for the time being, the Arab League and Egypt dismissed the idea as premature.[24]

---

19. *Asharq Al-Awsat*, December 17, 1996, p. 1.

20. Kenneth R. Timmerman, "How to Respond to the Dhahran Bombing," *Wall Street Journal*, January 3, 1997, p. 6.

21. See the commentary on the Tehran-Kuwait negotiations over their common borders in the shelf in *Asharq al-Awsat*, February 24, 1997, p. 9.

22. *U.S. Information and Texts*, 037/September 18, 1996.

23. Malcolm Rifkind, "Blueprint for a Region at Peace," *Times* (London), November 5, 1996, p. 20. For Netanyahu, see BBC, *Summary of World Broadcasts*, ME 2784 MED/6, December 2, 1996.

24. For Iran, see Ali Akbar Dareini, "UAE and False Expectations," *Kayhan-e*

Nevertheless, the link between the Middle East and the Gulf is a fact for all Arab states. The GCC countries consider it irreversible, and since they have always feared spillover effects from the Palestine problem, the peace process gives them a sense of relief. Their decision of September 30, 1994, to no longer enforce the secondary and tertiary aspects of the Arab League boycott against Israel was a clear sign of this change. In December 1994, Yitzhak Rabin visited Oman, the country which, of all the GCC states, has the best relations with Iran; and in April 1996, Shimon Peres went to Oman and Qatar. Qatar even authorized a U.S. company to deliver annually 2.5 million tons of Qatari gas to Israel.[25]

The link between the Near East and the Persian Gulf region is undeniable, but Israeli views should not be allowed to be the sole decisive determinant of American and European perceptions of the Gulf. Israel views Iraq and Iran as dangerous countries of the "second circle," whose medium-range missiles pose a threat. In spring 1996, a wave of bomb attacks shocked Israel, and Iran was held responsible because of its support for Hamas. At that time the mood in Israel was anti-Iranian to the utmost and, because of "critical dialogue," Germany was blamed too. Thereafter the mood changed to a certain degree. Israel decided to re-examine its relations with Iran, the cause being mainly Iranian signals of willingness to assist in the search for the Israeli pilot Ron Arad.[26] After German intelligence helped Tel Aviv in the case in autumn 1996, Israel softened its criticism of critical dialogue: "In principle we are against the dialogue, but if we need it, we want the Germans to speak with Iran," a high ranking Israeli diplomat said.

The other important link goes to the north. For at least two decades, the main threat to the Gulf was thought to be the Soviet Union. After its demise, the Persian Gulf's link to the north became somewhat neglected. But it was precisely the policy of "dual containment" that opened a new window of opportunity for Moscow to come back as a player in that region. Russia wants its money back from its old clientele (weapons debts are an estimated $10–15 billion from Syria and $8 billion from Iraq), and is looking for new trading partners, especially in the Persian Gulf region. It views the peace process as essential to its

---

hava'i, December 4, 1996, p. 22. For the Arab League and Egypt: BBC, *Summary of World Broadcasts*, ME 2763 MED/16, November 7, 1996.

25. *Le Monde*, April 4, 1996, p. 2.

26. BBC, *Summary of World Broadcasts*, ME/2766 MED/8, November 11, 1996.

own interests and upholds the UN sanctions against Iraq despite its support for their relaxation. Thanks to its strategic relations to Iran, Russia is closer to the Persian Gulf than the Soviet Union ever was. Russian rebuilding of the Iranian nuclear reactor in Bushehr is seen with great concern by the West. Israelis are already speaking of a "Moscow-Tehran axis," and an unidentified Russian general in September 1995 even threatened to provide not only Iran, but also India, Iraq, and even Algeria with nuclear and missile technology if too much Western pressure was placed on Russia.[27]

Regardless of such eccentric views, more dangerous is the growing influence of old Cold War perceptions dividing the whole area south of Russia into pro-Russian and pro-Western countries. This perception is prompted by the U.S.-Russian rivalry over the rich energy resources in the Caspian basin (see Chapter 8 in this volume, especially the section on the Caspian by Friedemann Müller) and by the American policy of building "bridgeheads" in the region. To speak of a pro-Western axis between Tashkent and Kabul or Pakistan, and a pro-Russian axis from Tehran via Dushanbe to Moscow has become common talk. The United States should be mindful of these developments, and the European countries should use their relations to all the countries of the respective areas to counter them. In order to reach peaceful development in the region, it is not helpful if Moscow feels subject to a U.S. containment policy in the energy field. Many in Russia view the growing Western and U.S. competition in that field, where the Soviet Union once had a monopoly over a huge territory, exactly that way. The view is widespread that American energy policy in the south of Russia is aimed at keeping Russia down, and the sanctions against Iran are seen as just a part of a global U.S. energy strategy.

What Kind of an Alliance?

Differences over Gulf policies, in particular towards Iran, prompted the conclusion that the Transatlantic alliance of the Gulf War was dead. But in 1990, the goal was to stop Saddam Hussein's aggression and to expel him from Kuwait. The demand that the alliance work for a longer period as an instrument of coordinated policies for regulating the various aspects of Gulf security would simply overburden it.

27. Lowell Bezanis, "Exploiting the Fear of Militant Islam," *Transition*, December 29, 1995, p. 10.

Oil has become a world market commodity. To ask Europe and Japan for a higher contribution to Gulf security because they are likely to need it even more than the United States, which will apparently have a large force in the region indefinitely, means overlooking the fact that European contributions to Gulf security must be different for structural reasons. The United States is one country with one decision-making center. Europe is not, does not wish to be, and will not be a similar "United States of Europe." Sometimes this fact seems to be forgotten even by Europeans. Since any alliance is a process of integrating different approaches, means, and capabilities toward a common challenge, one may even wonder whether the alliance of the Gulf War could have worked if the structures and capabilities of the partners had not differed. The success of the alliance is difficult to imagine if Germany and Japan had contributed mostly troops rather than money and, in the case of Germany, logistics.[28]

Even a brief glance at the framework of the EU as the economic organization of the European countries reveals why it is unrealistic to expect it to have more political or military coherence. Having come into existence as an economic organization, its principal level of common foreign policymaking is still in the areas of commerce, agriculture, and regional development. Most relevant for Middle East policy is the "cooperation level," where Common Foreign and Security Policy (CFSP) is placed. Here, "soft cooperation" is the rule; that is, cooperation is not obligatory.[29] These "deficiencies" in the formulation and conduct of foreign policy, together with the fact that the EU is preoccupied with Eastern Europe and will undertake vast reforms in coming years, leave little scope for Europe to be active in Gulf affairs. The agreement on the New Mediterranean Policy (NMP), shaped in 1989 and concluded in the face of the Gulf crisis, has been overtaken by events.

Notwithstanding Europe's high dependence on Gulf oil and trade with the Gulf countries, the Persian Gulf region figures only as an appendix of Europe's policies toward the Middle East. Consistent with the Gulf's history and geostrategic diversity, policies are not

---

28. For a most detailed analysis of the functioning of the alliance, see Andrew Bennett, Joseph Lepgold, and Danny Unger, "Burden-sharing in the Persian Gulf War," in *International Organization*, Vol. 48, No. 1 (Winter 1994), pp. 39–75.

29. Martin Landgraf, "The Impact of the Second Gulf War on the Middle Eastern Policy of the European Union," in *Orient* (Hamburg), Vol. 35, No. 1 (1994), pp. 89ff, and p. 93, Graph 2, "Foreign Policy Levels of the European Union: Levels of Decisionmaking and Relevant Policy Areas."

directed toward the Gulf in its entirety, but toward individual countries. For example, Germany's presence in the Gulf was not based on a broad political concept, but was the result of specific economic relations with individual Gulf states. Preoccupied with reunification, Germany found it difficult to join the alliance of the Gulf War in "out-of-area" operations.[30]

Negotiations for the establishment of a free trade zone between the EU and the GCC states have been conducted since the end of the 1980s. At the latest ministerial meeting between the two groups in Doha, Qatar in February 1997, expectations were expressed that they will be finished in 1998. A customs union is still out of sight.[31] Great Britain and France conduct much arms trade with the GCC; Germany, due to historical and political reasons, is nearly non-existent in this field.[32] The criminal and clandestine business of providing Iraq with material for building weapons of mass destruction during the 1980s was quite contrary to official German policy.

SANCTIONS VERSUS CRITICAL DIALOGUE

The U.S. sanctions against Iran and the European critical dialogue are where the policies of the United States and Europe toward the Persian Gulf differ most. At the EU summit in Edinburgh in December 1992, critical dialogue became official European policy. Its aim is to maintain contact with Iran as an important regional power and to use moral persuasion to convince Iran that it harms its own interests by crossing the limits of internationally recognized civilized behavior. Human rights, particularly the case of the British author Salman Rushdie, which was a significant prompt for critical dialogue, and terrorism are specifically addressed by this dialogue.

The European governments by now recognize that the critical dialogue has had nearly no positive effect. However, the chances that sanctions will have more convincing effects are very slim, too. Their aim is "to deny Iran the ability to support acts of international terrorism and to fund the development and acquisition of weapons of

---

30. Udo Steinbach, "Germany and the Gulf," in Shahram Chubin, ed., *Germany and the Middle East: Patterns and Prospects* (London: Pinter, 1992), pp. 220–224.

31. *Europe*, No. 6920 (February 22, 1997), p. 8.

32. *SIPRI Yearbook 1996* (Oxford: Stockholm International Peace Research Institute, 1996) Appendix 11B, "Register of the trade in and licensed production of major conventional weapons, 1995," p. 503. Germany delivered only to the UAE some training material worth $5.5 million.

mass destruction and the means to deliver them by limiting the development of Iran's ability to explore for, extract, refine, or transport by pipeline petroleum resources of Iran."[33] Despite clarifying statements of the U.S. administration, in public discourse these goals are much mixed with far-reaching ideas of dual containment, that is, political isolation not only to change the rogue behavior of Iran's government, but to change the government itself and the ruling system. Critical dialogue (which over time degenerated into an institution of ritually accusing Iran and therefore can no longer really be called a dialogue) was overburdened with the general aim of a change of government, too. Neither sanctions nor dialogue work as "carrots and sticks" in an international division of labor. The overheated debates on sanctions versus critical dialogue have prevented the United States and Europe from developing a common strategy.[34]

It is to be hoped that after the Mykonos trial, in which the Iranian government was found to be responsible for the assassinations of Kurdish opposition leaders in Berlin in 1992, a European policy worthy of this name toward Iran as a highly problematic country will be developed. This policy on the one hand should include a harmonization with U. S. strategies, but on the other hand should avoid the trap of pure demonization of Iran by following only the sweeping approach of sanctions and boycott. Harmonization of European and U. S. strategies should be worked out not only with specific goals but also with clear incentives. The United States should give up on sanctions and develop with the Europeans a case-by-case strategy working on the principle of "carrots and sticks." The relation between the reasons for the sanctions on the one hand and what would be required in order to lift them on the other hand presently lacks necessary rigor and specificity which, for example, existed in the case of the sanctions against South Africa because of apartheid. The example of Syria, enjoying good contacts with the U.S. administration while it is accused of state terrorism, is counterproductive for gaining long-term political effects of the sanctions. Hopes that the economic hardships within Iran caused by the sanctions will eventually lead to a conflict of "population versus government" should be abandoned, first, because the sanctions are too late. When the U.S. boycott of Iran

---

33. Iran and Libya Sanctions Act of 1996, section 3(a).

34. Peter Rudolph, *Konflikt oder Koordination? Die USA, Iran und die Deutsch-Amerikanischen Beziehungen* (Ebenhausen: Stiftung Wissenschaft und Politik AP 2976, 1996), pp. 26–30.

under dual containment was started, Tehran put much effort into diversifying its economic relations and has been able to diminish the effects of the sanctions to a considerable degree. In addition, even before the sanctions, the Iranian population had already learned to blame internal mismanagement and rivalries within the ruling elite for frustrating their hopes for reconstruction and effective economic development following the war with Iraq. Second, the Iranian government is not monolithic; the country is ruled by an elite, too incoherent to allow a conflict of "people versus government" to appear. The old dividing line between "pragmatists" and "radicals" does not fit the situation any longer. There are not only regular government institutions working against revolutionary ones; there is also infighting between the political and the clerical groupings and institutions, and even among the clergy and their own institutions. Therefore, even the demands of the opposition in exile for an end of the "mullah regime" are somewhat out of step with current realities.

American and European politicians should be aware that a "carrots and sticks" approach based on a "good cop–bad cop" philosophy (as proposed by Geoffrey Kemp in Chapter 5) has political and psychological implications that might be counterproductive. The United States and Europe are not, in fact, the policemen of the world, and viewing them as such would run contrary to the self-images of Third World countries, and in particular of a country like Iran with a revolutionary tradition. Iranians still view the revolution as a fundamental achievement in their modern history, whatever they may think about its outcomes. The "good cop–bad cop" philosophy would be viewed in Iran as another proof of Western arrogance. And to list "carrots" and "sticks," as reasonable as they might be from a pragmatic point of view, without even mentioning the Iranian assets frozen by the U.S. government, would make it very difficult for any Iranian government to give the incentives serious consideration.

Conclusion: A Vision and a Challenge

There are clear indications that the Europeans tend to view the Gulf region more as a region with its own dynamics than does the United States, which is more inclined to "bridgehead" thinking and "friend-foe" perceptions. However, in order to reach a more harmonious policy between the two in order to save their common interest, a better coordination of efforts in the sense of constructive competition is called for in respect to the Gulf region, just as it is demanded for the peace process (see Chapter 4 by Volker Perthes in this volume). This can be reached only if the Europeans become more explicit in their positions.

However, there is only one lasting guarantee for stability in the Persian Gulf region, and this is a broad security agreement including all of the Gulf states. Given today's military and political situation in the area, this may seem like a vision beyond serious political consideration. But for both Europe and the United States to have a clear awareness of this goal and to promote it in the various dealings with the countries of the region instead of dismissing it out of hand as a practical impossibility would be an important first step.

This idea is being considered in debate; political developments mentioned above warrant the conclusion that cooperation can have a chance. There is no doubt that the region is constituted to a high degree by conflict interaction, not only between Iraq, Iran, and the GCC, but also among the GCC countries. To overcome the burden of historical and political distrust between Arabs and Iranians as well as between Sunni and Shi'ite Muslims may seem to be an insurmountable task. However, all of these countries are bound by the same economic interest: to sell their oil. This provides a strong incentive for mutual cooperation.

Prospects for reaching this goal are not rosy. The fate of the Damascus declaration by Egypt, Syria, and the GCC states of March 6, 1991, has shown that security arrangements that omit the two important powers of the Gulf, Iraq and Iran, have no chance at all. The Damascus declaration was basically conceived to bring the GCC states together with Syria and Egypt in order to create a "new Arab order,"[35] but from the beginning it was also understood by many, particularly by Iran, as a security arrangement for the Gulf. As such, it was ill-fated. It should be added that any proposal excluding the role of the West, and foremost the United States, in sustaining a military balance stands no chance, at least in the foreseeable future.

Against the background of a possible change in the political climate of the region, the discussion of confidence-building measures by Iranian as well as Arab strategic institutes[36] should be regarded as

---

35. Volker Perthes, "Regionale Auswirkungen des zweiten Golfkrieges: Probleme der Sicherheit und Zusammenarbeit im arabischen Raum und die Optionen europäischer Politik," *Interdependenz*, No. 6 (Bonn: Friedrich-Ebert-Stiftung, 1991), pp. 26–31.

36. Jamal S. Al-Suwaidi, "Gulf Security and the Iranian Challenge," *Security Dialogue*, Vol. 27, No. 3 (1996), pp. 277–294 (the author is director of The Emirates

a first necessary step toward the goal of reaching a regional security arrangement. The lack of an institutional framework for conceptualizing this idea, not to mention formulating it into practical terms, is a serious impediment. Until now, Arab and Iranian reactions to the Rifkind proposal cited above are not encouraging. Nevertheless, ideas for creating some kind of an institutional framework are in the air. European countries that trade with all the countries of the region can do a lot in promoting the idea. To think of an institutional framework seems premature unless the first step is done, which is to view the Gulf as a region that has much more positive interaction than just conflict. It should be remembered that it was a necessary—even if insufficient—contribution to the peace process when the Israeli-Arab conflict began to be seen as a conflict within a region, with its own dynamics and interaction, instead of merely as a deep enmity between two sides within the context of the Cold War. A similar conceptual change would be the first step toward a regional security arrangement, which would be in the long-term interests not only of the Gulf region but of the entire world.

Center for Strategic Studies and Research, Abu Dhabi, UAE); Saleh A. Al-Mani, "Gulf Security and Relations with Our Neighbors," ibid., pp. 295-301 (the author is Chairman of the Department of Politics, King Saud University, Riyadh, Saudi Arabia). For Iran, *The Iranian Journal of International Affairs* of the Institute for Political and International Studies (IPIS) has published many articles on the questions of security in the Persian Gulf and confidence-building measures, including articles by non-Iranian authors; see, e.g., Lawrence G. Potter, "Confidence-Building Measures in the Persian Gulf," in *The Iranian Journal of International Affairs*, Vol. 8, No. 2 (Summer 1996), pp. 353–367; and Peter Jones, "Maritime Confidence and Security-Building Measures in the Persian Gulf Region," ibid., pp. 368–392. Most noteworthy is the idea of putting the security concerns of all the countries of the region on the table as a first realistic step towards confidence-building measures; this has been presented by leading members of this institute, Sohrab Shahabi and Farideh Farhi, in "Security Considerations and Iranian Foreign Policy," ibid., Vol. 7, No. 1 (Spring 1995), pp. 89ff.

Chapter 7

U.S. and European Policy toward Turkey and the Caspian Basin

F. Stephen Larrabee

The collapse of communism in Eastern Europe and the disintegration of the former Soviet Union have created a new set of strategic challenges facing the United States and its European allies. During the Cold War, the main challenges to Western interests were located in Europe, particularly along the former West German–East German border. Today the key security challenges facing the Western coalition of democracies lie increasingly on Europe's periphery and beyond Europe's borders. This shift in the locus of strategic threats and challenges poses new policy dilemmas for U.S. and European policymakers. How well they succeed in addressing these challenges will have a significant impact on the future of security in Europe and the future of the Transatlantic relationship.[1]

This is particularly true in the case of Turkey and the Caspian basin. Both areas are emerging as critically important in the effort to create a stable post–Cold War security order. Indeed, the energy-rich Caspian region could become the focus of increased political rivalry between Russia, Iran, and Turkey. However, Western policy toward both areas is unclear and in many instances contradictory.

In the case of Turkey, the old Cold War certainties no longer hold. In foreign policy, Turkey continues to look west, but it is being

The views expressed here are the author's own, and not those of RAND or any of its sponsors.

1. For a detailed discussion, see F. Stephen Larrabee, "Security Challenges on Europe's Eastern Periphery," in David C. Gompert and F. Stephen Larrabee, eds., *America and Europe: A Partnership for a New Era* (New York: Cambridge University Press, 1997), pp. 166–190.

increasingly pushed east and south by the new political dynamics unleashed by the end of the Cold War. Domestically, many of the basic tenets of the Ataturk revolution, particularly secularism, are under growing assault. These developments have raised new questions about Turkey's long-term domestic and foreign policy evolution.

At the same time, new fault lines have begun to emerge in Western policy. During the Cold War there was a broad consensus within the Western alliance about Turkey's strategic importance. Ankara was regarded by Western policymakers as a key bulwark against the expansion of Soviet military power. Turkish forces tied down some twenty-four Soviet divisions that might otherwise have been deployed on the Central Front. Turkish facilities were also important for the projection of U.S. and North Atlantic Treaty Organization (NATO) power into the Middle East, as well as for verifying arms control agreements with Moscow.

With the end of the Cold War, however, this consensus has begun to erode. For U.S. policymakers, Turkey remains a critical political actor and a key strategic ally. As former U.S. Assistant Secretary of State Richard Holbrooke has noted, Turkey is at the crossroads of almost every issue of importance to the United States on the Eurasian continent, including NATO, the Balkans, the Aegean, Iraqi sanctions, Russian relations with the newly independent states of the former Soviet Union, peace in the Middle East, and transit routes for Central Asian oil and gas.[2] Hence, keeping Turkey tied tightly to the West remains a strong U.S. priority.

For Europe, on the other hand, Turkey is increasingly seen as a problem—as odd man out—in the emerging new post–Cold War European security architecture. Moreover, with the end of the Cold War, non-strategic factors, especially human rights and the Kurdish issue, have begun to exert a stronger influence on European attitudes and policy toward Turkey. These have led to increasing strains in Turkey's relations with the European Union (EU) and a weakening of Turkey's ties to Europe. In addition, Turkey's growing involvement in the Middle East and Caspian basin have tended to reinforce Turkey's geographic distinctiveness and raise new questions about whether Turkey is really a part of "Europe" or not.

The collapse of the former Soviet Union has also thrust the Caspian region and Central Asia onto the U.S., Turkish, and European security

---

2. See his testimony to the Subcommittee on Foreign Operations of the Senate Appropriations Committee, March 3, 1995, p. 12.

agendas. The Caspian region is a major source of gas and oil. The search for new sources of energy in the region has sparked a new rivalry and struggle for influence between Turkey, Russia, and Iran. Indeed, in many ways the nineteenth-century "Great Game" is being replayed in a new geopolitical context. How this game evolves will have a major impact not only on Turkey's policy but on the political evolution of the Middle East and the whole post-Soviet space.

These developments illustrate the way in which the post–Cold War Transatlantic strategic agenda is changing. At the same time, they raise important questions for Western policymakers. How are domestic changes in Turkey likely to affect Turkey's long-term foreign policy orientation? Is Turkey moving away from the West? Where do Turkey and the Caspian region fit into Western policy today? Are U.S. and European policies toward Turkey and the Caspian region broadly convergent, or are there significant policy differences? How can U.S. and European policy be more closely harmonized?

This chapter examines U.S. and European policy toward Turkey and the Caspian basin. The first two sections discuss the impact of the end of the Cold War on Turkey's foreign and domestic policy, particularly Turkey's growing involvement in the Middle East and Caspian basin. The third section examines Turkey's role in the new U.S. strategic agenda, while the fourth and fifth sections focus on Turkey's increasingly troubled relations with Greece and with Europe. The sixth section discusses the growing importance of the Caspian region in U.S., European, and Turkish policy. The final section focuses on the implications of recent trends for Western policy and Transatlantic relations.

Turkey's Expanding Strategic Horizons

The end of the Cold War has had a profound effect upon Turkey's strategic environment, and has forced Turkey to reassess its national interests and security requirements in light of changed circumstances. While Turkey remains firmly tied to the West through its membership in NATO and its close ties to other Western institutions such as the EU and the Western European Union (WEU), its foreign policy horizons—and strategic exposure—have visibly expanded. Where once it focused primarily on its ties to the West, Ankara now has to balance its interests in the West carefully with its interests in other areas, particularly the Middle East and Caspian region.

The end of the Cold War has changed Turkey's strategic environment and strategic agenda in several important ways. First, it has led to a shift in Turkish threat perceptions and security concerns. With the elimination of the Soviet threat, Turkey's main security concerns have shifted southward. Today Turkey sees the main threat to its security not from Russia—though Moscow remains an important residual concern—but from Iraq and Syria (and to a lesser extent Iran). The Gulf crisis reinforced a trend already under way toward the reorientation of Turkish defense priorities from Thrace and the Soviet-Turkish border to threats along Turkey's southern border.

This does not mean that Turkey is no longer worried about Russia. On the contrary, Turkey takes a much more wary and conservative view of Russian ambitions, particularly in the Caucasus, than do most members of NATO. But Russia does not represent the type of existential threat that the Soviet Union once did. At the same time, Turkey's more cautious and conservative view of Russian policy as well as its exposed geographic position on the flanks distinguish it from the rest of the alliance (with the exception of Norway) and have caused differences with its Western allies particularly over Russia's demand for changes in the Agreement on Conventional Forces in Europe (CFE) flank limitations and the disposition of its forces in the Caucasus. At the moment these differences are muted, but they could reemerge with the beginning of the CFE II negotiations.

Second, the end of the Cold War has opened up new opportunities and options in Central Asia and the Caucasus.[3] With the collapse of the former Soviet Union, a whole new "Turkish world" has opened up that was previously closed to Turkish policy. While Turkey has been relatively cautious about exploiting these possibilities, the reemergence of Central Asia and the Caucasus has given a new geopolitical dimension to Turkish policy which did not exist earlier. It has also prompted an internal debate in Turkey about Turkish national interests which could have important implications for Turkish policy over the long run, especially if pro-Islamic forces in Turkey continue to gain strength.

Third, since the end of the Cold War, Turkey has evinced a new interest and activism in the Balkans.[4] While Turkish policy in the

---

3. For a comprehensive discussion, see Graham E. Fuller, *Turkey Faces East: New Orientations Toward the Middle East and Old Soviet Union,* R-4234-AF/A, (Santa Monica, Calif.: RAND, 1992).

4. For details, see James F. Brown, "Turkey: Back to the Balkans," in Graham E. Fuller and Ian O. Lesser, eds., *Turkey's New Geopolitics* (Boulder, Colo.: Westview, 1993), pp. 141–162.

Balkans has been relatively cautious and restrained, the new Turkish activism in the area has caused some concern among its Balkan neighbors, especially Greece. Athens has tended to see Ankara's more active policy in the Balkans as part of a larger effort by Turkey to establish itself as a regional power in the Balkans and create a "Muslim arc" encircling Greece.[5] This has given a sharper focus to Greek-Turkish rivalry in the Aegean and on Cyprus.

Fourth, Turkey's relations with Europe have become more difficult and problematic. The end of the Cold War has underscored Turkey's distinctiveness and raised questions about where Turkey fits into the new emerging security order in Europe. At the same time, Turkey's prospects for membership have receded. The result has been a growing sense of disappointment and estrangement between Turkey and Europe which could have serious implications for Turkey's ties to the West over the long run.

Finally, improvements in the weapons of mass destruction (WMD) at the disposal of Turkey's Middle Eastern neighbors have heightened Ankara's perception of its vulnerability to new threats emanating from the Middle East.[6] The development by Iraq of longer-range missiles during the latter stages of the war with Iran and its use of Scuds against Israel in the Gulf War raise the prospect that Iraq may be able to hit targets with non-conventional payloads. In theory, much of Turkey is within range of missiles launched from Iraqi or Syrian territory. This has accentuated Turkey's concern about its own vulnerability and made it more sensitive to the need to maintain good relations with its Middle Eastern neighbors.

At the same time, Turkey's growing vulnerability to external threats in the Middle East has made the intensification of cooperation, especially military cooperation, with Israel more attractive. The burgeoning military cooperation with Israel was highlighted by the signing of a controversial military cooperation agreement with Tel Aviv in February 1996. The military cooperation with Israel is seen by many Turks, especially the Turkish military, as a means of putting pressure on Syria and of acquiring advanced military technology.

---

5. See Yannis Valinakis, *Greece's Security in the Post–Cold War Era*, SWP-5394, (Ebenhausen: Stiftung Wissenschaft und Politik, April 1994); and Yannis Valinakis, *Greece's Balkan Policy and the "Macedonian Issue,"* SWP-IP2746 (Ebenhausen: Stiftung Wissenschaft und Politik, April 1992).

6. See Ian O. Lesser and Ashley J. Tellis, *Strategic Exposure: Proliferation around the Mediterranean*, MR-742-A (Santa Monica, Calif.: RAND, 1996).

Some Turks also hope the cooperation will enable Turkey to exploit the political clout of the Israeli lobby in Washington to counter the influence of the Greek and Armenian lobbies on Capitol Hill.

Taken together, these factors have increased Turkey's foreign policy options as well as its strategic exposure. Turkey today has opportunities that it did not have a decade ago, above all in the Caspian region and Caucasus. But it also faces a number of new threats and challenges, both internal and external, which did not exist previously. This has complicated Turkey's relations with the West and raised new questions about where Turkey fits in to the emerging new security order in Europe.

Domestic Change in Turkey

These new foreign policy challenges have coincided with important domestic changes in Turkey, particularly the growing role of Islam in Turkish society, which could have an important impact on Turkish foreign policy over the long run.[7] The process of "re-Islamization" began in the 1950s and gathered strength in the 1980s.[8] It was given greater impetus by the democratization of Turkish society, which created greater public space for forces and ideas that had previously been banned or suppressed. Paradoxically, it was also aided and abetted by the Turkish military, which saw Islam as a means of countering communism and the spread of left-wing ideas.

---

7. For a good discussion of the impact of Islam in Turkish society, see Binnaz Toprak, *Islam and Political Development in Turkey* (Leiden: E.J. Brill, 1981); Ilkay Sunar and Binnaz Toprak, "Islam in Politics: The Case of Turkey," *Government and Opposition*, Vol. 18 (1983), pp. 421–441; and Binnaz Toprak, "The State, Politics and Turkey," in Metin Heper and Ahmet Evin, eds., *State, Democracy and the Military: Turkey in the 1980s* (Berlin: Walter de Gruyter, 1988), pp. 119–136. For a more recent treatment, see Metin Heper, "Islam and Democracy in Turkey: Towards a Reconciliation?" *Middle East Journal*, Vol. 51, No. 1 (Winter 1997), pp. 32–45.

8. As Bassam Tibi has noted, the term "re-Islamization" does not adequately describe what is happening in Turkey. Turkey was never really "de-Islamized." The reforms introduced by Ataturk in the 1920s were designed to depoliticize Islam and remove it from Turkish political life. In effect, what resulted was a process of enforced secularization from above. This process, however, remained relatively superficial. It affected state institutions and the Westernized—mostly urban—elite. Beneath the surface, however, Islam continued to exert a strong influence on Turkish society, particularly in the rural areas through the activists in various Islamic religious orders (Tarikat). The Tarikat were never eliminated; they were simply driven underground. See Bassam Tibi, "Schleichende Entwestlichung," *Frankfurter Allgemeine Zeitung*, March 5, 1997.

The increasing strength and electoral success of the pro-Islamic Welfare Party (Refah), led by Prime Minister Necmettin Erbakan, should be seen against this background. Refah's success, however, has been given greater impetus by the inability of the traditional main-stream parties to address Turkey's economic and social problems. Refah has capitalized on this failure and successfully sought to por-tray itself as the party of "clean government." Indeed, Refah's success has more to do with the Turkish public's disenchantment with the tra-ditional mainstream parties than it does with religious conviction. A Turkish poll in 1994, for instance, showed that only 30 percent of those who voted for Refah did so because it was an Islamic party.[9]

Refah's accession to power has given Turkey's Middle East policy a new dimension. Prime Minister Erbakan, the leader of Refah, has made rapprochement with the Islamic world a top priority. The high-light of this effort to cultivate the Muslim world was a $23 billion nat-ural gas deal concluded with Iran in August 1996. He also made a highly controversial visit to Libya in August 1996 and has sought to develop a Muslim economic grouping—the D-8—as an alternative to the G-7.[10]

However, Erbakan has been careful not to take any major foreign policy initiatives that would seriously jeopardize relations with the West. He has not tried to take Turkey out of NATO or keep it out of the EU, as he threatened to do when in opposition. He has also sup-ported the continuation of Operation Provide Comfort (OPC) in Northern Iraq—albeit in somewhat scaled-back form—and has not canceled the highly controversial military agreement signed with Israel in February 1996. And he quietly signed a $650 million deal with Israel for up-grading Turkish F-4s, despite his expressed misgivings.

These moves reflect a certain pragmatism as well as a clear desire not to anger the Turkish military, which remains highly suspicious of Erbakan and his party. Erbakan appears to recognize that with only 21 percent of the vote, he cannot afford to push a radical break with Turkish foreign policy. Moreover, he still is somewhat constrained by his electoral alliance with the conservative True Path party, led by Foreign Minister Tansu Çiller, who strongly supports Turkey's tradi-tional pro-Western orientation.

Refah's domestic policy, however, has caused greater concern. Since

9. Heper, "Islam and Democracy in Turkey: Towards a Reconciliation?" p. 35.

10. The D-8—or Developing 8—comprises eight predominantly Muslim coun-tries: Iran, Pakistan, Indonesia, Malaysia, Egypt, Bangladesh, Nigeria, and Turkey.

coming to power, Erbakan has proposed a number of moves that have upset both the military and Turkey's strongly secular elite, such as demanding an extension of Muslim teachings in schools and the lifting of the ban on the wearing of female head scarves in state institutions and universities. Erbakan also proposed the building of a mosque in Istanbul's historic Christian quarter, a bastion of secularism.

To be sure, these moves are largely symbolic gestures; they hardly suggest that Turkey is about to become a theocratic state. Indeed, if they occurred elsewhere in the Middle East no one would bat an eyelash. But Turkey is not just another Middle Eastern state. It is a member of NATO and aspires to be a member of the European Union. Thus it is judged by different standards than other Middle Eastern states that do not have such aspirations.

Turkey, however, is not likely to become a second Iran. The attachment to secularism remains strong among large parts of the Turkish population, especially the military, which is the most important political force in the country. The military see themselves as the custodians of democracy and Ataturk's legacy. They have intervened three times in the post-war period (1960, 1971, and 1980) and they could be tempted do so again if they felt the basic principles of Ataturk's legacy—especially the commitment to secularism—were seriously threatened.[11]

The military, however, would prefer to avoid direct intervention if possible. Direct intervention could lead to bloodshed and civil unrest; Refah, after all, did come to power by democratic means. Moreover, it would do little to solve Turkey's long-term economic and social problems. And it would provoke a strong outcry in Europe, especially among the European left, leading to Turkey's isolation and further diminishing Turkey's chances of entry into the EU.

Military intervention could also lead to a dangerous radicalization of Turkish society. Many Refah supporters might lose hope that they could achieve their aims by democratic means and turn instead to more militant Islamic movements. Thus Turkey could find itself facing a much more militant and dangerous Islamic threat, one possibly clandestinely supported by radical Islamic states like Iran and Libya.

For all these reasons, the military is likely to avoid direct military

11. For a good discussion of the role of the military in Turkish politics, see in particular Kemal H. Karpat, "Military Interventions: Army-Civilian Relations in Turkey Before and After 1980," in Heper and Evin, *State, Democracy and the Military*, pp. 137–158; and George Harris, "The Role of the Military in Turkey: Guardians or Decision-Makers?" in ibid., pp. 177–200.

intervention, preferring instead to work behind the scenes to ensure that Turkey remains closely tied to the West and does not depart significantly from the basic principles of Ataturk's legacy, above all secularism. However, there have been increasing signs of unease with Erbakan's policies within the military.[12] In February 1997, the National Security Council (MGK), which is dominated by the military, gave Erbakan a twenty-point ultimatum, calling upon him to check the spread of radical Islam in educational institutions and the civil service.[13] Whether this will succeed in arresting the growing strength of the Islamic forces remains to be seen. But if it does not, the military could be tempted to take stronger action.

The United States and Turkey: The Changing Strategic Agenda

Turkey had always been considered an important U.S. ally. However, with the end of the Cold War, the focus of U.S. interests has changed. During the Cold War, Turkey was important because it served as a bulwark against the expansion of Soviet power into the Southern Region. Turkey is important in the post–Cold War period because it plays a critical geo-political role in three areas that are of increasing strategic importance to the United States: the Middle East, the Balkans, and the Caspian basin. In each of these areas, Turkey's cooperation is critical to the achievement of broader U.S. strategic objectives.

The U.S.-Turkish agenda, however, has changed markedly since the end of the Cold War. During the Cold War, it centered primarily around Turkey's role in Europe, particularly Turkey's role in containing the expansion of Soviet power into the Mediterranean and tying down Soviet troops that might otherwise be used on the Central Front. The Greek-Turkish relationship also was high on the agenda because of the potential impact that the outbreak of conflict between the two countries could have had on NATO solidarity in the Southern Region.

After the end of the Cold War, the U.S.-Turkish agenda has been quite different. The key issues center around Operation Provide

---

12. John Barham, "Generals grow restless in Turkey," *Financial Times*, February 7, 1997; "Zeichen der Unruhe in der türkischen Armee," *Neue Zürcher Zeitung*, February 5, 1997; and Nicole Pope, "Tension en Turquie entre l'armée et le gouvernement," *Le Monde*, February 7, 1997.

13. John Barham, "Army aims broadside at Erbakan," *Financial Times*, February 28, 1997; Stephen Kinzer, "In Defense of Secularism, Turkish Army Warns Rulers," *New York Times*, March 2, 1997; and Kelly Couturier, "Turkish Leader Bows to Army on Islam," *Washington Post*, March 6, 1997.

Comfort and Northern Iraq, the Kurdish issue, the Caspian pipeline, the Balkans, and Iran. Turkey's relations with Greece remain an important U.S. concern, but they are less important than they were during the Cold War, when the dispute between the two NATO allies threatened to seriously erode the alliance's military cohesion and ability to deter a Soviet threat in the eastern Mediterranean.

This changed agenda highlights the way in which Turkey's strategic importance has shifted in Washington's eyes, away from Ankara's role in Europe and toward its pivotal role in the Persian Gulf, Middle East, and Caspian region. This is part of a broader shift in U.S. policy since the end of the Cold War. While Europe still remains important for the United States, it does not have the same centrality that it had during the Cold War.[14] U.S. defense planning is no longer focused on preventing an attack against Europe, but on regional contingencies in the Persian Gulf and Southwest Asia. The Bottom-Up Review (BUR), for instance, barely mentioned Europe.

Turkey fits well into this new U.S. strategic agenda. Indeed, the United States has become Turkey's strongest ally in the West. On the three issues of critical strategic importance to Turkey—the Caspian pipeline, membership in the EU, and Kurdish Workers' Party (PKK) terrorism—the United States has strongly backed Turkey, a fact which is recognized and appreciated in Ankara. European support on these issues, on the other hand, has been lukewarm or ambivalent and, in some cases, such as the Kurdish/PKK issue, even hostile.

At the same time, human rights issues impinge much more directly on U.S.-Turkish relations than they did a decade ago. The United States Congress, in particular, has been increasingly inclined to tie human rights issues to foreign and military assistance. At the end of November 1996, for instance, Turkey canceled plans to buy ten U.S. Cobra helicopters after the deal got bogged down in Congress as a result of congressional concerns that the helicopters might be used against the Kurds. The delivery of three frigates—which Turkey has bought and paid for—has also been held up due to congressional concerns about the military balance in the Aegean.

These examples illustrate the way in which human rights issues and other concerns have increasingly begun to intrude on the U.S.-Turkish agenda. Domestic "ethnic lobbies," particularly the Greek

---

14. See Ronald D. Asmus, Robert D. Blackwill, and F. Stephen Larrabee, "Can NATO Survive?" *Washington Quarterly*, Vol. 19, No. 2 (Spring 1996), pp. 79–101. For a broader discussion, see Gompert and Larrabee, *America and Europe*.

and Armenian lobbies, have exploited human rights concerns to pursue their own more narrowly focused goals. In June 1996, for instance, the House of Representatives, under pressure from the Armenian-American lobby, voted to prevent the Clinton administration from sending $25 million in economic assistance to Turkey on the grounds that Ankara was blocking the flow of humanitarian assistance to Armenia.

These developments resulted in a *de facto* embargo on U.S. military assistance to Turkey. As a result, Turkey has increasingly begun to look to Europe and Israel as alternative sources of military equipment. In addition, congressional cutbacks in economic and military assistance have reduced traditional sources of U.S. leverage.

NEW FAULT LINES

The shift in the U.S.-Turkish agenda toward greater emphasis on the Middle East, Persian Gulf, and Caspian basin has opened up new fault lines in U.S.-Turkish relations. Operation Provide Comfort (OPC), in particular, has been a source of friction in bilateral relations. The Turks have been concerned about the impact of the operation on their relations with Iraq and other neighbors in the Middle East. In addition, many Turks fear that the operation is, intentionally or unintentionally, leading to the creation of a *de facto* independent Kurdish state in Northern Iraq, a development that could have serious consequences for Turkish security. This has resulted in repeated calls in the Turkish Parliament—including from Erbakan when he was in opposition—for the termination of the operation.

In response to Turkish concerns, new arrangements were introduced at the end of 1996. Under the new arrangements, OPC—renamed "Northern Watch"—was scaled back and limited to air operations.[15] The ground component, the Military Coordination Center (MCC), which had been a key Turkish concern, was terminated, and U.S. humanitarian assistance agencies were withdrawn from Northern Iraq. In addition, the Turkish government was given greater say in working out the rules of engagement for the air patrols.

These changes should help to remove OPC as a major irritant in U.S.-Turkish relations. However, the OPC experience highlights a broader trend in Turkish policy toward an increasing reluctance to allow its facilities to be used in Middle East and Persian Gulf contin-

---

15. See Kelly Couturier, "Turks Agree to Continued Air Patrols," *Washington Post*, December 26, 1996.

gencies, except in cases where Turkish interests are at stake.[16] As Turkey's interests in the Middle East grow, this reluctance is likely to become more pronounced, making the use of these facilities by the U.S. or NATO in Middle East contingencies increasingly questionable.

Moreover, the continued sparring over OPC reflects broader differences between Washington and Ankara over policy toward Iraq. U.S. policy and Turkish policy are fundamentally at odds with one another. U.S. policy is designed to isolate Iraq and promote Saddam Hussein's overthrow. Turkey, on the other hand, fears that Saddam Hussein's overthrow will lead to the disintegration of Iraq and the creation of an independent Kurdish state.

In addition, Turkey has a strong economic interest in trade with Iraq. Before the imposition of UN sanctions, Iraq was Turkey's third largest trade partner and its largest oil supplier. According to Turkish sources, the embargo has cost Turkey about $30 billion in lost revenue. Turkey thus has a strong economic interest in seeing the sanctions lifted and Iraq's economic isolation ended.[17]

Indeed, on policy toward Iraq, Turkish perspectives are closer to those of Europe than to those of Washington. Like Turkey, most European states, especially France, are uncomfortable with Washington's policy toward Iraq and favor an easing of the sanctions.[18] Thus the differences with Turkey reflect broader fault lines within the alliance, which may make it increasingly difficult for the United States to get allied support for its Iraqi policy in the future.

A similar fault line exists between Ankara and Washington over policy toward Iran. U.S. policy is designed to isolate Iran. Turkey, however, has a strong interest in maintaining good relations with Iran because of the Iranian government's support for and ties to the Patriotic Union of Kurdistan (PUK), led by Jalal Talabani, one of the

---

16. This trend was well illustrated by Turkey's refusal to allow the United States to use the air base at Incirlik for air attacks against Iraq in response to the incursion of Saddam Hussein's forces into Northern Iraq in September 1996.

17. Turkey worked hard behind the scenes to promote the oil-for-food deal, which allows Iraq to sell $2 billion worth of oil during the first six months of 1997 to buy food and medicine; Turkish companies were quick to exploit the partial lifting of UN sanctions in December 1996. Ankara hopes to earn transit revenues from Iraqi oil exported through its pipeline. Ankara also hopes that Iraq will be able to purchase goods from Turkey and thus give new impetus to Turkish-Iraqi trade.

18. For a trenchant French critique of U.S. policy toward Iraq, see Eric Rouleau, "America's Unyielding Policy Toward Iraq," *Foreign Affairs*, Vol. 14, No. 1 (January/February 1995), pp. 59–72.

rival Kurdish factions operating in Northern Iraq. Iran's incursion into Northern Iraq in the summer of 1996 to destroy the base camps of the Iranian-Kurdish rebels has shown that Iran is a key player in the region, a fact that Turkey cannot ignore.

In addition, Turkey's growing energy needs give it a strong incentive for maintaining good economic ties to Iran, which has the world's second largest gas reserves (behind Russia). Turkey's current annual gas needs of 8 billion cubic meters are expected to increase to 30 billion cubic meters by the year 2005 and to 40 billion by 2010.[19] Hence, for Turkey, increasing ties to Iran in the energy field makes good economic sense.

These interests exist regardless of the nature of the government in Ankara. However, the advent to power of Refah and Prime Minister Erbakan has given relations with Iran a new dimension. Erbakan has made rapprochement with the Islamic world, especially Iran, a high priority. He made his first official visit abroad as prime minister to Tehran in August 1996, where he signed a controversial $23 billion natural gas deal. This was followed by a visit to Ankara by Iranian President Hashemi Rafsanjani in December.

The Turkish military, however, remain an important constraint on Erbakan's freedom of maneuver. The military are highly suspicious of Iran because of Tehran's support of terrorism and the PKK. They are willing to tolerate greater economic cooperation with Iran—which they see as being in Turkey's interest—but have blocked plans for defense-industrial cooperation, fearing that such cooperation could have a detrimental impact on Turkey's relations with NATO.[20]

Turkey's rapprochement with Iran—especially the gas deal—has raised alarm bells in Washington and could undercut U.S. efforts to isolate Iran. The Clinton administration has taken a relatively pragmatic and business-like approach to dealing with Erbakan, hoping that the military will constrain him or that his government will eventually collapse of its own weight. But if Erbakan pushes the incipient rapprochement with Iran too far—especially if he tries to establish defense ties to Tehran—U.S.-Turkish relations could seriously deteriorate.

Turkey's relations with Syria also impinge on the broader framework of U.S.-Turkish relations and U.S. interests in the Middle East.

---

19. See Cenk Bila, "Trade Over Politics," *Turkish Probe*, November 8, 1996.

20. See "Rafsandschani besucht die Türkei," *Frankfurter Allgemeine Zeitung*, December 20, 1996; and "Ankara und Teheran wollen kooperieren," *Frankfurter Allgemeine Zeitung*, December 23, 1996.

Here again U.S. and Turkish interests do not entirely coincide. Turkey has been wary of Washington's attempt to court Syria as part of its effort to obtain an Israeli-Syrian accord in the Middle East. Ankara wants Syria to renounce financial and political support for the PKK and stop giving refuge to PKK leader Abdullah Öcalan, who has his headquarters in Damascus. The United States, on the other hand, has to balance Turkey's concerns about the PKK against its broader interest in obtaining a Middle East settlement, for which Syria's cooperation is critical.

The Greek-Turkish Dispute

While U.S. interests in Turkey are increasingly focused on the Middle East and Caspian regions, Turkey's relations with Greece continue to be a major American concern. U.S. officials worry that an unanticipated incident could lead to a confrontation between the two countries, as almost happened in February 1996 when the two countries nearly went to war over a deserted islet in the Aegean. Only last-minute high-level U.S. intervention prevented the incident from leading to a military confrontation.

A Greek-Turkish conflict would seriously undermine security in the Eastern Mediterranean. It could also affect broader U.S. interests in NATO, possibly derailing NATO enlargement. Faced with an outbreak of conflict between Greece and Turkey, many European countries could be even more reluctant to enlarge NATO, fearing that such a move would result in importing new ethnic conflicts into NATO's midst.

Consequently, the United States has stepped up its behind-the-scenes diplomatic efforts to reduce tensions between the two countries and encourage them to resolve their outstanding bilateral differences.[21] The U.S. approach has focused on confidence-building measures (CBMs) and a package deal between the two capitals, whereby Athens would drop its claim to the right to declare a twelve-mile national limit over Aegean airspace in return for Turkey's acceptance of the present situation in the Aegean. In addition, Washington

---

21. For a comprehensive analysis of the Greek-Turkish dispute over the Aegean, see Andrew Wilson, *The Aegean Dispute*, Adelphi Paper No. 155 (London: International Institute for Strategic Studies [IISS], 1979–80); and Dimitri Constas, ed., *The Greek-Turkish Conflict in the 1990s: Domestic and External Influences* (New York: St. Martin's Press, 1984).

has been working on a new Cyprus initiative designed to give inter-communal talks on Cyprus new movement.

The European Union has also been pushing hard behind the scenes to help dampen Greek-Turkish tensions. These efforts have shown some small signs of success. In April 1997, Greek Prime Minister Costas Simitis agreed to inititate direct contacts with Turkey at the level of experts—a move his predecessor, Andreas Papandreou, had persistently rejected. Simitis seems genuinely interested in reconciliation with Turkey, in part because he needs to reduce defense expenditures if Greece is to have any chance of join-ing the Economic and Monetary Union (EMU). However, he faces significant resistance within his own party to any far-reaching com-promise with Turkey, especially from hard-core supporters of former prime minister Papandreou.

The political crisis in Turkey, moreover, may make it difficult for Ankara to respond to the new positive signals from Athens. In addi-tion, there is no strong domestic constituency in Ankara pushing for reconciliation with Athens. Prime Minister Erbakan was deputy prime minister in 1974, when Turkey invaded Cyprus. He is even more of a hawk on the Cyprus issue than Rauf Denktash, the leader of the Turkish Cypriot community. Indeed, there is a danger that Erbakan could view the Cyprus issue as a means of bolstering his nationalist credentials and diverting attention from Turkey's mount-ing internal problems. The Turkish military also opposes any com-promise that could endanger the security of the Turkish Cypriot population. Thus the prospects for a settlement of the Cyprus issue in the near term do not look particularly promising.

The Cyprus issue, moreover, has become caught up in the politics of EU enlargement. In order to get Greece to drop its objections to the conclusion of the Turkish-EU customs union, the EU agreed to open accession talks with Cyprus six months after the end of the intergov-ernmental conference (IGC) in Turin. However, there is little chance that Cyprus will be admitted into the EU as long as there is no satis-factory settlement of the Cyprus issue.

The United States and Europe both share a strong interest in a set-tlement of the Cyprus issue and a general dampening of Greek-Turkish tensions. However, European policy is hampered by the fact that Greece is a member of the EU and has a veto over EU policy, while Turkey is not an EU member. Thus the EU is not viewed as an impartial mediator by Turkey. This inhibits the effectiveness of EU diplomacy. Moreover, as long as the door to EU membership appears shut, Ankara has little incentive to make major concessions to facilitate a resolution of either dispute.

The United States, on the other hand, has good relations with both Greece and Turkey. Moreover, it has traditionally played a more active role in the eastern Mediterranean, whereas the EU has taken a stronger interest in the western Mediterranean. Washington is thus in a better position to act as a mediator and to facilitate a settlement of the Greek-Turkish dispute. However, it is unclear how much political capital the Clinton administration will be willing to expend to achieve a resolution of the Greek-Turkish dispute, given all the other first-order issues on its plate, such as NATO enlargement, the Russia-NATO charter, China, and Iran.

Turkey and Europe

While Turkey's strategic importance has increased in U.S. eyes, Turkey's relations with Europe have become more difficult and problematic. As long as the Soviet Union was perceived as a major threat, strategic considerations were given a high priority in Europe's relations with Turkey. While many Europeans had doubts about Turkey's "Westernness" and the degree to which Turkey could be fully integrated into the European Community (EC), these doubts took a back seat to the overriding strategic need to bind Turkey closely to the West.

However, the end of the Cold War has reduced Turkey's strategic importance for Europe. At the same time, economic, political, and cultural issues have become more important in Europe's relations with Turkey. Today the main European concern is not deterring the Soviet threat but creating an economic and monetary union and forging a common European foreign and security policy. This has highlighted Turkey's "distinctiveness" and raised questions about where Turkey fits into the overall European architecture.

Turkey stands outside the general trend toward Europeanization that has characterized developments in the rest of the Southern Region.[22] While all countries in the Southern Region want to see a strong NATO, Turkey's stake is the strongest of all because participation in the creation of a European defense identity remains closed to it as long as it is not a member of the EU. Hence Ankara wants to

---

22. See Ian O. Lesser, *Mediterranean Security: New Perspectives and Implications for U.S. Policy*, R-4178-AF (Santa Monica, Calif.: RAND, 1992).

see NATO, not the EU or WEU, be the dominant security organization in Europe.

Unlike most European members of NATO, Ankara opposes the "Europeanization" of the alliance because it fears this would diminish the U.S. role and could lead to a weakening of Article 5 (on collective defense). Ankara, for instance, has strongly backed the United States in the dispute with France over control of the southern command (AFSOUTH) in Naples. Turkish officials fear that if a European (especially a Frenchman) is appointed to lead NATO in southern Europe, the delicate balance between Turkey and Greece could be jeopardized.[23]

Turkey's exclusion from the EU also colors its view toward NATO enlargement. Ankara has sought to link NATO enlargement to EU enlargement and threatened to veto NATO enlargement unless Turkey is included in the list of potential candidates for EU membership along with the East European countries, the Baltic states, and Cyprus.[24] While Turkey is unlikely to follow through with its threat, the move has angered many European members of the alliance who regard it as a form of political blackmail. At the same time, it underscores how closely linked the two issues have become in the Turkish mind.

This is in part because Turkey's relations with the EU have become more problematic.[25] The end of the Cold War has reduced Turkey's chances—which were never very good—of gaining membership in the EU. Turkey must now compete with a whole host of new applicants from Eastern Europe who have jumped the queue and whose chances of obtaining membership in the EU are considerably better than Turkey's. This has caused considerable bitterness in Ankara and led to a growth of anti-EU sentiment in Turkey, even among the traditionally pro-EU Westernized elite.

For Turkey, EU membership is more than an economic issue; it is intimately tied to Turkey's "Western vocation." Ankara has seen full membership in the EU as a symbol of the successful completion of the Ataturk revolution. EC and EU attitudes, by contrast, have been more ambivalent. The EC was never exactly sure how intensive a

---

23. See Ilnur Cevik, "Turkey Eyes French-U.S. NATO Command Debate with Concern," *Turkish Daily News*, December 13, 1996.

24. See Lionel Barber, John Barham, and Bruce Clark, "Turkey in NATO Enlargement Threat," *Financial Times*, January 20, 1997.

25. For a comprehensive discussion, see Heinz Kramer, *Die Europäische Gemeinschaft und die Türkei* (Baden-Baden: Nomos Verlag, 1988).

relationship it wanted with Turkey and what the exact final goal should be. Indeed, many Europeans see the customs union, which went into force in January 1996, as a substitute for Turkish membership rather than as a step toward it.

Many Turks fear that Greece will use its veto to block Turkey's entry into the EU. Greece, however, is not the real obstacle to Turkey's membership in the EU. Greece provides a convenient pretext behind which many Europeans hide their own deep reservations about Turkey's qualifications for EU membership. Many Europeans have strong doubts whether Turkey really is a part of Europe. As Eberhard Rhein notes in Chapter 2 of this volume, "Turkey has never been fully considered a European country, but neither is it considered fully Asian. It is at the crossroads between two continents, two cultures, and two destinies."

These doubts about Turkey's "Europeanness" were always present. However, they have come more strongly to the fore since the end of the Cold War. Many Europeans feel that Turkey's human rights record does not meet European standards. But behind these concerns lies a larger "civilizational" issue. As Dutch Foreign Minister Hans Van Mierlo put it in early 1997: "There is a problem of a large Muslim state. Do we want that in Europe? It is an unspoken question."[26]

Turkey's increased diplomatic involvement in the Middle East has also reinforced European reservations about Turkish EU membership. Many Europeans fear that Turkish membership in the EU would expose them to new risks and could import Middle East conflicts into the EU. A security guarantee against an attack by the Soviet Union is one thing; a guarantee in case of attack by Iran or Syria quite another.[27]

Turkey's growing vulnerability to ballistic missile threats from Iraq and Syria is likely to exacerbate these concerns. As the Gulf War underscored, many of Turkey's European allies regard NATO as essentially

---

26. Quoted in Stephen Kinzer, "Turkey Finds European Union Door Slow to Open," *New York Times*, February 23, 1997.

27. These concerns were reflected in Germany's grudging response to Turkey's request for Allied Mobile Force–Air reinforcements during the Gulf crisis. To many Germans, deterring a possible attack by Iraq against Turkey was not what NATO was all about. To many Turks, on the other hand, Germany's ambivalent response called into question the validity of Article 5 (collective defense) of the Washington treaty and raised broader doubts about the utility of NATO membership. See Ian O. Lesser, *Bridge or Barrier: Turkey and the West After the Cold War*, R-4204-AF/A (Santa Monica, Calif: RAND, 1992), pp. 14–15.

a "European alliance" to deter threats against the European mainland. They view Turkey's problems with Iraq and Syria as part of a strategic equation in the Middle East which has little to do with European security. They are thus likely to be reluctant to see NATO or the EU drawn more deeply into the Middle East by Turkey's growing exposure to missile threats from its Middle Eastern neighbors.

European efforts to create a distinct European security and defense identity also threaten to increase Turkey's isolation from Europe. Turkey is a member of NATO but not a member of the EU. Thus, it does not directly participate in the debate on European defense and security policy. In addition, Turkey is not part of the general trend toward Europeanization that has characterized the rest of the southern region. This sets it apart from the other members of the region and has tended to reinforce Turkey's distinctiveness and isolation from the broader trends affecting European security.

This sense of marginalization could intensify in the future as the EU moves toward the creation of a stronger common foreign and security policy (CFSP) within the EU from which Turkey is excluded. If Turkey does not join the EU in the near future—which seems to be likely—Ankara could find itself excluded from the key decisions that affect Europe's—and its own—security. This, in turn, could contribute to Ankara's further estrangement from Europe, as well as deeper discord with the United States, which strongly supports Turkey's bid for EU membership.

The Caspian Connection

While the end of the Cold War has led to increased strains in Turkey's relations with Europe, it has also opened up new prospects for the expansion of Turkish influence in Central Asia, the Caucasus, and the Caspian region. Turkey is seen by many of these countries as a model and a source of economic assistance. While Turkey has been relatively cautious about exploiting these new opportunities for fear of antagonizing Russia, it has stepped up economic assistance and cultural ties to many of the newly independent states in the region. These expanding ties have given Turkish policy a new geopolitical focus and sparked a lively debate within Turkey about Turkey's national interest and national identity.[28]

---

28. See Ola Tunander, "A New Ottoman Empire?" *Security Dialogue*, Vol. 26, No. 4 (December 1995), pp. 413–426.

The energy issue, moreover, has given Turkish interest in Central Asia and the Caucasus a sharper focus. The Caspian region is a major source of gas and oil that Turkey needs to meet its increasing domestic requirements.[29] Ankara is particularly interested in the construction of a pipeline to carry Caspian oil through Turkey. This would not only help assure Turkey's growing domestic energy needs, but would increase its political influence in the region over the long run. Whoever controls the transport of oil and gas is likely to be the dominant political actor in the region.

Indeed, control over the energy resources of the Caspian region is becoming one of the central issues of post–Cold War politics and the struggle for influence in the post-Soviet space. In a certain sense, the old nineteenth-century "Great Game" is being reenacted in a new geopolitical setting.[30] However, whereas in the nineteenth century the Great Game pitted British interests against those of the Russian Empire and German Reich, the new Great Game has a more diverse group of players which includes not only Russia but also Turkey, Iran, Saudi Arabia, and Western oil companies. In the new Great Game, oil and pipelines have replaced the railroad as the key geostrategic factors.

The United States and Europe also have strong stakes in the outcome of this new Great Game. The resources from the Caspian region will be important in ensuring economic prosperity in the twenty-first century and in reducing the West's dependence on Persian Gulf oil. Moreover, oil revenues can help to ensure the independence of the neighboring Caspian basin and allow these states to reduce their dependence on Russia. In short, much more is at stake than simply hard currency earnings from the export of gas and oil. The outcome of the various Caspian pipeline negotiations will have a profound effect on the geopolitics of the whole Caspian region and Central Asia in the next century.

The United States has emerged as a key player in the new Great Game. Washington has pursued three main policy goals in the

29. For a detailed discussion of the Caspian energy issue, see Rosemarie Forsythe, *The Politics of Oil in the Caucasus and Central Asia*, Adelphi Paper No. 300 (London: IISS, May 1996).

30. See Ariel Cohen, "The 'New Great Game': Pipeline Politics in Eurasia," *Eurasian Studies*, Vol. 3, No. 1 (Spring 1996), pp. 2–15; and Michael P. Croissant, "Oil and Russian Imperialism in the Transcaucasus," in ibid., pp. 16–25. On the nineteenth century struggle for influence in Central Asia and the Caucasus, see Peter Hopkirk, *The Great Game* (New York: Kodansha International, 1990).

region:[31] first, support of the sovereignty and independence of the newly independent states in the region; second, support of its own commercial involvement in the region's oil production and export; and third, reduction of future dependence on Persian Gulf oil.

In addition, the United States has sought to support Turkey as a balancing factor in the Caspian against the expansion of Russian and especially Iranian influences. Washington openly backed the construction of an oil pipeline route from the Caspian basin through Turkey as part of its policy to support multiple pipelines in the region. European countries, by contrast, have not been explicit in their policy pronouncements on Caspian oil issues, especially regarding pipeline issues.

At the same time, the United States has sought to contain Iran due to its support for terrorism and its effort to sabotage the Middle East peace process. Iran was excluded from the lucrative Azerbaijani International Operating Company (AIOC) deal in September 1994, largely due to U.S. objections. Similarly, in October 1995, Azerbaijani President Gaidar Aliyev reportedly decided against a pipeline through Iran to transport Azerbaijani oil after a phone call from President Clinton. Kazak President Nursultan Nazarbayev was also persuaded by strong U.S. lobbying to abandon the idea of transporting oil through Iran.

Europe has been less active in the region. The EU provides considerable humanitarian and technical assistance to the region, but it has not provided assistance to the gas and oil sector.[32] However, recently Europe has begun to show greater interest in the Caspian region. John Brown, the British engineering subsidiary of Norway's Kvaerner group, is rebuilding a pipeline linking Georgia with the offshore waters of Azerbaijan, and a consortium led by British Petroleum has won an $8 billion contract to exploit these waters. France has also recently begun to show more active interest in the region, in part to offset the impression that it favors Armenia in its conflict with Azerbaijan.

But these efforts have been *ad hoc* responses to opportunities rather than part of a coherent Western strategy. Moreover, there is no strong agreement among the United States and its European allies on what Turkey's role in the region should be. Turkey is seen by some countries, especially the United States, as a potential

31. See Forsythe, *The Politics of Oil in the Caucasus and Central Asia,* pp. 17–18.
32. Ibid., p. 29.

Western "bridge" to the Caspian region and Central Asia due to its cultural and ethnic ties to many of the countries of the region. Indeed, many of the Muslim countries in Central Asia see Turkey as a possible model.

However, as Turkey itself has found out, there are limitations to Ankara's ability to act as a bridge and role model in the Caspian region and Central Asia. First, Turkey does not have the resources to satisfy the development needs of these states, most of which are very poor. Second, Turkey initially overestimated its ethnic and linguistic affinity with the Turkish-speaking states in the Caspian region and Central Asia. In actual fact, the similarity between Turkish and many of the Central Asian Turkic languages is less than between Danish, Swedish, and Norwegian.

Third, since 1993 Russia has more forcefully reasserted its interests in the Commonwealth of Independent States (CIS), and especially in the Caucasus. The ouster of Azerbaijani President Abulfaz Elchibey in June 1993—in which Moscow is thought to have had a hand—was a strong blow to Turkish interests in the region. Elchibey had been the most pro-Western and pro-Turkish leader in the region. Since then, Russia has also reasserted its influence in Georgia.[33] This has reduced the potential for Turkish inroads in the region.

These factors have served to dampen Turkey's initial high expectations about the short-term prospects for the expansion of Turkish influence in the Caspian region and Central Asia. Turkey has by no means given up its aspirations to play an important role in the region—on the contrary, strengthening ties to the Caucasus is a major Turkish priority—but today there is a more realistic understanding of the difficulties involved and the length of time that the process may take.

In addition, there is no consensus between the United States and its European allies about Iran's role in the development of the Caspian region's energy resources. The United States has sought to block Iran's involvement in projects that would lead to an expansion of Iranian influence in the Caspian region or result in significant material benefit to Tehran as part of its broader policy of containing Iran. However, many U.S. allies, especially France and Germany, have strong doubts about the wisdom of U.S. policy toward Iran and continue to favor conducting a "critical dialogue" with Iran despite

---

33. For details, see Cohen, "The 'New Great Game': Pipeline Politics in Eurasia"; and Croissant, "Oil and Russian Imperialism in the Transcaucasus."

strong evidence linking the Iranian regime to terrorism.[34] Thus it is by no means clear that they will go along with the U.S. policy of isolating Iran in the Caspian region and Central Asia.

Moreover, as Heinz Kramer and Friedemann Müller point out in Chapter 8 of this volume, the U.S. policy of isolating Iran is beginning to erode. Kazakstan, Russia, and Turkey have all recently signed agreements with Iran for the exploitation or transport of oil or gas from the Caspian region. This will not only put greater pressure on Azerbaijan to follow suit, but also reduces the incentive for European countries to go along with the U.S. policy of excluding Iran from Caspian energy deals.

For Turkey as well, cooperation with Iran in the energy field has strong appeal. The alternative for Ankara is to increase its reliance on oil and gas from Russia or Algeria. Neither of these prospects is particularly attractive. Thus, expanded cooperation with Iran in the energy field is likely to occur in any case, regardless of whether a Refah government is in power or not. This too will make the policy of isolating Iran harder to enforce.

Toward a Broader Western Strategy

These developments highlight the need for a broader Western strategy toward Turkey and the Caspian region. The end of the Cold War has unleashed a new set of geopolitical dynamics and changed the way Western policymakers need to think about both regions. Many of the old paradigms no longer work and are in need of revision.

This is particularly true in the case of Turkey. In many ways the Cold War arrested Turkey's political evolution by legitimizing the special role of the military in Turkish politics and reinforcing its preference for controlled or "guided" democracy. At the same time, it made it easier to suppress certain political forces, particularly Islam and Kurdish nationalism.

---

34. For recent critiques of U.S. policy, see Fawaz Gerges, "Washington's Misguided Iran Policy," *Survival*, Vol. 38, No. 4 (Winter 1996–97), pp. 5–15; Shahram Chubin, "U.S. Policy Toward Iran Should Change—But It Probably Won't," ibid., pp. 16–18; and F. Gregory Gause III, "The Illogic of Dual Containment," *Foreign Affairs*, Vol. 73, No. 2 (March/April 1994), pp. 56–66. On U.S.-European differences over Iran, especially with Germany, see Charles Lane, "Germany's New Ostpolitik," *Foreign Affairs*, Vol. 74, No. 6 (November/December 1995), pp. 77–89; and Peter Rudolf, *Konflikt oder Koordination: Die USA, Iran, und die deutsch-amerikanschen Beziehungen*, SWP-AP 2976 (Ebenhausen: Stiftung Wissenschaft und Politik, October 1996).

With the end of the Cold War and the increased democratization of Turkish society, these forces have come more strongly to the fore. As a result, Turkish domestic politics have become more complicated. The genie is out of the bottle, however, and it cannot be forced back in. These forces have become an important part of contemporary Turkish reality. They cannot simply be suppressed. Instead they will have to be politically accommodated.

In short, Western policymakers need to recognize that Cold-War Turkey—pro-Western, étatist, and largely ruled from above by a Westernized elite—is not the Turkey that they will deal with in the future. The "new Turkey" is likely to be a much more complex and difficult partner, especially when it comes to asserting its own interests. This is particularly true as far as the Middle East is concerned. As Turkey's involvement in the Middle East increases, it is likely to become more cautious about letting the United States or NATO use its facilities for Middle Eastern or Persian Gulf contingencies unless there is a clearly perceived Turkish interest.

Similarly, it would be a mistake to view Refah's political upsurge as some sort of aberration. Refah represents strong forces in Turkish society. These forces are not likely to disappear if the present Refah-led coalition collapses or is ousted from power. Indeed, there is a strong possibility that Refah could increase its strength in the next general elections. Thus, while Western policymakers may not like Refah, they are going to have to deal with the forces it represents.

These developments present several dilemmas for Western policymakers. One of the most vexing is how to deal with Refah. What should Western policy be? Should the United States and its European allies try to get along with Refah, and thereby indirectly legitimize it and possibly contribute to its growing strength? Or should they seek to isolate Refah or encourage efforts to oust it from power?

This question would be easier to answer if there were a strong reform-oriented center that could act as a viable alternative to Refah, but this is not the case. The Turkish mainstream parties are largely discredited and viewed as ineffective and corrupt by many Turks. They have persistently failed to address Turkey's mounting economic and social problems, and there is little reason to believe that they will succeed in doing so in the future.

Thus the alternative to Refah staying in power is either a weak coalition of mainstream parties or a military intervention. Neither of these, however, would resolve Turkey's problems. Indeed, military intervention would exacerbate them. It would lead to Turkey's isolation and doom Ankara's chances of joining the EU. It could also lead to a dangerous radicalization of Turkish politics.

Hence, an attempt by Western governments to overtly undermine Refah makes little sense and could be counterproductive. Instead, Western policymakers should make it clear that they are prepared to deal with any government in Turkey—including one dominated by Refah—as long as it is fairly and democratically elected and as long as it respects the Turkish Constitution. In addition, they should stress that their attitude toward Refah will be determined by its demonstrated willingness to live up to several criteria: respect for secularism, respect for human and minority rights, democratic pluralism, and fulfillment of Turkey's alliance obligations. In short, the basic guideline for Western policy should be "engage, but don't embrace."

In addition, the United States and its European allies should make clear their strong opposition to direct military intervention (unless there is a clear and overriding danger to the Turkish state). As noted earlier, military intervention would solve little and would lead to Turkey's isolation. Many Europeans would see it as a convenient excuse to reject Turkey's application for EU membership. Intervention would also create problems with the U.S. Congress and could lead to further restrictions on economic and military assistance. Thus the cure would be worse than the disease.

At the same time, Western policymakers should press the mainstream Turkish parties to undertake structural political and social reforms, and particularly an improvement in Turkey's human rights performance. The best way to diminish the appeal of radical Islamist movements is by getting on with long-overdue reforms in the economic, political, and social arenas. This is as true for Turkey as it is for other countries in the Middle East. Refah has been able to increase its political appeal largely because the mainstream parties have failed to undertake the political and economic reforms necessary to address Turkey's growing social and economic problems. Unless the mainstream parties begin to address these problems seriously, Refah's strength will continue to increase.

Finally, Western policymakers need to push the Turkish government to find a political solution to the Kurdish problem. The Kurdish issue remains a major obstacle to an improvement of relations with Europe and Turkey's ties to the EU. The longer the issue is allowed to fester, the more damaging its impact on relations with the West, including the United States, will be. What is needed is a return to some of the initiatives undertaken by Turgut Özal in his last few years directed at meeting the aspirations of the moderate Kurds, especially regarding the use of the Kurdish language.[35] Most Kurds do not support the PKK's separatist goals or violent methods. However, many feel that the PKK is the only organization that articulates and defends Kurdish interests. Thus, encouraging a moderate alternative to the PKK and granting some greater degree of linguistic autonomy could undercut support for the PKK and defuse separatist pressures over the long run.

On the external front, Western and especially European policymakers need to do more to anchor Turkey more firmly to the West. Here the most critical issue is giving Turkey a clear prospect of EU membership. While there are good reasons why Turkey cannot become a member of the EU in the near term, the long-term prospect of EU membership should be kept open. EU membership is seen by Turkey as a symbol of Turkey's Western orientation. If Turkey comes to believe that it has no chance of getting into the EU, this could spark a domestic backlash and strengthen anti-Western forces in Turkish society.

Moreover, the prospect of membership—however far in the future—offers an important means of influencing Turkish policy. If Turkey believes it has no prospect for EU membership, Ankara will have less incentive to improve its human rights record and make concessions that could lead to resolution of its differences with Greece over Cyprus and the Aegean. Thus, it is important to keep the European Union option open even if Turkey may not be ready for admission for a long time.

Turkey needs to feel that there is a firm European commitment to its eventual accession to the EU. To give Turkey this feeling, the EU should, as Heinz Kramer and Friedemann Müller suggest in Chapter 8, officially reaffirm its commitment to Turkish membership in the EU as laid down in the 1963 Association Agreement, and put Turkey on an equal footing with the other East European and Baltic countries. Turkey should also be included in the structural dialogue and all other measures established in order to prepare the applicant countries for membership.

This would not mean that Turkey would be among the first countries with whom accession negotiations would be opened. Turkey would have to do much more to improve its human rights record and

---

35. See Henri J. Barkey and Graham E. Fuller, "Turkey's Kurdish Question: Critical Turning Points and Missed Opportunities," *Middle East Journal*, Vol. 51, No. 1 (Winter 1997), pp. 59–79.

treatment of minorities before accession negotiations could be initiated. But such a move would be a strong indication that Turkey was an integral part of the new European security order and would significantly change the nature of the debate. As Kramer and Müller point out, the issue would no longer be *if* Turkey will become a member of the EU, but *when* and *how*. At the same time, such a move would strengthen the hand of the Westernizers in Turkey and would deprive the Islamists of one of their most potent arguments: that Turkey's European option is an illusion and that Turkey's true salvation lies in an intensification of ties to the Islamic world.

In addition, the EU needs to improve the functioning of the EU-Turkish customs union, introduced at the beginning of 1996. The customs union represents an important way station on Turkey's march toward closer ties to Europe. However, Turkey has received few visible benefits from the customs union so far. Turkey's trade gap with the EU has grown, while foreign investment has declined.[36]

The lack of tangible benefits from the customs union has caused growing disillusionment in Turkey, even among those members of the Turkish elite who spearheaded the drive for Turkish integration. At the same time, the anti-Western forces have pointed to these difficulties as proof that joining the customs union was a mistake and has brought few benefits. The EU needs to make greater efforts, therefore, to ensure that the customs union benefits Turkey in the way it was originally intended to do.

Several other steps need to be taken to anchor Turkey more firmly to the West and reduce Ankara's growing estrangement from Europe. First, the requirements for membership in the WEU should be changed to allow Turkey (as well as Iceland and Norway) to become a full member of the WEU without first becoming a member of the EU. This would remove an important point of friction in relations with the EU and integrate Turkey more fully into the mainstream of European security planning. Such a revision is all the more important in light of the decisions at the NATO Ministerial in Berlin in June 1996 that allow the Europeans to draw on NATO assets to conduct operations under

---

36. Turkey's trade gap with the EU grew 273.7 percent in the first quarter of 1996 in comparison to the same period in 1995, while foreign investment dropped 35.2 percent in the first eleven months of 1996 compared to 1995. See "Turkey Not Benefiting from Customs Union," *Turkish Daily News*, December 13, 1996. See also "On Customs Union Anniversary, Expectations Still Not Met," *Turkish Daily News*, December 12, 1996.

the aegis of the WEU in crises in which the United States does not want to participate.

Second, an institutional mechanism should be set up to allow Turkey to participate in the Transatlantic dialogue between the United States and the EU. Many of the issues discussed in the dialogue are of direct concern to Turkey and touch on important Turkish interests. Such a forum would help to harmonize U.S., EU, and Turkish interests. It would also help to reduce the strong sense of exclusion that currently prevails in Turkey and which is a source of friction in relations with both the United States and the EU.

Third, the problem of the proliferation of weapons of mass destruction should become an integral part of the bilateral and multilateral dialogue with Ankara. If Turkey's security concerns are not addressed, there is a danger that Turkey could be tempted to take unilateral steps to develop nuclear weapons or other weapons of mass destruction. Such a development could heighten regional instability, particularly in the Balkans.

Fourth, the United States and Europe should undertake new initiatives designed to promote a settlement of the Cyprus issue and of the Greek-Turkish dispute over the Aegean. A Greek-Turkish confrontation over Cyprus would be a major blow not only to security in the Mediterranean but to NATO's larger security agenda. The EU should make accession by Cyprus conditional on significant progress toward a settlement of the outstanding issues between the two Cypriot communities. At the same time, the EU should make clear its commitment to bringing Turkey into the EU once it has fulfilled the requirements for membership. This would provide an incentive for Turkey to take a more conciliatory approach to an eventual settlement.

Fifth, Western policymakers should encourage Greece and Turkey to implement the confidence-building measures in the Aegean agreed upon between the late Turkish President Turgut Özal and former Greek Prime Minister Andreas Papandreou in Davos in 1988. These could be supplemented by other CBMs. For instance, a trade-off between the demobilization and disbandment of the Turkish Fourth Aegean Army and the demilitarization of the Greek Aegean islands might be possible. Similarly, an "open skies agreement," comparable to the one signed between Romania and Hungary in May 1991, could help to reduce tensions and lay the groundwork—as it did in the Romanian-Hungarian case—for a broader improvement of political relations later on.

Finally, the United States and its European allies should encourage a direct dialogue on security issues between the Greek and Turkish military. Many Greek military officers oppose such a military-to-military dialogue on the grounds that the Turkish military does not have the same status as the Greek military (i.e., there is less civilian control over the military in Turkey). But any resolution of Greek-Turkish differences will require the support of the Turkish military. Thus, it is important that the Turkish military be part of the bilateral security dialogue, not excluded from it.

THE CASPIAN REGION

In the Caspian region as well, there is a need for new thinking on the part of Western policymakers. The Caspian region and the Caucasus are emerging as part of a new geopolitical space that cuts across old geographic and political boundaries. Old historical and cultural influences, long suppressed under seventy-five years of Soviet communist rule, are now beginning to reassert themselves. Russia will remain an important actor in the region but other countries, particularly Turkey, Iran, and China, are likely to play an increasingly important role.

Western policymakers therefore need to change how they think about the Caspian region. Rather than regarding the region as an appendage of Russia or a Russian sphere of influence—though Russian influence will remain strong in the region—they need to begin to view it as an important geopolitical entity in its own right. At the same time, they need to recognize the important geopolitical linkages that are beginning to reassert themselves with neighboring states such as Turkey, Iran, Pakistan, and China. These will have a strong impact on the region's future over the long run. This means that policy toward the Caspian region, Turkey, Iran, and Russia cannot be seen in isolation; the various elements are closely connected and part of a larger geostrategic mosaic. In formulating a strategy toward the region, Western policymakers need to take these interconnections into account.

The main goals of Western policy should be to assure full and open access to the energy reserves of the Caspian region, and to promote the independence and sovereignty of the countries of the region. To achieve these goals, the United States and Europe need to harmonize their policies more closely. In particular, assistance to the energy sector should be coordinated in order to avoid duplication. In addition, the Western partners should take several other steps.

First, the United States and Europe should support multiple transit routes for the short-term and long-term export of oil. This would help the countries of the Caspian region to avoid becoming dependent on any one country for their energy supplies, thereby enhancing their ability to maintain their territorial integrity and independence.

Second, the members of the Western alliance should strongly support the reform process in Russia and encourage Russia's broader integration into the world economy. This can strengthen the hand of those forces in Russia that favor cooperation with the West in developing Caspian oil resources as a means of ensuring Russia's access to Western capital and advanced technology, and establishing a firm foothold in world oil markets. At the same time, Russia should be encouraged to abide by accepted international standards in dealing with its neighbors in the region. This is particularly important in the case of the Caspian demarcation issue, where Moscow has used strong-arm tactics to try to pressure and intimidate some of the Caspian states.

Third, the United States and Europe should undertake more strenuous diplomatic efforts to help resolve ethnic and regional conflicts in the Caucasus and Caspian basin, particularly the conflict in Nagorno-Karabakh. A resolution of these disputes would contribute significantly to the development of a stable energy regime in the Caspian basin over the long run. Moreover, Russian attitudes toward resolving these disputes have begun to shift lately. While Russia continues to regard the CIS as its own special area of responsibility, it has recently shown a greater willingness to accept mediation by the Organization for Security and Cooperation in Europe (OSCE) to help settle disputes on the territory of the CIS. This more conciliatory Russian approach could open up new possibilities for Western diplomacy to work with Russia to help dampen regional disputes in the Caucasus and Caspian region.

Fourth, the Western partners should make more assistance available to develop the region's energy infrastructure. The EU, in particular, should increase its assistance to the Caspian region. The EU provides significant amounts of humanitarian and technical assistance to Caspian states. However, thus far, it has not provided assistance in the gas and oil sectors. Greater EU support for gas and oil ventures in the Caspian region could help to diversify the supply routes and contribute to greater regional stability over the long run.

Fifth, international institutions like the World Bank and European Bank for Reconstruction and Development should also become more actively engaged in developing the region's oil and gas supplies. The main emphasis should be on developing the region's infrastructure, legal framework, and technical expertise. The World Bank has already initiated projects to help several Caspian countries develop their energy structures and legal frameworks. In early 1995, it granted Azerbaijan and Kazakstan technical assistance loans of several million dollars to develop their management of oil resources.[37] Such projects can help to enhance the viability and independence of the Caspian states.

Sixth, NATO should promote the greater involvement of the states of the Caucasus and Caspian region in the Partnership for Peace program (PfP). This would help to enhance their viability and independence and give them a strong anchor to the West. In developing ties to the Caspian states, however, NATO needs to proceed cautiously and bear in mind Russian sensitivities. Russia remains highly sensitive regarding the development of ties between NATO and the states of the CIS, as the sharp Russian reaction to NATO Secretary General Javier Solana's visit to Georgia, Armenia, Azerbaijan, and Moldova in February 1997 underscores.[38] Thus NATO will need to balance its desire to strengthen ties with the Caspian states with its broader objectives of developing a cooperative partnership with Russia.

Finally, the Clinton administration should work with its congressional allies to get Section 907 of the Freedom Support Act—which restricts all aid to Azerbaijan—lifted. The provision significantly restricts the ability of the United States to become involved in the development of Azerbaijan's strategic oil sector or to offer advice on economic and democratic reform. In addition, it prevents the United States from acting as an effective mediator in the Nagorno-Karabakh conflict.

---

37. See Forsythe, *The Politics of Oil in the Caucasus and Central Asia*, p. 29.

38. See "La visite du secrétaire général de l'OTAN dans le Caucase irrite Moscou," *Le Monde*, February 14, 1997.

Chapter 8

Relations with Turkey and the Caspian Basin Countries

Heinz Kramer and
Friedemann Müller

Turkey and the Caspian basin are not part of the Middle East. They are, however, related to the region to different degrees. Turkey has difficult relations with Syria, Iraq, and Iran, all of which are countries that play an important role for future regional development. Growing economic, political, and even military relations with Israel and Egypt are linking Turkey to other important Middle Eastern political actors. At the same time, being a member of the Atlantic alliance with a special relationship to the United States further contributes to the country's importance with respect to the Middle East, given the strong American strategic interest in the region.[1] The European Union (EU) and its member states, however, do not seem to put that much emphasis on Turkey's Middle Eastern role in their relations with Ankara. For them, Turkey's European vocation and its implications for Turkey's role in and for Europe remain the predominant issue of concern.

The Caspian basin region is even less directly linked to the Middle East than Turkey. Its wealth of energy resources, reanimated historical ties, religious and ethnic relationships, and strategic interests have drawn Iran, the United States, Turkey, and above all Russia into the

---

This article is a common effort in which Heinz Kramer wrote the discussion of Turkey, whereas the Caspian basin discussion was written by Friedemann Müller.

---

1. More details of Turkey's multifaceted position in the Middle East can be found in Soli Özel, "Of Not Being a Lone Wolf: Geography, Domestic Plays, and Turkish Foreign Policy in the Middle East," in Geoffrey Kemp and Janice Gross Stein, eds., *Powder Keg in the Middle East: The Struggle for Gulf Security* (Washington, D.C.: American Association of the Advancement of Science, 1995), pp. 161–194.

politics of the Caspian basin. The EU and most of its member states are conspicuously absent from the scene. The strategic game that is played here is largely decoupled from the Middle Eastern arena, although its substance is also strategic influence, via control over the production and distribution of large energy resources. Hence, this chapter is divided in two separate parts that are linked by overlapping political actors.

In the first part, we outline the importance of Turkey for the realization of Western strategic interests. We develop some ideas for a revision of European policies toward Turkey that seem necessary in order to prevent lasting damage to already strained relations with Ankara. Turkey's place in the emerging European security architecture, the Cyprus problem, and the Kurdish question are identified as especially crucial issues. Throughout the discussion of these issues, we also address the problem of U.S.-European differences in relations with Turkey and of ways to overcome them.

The second part deals with the Caspian region. The dissolution of the Soviet Union created, besides Iran, four new littoral states: Russia, and the three newly independent states (NIS) of Azerbaijan, Kazakstan, and Turkmenistan. The NIS are ethnically linked with Turkey; however, their major challenges are their new sovereignty and their energy wealth, which, in order to yield its benefits, must be transported from this landlocked region, without a common border with Turkey, to the world market. The United States and Europe follow, with much less European engagement, different strategies. While the common goals of a secure energy supply and support for the independence of the NIS are undisputed, different priorities are given to carrots and sticks as classical geopolitical instruments, or to the gradual build-up of a regulatory regime. These different strategies also affect the treatment of Iran.

Relations with Turkey: How to Meet the Challenge of Rising Alienation

For decades, Turkey was taken for granted by its Western allies. This changed with the advent to power of Necmettin Erbakan's Welfare Party (Refah) in June 1996. The future political course of a strategically important ally has become dubious. Europe and the United States are trying to adapt to the new situation and are looking for ways to prevent a serious and lasting deterioration of their relations with Turkey.

For a better understanding of the actual challenges that are inherent in Western relations with Turkey, we start with a short analysis of Turkey's fundamental domestic problems, which influence its foreign policy abilities and especially its relations with its Western allies. Although a solution to these problems can only marginally be influenced from the outside, Turkey's partners in Europe and America should, nevertheless, try to get an enlightened understanding of the issues, and start a comprehensive and continuous dialogue with their Turkish counterparts about possible contributions of the Europeans and the United States to an alleviation of Turkey's domestic problems.

DOMESTIC CLEAVAGES AND INSTABILITY

Three clearly identifiable cleavages tend to endanger Turkey's social and political stability: Kemalist modernizers (secularists) versus religious traditionalists (Islamists); Turks versus Kurds; and Sunni Muslims versus Alawites. Domestically, these issues form an important part of the current debate about the general orientation of Turkey's society between the republican tradition of "Westernization" and a more self-centered way based on national and religious traditions.[2] With regard to foreign policy, the way these cleavages are bridged will also to a large extent influence the future of Turkey's relations with its Western allies.

Although Turkey's political and economic elite is genuinely Western by character, and the basic rules of a democratic system and capitalist economy are fairly well entrenched in the political and social outlook of the majority of Turks, the complete body of Kemalist ideas never took hold in the Turkish masses.[3] To the contrary, there have been ample indications that some of the more traditional, religiously based habits and attitudes, including a certain following for ideas of an explicitly political Islam, have survived under the surface of Kemalist modernization politics.[4]

---

2. This debate is reflected in two recent analyses by Shireen T. Hunter, *Turkey at the Crossroads: Islamic Past or European Future*, CEPS Paper 63 (Brussels: Centre for European Policy Studies, 1995); and Andrew Mango, *Turkey: The Challenge of a New Role*, Washington Paper No. 163 (Westport, Conn.: Praeger Publishers, 1994).

3. An interesting discussion of the mechanisms of Turkey's "Westernization" can be found in Metin Heper et al., eds., *Turkey and the West: Changing Political and Cultural Identities* (London: Tauris, 1993).

4. For a discussion of Islam in Turkish social and political life, see the contributions in Richard Tapper, ed., *Islam in Modern Turkey: Religion, Politics and Literature*

The division of Turkish society into convinced modernizers and so-called traditionalists or Islamists has led, under the circumstances of a democratic multi-party competition, to a gradual dilution of the principle of secularism as a basic element of the republic's social and political structure. However, as long as the established political parties of Turkey, in cooperation with the state elite, were able to satisfy the social and economic needs of the people's majority, the politics of Westernization could go ahead almost unchallenged.

However, change started in the 1980s when, under the rule of Turgut Özal, Turkey was simultaneously confronted with a fundamental and far-reaching wave of economic and social change and with a political revaluation of religious values and habits.[5] Then, with the end of the Cold War and the consequent demise of the Soviet empire, Turkey was thrown into another maelstrom of enormous internal and external change. Growing political fragmentation and rising economic problems led to a serious deterioration in living conditions in large parts of Turkish society. The country's established political class, however, showed itself unprepared to meet the new challenges. The consequence was a tremendous loss of public confidence in its politicians. Alternative, religiously based political concepts gained ground, culminating in the rise to power of Erbakan's Welfare Party. Thereafter, an open fight between secularists and Islamists for political dominance broke out. On February 28, 1997, this fight caused the military leadership to issue a serious warning to Erbakan and his party not to overstep the constitutional limits of the secular republic.

It was not only the myth of the secular republic that was questioned in the course of the economic, social, and political change that Turkey has experienced since the mid-1980s. The myth of the one-and-undivided nation came also under attack when, in 1984, the separatist Kurdish Workers' Party (PKK) started its terrorist activities against the suppression of Turkey's Kurdish population. As a result of the state's purely military reaction to the PKK activities, public awareness of the Kurdish question grew constantly, as did ethnic

in a Secular State (London: Tauris, 1991); and Mehmet Ali Agaogullari, *L'Islam dans la Vie Politique de la Turquie* (Ankara: Ankara Üniversitesi Basimevi, 1982).

5. First evaluations of the Özal period can be found in Feroz Ahmad, *The Making of Modern Turkey* (London: Routledge, 1993), chap. 9; and Erik J. Zürcher, *Turkey: A Modern History* (London: Tauris, 1993), chap. 15.

self-consciousness among Turkey's Kurds.[6] The possibility of a division of Turkey's society between Turks and Kurds is much greater in 1997 than in 1984, whereas the probability of a territorial separation has not increased. Only Erbakan's Welfare Party seems to favor a different, i.e., political, conception for dealing with the issue.[7] However, as long as the public debate about the correct way of handling the problem continues, together with unrestricted military activities in the southeast, Turkey will experience another important division of its polity, which tends to undermine the country's political stability.

The continuing growth of traditional political Islam in the public sphere of Turkey has contributed to the revival of another social and political cleavage which had been rather dormant for decades: the division of Turkey's Muslims into a Sunni majority and an Alawite minority of about 25 percent of the population. Turkey's Alawites (distinct from Syrian Alawites or Iranian Shi'ites) have a long history of religious, social, and political discrimination dating from the Ottoman empire. For them, the concept of the secular republic opened a chance for religious freedom and social non-discrimination, although the republican regime was far from granting them equal status.[8] The recent rise to power of traditional, i.e., Sunni, political Islam changed this situation. Islamic militants of the Welfare Party and within the police and the paramilitary forces (Jandarma) have started to persecute Alawites whom they regard as heretics and "leftists."

This development induced Turkey's Alawites to reconsider their political and social situation, resulting in attempts at gaining a higher public profile for Alawite groups and representatives. Their aim is official equality with the Sunni element of Turkish Islam

---

6. For an overview of Turkey's Kurdish problem, see Henri J. Barkey and Graham E. Fuller, "Turkey's Kurdish Question: Critical Turning Points and Missed Opportunities," *Middle East Journal*, Vol. 51, No. 1 (Winter 1997), pp. 59–79. On the PKK, see especially Ismet G. Imset, *The PKK: A Report on Separatist Violence in Turkey (1973–1992)* (Ankara: Turkish Daily News Publications, 1992).

7. On August 22, 1996, Erbakan's speaker revealed a comprehensive package for approaching the Kurdish question, which tried to balance Kurdish aspirations for a wider acceptance of their ethnic identity within the Turkish state and the state's security-related interest in preserving internal stability and territorial integrity. This approach was, however, scrapped by the National Security Council. See *Turkish Daily News* (Electronic Edition), August 23, August 27, and August 29, 1996.

8. For a short overview, see Mark Soileau, "The Changing Face of Anatolian Alawism," *Turkish Daily News* (Electronic Edition), September 11, 1996.

regarding public recognition and representation.[9] If the Alawites can keep the momentum of their newly found self-consciousness, and if the hostility of radical Sunni (which are also represented among municipal authorities of the Welfare Party) continues, this religious cleavage adds another element of instability to the country's mid-term development.

The multifold social and political division of Turkey demands forceful political leadership in order to keep the country on track. The way Turkey's politicians and parties actually present themselves, however, gives cause for serious concerns. The center-left has been in decline for years and is paralyzed by petty political infighting. The center-right is not in much better shape, given the ongoing personal rivalry between the Motherland Party's chairman, Mesut Yilmaz, and the chair of the True Path Party, Tansu Çiller.[10]

This domestic situation does not leave the country's foreign policy unaffected. In recent years, relations with the United States and Europe have increasingly been overshadowed by the negative image created by Turkey's lasting domestic problems, especially regarding the Kurdish issue and insufficient realization of human rights. The United States has repeatedly turned down previously agreed arms delivery to Turkey, whereas the European Union takes Turkey's disappointing human rights record as a cause to keep the country at arm's length. Besides this, Turkey's governments have tended to use foreign policy issues for domestic policy interests, which has often led to an unnecessary emotional overload of foreign affairs, especially in relations with the EU and Greece.

A DIVIDED FOREIGN POLICY

The demise of the Soviet Union caught Turkey unprepared and left the country with a radically transformed international environment. Since then, Turkey has tried to adapt itself to the new situation. In doing so, it does not perceive itself as a winner of the end of the Cold War although, in Ankara's view, the new situation has widened Turkey's potential room for maneuver in foreign policy. This coincides, however, with increases in the external risks to the country's

9. See, for more details, Krisztina Kehl-Bodrogi, "Die 'Wiederfindung' des Alevitentums in der Türkei: Geschichtsmythos und kollektive Identität," *Orient*, Vol. 34, No. 2 (1993), pp. 267–282.

10. See Ümit Cizre Sakallioglu, "The Energy, Fragility and the Lethargy of Turkey's Politics," *Private View*, Vol. 1, No. 1 (Winter 1996), pp. 30–39.

security, especially in its immediate neighborhood to the north and southeast.[11] In this difficult situation, Turkey's traditional foreign policy elite feels itself increasingly left alone or insufficiently supported by its Western allies. Turkish criticism in this respect is directed against Europe's policy of keeping Turkey at arm's length, American neglect of Turkish interests concerning Iraq, and Western indulgence *vis-à-vis* Russian aspirations in the Caucasian and Caspian regions.

This evaluation is, however, not shared by the major party of the coalition government. The leadership of the Welfare Party, especially Prime Minister Erbakan, believe that Turkey not only has a special mission to fulfill as a leading country of the Islamic world and as an important bridge between the West and the Islamic states, but also that the country is fully equipped to meet this challenge. They argue that Turkey only needs to realize its true strength and develop the political will to make the correct use of it. Furthermore, they do not seem to be extremely bothered by Western attitudes or behavior towards Turkey and its foreign policy goals.

Hence, the internal political division of Turkey is reflected in the government's foreign policy outlook. This division is also visible in foreign policy practice: whereas Foreign Minister Tansu Çiller, from the junior coalition partner True Path Party, shares the responsibility with the military leadership for upholding the traditional vision of Turkey as a committed member of the Western system, it is Erbakan's responsibility to show the new vision of a more independent, self-assertive Turkey amid the group of Islamic "rising stars" on the international scene.

If Erbakan sees any impediments that may hinder Turkey from playing its international role, these result from an overextended link to the Western system. Therefore, he undertakes great efforts to strengthen Turkey's ties with other large Islamic countries. To the great concern of the U.S. government and the Turkish military leadership, he is trying especially to forge a special relationship with Iran in the economic field by concluding important gas deals with Tehran. In addition to that, his efforts at creating an economic bloc of large Islamic countries—the so-called group of D-8—as an interna-

---

11. More details of this perception can be found in Duygu B. Sezer, "On the Faultlines of the Post–Cold War Disorder," *Private View*, Vol. 1, No. 1 (Winter 1996), pp. 42–49.

tional counterpart to the G-7 has caught attention in Turkey and abroad.[12] The Welfare Party's fundamentally different orientation from the mainstream of Turkey's elite will create growing strains on the country's ability to conduct a coherent and rational foreign and security policy in the longer term. The competition for influence between the old and the new foreign policy elites within Turkey's political establishment will increasingly contribute to the West's feeling of uneasiness.

EUROPEAN AND AMERICAN INTERESTS IN RELATIONS WITH TURKEY

Europe's interest in Turkey's strategic position and role, so much esteemed during the Cold War era, has kept its momentum in the new international situation of Europe and Turkey after the demise of the Soviet Union. Although Turkey's current security policy function is less one-dimensional than it was during the East-West conflict, when the country was regarded as the southeastern pillar of the North Atlantic Treaty Organization (NATO), and the main barrier against the Soviet drive toward the Mediterranean and the Middle East, there is a general consensus among European governments that Turkey remains a partner of great strategic importance.[13]

Many regional developments that are critical to Europe's security concerns will be decisively influenced by Turkey's policy. This especially applies to:

- the Cyprus question;
- Greek-Turkish differences in the Aegean;
- developments in the former Yugoslavia, the Balkans, and the Black Sea region;
- the broader Kurdish problem and the future of northern Iraq;
- the Middle Eastern water problem, which will become an ever more urgent issue for the region;

---

12. The "Developing 8" (D-8) are Turkey, Iran, Malaysia, Pakistan, Bangladesh, Indonesia, Egypt, and Nigeria. For Erbakan's intentions regarding the D-8, see *Turkish Daily News* (Electronic Edition), January 5, 1997.

13. This was clearly revealed by the European debate about the appropriateness of the conclusion of the customs union agreement with Turkey in 1995. The main argument put forward by the EU's governments for the necessity of strengthening the integration with Turkey was built upon the country's strategic importance for Europe's security. See Heinz Kramer, "The EU-Turkey Customs Union: Economic Integration Amidst Political Turmoil," *Mediterranean Politics*, Vol. 1, No. 1 (Summer 1996), p. 70.

- the settlement of the Caucasian and Transcaucasian crises (Nagorno-Karabakh, Georgia-Abkhazia, Chechnya);
- Caspian and—to a lesser extent—Central Asian gas and oil resources; and
- the future of the newly independent states of Central Asia.

Moreover, due to its NATO membership, its membership in the Organization for Security and Cooperation in Europe (OSCE), and its associate membership status in the Western European Union (WEU), Turkey also has a direct influence on the final shape of Europe's new security architecture. Hence, Europe's interest in having a stable security architecture and a peaceful and prospering neighborhood to its east and south cannot be realized without Turkish cooperation. In this respect, Europe and Turkey share common interests with regard to crisis prevention, conflict resolution, and regional stability.

The commonality of European and Turkish interests should, however, not be taken for an identity of interests. Whereas many of the issues mentioned are of strategic national interest for Turkey, they are of only more general security concern for the Europeans. Nevertheless, there are many reasons to conclude that the new European security architecture in a broad sense can be better achieved together with Turkey than without it.

This view is also shared by the United States. The general U.S. security interest in relations with Turkey does not really differ from the European one: to keep Turkey in the Western camp and to use it, as much as possible, for the realization of Western interests. What is different, however, is the resulting policy agenda in terms of priorities. Concerning Turkey's domestic situation, the U.S. government is mainly interested in a "stable and democratic Turkey," whereas the driving European interest seems to aim at a "democratic and stable Turkey." With respect to foreign policy, in the American view, Turkey is today mainly regarded as a factor of the Middle Eastern political arena, which is America's direct national interest. For Europe, the Middle East is of only secondary strategic importance compared to the task of reconstructing Europe after the end of the Cold War. It is mainly in this connection that relations with Turkey enter Europe's security policy agenda, the focus of discussion being the contentious issue of Turkey's inclusion in Europe.

This issue concerns the U.S. administration only with regard to possible repercussions for American national interests; it is of an instrumental character. The more firmly Turkey is bound into the Western security system, the more it is expected to be prepared to help realize

American interests in the Greater Middle East. For many Europeans, however, relations with Turkey include elements that are much more connected with the issue of "European identity" and are of a very fundamental character. This especially applies to those European political circles for whom the notions of European integration and European Union mean more than just a special way of cooperation, but bear a distinct connotation of political community building.

The difference between the American and the European view on Turkey is also reflected in Turkey's political approaches toward its allies: Washington is mainly confronted with demands for political support for Turkey's various foreign policy interests and assistance in terms of military equipment. In contrast, Europe is, first and foremost, confronted with the Turkish demand for EU membership, the issue of assistance either being part of that demand or relegated to secondary importance. Thus, American and European approaches to relations with Turkey are bound to differ in substance and in emphasis as a result of different policy agendas for Turkey on either side of the Atlantic; and different demands on its allies put forward by Turkey.

The shared general European and American interest in keeping Turkey in the Western camp during a period of difficult domestic and external situations for Ankara should, nevertheless, induce coordination of European and American approaches towards Turkey and cooperation where possible. For this purpose, relations with Turkey should be included as a topic in the regular policy meetings between the United States and the European Union, as well as between Washington and its main European allies.

KEY ISSUES OF EUROPEAN-TURKISH RELATIONS

Three issues stand out on the agenda of European relations with Turkey, which are also of interest for the United States and its relations with Turkey. These are Turkey's place and role in the new European architecture; the Cyprus problem, which is also part of the broader Greek-Turkish dispute; and the Kurdish question. All of them should become part of efforts at Transatlantic policy coordination. Most important, Europeans and Americans should upgrade their level of coordination regarding contacts with Ankara over the Cyprus question and the Kurdish issue.

Other issues such as relations with Iran or Iraq, relations with Israel and the Middle East peace process, or the settlement of the Transcaucasian problems, including the mapping of oil and gas pipelines, are also of importance to Europe, Turkey, and the United

States. Cooperation or coordination of policies among the three sides or just among pairs of them are, however, more problematic due to policy differences or differences of priority, as F. Stephen Larrabee demonstrates in Chapter 7 of this volume. Nevertheless, the United States, the EU, and its leading member states should maintain a constant political dialogue with Turkey on these issues as well in order to mitigate Turkish fears of Western neglect of Turkey's broader foreign and security policy concerns.

TURKEY AND THE EMERGING NEW EUROPEAN ORDER. Europe's future security architecture will be based mainly on a combination of a reformed and extended NATO and an enlarged EU plus their respective relations with Russia. The main question concerning Turkey's place and role in the new European order is that of its inclusion in the specific European elements of that system, whereas its position in the Atlantic alliance remains firmly defined. Two closely related issues have to be addressed in that respect: Turkey's eventual full membership in the EU and in the WEU. Only when it is part of both will Turkey be an integral component of Europe's future security architecture.

The United States clearly has spoken out in favor of both without, however, showing much concern for the problems that may arise for Europe after Turkish EU membership. The European attitude is much more ambiguous. Germany, especially, shows great reluctance with regard to Turkey's full membership in the EU or WEU. This position can, to a certain extent, be explained by Germany's experience with its large minority of about two million Turkish citizens who have lived in the country for decades as a result of past labor migration. Problems of integrating this group into German society are projected misleadingly onto the issue of integrating Turkey into the EU: the political, social, and cultural cohesion of the EU is seen as being endangered by the inclusion of almost seventy million Muslim Turks. For similar reasons, other important member states of the EU are only slightly more enthusiastic with regard to Turkish membership.[14]

This reluctance might have been justified as long as the EU's basic rationale was the creation of a new and special political actor whose main task was to ensure economic prosperity for its member states

---

14. A striking example of this was the declaration of six mainly Christian-Democrat heads of governments of March 4, 1997, that they oppose a Turkish EU membership also because of cultural differences. *Financial Times,* March 5, 1997, p. 2.

and to bring Europe's weight to bear in international economic and political relations. In the future, however, the main task of the Union will be to organize and guarantee stability and security for all of Europe. The arguments brought forward as justifications for the fairly rapid eastern enlargement of the EU give ample evidence of that shift of rationale of European integration.[15] Moreover, the original goal of an "ever closer union" among the people of Europe will become obsolete with the envisaged enlargement of the EU to twenty-five members over the next decade or so. Hence the issue of Turkey's participation should be re-evaluated under that perspective.

Given Turkey's considerable importance for security and stability in important parts of Europe and its immediate neighborhood, the EU should actively support a policy of Turkey's inclusion in the European security order. Consequently, it should officially put Turkey on equal footing with those other eleven European states that are accepted as candidates for membership.[16] The EU should formulate conditions for Turkey's accession similar to those stipulated for the central and east European states by the meeting of the European Council at Copenhagen in 1993. Furthermore, Turkey should be included in the so-called "structured dialogue" and all other measures established to prepare the applicant countries for membership.

Such a move would not imply quick Turkish accession to the EU, but it would help to consolidate Turkey's links with the rest of Europe. Beyond that, it would contribute to the strengthening of the domestic position of Turkey's Westernizers; it would revive the European orientation of Turkey's public; and it would force Erbakan and his followers to take a more unequivocal position with respect to Turkey's position in Europe. The element of a self-fulfilling prophecy that is part of Europe's doubts about Turkey's future European orientation would be eliminated and the process of Turkey's creeping alienation from Europe could be reversed. European criticism of Turkey's domestic affairs would become less hypocritical in the eyes

---

15. For a short discussion of this issue, see Werner Weidenfeld and Manfred Huterer, *Eastern Europe: Challenges, Problems, Strategies* (Gütersloh: Verlag Bertelsmann Stiftung, 1992); and Heinz Kramer, "The European Community's Response to the 'New Eastern Europe'," *Journal of Common Market Studies*, Vol. 31, No. 2 (June 1993), pp. 213–244.

16. The current list of accepted applicant countries contains Poland, Hungary, the Czech Republic, Slovakia, Estonia, Latvia, Lithuania, Bulgaria, Romania, Slovenia, and Cyprus.

of many Turks. Moreover, a clear prospect of EU membership would also influence the dynamics of Turkey's other domestic and external problems. The prospects for an acceptable solution of the Kurdish problem as well as of the Cyprus issue would brighten.

If, however, the European states continued their policy of keeping Turkey at arm's length while proceeding with the establishment of the new European security architecture, relations could quickly turn sour. Turkey could, indeed, try to block NATO enlargement, and it would most likely end the customs union with the EU by re-establishing barriers to trade for European exports.[17] If, under such circumstances, Erbakan's Welfare Party further gained in popularity, a more far-reaching break in relations with the West could result. Otherwise, Turkey would try to intensify its relations with the United States.

This could put Washington into a delicate position *vis-à-vis* its European allies and also in its relations with Turkey, given the existing U.S. problems with fully meeting Ankara's current expectations as Larrabee explains (Chapter 7). However, there is little the United States government can do to bring about a change in Europe's approach toward Turkey beyond trying to persuade European opinion leaders of the wisdom of such a move. At the same time, the U.S. government should try to use its influence in Ankara to convince the Turkish leaders that a more sober approach to the issue of EU membership would only improve Turkey's chances to be accepted as a candidate. It would be especially helpful if the Americans would join the Europeans in their demand for certain domestic policy changes in Turkey, such as an improvement of the human rights situation and a political solution of the Kurdish problem, as conditions for the eventual opening of membership negotiations.

THE CYPRUS QUESTION AND OTHER GREEK-TURKISH DISPUTES. A much closer coordination of policies between European governments and the United States is necessary regarding the Cyprus question. This is mainly a consequence of the new dynamism brought about by

---

17. The customs union, which came into effect on January 1, 1996, established a common economic area between Turkey and the EU, with no barriers to internal trade and with a common external customs tariff and foreign trade policy. It is the strongest form of economic integration short of full EU membership, and Turkey is the only country with which the EU has engaged in such a form of economic integration. For more details, see Kramer, "The EU-Turkey Customs Union," and William Hale, "Turkey and the EU: The Customs Union and the Future," *Bogaziçi Journal*, Vol. 10, No. 1–2 (1996), pp. 243–262.

the European Union's decision of 1995—taken in order to get Greek assent to the establishment of the EU-Turkey customs union—to open accession negotiations with Cyprus six months after the end of the EU's Intergovernmental Conference (IGC) for the revision of the Treaty of Maastricht. Hence, negotiations will probably be due at the beginning of 1998. Since the EU dropped the condition of a prior solution of the Cyprus problem for the opening of accession negotiations, it upset the delicate balance of influence that had been established between Greek and Turkish Cypriots, Greece, and Turkey with regard to the political situation in the extended Aegean region.[18]

By basing its new policy on the formula that an eventual EU membership for Cyprus would require a prior solution to the Cyprus problem, but that Turkish Cypriots should not be given a right of veto over the membership issue, the Europeans hoped to create enough momentum for both sides to engage in a serious effort at reaching a compromise under UN guidance. The main result, however, has been a rise of tensions, both on the island between Greece and Turkey and in EU-Turkish relations. The situation has been further worsened by the Greek Cypriots' intention to buy state-of-the-art Russian S-300 anti-aircraft missiles, which, in turn, provoked the Turkish announcement that it would undertake a preemptive military strike if the missile systems were deployed in the first half of 1998.

Quick and easy solutions to the Cyprus problem are prevented by the existing fundamental differences between the Greek and Turkish sides.[19] Furthermore, both sides believe they have some additional instruments of political leverage, which makes them hope to reach their respective goals without much further compromise. Turkey and the Turkish Cypriot government have declared their intention to start negotiations about integration of northern Cyprus with Turkey at the same moment that Brussels starts membership negotiations with the government of the (Greek) Republic of Cyprus without a prior change of the situation on the island. This would finalize the division of the island. Also, the Turkish side, mainly for security reasons, links Cyprus's EU membership to Turkey's accession to the Union. Hence,

---

18. For details, see Tozun Bahcheli and Nicholas X. Rizopoulos, "The Cyprus Impasse: What Next?" *World Policy Journal*, Vol. 13, No. 4 (Winter 1996/97), pp. 27–39.

19. For a succinct summary, see Costas Melakopides, *Making Peace in Cyprus: Time for a Comprehensive Initiative* (Kingston: Centre for International Relations, Queen's University, 1996), pp. 31ff.

chances for a solution to the Cyprus question may be improved by the full inclusion of Turkey in the emerging European security architecture as suggested above.

The Greek side would be in a fairly comfortable situation if it were ready to cede the northern part of the island to the Turks as a price for EU membership. Greece could then try to enforce Cyprus membership in the EU without a prior solution on the island, by threatening not to ratify the results of the IGC or by linking Cyprus's accession to the so-called eastern enlargement of the EU. Greece and the Greek Cypriots may be tempted to pursue such an approach in the hope of a further alienation of Turkey from Europe by these developments. This could in turn result in stronger EU support for the Greek side in the overall Turkish-Greek dispute, as well as with respect to the continuous Greek and Greek Cypriot efforts at gaining international support for the withdrawal of the Turkish troops presently stationed in northern Cyprus.

Any such developments would sharply increase the tensions between the Aegean adversaries and on Cyprus itself. The likelihood of a military confrontation would rise. Turkey's temptation to turn its back on Europe—and probably also on the United States—would increase, especially with a Welfare Party–led government. Anti-Western sentiment in Turkey would rise; the influence of the established power elites would decrease; and Erbakan's chances of increasing his margin of victory in the next elections would rise. In the longer term, Turkey's involvement in the Western system would be seriously jeopardized, and the whole geostrategic configuration of the region could be changed in a dramatic way. All of this would run directly contrary to European and U.S. security interests concerning the larger Middle East and southeastern Europe.

Turkey's allies, therefore, have ample reason for increasing their efforts at bringing about a compromise between Turkish and Greek Cypriots concerning the issues dividing the island. In doing so, the Europeans in many respects will not be able to make use of the EU, which due to Greece's membership is regarded by the Turks as biased. Hence, interested European governments and the U.S. administration should upgrade their coordination with each other and with the UN, especially concerning issues related to the security on the island, by establishing regular meetings of the various special envoys to Cyprus. They should establish provisions for a constant exchange of information on the results of their contacts and talks with the parties to the conflict in the region. Interested European governments should join

Washington's efforts at suggesting a comprehensive package of confidence-building measures on Cyprus and in the Aegean in order to bring about a lasting defusion of tension between the two sides on Cyprus as well as between Greece and Turkey.

Another important issue that can only be solved with the help of third parties is safeguarding security on Cyprus after an eventual reunification of the island. As a UN formula would most likely be unacceptable to the Turkish side, other institutions such as the WEU or NATO will have to be considered. Here, again, Transatlantic policy coordination and eventual cooperation should start as soon as possible.

Parallel to this, the Europeans have to address the twofold task of convincing the Turkish Cypriots of the longer-term advantages for them of entry into the EU of the whole island, and of convincing the Greek Cypriots to accept participation of Turkish representatives in entry negotiations with Brussels. If Greece should be tempted to block such EU initiatives in the Union's Council of Ministers, its partners should not hesitate to stall the beginning of entry negotiations with Cyprus or suspend them indefinitely immediately after their start. The leading EU member governments should make it very clear that they are not ready to accept Cyprus's membership without a solution on the island, even if this would mean a certain delay of the EU's eastern enlargement.

THE KURDISH QUESTION. For many years, the Kurdish problem has been another factor contributing to the alienation between Turkey's political and military elites and their Western partners. Especially since the fight against the PKK turned into a form of low-level civil war accompanied by recurrent violations of human rights, Turkey's European and American allies have often been forced by public opinion to protest the behavior and policies of the Turkish authorities. European criticism is, however, generally more harsh and pronounced than that from the United States because the U.S. government seems to be more aware of the regional strategic impact of the Kurdish issue, which also affects American national interests in the wider Gulf area. Nevertheless, what for many Turks is a question of preserving the national and territorial integrity of the republic, is for most in the West merely a problem of correct treatment of a non-negligible minority. This difference in perception is difficult to overcome, especially as both sides do not seem to be fully prepared to accept the other's view as serious. Many Europeans, especially, regard the Turkish way of arguing as nothing but a pretext for upholding a basically authoritarian military rule in disguise, where-as even many of the "Westernized" Turks see the European criticism as a barely veiled promotion of Turkey's partition.

The situation is aggravated by the presence of about half a million Kurds in Europe, mainly in Germany. Only a tiny minority of them are active PKK supporters. However, there is a large group of politically conscious Kurds, many of them political emigrants from Turkey. Over the years, they have succeeded in developing a network of Kurdish associations, from self-help groups at the local level to more politically oriented umbrella organizations at the national level. These organizations are an important factor in shaping European public opinion on the Kurdish problem because they have established working relationships with many parts of European civil society.[20] Hence, the Turkish government finds it difficult even to communicate its position on the issue to the European public and the political circles, let alone have it accepted.

If the Turkish government were, however, able to develop and implement a non-military approach for the solution of the Kurdish question, it could simultaneously stabilize the domestic situation, channel a considerable part of the budget toward more productive uses, and eliminate a source of constant tension in relations with its Western allies.

Turkey's European and American partners should, therefore, undertake greater efforts to convince the reluctant parts of the Turkish political elite of the necessity and the advantages of applying a comprehensive non-military solution to the Kurdish question. For this purpose, non-governmental actors such as German political foundations or U.S. policy-related academic institutions should try to establish dialogues between moderate Kurdish groups and "enlightened" Turkish political representatives. Europeans and Americans should, however, make clear that this does not mean support of PKK terrorist activities nor of separatist tendencies of whatever kind. Furthermore, Turkey's European and American partners should underline the seriousness of their engagement regarding the Kurdish problem by developing a co-sponsored and co-financed "Southeast

---

20. A comprehensive overview of the situation of the Kurdish exiles in Europe can be found in Berliner Institut für Vergleichende Sozialforschung, ed., *Kurden im Exil: Ein Handbuch kurdischer Kultur, Politik und Wissenschaft*, 2 vols. (Berlin: Edition Parabolis, 1991).

Anatolia Relief Program" of financial and technical assistance for the rehabilitation of the war-ravaged southeastern provinces of Turkey, on the condition that the Turkish government implements a similar program of its own.

The Emerging Attention to the Caspian Basin Region

With the dissolution of the Soviet Union, the Caspian basin region shifted from the periphery of a huge empire to become the focus of a new regional orientation and order. Its energy wealth has provoked the desire of neighbors and multinational companies. The need to transfer this oil wealth to harbors where it can be traded under world market conditions makes cooperation indispensable and coalition building opportune. The potential for crises to the west in the Caucasus region, to the south in the Persian Gulf, and to the east in Tajikistan and Afghanistan makes this balancing even more delicate. The "Great Game" of the nineteenth century has been revived in numerous headlines. Azerbaijan and Turkmenistan have claimed to be the new Kuwait, and the title "Persian Gulf of the twenty-first century" is even sometimes awarded to the Caspian basin region.

Undoubtedly this region can be considered one of the last playgrounds of classical geopolitics. Russia is sending mixed signals about its claims; Iran and Turkey are still obvious rivals; Pakistan wants to reserve a piece of the cake for itself; Saudi Arabia is involved with its quiet diplomacy. The United States, however, seems to be the only power that understands the game as a whole, while Europe has its interests but no policy. The common understanding, however, is that the Caspian region must be treated as a potential crisis area as well as a potential future cooperation track. It is the gate to Central Asia and beyond.

THE POTENTIAL OIL RESOURCES

Caspian oil resources are divided into three regions with different potential: the offshore oil fields east of Baku, the Caspian shelf oil fields in the northeastern part of the sea, and the Kazak on-shore fields around Tengiz. Most of the international attention has been drawn to the Azerbaijan oil deals. On September 20, 1994, the Azerbaijani International Operating Company (AIOC), including eleven mainly Western companies but also Russia's Lukoil, came to an agreement in Baku on the "deal of the century" with an estimated investment of $7.8 billion and an extraction potential of 500 million tons of oil. Three smaller contracts and a further negotiation process followed, about two-thirds the size of the first deal in investment and extraction volume.[21] The reserves of that region have been estimated at about 1 billion tons; later estimates, however, indicate that they might be as much as 2.5 billion tons.[22]

The Caspian shelf oil resources are not well explored. A seismic survey done by Western firms says it is unlikely that the reserves will exceed 3.5 billion tons.[23] Other Western estimates reach 5.5 to 8.2 billion tons.[24] The government of Kazakstan, however, is confident that its share of the treasure under the Caspian Sea is close to 10 billion tons.[25]

The Kazak on-shore oil field reserves in the Tengiz area are between 1 billion tons (proven) and 5 billion tons (probable or possible). In 1993 the largest deal yet between a former Soviet country and a Western firm was concluded: the U.S. firm Chevron agreed with the state of Kazakstan to exploit approximately one billion tons of oil in the Tengiz field, requiring a total investment of $20 billion. Due to uncertainties about the transportation of the oil, however, this project has had a slow takeoff.

The total oil reserves in the Caspian area might exceed 10 billion tons; high estimates reach as much as 25 billion tons (proven reserves are 6 billion tons).[26] Recent calculations tend, however, more toward slightly below 10 billion tons.[27] That means that the share of the

---

21. The second deal signed with the Cipco consortium is dominated by Lukoil (32.5 percent); investment is $2 billion, and potential resources are 140–420 million tons. Shakh-Deniz is the third deal, of 250–500 million tons and $4 billion investment; it is dominated by British Petroleum and the Norwegian company Statoil. *Handelsblatt*, November 13, 1996, p. 16. The fourth project is on the Dan Ulduzu and Ashrafi fields, with investment of $2 billion and resources of 150 million tons, signed on December 14, 1996. *OMRI Daily Digest*, No. 241, Part I (December 16, 1996). Negotiation led by the French group Elf is under way to develop the Lenkoran Deniz and the Talish Deniz fields. The deal is said to be worth $2 billion. For the first time a German firm, Deminex, is likely to get involved. *OMRI Daily Digest*, No. 247, Part I (December 31, 1996).

22. *Handelsblatt*, November 13, 1996, p. 17.

23. *Petroleum Economist*, No. 8 (August 1996), p. 53.

24. Matthew J. Sagers, "The Oil Industry in the Southern Tier Former Soviet Republics," *Post-Soviet Geography*, Vol. 35, No. 5 (1994), pp. 265–298; and *Financial Times*, March 11, 1996, p. 2.

25. *Petroleum Economist*, No. 8 (August 1996), p. 53.

26. *The Economist*, May 6, 1996, p. 61.

27. In comparison, proven oil reserves in the North Sea are 3 billion tons; Iraq, 13

Caspian region is less than 5 percent of proven world oil reserves. Further explorations might increase this; there will, however, definitely be nothing like a "Persian Gulf of the twenty-first century."

Natural gas might be a slightly different story. Turkmenistan's resources could be in the range of 12 (proven) to 21 trillion m^3 (9–16 billion tons of oil equivalents).[28] This would be close to 10 percent of the world's natural gas resources.

THE LEGAL STATUS OF THE CASPIAN SEA

The legal status of the Caspian Sea was relatively clear before 1991, although the agreements signed in 1921 and 1940 by the Soviet Union and Iran regulated principally fisheries, trade, and navigation, not property rights. The dissolution of the Soviet Union in 1991 raised the number of littoral states to the Caspian Sea from two to five, and thus provoked new claims. The newly independent states of Azerbaijan, Kazakstan, and Turkmenistan recognized the opportunity to substantiate their new sovereignty by exploiting the offshore treasures. The Soviet Union unilaterally drew a line between the borders at the west and east coasts as a dividing line of territorial waters and protected this line with coastal guards, but even this divide had to be given up after Iran protested against it in 1980.[29] The lack of regulation applies most of all to the property rights on offshore resources. Since 1991, Russia has favored a condominium regime applied to some of the inland waters (like Lake Constance between Germany, Austria, and Switzerland), according to which only a coast strip to 25 meters water depth belongs to the neighboring territory, with the main water administered in common.[30] This principle also corresponds with the interests of Turkmenistan. Azerbaijan and Kazakstan prefer a solution on the basis of treating the Caspian Sea according to the Law of the Sea Treaty, implying a 200-mile zone or, if the coast to

---

billion tons; Iran, 13 billion tons; Kuwait, 14 billion tons; Saudi Arabia, 35 billion tons; the Gulf region, 85 billion tons; and the world as a whole, 136 billion tons. Federal Ministry of Economics, *Energiedaten '95: Nationale und internationale Entwicklungen,* Bonn, September 1995, p. 90.

28. *Financial Times,* March 3, 1996, p. 5; and *Neue Züricher Zeitung,* October 1, 1995, p. 11.

29. Vladimir Razuvaev, "Russian Interests in the Caspian Region: The Energy Dimension," Stiftung Wissenschaft und Politik, SWP-IP 2956, May 1996, p. 9.

30. Henn-Jüri Uibopuu, "Das Kaspische Meer und das Völkerrecht," *Recht in Ost und West,* Vol. 39, Heft 7 (September 1995).

coast distance is less than 200 miles, the application of the equidistance principle; the latter would be valid for the Caspian Sea, due to the fact that it is less than 200 miles broad. According to the condominium principle, all neighboring countries would get a share in the offshore energy wealth, while the second approach would reserve this wealth for Kazakstan and Azerbaijan.

Kazakstan made a proposal in September 1994 to apply the Law of Sea Treaty to the Caspian Sea. Iran and Azerbaijan had already presented a draft convention by the end of 1993.[31] The Russian government was not unanimous in refusing the planned offshore exploitation activities. While the foreign ministry under Andrei Kozyrev and the secret service chairman Yevgeni Primakov tried to convince President Boris Yeltsin to intervene against any agreement,[32] Prime Minister Victor Chernomyrdin supported the Azerbaijani activities, including the involvement of the Russian company Lukoil. Nevertheless, the diplomatic dispute started in October 1994 immediately after the signing of the "deal of the century" in Baku. Russia asked the United Nations, by memorandum on October 5, 1994, to prevent any illegal acts; if this was not done, Russia might decide to restore the former status "by any means."[33] On the other hand, Russia promoted a negotiation process that led to an agreement signed on November 12, 1996, in Ashgabat by four of the five coastal states, omitting Azerbaijan.[34] It grants each state an exclusive 45-mile offshore zone. For Kazakstan, this is enough to keep practically all of the offshore fields that it could claim according to the 200 miles/equidistance principle. However, Azerbaijan would have to share its major fields with the other littoral states. This agreement was quite an achievement for Russia, demonstrating its ability to compromise in a civilized way to reach a peaceful settlement of a disputed matter in this region with diplomatic means. However, as long as the main loser under the agreement cannot be convinced to sign it, the agreement is

31. Sergei Vinogradov and Patricia Wouters, "The Caspian Sea: Current Legal Problems," *Zeitschrift für ausländisches öffentliches Recht und Völkerrecht,* Vol. 55, No. 2 (1995), pp. 604–623.

32. Kozyrev and Primakov convinced Yeltsin to sign Secret Decree No. 396 on July 21, 1994, "On protecting the interests of the Russian Federation in the Caspian Sea." Robert V. Barylski, "Russia, the West, and the Caspian Energy Hub," *Middle East Journal,* Vol. 49, No. 2 (Spring 1995), pp. 217–232.

33. *Le Monde Diplomatique,* July 27, 1995, p. 18.

34. *OMRI Daily Digest,* Part I, No. 219 (November 12, 1996).

legally meaningless. Nevertheless, the very fact that the Russian oil company Lukoil is a shareholder in the first Baku deal of 1994 and became the leader of the consortium in the second deal makes it improbable that Russia will use force or produce major tensions to enforce any legal claims unilaterally.

ECONOMIC INTERESTS AND THE TRANSPORTATION PROBLEM

The newly independent states are landlocked and need comprehensive agreements with difficult neighbors on how to get energy resources to the world market. This dependence on agreements means not only a heavy burden for the newly independent states, but has also provoked the interests of all neighbor states, since it affects the future balance of power in the region. The region, however, is in the vicinity of such sensitive regions as the Persian Gulf and the Caucasus, with their numerous conflict constellations. Thus, the balance in the Caspian region has a major impact on the neighboring regions, and therefore the United States as a global power is engaged and Europe is interested.

The short history since 1991 of evaluating the options for pipeline routes is full of evidence of the dominance of geopolitics over economic rationality, and of the importance given to these questions not only by regional powers, or those who would like to be, but also by those who consider influence in the Greater Middle East to be of global importance. In 1992, Azerbaijan as well as Kazakstan indicated their preference to transport Caspian oil via Iran, either to the Persian Gulf or by a pipeline through Turkey to the world market. In both cases, pressure and incentives from the United States caused them to change their policies. Kazakstan's President Nursultan Nazarbayev changed his position after a visit to the White House in early 1994. Azerbaijan's President Gaidar Aliyev was convinced after a phone call from President Clinton in early October 1995 that the preferred route to transport the "deal of the century" oil should go west or north, but not south through Iran. A year earlier, under U.S. advice, he gave up his plans to offer Iran a five percent share in the AIOC.

The fact that Iran, for the time being, was excluded as a transit country brought Russia into a very strong position. The only remaining route apart from Russian territory was via the Transcaucasus, but this would serve only for Azerbaijani oil. Kazakstan considered constructing a pipeline through the Caspian Sea to Baku or transporting the oil by tanker, but this would require complicated harbor construction; moreover, the legal status of the Caspian Sea, particularly in the case of an underwater pipeline, would have to be resolved first and agreement with Russia achieved. Under these conditions, the best solution the United States could reach was a compromise with Russian interests that allows for both the northern and western routes for the Azerbaijani oil.

On October 9, 1995, the twin agreement was signed in Baku according to which the AIOC committed itself to transport its oil via Georgia to the Black Sea harbor of Supsa, as well as via the Russian regions of Dagestan and Chechnya to the Russian Black Sea harbor of Novorossisk. Both existing pipelines are to be overhauled for the "early oil" of about 80,000 barrels per day (bpd) running from 1997 on. The peak capacity of 700,000 bpd after the year 2000 from the "deal of the century" alone will require, however, new pipelines which are not yet in an advanced stage of planning. The western route depends very much on what happens with the oil after arriving at Supsa, the Georgian Black Sea harbor at the Georgian-Turkish border; this is uncertain. Turkey has not yet made a decision whether the oil can be transported by pipeline through the mountains and Kurdish territory to its Mediterranean harbor of Ceyhan, or by tanker to Sinop, the Black Sea harbor north of Ankara, and from there via pipeline to Ceyhan. The second solution would be technically less demanding and politically less risky, but the cost of loading the oil onto tankers in Supsa and back to the pipeline system in Sinop adds considerable cost.

Russia, on the other hand, has a similar problem with getting the oil from Novorossisk to the world market. Turkey refuses to accept major additional oil transportation through the Bosporus due to the risk of an accident that could affect the ten million people of Istanbul. The legal situation, based on the Montreux Convention of 1936, supports the Russian argument for free transportation; the political effects of enforcing the right in this case, however, are high. Therefore, Russia is preparing an alternative, a bypass pipeline to the Bosporus from Bourgas, Bulgaria, to Alexandropolis, Greece. Many speculations in Russia and the Western media are connected with this "orthodox axis."[35] As in the Turkish case, transfers of the oil from pipeline to tanker in Novorossisk, to pipeline in Bourgas, and then to tanker in Alexandropolis would be expensive. The advantage for Russia would

---

35. Takis Michas, "Russian-Greek Pipeline Will Carry More," *Wall Street Journal*, September 22, 1995, p. 8.

be the economies of scale. Since, in addition to the Baku oil, Novorossisk will also receive Tengiz oil from 1999 on, much more oil will be transported from Novorossisk than from Supsa.

In the long run, this Tengiz oil and the offshore oil from the North Caspian Sea will be more important than the Baku oil. After years of dispute between Chevron, the state of Kazakstan, and Russia, the Caspian Pipeline Consortium (CPC) signed an agreement on December 6, 1996, on the construction of a pipeline from Tengiz to Novorossisk. Construction will begin in 1997 and be finished in 1999 at a cost of $1.5 billion, with an initial transportation potential of 28 million tons per year. Russia, Kazakstan, and Oman reduced their stakes in the original consortium in favor of oil companies, particularly Chevron (15 percent) and also the two Russian companies Lukoil (12.5 percent) and Rosneft (7.5 percent), as well as Mobil (7.5 percent) and others.[36] This deal was in line with the 1995 twin deal on Baku oil, and it shows that Russia principally defends its economic interests by playing with its geographic advantages. However, it also indicates that the harsh line of the Russian foreign ministry and other influential groups in Moscow promoting the "near abroad" philosophy during earlier negotiations[37] could not completely dominate the Russian position.

A side effect of the long-lasting negotiation process is that the U.S. doctrine of isolating Iran is eroding. Kazakstan and Iran signed an agreement on August 10, 1996, that gives Kazakstan access to Iranian ports on the Persian gulf. Kazakstan will ship two million tons of crude oil annually to Iranian ports on the southern coast of the Caspian Sea.[38] On November 13, 1996, Russia, Turkmenistan, and Iran signed a memorandum on cooperation in developing the Caspian Sea oil resources, and established a joint company for further exploration in the Caspian Sea.[39] Russia and Iran signed an agreement on joint exploration and exploitation of Caspian Sea oil on December 3, 1996.[40] Turkish Prime Minister Erbakan signed, during his visit to Tehran in August 1996, a $20 billion natural gas deal, starting with 2 billion m³ deliveries from Iran to Turkey in 1998 and increasing to 10 billion m³

---

36. *OMRI Daily Digest*, Part I, No. 238 (December 9, 1996).

37. Barylski, "Russia, the West, and the Caspian Energy Hub," pp. 217–232.

38. *OMRI Daily Digest*, Part I, No. 155 (August 12, 1996).

39. *OMRI Daily Digest*, Part I, No. 220 (November 13, 1996).

40. *DW Monitor Dienst*, December 5, 1996.

in 2004, and opening an option for an additional 8 billion m³ delivery from Turkmenistan via Iran to Turkey. The construction of the pipeline has already begun.[41] Turkey's Energy Minister Recai Kutan confirmed this project during a visit to Tehran in December 1996. Considering that Turkey's total natural gas consumption amounted to 9 billion m³ in 1996, this project plays an important role in Turkey's ambitious economic development. All these deals with Iran put pressure on Azerbaijan to be open as well, and not to follow the U.S. position of excluding Iran from any energy deal.

The situation concerning Turkmenistan's natural gas is rather unclear. The world's third largest natural gas resources are not well exploited due to the unsolved transportation problem. Production fell after the dissolution of the Soviet Union from 82 billion m³ in 1990 to 31 billion m³ in 1995, with only a minimal recovery in 1996.[42] The only transportation route is the Russian network. While Ukraine is interested in buying Turkmenistan's natural gas, it is unable to pay world market prices. To those who pay, namely the European countries, Russia lets only a limited amount through its pipelines. Huge pipeline projects, including an $8.7 billion pipeline to Europe[43] or a $12 billion pipeline through China to the Pacific coast are under consideration, with studies in progress by Exxon and Mitsubishi, as well as China's state oil company.[44] However, political uncertainties and economic risks are so high that investors are not yet seriously interested. The Erbakan government, however, is testing the option of constructing the long-planned 1,320 km "friendship pipeline" from Iran to Turkey, the most critical part of a pipeline from Turkmenistan to Europe.[45] It is, however, quite uncertain whether there will be a demand in Europe for natural gas beyond the traditional supply from Norway, the Netherlands, Russia, and Algeria. At the least, this new offer would have to adjust to very competitive conditions.

Demand on the Indian sub-continent is different from the European

---

41. *Turkish Daily News,* February 18, 1997.

42. The increase during the first half of 1996 was 1 percent more than the first half of the previous year. *Petroleum Economist,* No. 11 (November 1996), p. 42; and *Petroleum Economist,* No. 1 (January 1997), p. 56.

43. Institute of Current World Affairs, ASA-4, January 27, 1995, p. 11.

44. *Financial Times,* March 20, 1996, p. 5; *New York Times,* September 9, 1995, p. 1; *Neue Zürcher Zeitung,* October 1, 1995, p. 11.

45. "Turkey-Iran Gas Pipeline Triggers U.S. Alarm Bells," *Financial Times,* August 30, 1996.

market. Therefore, the American company Unocal and the Saudi Arabian company Delta are competing with the Argentine-British company Bridas for the right to construct a pipeline from Eastern Turkmenistan via Afghanistan to Pakistan, and from there into India.[46] The political risk of constructing a pipeline through Afghanistan is obvious, but it is also possible that such an investment could bring some stability into the country. It also could create pressure on outsiders to support a domestic political group that is not otherwise favored, such as the Taliban regime, in order not to jeopardize the reliability of this transportation system.

GEOPOLITICS VERSUS THE REGULATORY REGIME

The United States is an important player in the Caspian region, while neither Europe nor its member states is. Even countries like Great Britain, France, Italy, and Norway, whose companies are involved in the exploitation of the energy, are not visible political players. That does not mean that Europe has no interest and no strategy. The United States acts based on its responsibility as the only world power, while Europe sees a chance to export Western-type principles as a contribution to stability and efficient cooperation.

U.S. diplomat Rosemarie Forsythe has written a study on the politics of oil in the region.[47] She identifies three main U.S. policy goals: support for the sovereignty and independence of the countries of the region; support for U.S. commercial involvement; and support of the diversification of world oil supplies to reduce future dependence on Persian Gulf oil.[48] These goals are shared without qualification by European governments, the second one by analogy. Forsythe makes, however, a distinction between goals; diplomatic, commercial, technical, and financial instruments; and parameters. One of the parameters within which political and commercial decisions will be made is "opposition to projects that give Iran significant political, material and economic benefits. The U.S. has encouraged Caspian countries to minimize Iranian involvement in oil projects as part of an overall effort to contain Iran."[49]

---

46. *The Independent,* March 14, 1997, p. 11.

47. Rosemarie Forsythe, *The Politics of Oil in the Caucasus and Central Asia,* Adelphi Paper No. 300 (London: IISS, May 1996). The study expresses her own views, not those of the U.S. government.

48. Ibid., pp. 17–18.

49. Ibid., pp. 19–20.

These goals are undisputed in the Western world; however, even after the "Mykonos" trial in Berlin, this particular "parameter" and the instruments to enforce it might be disputed. The difference seems to be that the United States prefers the application of carrots and sticks in a region where classical geopolitics still is an option, while the Europeans have a stronger belief in designing a regulatory framework accepted equally by the participating parties. Thus the two poles of U.S.-European differences are geopolitics versus a regulatory regime.

What is the European approach of a regulatory framework? In 1990, when the opportunity for a new European order became visible, the European Union initiated a European Energy Charter in order to integrate the Soviet Union into a Western-type regime of energy extraction, transportation, and consumption, including its environmental implications. After a one-year negotiation, the charter was signed on December 17, 1991 by all Organization for Economic Cooperation and Development (OECD) countries, including the United States and Japan, and all Central and Eastern European countries including all republics of the Soviet Union.[50] The charter designed a further negotiation process for a legally binding treaty, which was negotiated over three years. The "Treaty of the Charter" was signed in December 1994[51] by all European states and also by Russia, which, however, has not yet ratified it. The United States did not sign it, after participating in the negotiations. The treaty regulates international investment and trade in the energy sector according to free market rules; it prohibits the interruption of energy flow by transit countries (Article 7.6); and implies a dispute-settlement process (Article 7.7). Thomas Waelde writes, in a thorough evaluation of the treaty:

The game is about helping effective institutions emerge, along with the culture that civil societies with market economy structure have, under the rule of law. In the context of international investment law, the Treaty is but the contemporary expression of the current primacy of economic liberalism, with its emphasis on equal competition, open door attitudes and protection of investment, adapted to the particular East/West context.[52]

---

50. *Europe Documents* (Brussels), No. 1754 (December 21, 1991).

51. The Energy Charter Treaty, *Bundesrat Drucksache* 963/96, August 16, 1996.

52. Thomas Waelde, "International Investment under the 1994 Energy Charter Treaty," *Journal of World Trade*, Vol. 29, No. 5 (October 1995), p. 71. Thomas Waelde is Jean Monnet Professor of European Energy and Economic Law, University of Dundee.

The European Union has done little to promote the influence of this treaty. The EU invited the Caspian littoral states and the potential transit countries that signed the treaty to Brussels in November 1995, where the participants agreed to establish a working group. Russia refused to transfer any negotiation power to this working group and considered its own position to be that of an observer. It is quite obvious that this process has no chance to become influential as long as the United States is not a participant but is determining the rules of geopolitics in the region. However, as Waelde puts it: "The Treaty cannot be seen in isolation. In the East/West context, it is just one of many instruments to inject Western values and methods into the transition process."[53] Even Iran, which has not yet been invited to sign the treaty, would probably find it much more acceptable to submit to a regulatory regime than to U.S. pressure.

Under current conditions, neither the U.S. nor the European strategy is successful. The isolation of Iran, whose high point was reached in 1994–95, is obviously crumbling; this is bad news, if the isolation of Iran is the ultimate goal, but good news for breaking open Russia's near-monopoly. The forces of the new economic gravity zone will be stronger than a containment policy to which the neighbors of Iran are not committed. The lack of effect of the Treaty of the Charter is obvious. Therefore, it might make sense to link the two approaches instead of letting them paralyze the respective policies of the two Western partners.

Obviously, in the short run the U.S. presence with its instruments is helpful. Otherwise the "near-abroad philosophers" in Moscow might gain support. It would, however, be very useful if the United States would commit itself to the goals of the Energy Charter and support the implementation of the Treaty of the Charter, and even invite Iran to sign it and become a partner. The advantage of such a regulatory policy is that its application can bring only benefits, while there are risks involved in a policy of supporting one group, such as the Taliban regime, to beat an even worse regime. If the United States would support the idea that only by observing the rules of the game, designed in the Energy Charter process, is an efficient and stable cooperation possible in the region, this certainly would impress the Russians and all other signatory states of the treaty.

---

53. Ibid., p. 71.

Chapter 9

The United States, Europe, and Weapons of Mass Destruction

Richard A. Falkenrath

For the industrialized democracies of the West, no development presents a greater long-term threat to their security or freedom of action than the proliferation of weapons of mass destruction (WMD)—nuclear, biological, and chemical weapons, and the advanced means for their delivery. The strategic impact of WMD proliferation is nowhere more visible than in the Greater Middle East; the region contains the world's densest concentration of proliferants and potential WMD flash points.

Yet as one surveys the efforts of the American and European allies to respond to the proliferation threats in the Greater Middle East, two related problems emerge.

First, the European allies have demonstrated little political will to cope with the most important proliferation problem of the coming decades: the clandestine WMD programs in the states most likely to pose a threat to international security.[1] This is manifested most clearly in the general unwillingness of the Europeans to attempt to change the behavior of known or suspected proliferant states through the exercise of collective political, economic, or military pressure in concert with the United States. European nonproliferation policies remain focused on refining the details of existing, largely voluntary,

The author wishes to thank the editors and other chapter authors of the volume, as well as Ash Carter, Shai Feldman, Joachim Krause, and Doug MacEachin, for their comments on early drafts of this paper. The author alone is responsible for the views expressed.

1. There are important differences among the European states on these topics, but for the sake of brevity and argument, these are distilled into a simplified "European" view.

and generally low-cost nonproliferation instruments, such as the Euratom Treaty, International Atomic Energy Agency (IAEA) safeguards, the Nuclear Non-Proliferation Treaty (NPT), the Chemical Weapons Convention (CWC), and the Biological Weapons Convention (BWC). These international legal instruments are important, but they are not sufficient as a nonproliferation agenda. The area where greater contributions from the major European states are needed most is in the prevention, reversal, and deterrence of specific states' clandestine WMD programs.

Second, the North Atlantic alliance does not add enough to the international effort to cope with the specific security problems posed by WMD proliferation. There is no clear political consensus within the North Atlantic Treaty Organization (NATO) on how the alliance's collective power should be used to reduce the shared risks associated with WMD proliferation. Operationally, the alliance has only recently begun to consider how NATO's integrated and national military resources should be adapted to enhance their relevance to the full range of possible WMD-related contingencies. While NATO has already begun to play a role in educating the allies' national security communities on the WMD threat, the alliance has remained focused on distinctly European missions and has been reluctant to take up the WMD agenda in an ambitious or aggressive fashion.

The allies on both sides of the Atlantic share an interest in preventing WMD proliferation, rolling it back where it does occur, and ensuring against any possible WMD use or threat of use. Although the Europeans' appreciation for the seriousness of the WMD proliferation problem appears to be growing, there are significant differences between the American and European approaches to the WMD problem. Many factors explain these American and European differences, but the effects of this policy divergence are clear: shaky American elite support for the Transatlantic security partnership; a NATO with limited relevance to one of the most important strategic challenges of the contemporary era; and missed opportunities for joint action and the pooling of resources among allies who share a common danger.

This chapter begins by surveying what is publicly known about the current extent and likely future trends of WMD proliferation in the Greater Middle East; it then explores the American and European policy responses to three key WMD-related issues in the Greater Middle East: Iran, Libya, and counterproliferation; and it analyzes several explanations for the differences between the American and European approaches. The final section focuses on specific policies that U.S.-European cooperation on WMD issues in the Greater Middle East should include.

Overview of the WMD Environment in the Greater Middle East

The sections below briefly describe what is publicly known about the WMD capabilities and designs of the region's seven key proliferant or potentially proliferant states: Iran, Iraq, Libya, Israel, Syria, Egypt, and Algeria. No attempt is made to place these capabilities and programs in their broader strategic and political context, and five caveats should be borne in mind while reading the synopses below. First, the purpose here is only to provide a basic overview of the distribution of WMD capabilities around the Greater Middle East.[2] Second, reliable information on clandestine WMD programs is difficult to acquire. WMD acquisition programs are generally conducted on a clandestine basis, so their existence must be inferred from their externally observed features. As revealed in Iraq after the Gulf War, the true extent of even a large WMD program can be successfully concealed. Third, although nuclear, biological, and chemical (NBC) weapons can be delivered in many different ways, most American military thinkers assume that short- and intermediate-range ballistic missiles will be the delivery means of choice for regional proliferants.[3] However, ballistic missiles present only one means of NBC delivery. Depending on the attacker's objectives and the type and sophistication of weapon used, delivery options include aircraft, cruise missiles, artillery, helicopters, and covert, clandestine, or terrorist methods. Fourth, the mere possession of biological or chemical weapons does not necessarily translate into a significant, or even a usable, operational capability. (Nuclear weapons, on the other hand, present such a serious military threat that their possession by any state will almost certainly be regarded as profoundly significant.)

---

2. The key sources on WMD proliferation in the Greater Middle East used here are Office of the Secretary of Defense (OSD), *Proliferation: Threat and Response* (Washington, D.C.: Department of Defense, April 1996); U.S. Congress, Office of Technology Assessment (OTA), *Proliferation of Weapons of Mass Destruction: Assessing the Risks*, OTA-ISC-559 (Washington, D.C.: U.S. Government Printing Office [U.S. GPO], August 1993); and Russian Federation Foreign Intelligence Service Report, *A New Challenge After the Cold War: Proliferation of Weapons of Mass Destruction*, JPRS-TND-93-007 (Joint Publications Research Service).

3. Short-range ballistic missiles are generally defined as those with ranges of less than 500 kilometers.

Finally, weapons of mass destruction become a threat mainly in cases of problematic behavior on the part of their owners, such as interstate aggression, religious extremism, unstable domestic political rule, or the sponsorship of terrorism.

IRAN

In recent years, Iran has presented the most serious proliferation problem in the Greater Middle East. Since being the victim of Iraqi chemical weapons attacks in the early 1980s, Iran has developed a very large chemical weapons stockpile and production capability and has trained its armed forces in offensive and defensive chemical warfare.[4] Iran is believed to possess a growing biological weapons program[5] and is reported to have received a large quantity of Iraqi biological weapons agents during the 1990–91 Persian Gulf War.[6] Iran does not yet possess nuclear weapons or the technical capacity to produce them, but U.S. intelligence sources believe that Iran is committed to a clandestine nuclear weapons program based on indigenous training and development, the purchase of facilities ostensibly intended to support a civilian nuclear energy program (e.g., Russian reactors), and the illicit acquisition of controlled technologies and materials (possibly including fissile materials from the former Soviet Union) through an organized covert buying program.[7] To date, however, there is no evidence that Iran possesses a uranium enrichment or a plutonium reprocessing facility, and the United States has concluded that "Iran will not be able to produce sufficient plutonium to create a weapon until well into the next century, unless it receives significant foreign assistance."[8]

Iran possesses a variety of short-range ballistic missiles purchased from China and North Korea. Iran's existing ballistic missile arsenal

4. OSD, *Proliferation: Threat and Response*, pp. 15–16; Barbara Starr, "Iran Has Vast Stockpiles of CW Agents, Says CIA," *Jane's Defence Weekly*, August 14, 1996, p. 3.

5. Tony Capaccio, "CIA: Iran Holding Limited Stocks of Biological Weapons," *Defense Week*, August 5, 1996, p. 1.

6. This report, derived from unevaluated human sources, was initially released to the public on the Pentagon's GulfLINK web site for Gulf War syndrome veterans. The Department of Defense later withdrew some of the documents which were found to reveal classified material, but these documents are now available on a private website (http://www.insigniausa.com).

7. See also Shahram Chubin, "Does Iran Want Nuclear Weapons?" *Survival*, Vol. 37, No. 1 (Spring 1995), pp. 86–104.

8. Quoted in Capaccio, "CIA: Iran Holding Limited Stocks of Biological Weapons."

allows it to attack the ports, oil fields, and cities along the full length of the Persian Gulf coast to the south, and Iran is trying to extend this range by acquiring intermediate-range ballistic missiles through additional foreign purchases and domestic production.

Notwithstanding its known and suspected WMD programs, Iran is a signatory of the Nuclear Non-Proliferation Treaty, Biological Weapons Convention, and Chemical Weapons Convention. Iran's declared civilian nuclear facilities are subject to International Atomic Energy Agency inspection, and the IAEA has never detected or declared an Iranian breach in the safeguards regime.[9] In the 1995 NPT review and extension conference, Iran did not campaign against the indefinite extension of the treaty, as some feared it would. Iran has also played an active and generally helpful role in the establishment of the Organization for the Prohibition of Chemical Weapons (OPCW), which will enforce the CWC.

IRAQ

Perhaps more than any other single factor, the revelations about Iraq's nuclear, biological, chemical, and missile programs that followed the Gulf War have shaped Western—especially American—attitudes toward WMD proliferation. The Gulf War revealed how poorly the coalition was prepared for Iraqi WMD use, and later generated considerable embarrassment because of the revelations that Iraq had developed its WMD capabilities with extensive Western commercial assistance, especially from German companies.[10]

Before the Gulf War, Iraq was known to have a large chemical weapons stockpile, as well as a large number of mobile, extended-range Scud missiles. Iraq was also suspected of having clandestine nuclear and biological weapons programs, but after the war both were revealed to be far more sophisticated and extensive than expected. Because of Saddam Hussein's history of using chemical weapons—first against Iran in 1983–88, and then in 1988 against Iraq's own Kurdish population—the potential for Iraqi chemical (or

---

9. The IAEA has conducted two "visits" (not inspections) at sites suspected to conceal undeclared nuclear activity, and found no evidence of Iranian non-compliance with the safeguards regime. See Vahe Petrossian, "Watchdog Fails to Find Nuclear Bombs: International Atomic Energy Agency's Inspection of Iran's Nuclear Facilities," *Middle East Economic Digest*, Vol. 39, No. 11 (March 17, 1995), p. 7.

10. See Harald Müller, Matthias Dembinski, Alexander Kelle, and Annette Schaper, *From Black Sheep to White Angel? The New German Export Control Policy*, Peace Research Institute Frankfurt (PRIF) Report No. 32, January 1994, pp. 1–2.

even biological) weapons use was of great concern to the coalition partners. Iraq attacked Saudi Arabia and Israel with Scud missiles, but these were armed only with conventional warheads.

UN Security Council Resolutions 687 and 715 prohibit Iraq from possessing nuclear, biological, or chemical weapons; facilities dedicated to producing them; or ballistic missiles with a range greater than 150 kilometers. Since 1991, these resolutions have been actively and generally effectively enforced by the UN Special Commission (UNSCOM) which, despite Iraqi interference and non-cooperation, has supervised the dismantling of Iraq's nuclear programs as well as the destruction of Iraq's chemical weapons and most or all of its prohibited ballistic missiles.[11]

Although Iraq's WMD programs have suffered a significant setback, most American observers believe that much of the Iraqi WMD capability could be reconstituted if the UNSCOM inspections are terminated, especially if UN economic sanctions are also lifted. With respect to its chemical and biological weapons capability, Iraq has retained many of the personnel, infrastructure, and dual-use technologies that it used to build its original arsenal.[12] Iraq would be hard pressed to recreate the ballistic missile capability it had before the Gulf War, but it is currently developing a 100–150 kilometer missile that has the potential for range extension.[13] Moreover, after UN sanctions and inspections are lifted, Iraq is expected to attempt to import longer range ballistic missiles, probably from North Korea or China. Iraq's clandestine nuclear weapons program will be most difficult to reconstitute because of the physical destruction of Iraq's fissile material production facilities. However, Iraq retains significant expertise and infrastructure relevant to the fabrication of simple nuclear weapons, and should therefore be regarded as a high-risk candidate for the illicit acquisition of fissile material abroad, possibly from the former Soviet Union.

---

11. With respect to biological weapons, UNSCOM has not been able to confirm that it has accounted for and destroyed all of Iraq's BW agent. With respect to ballistic missiles, "the United States believes Iraq has hidden a small number (6–16) of mobile launchers and several dozen SCUD-type missiles produced before Operation Desert Storm." OSD, *Proliferation: Threat and Response*, p. 24.

12. Dual-use technologies are those with civilian applications as well as military ones.

13. OSD, *Proliferation: Threat and Response*, p. 24.

LIBYA

One of the most problematic states in the Greater Middle East region, Libya has a long-standing interest in acquiring WMD capabilities. Although Libya is a signatory of the NPT, Muammar Qadhafi's interest in acquiring nuclear weapons dates to the early 1970s. Libya has, however, been largely unsuccessful at acquiring the facilities, expertise, infrastructure, or foreign-supply relationships needed for the indigenous production of nuclear weapons. In the 1970s and 1980s, Libya attempted to purchase complete nuclear weapons from the Soviet Union and China, and to acquire advanced nuclear technology from India and Pakistan. Because of its past record, Libya is a potential risk for illicit nuclear acquisition from the former Soviet Union. Libya is also believed to be attempting to establish a clandestine biological weapons program, but according to the U.S. Department of Defense, Libya's "technical shortcomings, combined with limitations in Libya's overall ability to put agents into deliverable munitions, will preclude production of militarily effective biological warfare systems for the foreseeable future."[14]

Libya's chemical weapons program presents the greatest current challenge to the international community. Libya first used Iranian-made chemical weapons to avert military defeat by Chadian troops in 1987.[15] Libya has also developed a large-scale chemical weapons production facility with extensive foreign—especially German—assistance.[16] During 1988–90, Libya is estimated to have produced 100 tons of blister agent and nerve gas at its Rabta chemical plant, which has now been partially disabled by a fire of suspect origin. However, Libya is in the process of constructing a large underground production complex at Tarhunah, which U.S. intelligence believes Libya intends to use as a secure CW production facility. Libya adheres to the Arab League decision not to sign the CWC so long as Israel does not accede to the NPT.

Finally, Libya possesses a number of 300–kilometer range Scud missiles acquired from the Soviet Union in the 1970s. The range of these missiles is not great enough to allow Libya to strike targets in Europe or Israel. Libya also currently lacks the technical capacity and

---

14. Ibid., p. 27.

15. OSD, *Proliferation: Threat and Response*, p. 25.

16. See Dan Petreanu, "The Business That Backfired," *Jerusalem Post*, January 27, 1989; and Aharon Levran, "The Libyan-German Chemical Axis," *Jerusalem Post*, March 16, 1990.

foreign-supplier relationships to produce longer-range ballistic missiles indigenously. However, like Iran, Libya is believed to be interested in acquiring longer-range ballistic missiles from foreign suppliers willing to ignore the Missile Technology Control Regime (MTCR)—specifically North Korea. If Libya were to acquire the Nodong missile from North Korea—which, although not yet produced, will have an estimated range of up to 1,000 kilometers—Qadhafi would be able to jeopardize targets in France (Corsica), Italy, Greece, Turkey, and Israel.

ISRAEL

Israel is the Middle East's dominant conventional military power and only nuclear-armed state, possessing an estimated 70–80 nuclear weapons (some estimates are considerably higher), some of which may be enhanced-yield, tritium-"boosted" weapons.[17] Israel also possesses intermediate-range ballistic missiles, a significant chemical weapons arsenal, and possibly a biological weapons program. Despite all this, however, no Western state regards Israel's WMD capabilities as a major threat to regional security or stability, and Israel is not a focus of U.S. or European nonproliferation policy. In general, the West treats Israel's WMD programs with tacit approval because of Israel's character as an advanced industrial democracy, its important role as a strategic ally in the region, and the strong cultural and historical ties that bind Israel to the West. Israel is not a party to the NPT or BWC but has signed the CWC. In the U.S.-European context, Israel's WMD capabilities are significant not as a threat but as a complication to regional nonproliferation efforts.

SYRIA

Syria has a large chemical weapons stockpile and is believed also to have a clandestine biological weapons program. Syria has a modest but growing arsenal of Scud short-range ballistic missiles, some of which can be or have been equipped for chemical weapons delivery,[18] as well as an indigenous range-extension capability acquired from North Korea. Yet despite Syria's proximity to Israel, Syria's known and suspected WMD programs have not been a major political issue

---

17. Leonard S. Spector, Mark G. McDonough, and Evan S. Medeiros, *Tracking Nuclear Proliferation* (Washington, D.C.: Carnegie Endowment for International Peace, 1995), pp. 135–139.

18. Steve Rodan, "Chemical, Biological Threats Loom Large in U.S.-Israeli Talks," *Defense News*, December 2–8, 1996, p. 6.

in the West's relations with Syria. The main reasons for this lack of attention are Syria's critical role in the Middle East peace process and its lack of an attention-grabbing nuclear program. It is also assumed that Syrian WMD use will be held in check by Israeli deterrence. In recent years, Western policy toward Syria has focused instead on Syria's role in the Middle East peace process and its support of international terrorism. Syria is a party to the NPT and BWC but has linked its signing of the CWC to Israel's accession to the NPT as a non-nuclear weapons state.

EGYPT

In the early 1960s, Egypt had a nuclear research program that appeared to be aimed at developing a nuclear weapons capability, but this program was abandoned long ago, and Egypt has acceded to the NPT. Egypt is believed to possess a chemical weapons stockpile, is suspected of having a biological weapons program, and has a handful of short-range Scud ballistic missiles.

Of the Arab states, Egypt has been the most aggressive in calling attention to Israel's nuclear weapons program, and was the principal organizer of the Arab League's rejection of the CWC on the grounds that Israel must first renounce its nuclear capability and accede to the NPT as a non-nuclear weapons state. Egypt also has not signed the BWC. Egypt's chemical (and possible biological) weapons program has received even less international attention than Syria's. This is explained by several factors: Egypt does not support international terrorism, is at peace with Israel, and—like Syria—would probably be deterred from WMD use by Israel if hostilities resumed. With an annual contribution of approximately $2 billion to the Egyptian economy, the United States has a significant capacity to exert leverage over Egypt's WMD policies, as it did prior to the 1995 NPT review and extension conference, persuading Egypt to accept the indefinite and unconditional extension of the treaty.

ALGERIA

Although its internal struggle with Islamic fundamentalism holds the worried attention of most international observers (especially those in southern Europe), Algeria is no longer regarded as a particularly acute proliferation threat in the Greater Middle East. Algeria has no ballistic missiles and is not suspected of having a chemical or biological weapons program. Algeria has signed and ratified the CWC. However, Algeria does possess two nuclear research reactors (the larger bought from China, the smaller from Argentina) and a small plutonium reprocessing laboratory. These facilities were discovered by U.S. intelligence in 1991 in circumstances that gave rise to suspicions that Algeria's military government harbored secret nuclear ambitions.[19] Algeria's subsequent accession to the NPT and acceptance of IAEA safeguards at its nuclear facilities have reduced the international community's suspicions, but concerns remain.

Past U.S. and European Policy Responses

This section describes the differences and similarities in the U.S. and European policy responses to three specific WMD problems in the Greater Middle East: the question of Iran's clandestine nuclear program; the international response to the Libyan chemical weapons program; and the preparation of allied military forces for conflict against WMD-armed states, a mission referred to as "counterproliferation" in the United States.

IRAN

Policy toward Iran has presented one of the most poisonous U.S.-European disputes in recent memory. Since 1993, the Clinton administration has sought to isolate and weaken both Iran and Iraq through a policy of "dual containment."[20] This policy holds that Iran is an implacably hostile state bent on achieving regional hegemony and acquiring nuclear weapons, with a long record of sponsoring international terrorism and political assassinations abroad. On the other hand, the European Union and especially Germany regard Iran as too important to ignore, and have maintained a policy of "critical dialogue" with Iran. This policy seeks to moderate Iran's international behavior through extensive political and commercial engagement, which is expected to enhance the domestic influence of the Iranian moderates, represented by President Ali Akbar Hashemi Rafsanjani, over the extremists, represented by the clerics.

The WMD issue plays a role in both the American and European policies toward Iran, but it has not been a dominant consideration. For the United States, knowledge of the Iranian WMD programs serves mainly to confirm the policy impulses in the Clinton administration, which arise out of other concerns, especially Iran's sponsorship of

---

19. See Spector, McDonough, and Medeiros, *Tracking Nuclear Proliferation*, p. 113.

20. See Anthony Lake, "Confronting Backlash States," *Foreign Affairs*, Vol. 73, No. 2 (March/April 1994), pp. 45–55.

terrorism and the personal animosity toward Iran felt by some U.S. officials. U.S. policy toward Iran has been harshly criticized by the Europeans for what they see as its empty rhetoric, incoherence, and "unhealthy obsession" with Tehran.[21] Since U.S. firms had become heavily involved in Iran's oil trade by 1993–94, the Europeans resented being lectured by the United States about their commercial ties with Iran.[22]

In response to the allies' charges of hypocrisy, congressional pressure, and several new terrorist incidents with possible Iranian connections, the Clinton administration decided to curtail U.S. commercial ties with Iran in 1995. In March 1995, President Clinton signed into law the Iran Sanctions Act of 1995, which imposed a unilateral U.S. economic embargo on Iran (albeit with some exceptions for the transit of Caspian oil). The president also canceled a contract worth $600 million between Iran and the U.S. firm Conoco to develop two oil fields near Sirri Island in the Persian Gulf. (This contract was later acquired by a French firm.) Then, in August 1996, the president signed the Iran and Libya Sanctions Act of 1996, which imposes third-party punitive sanctions on foreign companies that invest more than $40 million in the Iranian energy sector. This last piece of legislation has provoked howls of protests from the allies, especially the Europeans, who have challenged the legality of these third-party sanctions and threatened retaliatory action.

The Europeans' policy of "critical dialogue" with Iran is coming under attack for different reasons. Germany, in particular, has deep commercial, political, and even intelligence ties to Iran, and Bonn has supported this relationship through an exchange of high-level visits, rescheduling Iran's $8.6 billion debt to Germany, and offering Iran extensive export credits for the purchase of high-technology German products.[23] But this policy has come under attack in Germany as the direct involvement of the Iranian government in the assassination of its political opponents in foreign countries has become more widely known. In particular, the "Mykonos affair," a

---

21. For a related critique, see Fawaz Gerges, "Washington's Misguided Iran Policy," *Survival*, Vol. 38, No. 4 (Winter 1996–97), pp. 5–15.

22. See Rick Atkinson, "Divergent Policies Toward Iran Strain U.S.-German Relations," *Washington Post*, June 27, 1996, p. A21; and Vahe Petrossian, "U.S. Escalates War of Words against Iran," *Middle East Economic Digest*, Vol. 40, No. 35 (August 30, 1996), p. 2.

23. For a full discussion of the German-Iranian relationship, see Charles Lane, "Germany's New Ostpolitik," *Foreign Affairs*, Vol. 74, No. 6 (November/December 1995), pp. 77–89.

September 1992 assassination of three Kurdish leaders in a Berlin restaurant, caused German federal prosecutors to issue an international arrest warrant in March 1996 for the head of the Iranian intelligence service, Ali Fallahian, who had been officially received at the Kanzleramt in October 1993.[24] In April 1997, a German court found the Iranian government guilty of having ordered the Mykonos assassinations, a finding which has greatly strained Iran's relations with Germany and most other European states. By the German government's own admission, the critical dialogue with Iran has shown few tangible results in terms of moderation in Iranian behavior.

The dominant factor in the Europeans' policy toward Iran has been exports and, more recently, the embarrassment caused by new evidence of Iran's sponsorship of assassination and terrorism abroad.[25] On the proliferation issue, the Europeans are generally more skeptical of intelligence reports on Iran's WMD programs than is the United States,[26] and most of the Europeans are less concerned by the prospect of a WMD-armed Iran because they do not anticipate being involved in military conflict with Iran. These differences have made it virtually impossible for the allies to formulate a constructive joint policy toward the Iranian proliferation problem, much less exercise any kind of collective coercive pressure to dissuade and deter Iran from pursuing its WMD ambitions.

LIBYA

The Americans and the Europeans are also divided in their policies toward Libya, though less severely than in the case of Iran. Like Iran, Libya has a long history of sponsoring international terrorism, opposing the Middle East peace process, pursuing regional adventures, and scheming to acquire WMD. This pattern of behavior has made the

---

24. For full details, see Thomas Sancton, "Iran's State of Terror," *Time*, November 11, 1996, p. 78.

25. It should be noted that the Europeans—especially the Germans—have been showing a greater willingness and ability than they did in the 1980s to limit exports of products having a clear potential to assist an Iranian WMD program. European exports are greatly assisting Iran to develop its conventional military and its overall technical infrastructure, but they do not appear to be directly contributing to WMD programs as they did in Iraq and Libya in the 1980s. See Müller, Dembinski, Kelle, and Schaper, *From Black Sheep to White Angel?*

26. In particular, European observers have tended to stress Iran's clean record with the IAEA, including two unprecedented "visits" to suspect but undeclared nuclear facilities in Iran. See Petrossian, "Watchdog Fails to Find Nuclear Bombs."

United States hostile toward Libya. Tripoli has been far less adept at courting European favor than Tehran. Muammar Qadhafi has managed to alienate much of Europe by harboring the terrorists who destroyed Pan Am Flight 103 over Lockerbie, Scotland; firing Scud missiles at Italian islands; attacking French forces in Chad; endorsing the Basque terrorists in Spain; and supporting the Irish Republican Army.[27] As a result of world condemnation of its support for international terrorism, Libya has been subject to an international arms and aviation embargo since January 1992,[28] as well as a limited freeze on Libyan government assets held abroad since November 1993.[29]

Despite some similarities in U.S. and European assessments of Libya, the United States has generally pressed for a more severe policy against Libya than the Europeans are willing to support. The United Nations sanctions on Libya, for example, do not apply to Libya's oil exports, not least because this step was opposed by the Europeans.[30] Concern that the Europeans were insufficiently committed to compelling Libya to renounce its support for terrorism and WMD programs was a key reason why the U.S. Congress decided to add Libya to the Iran and Libya Sanctions Act of 1996, which requires the imposition of third-party sanctions on foreign companies that invest in Libya's oil industry.

With respect to Libya's WMD programs, there are still differences between the United States and the Europeans, but export controls are no longer a highly divisive issue. The Libyan CW program was constructed with extensive assistance from European—especially German—companies. Since the revelation of this connection in the late 1980s, the Europeans have begun to improve their export control systems and to view industrial or chemical exports to Libya with greater suspicion.

The key issue that continues to divide the allies is preventive military action. This disagreement dates back to the 1986 air strikes against Libya, when France refused to allow U.S. aircraft to fly through its air space, and the United States was widely criticized around Europe for its "cowboy" foreign policy. More recently, however, U.S. Defense

---

27. See Robert Waller, "The Libyan Threat to the Mediterranean," *Jane's Intelligence Review*, Vol. 8, No. 5 (May 1, 1996).

28. United Nations Security Council Resolution 748, March 31, 1992.

29. United Nations Security Council Resolution 883, November 11, 1993.

30. Robert Waller, "Libyan CW Raises the Issue of Pre-Emption," *Jane's Intelligence Review*, Vol. 8, No. 11 (November 1, 1996).

Secretary William Perry stated in April 1996 that the United States would not allow Libya to complete construction of its underground chemical weapons plant at Tarhunah. Asked about the use of the U.S. military to achieve this aim, Perry stated, "I wouldn't rule anything out, or anything in."[31] The Europeans have been basically silent on this issue. Indeed, the Clinton administration never really seems to have expected or sought European support for its explicit threat against the Libyan CW program, and in fact invested considerably more political capital into securing Egyptian support for the hard-line policy than it did with the NATO allies.

It is, of course, not a foregone conclusion that the United States will take preventive military action against the Libyan chemical weapons program. An underground production facility at Tarhunah would be a very hard target to destroy by conventional means, and while the Department of Defense is making a major investment in improving its "hard and/or deeply buried target defeat capability" (HDBTDC),[32] there is little optimism that a reliable technique will be found to destroy a bunker protected by 30 meters of rock and reinforced concrete. The relevant political issue between the allies, however, is not so much one of planning for an attack, but instead of issuing a threat that the Libyan government must take seriously, with the hope that this threat will cause Qadhafi to decide against completing this underground facility or beginning chemical weapons production there. The fact that the United States must issue such threats alone, rather than in unison with its closest allies, reduces their gravity and thus their coercive power.

COUNTERPROLIFERATION

For the United States, a key lesson of the Gulf War was that U.S. military forces were ill-prepared to fight a war against an adversary able and willing to use WMD. Fortunately, Saddam Hussein did not use chemical or biological weapons against the coalition arrayed against him. Since most other potential military adversaries of the United States also possess some form of WMD, U.S. defense planners quickly identified the need to improve the U.S. military's capacity

---

31. "USA Warns Libya on CW," *Jane's Defense Weekly*, Vol. 25, No. 15 (April 10, 1996), p. 3.

32. See Counterproliferation Program Review Committee (CPRC), *Report on the Activities and Programs for Countering Proliferation* (Washington, D.C.: Department of Defense, May 1996), pp. 42–43.

to prevail in proliferated environments. Thus the "Defense Counterproliferation Initiative" was formally announced by former Defense Secretary Les Aspin in September 1993, and was shortly thereafter presented to the NATO defense ministers as a sensible thing for the alliance to undertake as well.

The emphasis of the counterproliferation initiative has been on distinctly military tasks: identifying specific battlefield deficiencies related to WMD use, developing action plans to remedy these deficiencies, and implementing these plans within the Department of Defense.[33] Although the counterproliferation initiative has engendered some controversy and resistance within the United States,[34] the Department of Defense is slowly improving its capacity to cope with WMD-related contingencies, especially in the areas of battlefield surveillance, passive defense, active defense (including theater missile defense), and hard-target counterforce. Given the U.S. desire to ensure that NATO's combined capacity to cope with WMD contingencies is at least roughly comparable to that of the United States, and more generally to ensure that the alliance remains relevant to the security threats of the future, the United States has pressed the allies to embrace counterproliferation as their own. To date, however, most of the European allies have been slow in doing so.[35]

After an initially frosty European reception of the Americans' counterproliferation concept,[36] in January 1994 the North Atlantic

---

33. In Chapter 12 in this volume, Joanna Spear essentially misses the point about counterproliferation, since she fails to note that this program of military innovations does not replace U.S. nonproliferation policy. It is absurd to suggest that U.S. nonproliferation policy is "decided at an abstract global level," and even if this were true, it would have nothing to do with the fact that the U.S. armed forces are in the process of improving their warfighting capabilities against a limited number of potential regional adversaries known or suspected of possessing WMD.

34. For a U.S. critique, see Leonard S. Spector, "Neo-Nonproliferation," *Survival*, Vol. 37, No. 1 (Spring 1995), pp. 66–85.

35. Great Britain and France have been considerably more engaged than other European states by the project of preparing their forces for proliferated environments, mainly because these two states have extensive experience with WMD programs themselves, and because they tend to take the idea of foreign military intervention seriously. See Robert Joseph, "Proliferation, Counterproliferation, and NATO," *Survival*, Vol. 38, No. 1 (Spring 1996), pp. 16–18; and David S. Yost, "U.S. Nuclear Weapons in Europe: Prospects and Priorities," Defense Programs at Sandia National Laboratory, Future Roles Series Paper No. 7, December 1996, pp. 18–26.

36. See Natalie J. Goldring, "Skittish on Counterproliferation," *Bulletin of the Atomic Scientists*, Vol. 50, No. 2 (March/April 1994), pp. 12–13; and Matthias

Council (NAC) directed the alliance governments to develop an agreed "policy framework" for addressing the proliferation problem, and created a Senior Political-Military Group on Proliferation and a Senior Defense Group on Proliferation (DGP). While the political group has done little, the high-level DGP has completed three major studies on proliferation issues for the alliance. The first was a December 1994 risk assessment, which drew on existing U.S. and other nations' intelligence estimates and identified the WMD threats to NATO territories, to NATO forces involved in regional interventions, and to NATO forces conducting peacekeeping or humanitarian missions. The second was a November 1995 needs assessment, which closely tracked the Department of Defense's previous studies of its own counterproliferation deficiencies. The third was a June 1996 report containing thirty-nine specific action plans for improvements in NATO's operational capacity to cope with WMD contingencies.[37] The alliance leadership has accepted each document, and NATO is now attempting to insert the recommendations into the alliance's complicated force planning process, which seeks to translate broad policy guidance into real operational capabilities.[38] This work is an important first step for NATO, which would not have been achieved without persistent American pressure.

While it is too early to pass judgment on NATO's effort at incorporating the ideas of counterproliferation into its own military structure, it is clear that this process will be a slow and difficult one. For one thing, real costs are involved in any systematic effort to improve a military force's capacity to cope with WMD-armed adversaries. While these costs are small as a percentage of aggregate expenditures, the competition for funding has grown especially stiff as defense budgets shrink throughout the alliance, and as NATO members contemplate significant expenditures related to enlargement. The alliance's two-year force planning process offers ample opportunity for delay, task avoidance, and the silent snuffing out of new

---

Dembinski, Alexander Kelle, and Harald Müller, *NATO and Nonproliferation: A Critical Appraisal*, PRIF Report No. 33, April 1994, pp. 42–45.

37. For a detailed treatment of this work, see Ashton B. Carter and David B. Omand, "Countering the Proliferation Risks: Adapting the Alliance to the New Security Environment," *NATO Review*, Vol. 44, No. 5 (September 1996), pp. 10–15; and Joseph, "Proliferation, Counterproliferation, and NATO," pp. 111–130.

38. See Guy B. Roberts, "NATO's Response to the Proliferation of Weapons of Mass Destruction: The Emerging Reality of NATO's Ambitious Program," U.S. Air Force Academy Institute for National Security Studies, September 1996, pp. 36–42.

ideas. More important, the NATO force planning process reflects rather than defines the defense priorities of the member states. Despite the alliance's acceptance of three important reports and a few joint statements, it is far from clear that countering WMD proliferation—much less fighting WMD-armed foes—is in fact a priority for most NATO governments and militaries.

NATO's ambivalence about counterproliferation is embedded in the larger debate about what the post–Cold War mission of the alliance ought to be. The dominant European view is that the purpose of the alliance is to create a stable new European security order built around an enlarged NATO. While the U.S. government clearly shares this goal, the United States has a broader strategic agenda, which has at its core a recognition of the threats to Western interests and freedom of action represented by WMD-armed adversaries in relevant regions. Weapons of mass destruction have little or no bearing on NATO's ability to fulfill the mission of greatest concern to the Europeans. A central conclusion of the DGP's December 1994 proliferation risk assessment was that the most serious near-term WMD threat was not to NATO territories or NATO forces on peacekeeping missions, but to NATO forces involved in regional interventions in the south.[39] Yet it is precisely this potential mission for NATO that most divides the allies. Because the Europeans have often disapproved of U.S. military activity in the Greater Middle East and have never consistently followed the U.S. lead in this region, there is a reluctance to see NATO modernized in a way which suggests it may be involved in a U.S.-led military intervention in North Africa, the Levant, or the Persian Gulf. Thus, until the issue of NATO's power projection role in the Greater Middle East is finally resolved, doubts and delays are likely to attend any effort to enhance the alliance's military capacity to prevail in WMD environments.

Yet even if NATO does not undertake joint planning and preparations for WMD contingencies, the counterproliferation dialogue within the alliance still serves the useful function of educating the European national security establishments on proliferation hazards in the emerging international environment. In this sense, NATO is serving as a conduit for updating the strategic assumptions of the European security elite. The effects of this long-term process will become visible principally in national nonproliferation policies, not in NATO's institutional adaptation. In this respect, the increasing

---

39. Ibid., pp. 40–42.

frequency of intelligence-sharing within NATO councils is playing an especially important role, since most of the NATO states cannot independently uncover reliable evidence of clandestine WMD programs abroad. This intelligence-sharing contributes to the Europeans' growing recognition of the extent and seriousness of the WMD proliferation problem.

Explanations for the U.S.-European Policy Differences

Most of the reasons that Americans and Europeans differ on proliferation issues in the Greater Middle East can be traced to six tendencies: different conceptions of the national interest; different domestic political importance of export markets; poor diplomacy; disagreements about the "facts" of proliferation in the Greater Middle East; disagreements about the most appropriate methods for dealing with known and suspected proliferants; and free-riding.

CONCEPTIONS OF THE NATIONAL INTEREST

Perhaps the most important explanation for the differences in the U.S. and European policy responses to WMD issues in the Greater Middle East is that the two sides conceive of their national interests in quite different ways.[40] It is clear, for instance, that American elite opinion regards an array of interests in the Greater Middle East as "vital": maintaining a reliable flow of oil from the Persian Gulf at reasonable prices; ensuring the survival of Israel; maintaining the freedom of naval movement and military action; and preventing and reversing WMD proliferation. It is conceivable that the United States would go to war to protect any of these interests—a good working definition of "vital." By this standard, however, it is not at all clear that the Europeans have retained any vital interests in the Greater Middle East (the French in North Africa being the main exception). The issues of most immediate importance to the European elites tend to be uniquely European tasks, such as achieving a European monetary union or promoting stability in Eastern Europe. While many European states see significant interests at stake in the Greater Middle East, there are few if any issues for which a European state would readily shed blood.[41] According to one close European

---

40. Indeed, some European states—Germany is the signal case—are reluctant even to talk about a distinctly national interest.

41. American and European leaders also often agree on which particular international outcomes are or are not desirable. (Thus there is no real disagreement that

observer of these issues, "public opinion in Western Europe is barely prepared, for the time being at least, to discuss risks and threats involving the proliferation of weapons of mass destruction."[42] Nonproliferation receives consistent rhetorical treatment in the foreign policies of the leading European states, but the substance of their policies and behavior belies the idea that nonproliferation—even in a nearby region like the Middle East—is a vital interest for Europe.

DOMESTIC IMPORTANCE OF EXPORT MARKETS

In general, the priority accorded to protecting or creating export markets relative to most other strategic or normative interests (e.g., nonproliferation or human rights) is higher in the Europeans' foreign policies than in U.S. foreign policy. As a result, the Europeans are both less committed to accepting or enforcing export controls on WMD-related goods to potential proliferants and regional aggressors, and less willing than the United States to exert political pressure or enact economic sanctions as part of a larger strategy of manipulating a state's behavior. This reduces the international community's ability to roll back proliferation where it occurs.

There are several possible explanations for this basic difference in European and American foreign policies. The first is that the Europeans have given priority to commercial interests because their alliance with the United States has made them exceptionally secure from external threats—a variant of the "free-riding" hypothesis discussed below. A second possible explanation lies in the relative importance of foreign trade to the U.S. and European economies: exports account for about 25 percent in the European Union's gross domestic product (GDP), but only about 10–11 percent of U.S. GDP. A third explanation lies in the nature of the European "social contract," which accords the state great responsibility for protecting the economic well-being of the citizenry. Most of the continental

---

democracy, human rights, and nonproliferation are preferable to their alternatives—a great help in the drafting of summit communiqués.) But there are major differences in the priorities attached to these interests, as well as the willingness to bear real costs for their defense. This has been especially apparent with respect to WMD proliferation, which has risen to the top of the U.S. security agenda and drives billions of dollars of U.S. expenditure on programs like Nunn-Lugar and the counterproliferation initiative, neither of which has any analog in any European state.

42. Joachim Krause, "Proliferation Risks and their Strategic Relevance: What Role for NATO?" *Survival*, Vol. 37, No. 2 (Summer 1995), p. 135.

European governments remain deeply committed to the continued viability of their manufacturing and industrial sectors, the source of the high-paying jobs for skilled labor that are seen as essential to the preservation of Europe's preferred social order. In contrast, there is less of a presumption that the U.S. government is responsible for protecting any particular type of job or industrial sector.

POOR DIPLOMACY

Poor diplomacy is another possible explanation for the different American and European approaches to the problems of WMD proliferation. In some cases, the allies may disagree simply because one side has not worked hard or skillfully enough at forging a common position. The European side often sees the United States as an imperious leader that refuses to accept the Europeans on an equal basis and that fails to understand the European governments' domestic political constraints. This critique of U.S. diplomacy implies that there may be times when a joint compromise position is possible but is not achieved for lack of effort or skill.

It is true that the United States is often unwilling or unable to compromise on its preferred approach to WMD issues. Sometimes this may result from a congressional mandate, other times from the hubris of a superpower. American policymakers also may feel that they know best how to cope with the specific WMD threats, and that even with highly effective diplomacy, the allies will simply refuse to go along with the preferred U.S. policies. Often, however, the United States does consult with the Europeans on these key issues—there is no shortage of workable communications channels—but its arguments leave the allies unmoved. The lack of cooperation has as much or more to do with the substance of the U.S. arguments as with the effectiveness of their delivery.

DISAGREEMENTS ABOUT THE FACTS

The fourth general reason why the United States and the Europeans have failed to cooperate more is that they sometimes disagree about the facts of WMD proliferation. Legitimate disagreements about proliferation facts can stem from two possible sources: different data, and dissimilar interpretations of the data. Between allies like the United States and the Western Europeans, the differing availability of data on WMD proliferation is basically an issue of intelligence-sharing, which the U.S. intelligence community has reluctantly begun to do on a limited basis within the alliance.[43] However, interpretations of inconclusive intelligence (especially if it has been supplied by an interested foreign power, such as the United States) will be influenced by the assumptions and biases of the interpreter. In the case of Iran, where the direct evidence of a clandestine Iranian nuclear program appears to be more suggestive than conclusive, there is little doubt that the Clinton administration's interpretation of the available data has been affected by the view that the Iranian theocracy is a fanatical, terrorist-sponsoring regime, implacably hostile to the United States. The prevailing European interpretation of Iran's nuclear program (as well as its sponsorship of terrorism) appears to be based on fairly benign assumptions about the intentions of the Iranian "moderates," which fits well with the Europeans' policy of engagement and critical dialogue.

DISAGREEMENTS ABOUT APPROPRIATE METHODS

The fifth set of explanations for the different U.S. and European approaches to WMD problems in the Greater Middle East has to do with different strategic theories or methods. In some cases, the United States and its European allies agree roughly in their assessments of the basic facts of a situation and also in their ultimate objectives, but still have quite different ideas for how they would like to see the issue resolved. This phenomenon is most graphically visible in the differences between U.S. and European policies toward Iran and, to a lesser extent, Libya, where there is a fundamental disagreement over the relative merits of engagement and isolation. Similarly, with respect to the counterproliferation issue, there remains a difference of opinion over the effects that a more militarized policy will have on consensual nonproliferation regimes.

FREE-RIDING

Finally, the lack of U.S.-European cooperation across a range of WMD proliferation issues can be at least partly explained as European "free-riding" on American efforts. Nonproliferation is a classic public good, like clean air or the freedom of navigation in the Persian

---

43. While the basic conclusions of an intelligence estimate can usually be revealed to allies, the hard evidence that supports these conclusions is often highly classified. This evidence would not normally be distributed even within a government, much less to a foreign one, but exceptions are sometimes made for close allies on important issues.

Gulf. This gives all other states an incentive to free-ride—that is, to refrain from contributing—on the American efforts to contain, reverse, or counter WMD proliferation.[44] The United States has underwritten European security for the past five decades, and there is no question that both sides have grown accustomed to this relationship. To some extent, therefore, Americans must simply accept a certain amount of free-riding on the collective security generated by U.S. power and presence. Indeed, leadership often depends on a willingness to bear a disproportionately large share of the costs involved in generating international public goods. Burden-sharing has always been contentious within the alliance. Hence, while this problem must be recognized and dealt with diplomatically, one should not make too much of it—so long, of course, as the allies do not go so far as to undercut the U.S. effort to limit the long-term WMD threat.

Policy Prescriptions

The United States and its European allies have slowly begun to consider their options for greater collaboration on a variety of WMD issues, but much more should be done in this area. This section presents five proposals for enhanced U.S.-European cooperation on WMD proliferation issues: first, improved U.S. diplomatic efforts to build consensus on WMD issues; second, a systematic effort to address the obstacles to routine intelligence sharing on WMD issues within the alliance; third, a joint effort to develop a common strategy of American and European policies toward Iran; fourth, the implementation of NATO's counterproliferation agenda already developed by the DGP, including the development of a joint U.S.-European acquisition and deployment strategy for theater ballistic missile defense; and fifth, the beginning of a strategic relationship between NATO and Israel. Underlying all of these recommendations is the imperative of continued strong security ties between the United States and Europe.

IMPROVE U.S. DIPLOMATIC EFFORTS TO BUILD CONSENSUS

The United States should give greater priority to securing European support and cooperation on WMD issues worldwide. Washington already devotes some effort to this task, but U.S.-European consulta-

---

44. For an explicit complaint by a U.S. official against European free-riding, see David E. Sanger, "U.S. Blames Allies for Undercutting its China Policy," *New York Times,* June 12, 1996, p. 1.

tion on WMD issues should be more systematic and should occur earlier, more frequently, and at higher levels in the policymaking process than has been the case. These issues should be discussed bilaterally as well as multilaterally (most importantly within NATO). Given the importance of the WMD issue to the United States, U.S. leaders should make every effort to convince their European counterparts of the gravity of the long-term proliferation threat, and of the importance of a more united international bulwark against the rising WMD tide. At the same time, though with greater subtlety, Washington should inform its allies that free-riding on U.S. nonproliferation and counterproliferation efforts is unacceptable.

A key element in the U.S. strategy of consensus-building on WMD issues should be a systematic effort to redirect and strengthen the individual allies' national security elites. The United States should take the lead in bringing all security researchers and officials in the alliance to focus on WMD proliferation and its long-term strategic consequences. Over time, Europe's own national security elites should come to play a much greater role in introducing WMD proliferation as a major issue for their countries' foreign policies. The U.S. government should use its influence to build WMD education into the curricula of all military academies, training facilities, and staff colleges in the alliance; direct NATO's funding of academic research and symposia for joint U.S.-European work on proliferation issues; and support much more extensive military-to-military and civilian-to-military collaboration on all aspects of the proliferation problem, from large-scale joint military exercises to small-scale policy development research.

The United States should also enhance the role of WMD issues in its own policy toward NATO. To date, the agenda for NATO reform has been driven for the most part by issues of greater strategic import to the European governments than the U.S. government, such as enlargement and Bosnia. Washington should press harder to include the issues of greatest concern to the U.S. national security community and should in general seek to build NATO into an institution that does more than promote democracy and stability in Europe. While European democracy and stability are important U.S. objectives, the parts of Europe that constitute NATO are already among the world's most reliably stable. The U.S. government should have a clear sense that the world's most significant alliance should not be excessively parochial or inward-looking, but should instead take up the most pressing strategic issues of the era. Just as the Europeans look to the

United States for the extension of a security guarantee to Eastern Europe or to bring peace to Bosnia, the United States should look to the Europeans to pull their weight on the nonproliferation front.

ADDRESS OBSTACLES TO INTELLIGENCE-SHARING

U.S.-European intelligence-sharing on proliferation issues should become routine and should be institutionalized in NATO. If the Europeans are to take the WMD problem seriously, they need to know more about it. The independent ability of most of the European allies to collect, process, and analyze intelligence on WMD proliferation abroad is limited. The effects of this on European proliferation policy are recognized by U.S. government officials, and some progress has been made toward sharing U.S. intelligence on proliferation with the allies. The United States has shared some intelligence on illicit Iranian purchases of sensitive nuclear technology with some allies on a bilateral basis (Germany, for example), and the July 1996 report of the DGP recommended the creation of a central NATO database on proliferation information. To date, however, most U.S. intelligence-sharing has resulted from discrete political impulses. Intelligence-sharing on proliferation issues is not a routine matter within NATO or between the United States and its allies, which reduces its impact on allied thinking and makes the U.S. motives for sharing information more suspect.

The key obstacles to a more formal intelligence-sharing process are bureaucratic in nature and can only be overcome through sustained political pressure. Habits of secrecy are deeply ingrained in all intelligence services, and are perpetuated by the concern that the sharing of high-quality intelligence might reveal something sensitive about the intelligence service's sources and methods. These concerns are partially justified, especially with respect to human intelligence, since different agencies and countries have different standards of internal security. But the answer to this problem should be an alliance-wide initiative to improve the quality and extent of intelligence-sharing, and to give national intelligence officials a greater stake in, and responsibility for, intelligence-sharing within the alliance on issues of high political importance, such as WMD. Senior representatives from NATO's intelligence and counterintelligence services should be ordered by their presidents and prime ministers to meet regularly and frequently to assess the quality and problems of intelligence cooperation within the alliance, and should be required to report on the specific improvements in national security procedures which they regard as necessary for more extensive information-sharing. Once the national intelligence bureaucracies become more accustomed to substantive collaboration, more ambitious ideas for intelligence-sharing should be considered, such as the establishment of a NATO proliferation risk and analysis center with a capacity to receive and process raw intelligence data provided directly by the NATO member states.[45]

DEVELOP A COMMON STRATEGY TOWARD IRAN

At the next NATO summit, the leaders of the alliance should instruct their governments to conduct a joint review of their collective policies toward Iran, and to formulate a proposal for a common policy by the time of the subsequent summit. It appears that both sides are approaching the realization that their policies toward Iran need to be rethought. Iran has been the single most divisive issue for the United States and its European allies in the Greater Middle East, and rather than allow this problem to fester, all concerned governments should give priority to the task of forging a common approach to Tehran.

In the interest of presenting Iran with a united international front, the Clinton administration should be prepared to compromise on its policy of strict isolation. The Clinton administration should be prepared to defy Congress on the third-party sanctions against European firms investing in the Iran oil sector. The Europeans, on the other hand, should recognize that their four-year policy of critical dialogue has failed to moderate Iran's foreign behavior. European policy toward Iran should de-emphasize commercial opportunism and elevate the larger strategic concerns of denying Iran access to greater WMD capabilities (most importantly nuclear weapons), halting Iran's sponsorship of terrorism, and improving the West's ability to deter Iran from acts that could destabilize the Persian Gulf.

The United States and the Europeans have major differences over Iran, but they also share several important objectives. For purely pragmatic reasons, therefore, both sides should accept that their bitter division over tactical issues impairs their capacity to influence Iran's behavior in any direction, and therefore that they would be better off with a combined approach to Iran. For this reason, NATO should conduct a joint review of policy toward Iran, and the alliance leaders should commit themselves to genuine collaboration and joint action *vis-à-vis* Iran. This joint policy should include clear perfor-

---

45. This proposal is made in Roberts, "NATO's Response," pp. 51–57.

mance criteria for Iran on the WMD and terrorism issues, as well as a commitment by the NATO partners to take retaliatory action against Iran if evidence of an Iranian transgression emerges.[46]

BUILD ON NATO'S COUNTERPROLIFERATION ROLE

NATO should proceed vigorously with its plans to improve its armed forces' capacity to cope with WMD contingencies, and should pursue the joint development, acquisition, and deployment of a theater missile defense system suitable to the alliance's needs. Through the work already done by the DGP, NATO has developed a reasonably comprehensive and detailed plan for improving its military forces' capacity to operate in proliferated environments. This should be implemented promptly to remedy the NATO armed forces' most glaring deficiencies in the WMD area. However, pushing this agenda through NATO's force-planning process will require a sustained, high-level commitment and a willingness by the NATO governments to bear substantial costs. It will also require the alliance to manage the familiar problem posed by the competing acquisition priorities of the alliance's defense industries. There are no simple solutions to these problems. Improved diplomacy and proliferation-education efforts will help over the long term, but in the near term these obstacles can only be overcome through aggressive political leadership, most importantly from Washington.

The alliance should also develop and implement a joint theater missile defense acquisition and deployment program. This issue has been discussed within the alliance, but no real progress has been made toward developing a NATO-based defense against the missile threat that is emerging along Europe's southern tier. The United States has a robust missile defense acquisition program, and because most of the systems being developed are mobile, the alliance can probably expect that U.S. theater missile defenses would be deployed in Europe to defend European cities against a missile attack in a North African or Middle Eastern crisis. From a U.S. perspective, however, this free-riding on U.S. missile defense capabilities is politically intolerable, and the Europeans should be expected to make a meaningful contribution to the development and deployment of a defensive system from which all NATO members potentially benefit.

Yet it is important to recognize that even if the alliance carries out the technical recommendations contained in the DGP's reports, the

---

46. For a related proposal, see Chapter 1 by Robert Satloff in this volume.

basic political problem of using NATO as a nonproliferation and counterproliferation instrument will persist. NATO is not a place where the allies can discuss and plan against real proliferation problems because the alliance remains ambivalent about its role outside of the European continent. This gets to the core of the debate about the future of NATO. If NATO is to play a truly significant role in the Middle East's WMD issues, the allies must first come to accept regional power projection—even if not explicitly authorized by the UN Security Council—as a legitimate and indeed important mission for the alliance. Unless this happens, NATO is likely to remain a bit player in the West's efforts to contain the proliferation threat in the Middle East, though some of the allies may come to do more on a bilateral or *ad hoc* basis.

DEVELOP STRATEGIC TIES BETWEEN NATO AND ISRAEL

Finally, NATO should establish a low-profile relationship with Israel based on the interests NATO shares with Israel in the Greater Middle East, including weapons of mass destruction.[47] Israel is the West's most important and reliable partner in the Middle East, and several individual NATO members already have security ties to Israel. The U.S.-Israeli security relationship is, of course, the most significant, but Israel also enjoys growing ties with Turkey. Unlike most of the European members of NATO, Israel does not have an abstract or detached perception of the WMD threat. Weapons of mass destruction in hostile hands are a reality in Israel's immediate vicinity, and NATO members stand to learn from the Israeli experience.

Israel has the potential to contribute to NATO's planning for Middle East contingencies involving WMD in several ways. If NATO ever does become involved in a regional contingency involving WMD, advance contingency planning with Israel could prove useful, especially if an Arab state seeks to use Israel to split a coalition arrayed against it. It would be helpful for all of the relevant actors to have some idea of how the others expect to respond in different scenarios. By sharing information on planning assumptions and preparations, both NATO and Israel could reduce the likelihood of a misunderstanding or conflicting action in a crisis. At an operational level, both could benefit from a more regular exchange of intelligence on regional WMD threats, or of technical information on WMD countermeasures.

---

47. A similar proposal is made in Shai Feldman, *The Future of U.S.-Israeli Strategic Cooperation* (Washington, D.C.: Washington Institute for Near East Policy, 1996), pp. 52–56.

Conclusion

This chapter has argued that the greatest deficiency in U.S.-European cooperation on WMD problems has been in the lack of a shared sense of mission, which is needed to exercise joint political or economic coercive pressure against proliferant states. The absence of a united front from the leading Western states creates an environment that is more permissive of WMD proliferation than it should be or could be. The Europeans have generally been good, if sometimes legalistic, partners in building international nonproliferation treaties and norms, but their performance leaves much to be desired when a specific state refuses to comply with its own nonproliferation commitments, when treaties or norms are inadequate to prevent WMD acquisition, or when a new problem emerges for which there is no relevant treaty or norm. The United States, on the other hand, has so far had minimal success at the diplomatic task of building a constructive U.S.-European policy consensus on key proliferation problems, and has failed spectacularly in at least one critical case, Iran. Moreover, the U.S. approach to WMD problems has often alienated the European elite for its militaristic and unilateral character. As a consequence, the potential for the United States and its key European allies to enhance the effectiveness of their nonproliferation and counterproliferation policies through joint action remains largely unfulfilled.

Chapter 10

Weapons of Mass Destruction

Joanna Spear

This chapter charts the evolution of European attitudes to weapons of mass destruction (WMD) proliferation over the course of the 1990s. A watershed event in shaping attitudes to the proliferation problem, particularly but by no means solely in connection with the Middle East, was the 1991 Gulf War. This was not only because of the salience of nuclear programs, chemical weapons (CW), and missile threats during the course of the conflict, but also because of the later disclosures on the extent of the Iraqi WMD programs, the role of European suppliers in aiding the programs, and how much had gone undetected. European policies on export controls, particularly on dual-use goods (that is, goods with both civilian and military applications) changed dramatically in the aftermath of the Gulf War.

In this chapter, the changing tide of Transatlantic relations on the issue of WMD in the Middle East is charted. The European allies have gradually heeded U.S. calls and tightened up their export controls over WMD equipment and technologies and dual-use items; a crucial determinant of European attitudes towards proliferation in the Middle East is the relationship with the United States. However, while the story thus far has been of the Europeans adopting proliferation policies in line with those of the United States, there is likely to be more discord between the allies on the future agenda for proliferation in the Middle East.

Export control issues, troublesome though they were, pale into insignificance beside the proliferation issues that now face the

The author would like to thank Professor Lawrence Freedman for his valuable advice and assistance with this chapter.

Transatlantic alliance. The proliferation of WMD in the Middle East affects the defense policies of the United States and Europe in two main ways. First, the fact that ballistic missiles are increasingly available in the Middle East, coupled with the difficulties encountered by the Gulf War allies in hunting down Iraqi Scud missiles, has led to increasing concerns about the effects of ballistic missiles on policies of force projection into the region. Although the ballistic missiles currently available are relatively unsophisticated, they nevertheless proved to be of great psychological importance during the Gulf War as weapons of terror out of proportion to their military effects. Moreover, the military utility of ballistic missiles is significantly enhanced if they are loaded with a nuclear, chemical or biological (NBC) payload. In such a situation, force projection into a region may be considered too risky to undertake, or may be conducted in the expectation of WMD attack, with countermeasures that significantly degrade military performance. If Iraq had achieved a nuclear capability prior to 1991, then there is good reason to believe that the allied response to the occupation of Kuwait would have been more circumspect. This sort of WMD capability offers the promise to a regional power of persuading external powers to stay away.

The second important influence results from the increased vulnerability of European territories to missile attack from within the Middle East.[1] The proliferation of longer-range ballistic missiles has profound defense implications for Europe.[2] For example, this raises the spectre of an attack by a Middle Eastern state on Europe. Such concerns are increasingly affecting French attitudes toward developments in Algeria, and Spanish, Portuguese, and British attitudes toward issues such as ballistic missile defense (BMD) systems.[3]

The issues now facing the alliance surround fundamental questions about force projection and the extent to which proliferation can be tolerated. Given the nature of these problems, more activism may be required in addition to supply-side solutions; this raises the danger

---

1. This issue has been discussed by the RAND Corporation, but only in the context of the willingness of European allies to join the United States in force projection operations. Ian O. Lesser and Ashley J. Tellis, *Strategic Exposure: Proliferation Around the Mediterranean* (Santa Monica, Calif.: RAND, 1996), pp. 19–30.

2. Michael Evans, "Growing Missile Threat to Europe," *Times* (London), On-line Edition, October 10, 1996.

3. "MoD Plans Laser Curtain Against Rogue Missiles," *Sunday Times* (London), March 2, 1997.

of the emergence of fundamental differences of approach between the United States and Europe. The greatest irritant in future Transatlantic relations on the WMD proliferation issue is going to be the combination of U.S. calls for greater activism and European reluctance to respond in the manner the United States wishes.

This chapter is divided into five sections. The first section examines WMD programs in the Middle East prior to the Gulf War, including the use of chemical weapons in the Middle East and the Israeli nuclear program. The following section discusses the United Nations' actions to dismantle Iraq's WMD production capabilities after the 1991 Gulf War, as well as the changes made to the export control policies of European states in the wake of the revelations about the major role played by the West in the Iraqi WMD programs. The third section considers two contemporary proliferation issues: Libya's chemical weapons program and the Iranian WMD programs. The fourth section lays out a number of factors that account for the differences in proliferation policies between the United States and Europe and the implications for future proliferation policies. The final section outlines policy recommendations designed to strengthen Transatlantic and wider cooperation on WMD issues.

WMD Programs in the Greater Middle East Prior to the Gulf War

The first WMD in evidence in the Middle East were chemical weapons. Both Iraq and Iran received help in developing their CW capabilities. In the 1970s, Iraq obtained the blueprints for a CW facility from a U.S. firm which was subsequently barred from exporting the machinery for construction of the facility. Many European firms had rebuffed initial Iraqi attempts to gain help in building CW production facilities. After this, Iraq set about a piecemeal acquisition of components, ostensibly for a pesticides plant. The first CW plant was completed by 1979. The Iraqi CW program was accelerated in 1982, and was greatly facilitated by cooperation with German and other foreign firms. The Iranian capability was developed in response to that of Iraq, but drew on many of the same sources. Although never as ambitious as the Iraqi program, the Iranians did develop production capabilities for mustard and nerve gas and for their means of delivery.[4]

4. Efraim Karsh, "Rational Ruthlessness: Non-Conventional and Missile Warfare in the Iran-Iraq War," in Efraim Karsh, Martin S. Navias, and Philip Sabin, eds., *Non-Conventional-Weapons Proliferation In The Middle East: Tackling the Spread of Nuclear, Chemical and Biological Capabilities* (Oxford, U.K.: Clarendon Press, 1993), pp. 32–34.

Iraq initiated the use of CW on the battlefield when the tide of the Iran-Iraq war seemed to have turned against it. The first documented Iraqi attacks came in late 1983, and in 1984 the United Nations sent a team to investigate the Iranian allegations.[5] The UN found incontrovertible evidence that the Iraqis had used both mustard gas and tabun.[6] Iraq had made no bones about its possession of CW (it is the third declared holder of CW) and had announced that they would be used if necessary to defend the state.[7] It was not until late in the war, possibly as late as 1988, that Iran was able to field its own CW. Even then, the scale of Iranian use of CW was dwarfed by Iraqi deployments. Iran claims it was attacked by Iraq with chemical weapons on 252 occasions during the Iran-Iraq war.[8]

Although Iraqi CW use was condemned by the international community, this was balanced by an anxiety lest Iraq be defeated by an Iran that was seen, during the 1980s, to be a much greater threat to international peace and security. However, by the time the war ended, most Western governments had developed intensive commercial as well as strategic interests in Iraq, and they did not want these to be jeopardized. This resulted in a muted response when the Iraqi CW arsenal was turned against its own civilians, most notably the Kurds at Halabja.[9]

Iraq's CW attacks on the village of Halabja on March 22, 1988, were widely reported in the Western press. It was the worst CW attack on civilians ever recorded. Five thousand people perished and many hundreds more were seriously injured.[10] The Iraqis were undeterred by the mild international response to their attacks on Halabja and a week later carried out CW attacks on Karadagh in which sixty-four civilians were killed.[11]

---

5. Karsh dates the first use of CW by Iraq to July 1982 in the battle for Basra, but the CW used were merely incapacitants. Karsh, "Rational Ruthlessness," p. 36.

6. John Sweeney, *Trading With The Enemy: Britain's Arming of Iraq* (London: Pan, 1993), pp. 26–28.

7. *Programme for Promoting Nuclear Non-Proliferation Newsbrief*, No. 10 (Summer 1990), p. 7.

8. *Tehran Voice of the Islamic Republic of Iran*, April 23, 1996, in *Foreign Broadcast Information Service–Near East Service* (FBIS-NES), April 24, 1996, cited in *Arms Control Reporter*, April 1996, Section 704.B.608.

9 . Sweeney, *Trading With The Enemy*; and Kenneth R. Timmerman, *The Death Lobby: How The West Armed Iraq* (London: Bantam, 1992).

10. Robin M. Black and Graham S. Pearson, "Unequivocal Evidence," *Chemistry In Britain*, July 1993, pp. 584–587.

11 . Sweeney, *Trading With The Enemy*, p. 83.

Until the Iraqi invasion of Kuwait in August 1990 and the assembling of an international coalition against the invader, international attitudes toward Iraqi use of CW were muted. When it became possible that CW would be used against coalition forces, international ire against Iraq was significantly heightened, and there was a reassessment of the significance of events such as Halabja and Iraqi deployments of CW in the Iran-Iraq war.[12]

THE ISRAELI NUCLEAR PROGRAM

Given the normal readiness of Europeans to distance themselves from American support for Israel, one might have expected that they would have been more ready to point the finger at Israel's nuclear program. However, this is an issue that the European states scrupulously avoid discussing, for fear of raising the wrath of a far more vital ally, the United States. There is therefore generally a silence on this issue, in contrast to the substantial discussions that generally surround issues such as unsafeguarded nuclear facilities and opaque proliferation.

There has been much debate over the actual number of nuclear weapons that Israel has manufactured, with estimates varying between fifty and two hundred.[13] This capability has been treated as a fact of life for almost three decades without ever being publicly admitted. In some ways it may even be said to have had a stabilizing effect on Arab-Israeli relations, in that it has made Arab governments aware of the special dangers of war with Israel. There is even some evidence that this deterred Iraq from using chemical warheads on Scud missiles directed against Israel during the Gulf War. Yet at the same time the supposed existence of this capability has provided a ready-made rationale for other proliferators. For example, Syria's claim that its ballistic missile and chemical capabilities are a response to Israel's nuclear capability are inherently plausible.

However, because this is Israel, no hue and cry has been raised in the United States. Since the Kennedy administration, U.S. policy has apparently involved taking Israeli denials of a nuclear weapons

---

12. Arguably the pendulum swung toward a rather crude assessment of Iraqi doctrine, as it was now regarded as likely to use CW in an indiscriminate fashion, whereas Karsh has demonstrated that Iraqi use of CW in the Iran-Iraq War was carefully calibrated, rational, and discriminate. Karsh, "Rational Ruthlessness," pp. 31–47.

13. Leonard S. Spector, "Nuclear Proliferation in the Middle East," *Orbis*, Vol. 36, No. 2 (Spring 1992), p. 193.

program at face value, despite evidence from U.S. intelligence agencies to the contrary. If the open secret were publicly acknowledged, then official responses would be required. The Israeli bomb highlights what could become a much more serious development should general proliferation in WMD take hold. The inclination of the United States seems to be to accept that friendly states have to look after their own security, and that this may involve the development of extreme capabilities. The acquisition of long-range missiles by Saudi Arabia could be seen in the same light. This could aggravate the divergence between attitudes taken to states perceived as generally hostile and those perceived as generally friendly.

In a sense, in Chapter 9, Richard Falkenrath endorses this approach in his policy recommendation for developing strategic ties between the North Atlantic Treaty Organization (NATO) and Israel on WMD issues. This recommendation also raises the question of whether the European NATO members would countenance such a link with Israel. In the eyes of European diplomats, the political costs of such a link would be likely to outweigh the benefits. Such ties would involve a clearer (albeit still implicit) acceptance of the Israeli nuclear capability, a situation the European states would be unwilling to accept, given their warmer relationships with the Arab states.

Iraq and UNSCOM

In January 1991, during the Gulf War air operations, the allies destroyed the research reactors at the Tuwaitha Nuclear Research Center near Baghdad. The raids were described as having "crippled Iraq's nuclear capacity." In early 1991, "most experts [were] of the opinion that Iraq was years away from any ability to produce weapons-relevant nuclear material and that, if it was indeed doing research towards that end, the work must have been at an embryonic stage."[14] Subsequent intelligence from Iraqi defectors and evidence from the UN Special Commission (UNSCOM) inspections proved this assessment to be worryingly inaccurate.

On April 3, 1991, the United Nations Security Council adopted Resolution 687, which set out the terms for a permanent cease-fire in the Gulf War. The Iraqis were to be denied all WMD and the means of making them. Iraq's compliance with the resolution was to be

14. *Programme for Promoting Nuclear Non-Proliferation Newsbrief*, No. 13 (Spring 1991), p. 1.

assured through a process of ongoing monitoring and verification. Soon after Iraq accepted the resolution, the Iraqi foreign minister wrote to the UN secretary general declaring that Iraq did not possess any nuclear materials that could be used in nuclear weapons, nor any of the other items listed in Resolution 687. The UNSCOM operation proved this statement to be a blatant lie.

The first inspection by an International Atomic Energy Agency (IAEA) action team took place in May 1991. This was followed by hundreds of inspections of different facilities. Iraq played a game of cat-and-mouse with the UNSCOM inspection teams.[15] Despite all the activities of UNSCOM, in October 1996 its deputy chairman reported that "serious problems" remained with the data that Iraq had provided about its WMD programs.[16] "Notwithstanding this unprecedented degree of access, UNSCOM inspections have almost entirely failed, in and of themselves, to uncover unambiguous evidence—the so-called 'smoking gun'—with respect to critical aspects of the prohibited Iraqi weapons programs."[17]

The information which led to revelations about the Iraqi WMD program did not result from the UNSCOM inspections themselves, but from the information provided by defectors from Iraq. Thus, initial inspections of Iraq's nuclear research facilities found no evidence of an illicit nuclear weapons program. However, an Iraqi engineer who defected to the United States provided vital information on secret installations where work was being done on the production of weapons-usable fissile materials.[18] Important information about the

---

15. David Albright and Mark Hibbs, "Iraq's Nuclear Hide-And-Seek," *Bulletin of the Atomic Scientists*, Vol. 47, No. 7 (September 1991).

16. "UN: 'Serious Problems' with Iraqi Compliance," *Jane's Defence Weekly*, Vol. 26, No. 15 (October 9, 1996), p. 31. For example, as of June 1996, the UNSCOM team in Iraq had been unable to verify Iraqi claims to have destroyed 25 warheads filled with the biological weapons (BW) botulinum toxic and anthrax. Iraq failed to provide any documentation relating to the destruction of the warheads, and UN investigators had been blocked and delayed from entering suspected missile storage sites. *Arms Control Reporter*, April 1996, Section 704.E.2143. There were similar questions over the veracity of Iraqi disclosures of its CW developments. For example, between December 1995 and April 1996, the Iraqis increased their totals for declared production of VX nerve gas by twenty percent. *Arms Control Reporter*, July 1996, Section 704.E-2.148.

17. Edward J. Lacey, "The UNSCOM Experience: Implications for U.S. Arms Control Policy," *Arms Control Today*, Vol. 26, No. 6 (August 1996), p. 11.

18. *Programme for Promoting Nuclear Non-Proliferation Newsbrief*, No. 14 (Summer 1991), p. 4.

existence of a centrifuge only came to light when a senior Iraqi, Hussein Kamel Hassan, defected in August 1995. Similar sources revealed Iraq's electromagnetic isotope separation (EMIS) program.[19]

The post–Gulf War revelations indicated the extent to which the Iraqi efforts were advanced through purchases of materials, equipment, and know-how from the West.[20] "Much of this trade has been conducted clandestinely, but some seems to have occurred with tacit governmental acquiescence."[21]

By 1992 German intelligence estimated that over three hundred firms and twenty-eight countries had contributed to the Iraqi nuclear weapons program, including twenty French firms, twelve from Italy, eighteen from Switzerland, seventeen from Great Britain, and twenty-five from the United States.[22] Preeminent was the role of German firms. Both German and UN sources suggested that 80 percent of the nuclear-related supplies received by Iraq came from Germany, including an estimated $198 million worth of dual-use items. There was also evidence that many of the German firms were aware that their supplies were destined for a nuclear weapons program.[23] Over fifty German firms were investigated for allegedly providing nuclear equipment or technology to Iraq. By late 1992, six

---

19. Spector, "Nuclear Proliferation in the Middle East," p. 182.

20. Part of the problem with the intelligence—and by extension with the inspection—was a lack of appreciation of the routes that Iraqi scientists might follow. The progress that Iraq had made using apparently outmoded techniques for uranium enrichment put the international community on notice that "bronze medal technology was enough." Peter D. Zimmerman, "Proliferation: Bronze Medal Technology Is Enough," *Orbis*, Vol. 38, No. 1 (1994), pp. 67–82. Indeed, the electromagnetic (calutron) enrichment process that Iraq was using had been considered so unpromising by the United States and other countries that the technologies had been declassified. Consequently firms such as the Hipotronics Company of Brewster, New York, had been able to export necessary components because they were not subject to U.S. export controls. *Programme for Promoting Nuclear Non-Proliferation Newsbrief*, No. 14 (Summer 1991), p. 4.

21. *Programme for Promoting Nuclear Non-Proliferation Newsbrief*, No. 11 (Autumn 1990), p. 7.

22. Cited in *Programme for Promoting Nuclear Non-Proliferation Newsbrief*, No. 17 (Spring 1992), p. 13.

23. Cited in *Programme for Promoting Nuclear Non-Proliferation Newsbrief*, No. 19 (Autumn 1992), p. 12. German complicity in this area had been noted prior to the Gulf War. See Dan Charles, "Exporting Trouble: West Germany's Freewheeling Nuclear Business," *Bulletin of the Atomic Scientists*, Vol. 45, No. 3 (April 1989), pp. 21–27.

German firms were on trial after equipment from these firms was found at various clandestine Iraqi sites. A German scientist, Karl-Heinz Schaab (who had previously worked for URENCO, a British-German-Dutch uranium enrichment consortium) is accused of selling Iraq blueprints for a sophisticated uranium-enrichment centrifuge (code named TC-11) in 1991. He is also suspected of helping to set up the centrifuge.[24] Evidence of German involvement in training Iraqi nuclear engineers prior to 1991 came to light in 1996. This apparently covered such areas as high-technology piping and welding practices "that would have been particularly useful in developing a nuclear weapons delivery system."[25]

EXPORT CONTROL POLICIES REASSESSED

Despite the evidence of European government complicity in many of these transfers through, for example, the granting of export licenses and the extension of trade credits, there was minimal political fallout from these revelations.[26] Nonetheless, after the Gulf War, European governments did move to tighten up export controls to problematic states. In February 1991, Germany announced that it had tightened export controls relating to nuclear weapons–related materials.[27] This was followed in January 1992 by the adoption of new legislation that stiffened export controls and imposed heavy

---

24. A German official stated, "This case is going to emerge as the most serious nuclear-export violation Germany has ever had to face." Quoted in Alan George, *The Observer*, January 28, 1996. Schaab is also under investigation for involvement in the Iranian program.

25. Steve Pagani in *Reuters*, February 2, 1996, cited in *Arms Control Reporter*, May 1996, Section 453.B-1.53. Other European countries played a role in providing training for Iraqi, Egyptian, and Palestinian engineers. Indeed, Dr. Jaffar Dhia Jaffar, the vice president of Iraq's Nuclear Energy Commission, who is thought to have had overall technical and administrative responsibility for the nuclear program, was trained in Britain. *Daily Telegraph* (London), October 3 and 4, 1991.

26. For example, in Britain the five-volume "Scott Report" on British trade with Iraq did not result in any resignations from the government and was a media issue for less than a week after its publication. This was due to careful media and parliamentary manipulation by the Conservative Government, and the indigestibility and impenetrability of the report, which was not accompanied by an overview or summary of conclusions. Davina Miller, *Export or Die: Britain's Defence Trade With Iran and Iraq* (London: Cassell, 1996).

27. *Die Welt*, February 7, 1991; *Frankfurter Rundschau*, February 7, 1991; and *Frankfurter Allgemeine*, February 9, 1991, all cited in *Programme for Promoting Nuclear Non-Proliferation Newsbrief*, No. 13 (Spring 1991), p. 2.

penalties for violations.[28] The speed with which the revised law was introduced was attributed to disclosures about German nuclear-usable exports to Iraq and the seizure in Germany of American nuclear-usable equipment supplied by a Dutch firm and intended for Libya.[29] Within the European Community, measures were taken to strengthen the community's nonproliferation policy.[30]

Multilateral and international control initiatives were also introduced in the wake of the war. The Bush administration launched several international initiatives. European countries were involved in all of them. The international export controls of the "Nuclear Suppliers Group" were tightened, and in July 1991 the Group of Seven (G-7), composed of the United States, Germany, Britain, France, Italy, Japan, and Canada, adopted "The Declaration on Conventional Arms Transfers and NBC Non-Proliferation" at its London Economic Summit.[31] "The old objections of some suppliers that 'ganging up' by the industrialized exporters would offend and alienate the developing countries had disappeared under the impact of the Gulf War."[32]

Chief among the Bush initiatives was "The Middle East Arms Control Initiative," also known as the "P5 Initiative," a reference to the group's membership, the five permanent members of the UN Security Council.[33] One aspect of the Middle East Arms Control Initiative was a call for cessation of the production of weapons-grade nuclear materials in the region. This initiative would have affected only Israel; thus it was the first time that the United States had pursued measures designed to constrain Israel's nuclear activities.[34] Launched in May 1991, the P5 Initiative resulted in several rounds of talks in 1991 and 1992 which were designed to set criteria for limiting arms transfers into the region, but participants were unable to agree

---

28. Release from the German Federal Ministry for Economic Cooperation, December 4, 1990, cited in *Programme for Promoting Nuclear Non-Proliferation Newsbrief*, No. 12 (Winter 1990/1991), p. 2.

29. *The Guardian*, January 24, 1992, cited in *Programme for Promoting Nuclear Non-Proliferation Newsbrief*, No. 17 (Spring 1992), p. 3.

30. Stockholm International Peace Research Institute, *SIPRI Yearbook 1992* (Oxford: Oxford University Press/SIPRI, 1992), pp. 98–99.

31. *Programme for Promoting Nuclear Non-Proliferation Newsbrief*, No. 15 (Autumn 1991), pp. 3, 15.

32. *SIPRI Yearbook 1992*, p. 97.

33. *Fact Sheet on Middle East Arms Control Initiative*, The White House, May 29, 1991, pp. 1–2.

34. Spector, "Nuclear Proliferation in the Middle East," p. 197.

on the way in which the group should operate.[35] The immediate reason for the demise of the talks was China's withdrawal following the U.S. decision to sell F-16 fighters to Taiwan. However, there were also tensions between the U.S. and European allies over the former's advocacy of arms transfer restraint even as it simultaneously agreed to massive arms transfer deals to the region.[36] For example, the day after President Bush announced the P5 Initiative, Defense Secretary Richard Cheney revealed that the U.S. would sell Israel ten F-15 fighters and had also promised Israel $200 million in research funding for a new missile system.[37] The collapse of the talks meant the loss of a Transatlantic negotiating forum for WMD issues.

Contemporary Proliferation Problems

This section reviews two current WMD proliferation issues, the WMD programs of Libya and of Iran.

LIBYAN CHEMICAL WEAPONS

As is often the case, the British and Americans have found their positions on the issue of Libya's CW program closer with each other than with their allies. This can be traced to a shared inclination to outlaw, rather than seek to engage, "renegade" states, as well as specific concerns about Libyan sponsorship of international terrorism. Britain has been concerned about the relationship between Libya and the paramilitary Irish Republican Army (IRA). Libya has been one of the main suppliers of conventional weapons and explosives to the PIRA, and the British fear that chemical weapons will get to the terrorists.[38] By contrast, other European states have seen their main links with Libya as essentially commercial in nature and became extremely hostile to U.S. and British pressure to sever trade links, even those which involved dual-use products.

As early as 1986, the United States accused Libya of employing chemical weapons against Chad. It was later discovered that the

---

35. Joanna Spear, "On the Desirability and Feasibility of Arms Transfer Regime Formation," *Contemporary Security Policy*, Vol. 15, No. 3 (December 1994), pp. 98–99.

36. Ibid., pp. 98–99.

37. John Adams, *Trading in Death: The Modern Arms Race*, 2nd ed. (London: Pan, 1991), p. xxvi.

38. Ibid., p. 243.

poison gas had been supplied by Iran in return for Soviet-made mines. The United States also suspected that Libya was attempting to create an indigenous chemical weapon capability. The British supplied evidence of this, as well as intelligence that special steels for weapons casing and chemicals were being shipped from West Germany and Italy to Libya. Despite this evidence, "for the next two and a half years many western governments including those of Japan, West Germany, France, and Italy deliberately ignored the clear information for simple financial gain."[39]

Meanwhile the United States, supported by Britain, spearheaded a campaign of international pressure to close the Libyan chemical weapons facility at Rabta. This led to disputes with the Federal Republic of Germany (FRG) when, in early 1989, the U.S. government accused a West German firm, Imhausen-Chemie, of building the Rabta plant. The FRG maintained that an international inspection of the plant, showing that its products were civilian, would provide evidence of its benign purpose. Although in January 1989 German customs confiscated more than two hundred tons of chemicals bound for Libya, only two months later West German firms were again shipping materials to Rabta. Soon after this exchange, there was apparently a fire at the Rabta facility, though subsequent reports suggested that the fire was a deliberate attempt to divert intelligence attention from the plant, which was still operational.[40] Further diversionary efforts came the next year when Libya closed, its CW facility in Rabta, but it immediately began secret work on an underground CW plant at Tarhunah, forty miles southeast of Tripoli.

The Tarhunah plant, located inside a mountain, is thought to be six miles square and to hold the Libyan stockpile of about one hundred tons of CW. The plant is expected to be completed in 1997 or 1998, when it should be able to manufacture tons of chemical agents per day. Much of the information on the Tarhunah plant has come from German intelligence; for example, German agents have reportedly obtained the construction blueprints for the plant.[41] This activity reflects a greater German readiness to take proliferation issues seriously following the embarrassment of the post–Desert Storm revelations.

---

39. Ibid., p. 243.

40. *Programme for the Promotion of Nuclear Non-Proliferation Newsbrief*, No. 9 (Spring 1990), pp. 7–8.

41. *New York Times*, February 25, 1996; and *Time*, April 1, 1996, both cited in *Arms Control Reporter*, April 1996, Section 704.E.2143.

In April 1996, U.S. Secretary of Defense William Perry stated that the United States would not allow the Tarhunah plant to become operational and would not rule out the use of force to prevent it. The statement came during a visit by Secretary Perry to Egypt, during which the United States gave information on the Tarhunah plant to Egyptian President Hosni Mubarak.[42] Perry's statement does not seem to have elicited any immediate response from European states. Libya responded by giving President Mubarak an extensive tour of the Tarhunah facility, after which he confirmed that the tunnels were empty when he visited. President Mubarak suggested that international inspectors be permitted to verify his findings, but as yet Libyan President Muammar Qadhafi has not responded to this suggestion. President Mubarak's findings have done nothing to assuage U.S. concerns.[43] Nor has the evidence that by June 1996 work at the plant seemed to have halted.[44]

The United States has taken a far more robust stance toward the Libyan CW facilities than have its European allies other than Britain. Nevertheless, over time other European allies have come to acknowledge concerns about Libya's CW capabilities, and some changes in export policies and practices have been instituted, though not with the degree of rigor that the United States would like. European moves toward tightening export controls have been rather grudging and piecemeal (despite efforts by the European Commission to propel the issue forward), reflecting the economic interests at stake in such moves.[45]

THE IRANIAN WMD PROGRAMS

Iran is not a simple case in terms of its attitudes toward weapons of mass destruction. It was, after all, a victim of chemical attack. The Iranians are widely suspected of seeking to acquire nuclear weapons. The Iranian nuclear program was initiated by the shah and continued

---

42. John Lancaster, *Washington Post*, April 4, 1996, cited in *Arms Control Reporter*, July 1996, Section 704.E-2.147.

43. Lancaster, *Washington Post*, May 30, 1996.

44. Bill Gertz, *Washington Times*, June 24, 1996, cited in *Arms Control Reporter*, July 1996, Section 704.E-2.147.

45. Whereas the United States has focused its attention primarily on the Libyan CW capabilities, the British are equally concerned about the Libyan nuclear weapons program. Despite the fact that Libya is a member of the NPT, British estimates suggest that Libya could have a nuclear device by 2004. *Arms Control Reporter*, January 1996, Section 453.A.4.

by the revolutionary government after his overthrow. The Khomeini regime worked on the program during the Iran-Iraq war, and in 1987 signed a deal with Argentina to supply 20 percent enriched (non–weapons grade) nuclear fuel for its research reactor in Tehran. By the late 1980s, there was increasing concern in the West about the Iranian nuclear weapons program, particularly as Iran's leadership was explicit about its intentions to obtain a nuclear capability. Iran's efforts to develop nuclear weapons were stepped up in the aftermath of the Gulf War, and Leonard Spector cites evidence suggesting that Iran was looking to Western Europe as the source for its requirements, using clandestine networks in order to obtain the hardware and technology.[46]

The German firms Siemens and Kraftwerk Union (KWU) were involved in a plan to build two 1,300-megawatt pressurized water reactors at Bushehr in Iran. Although construction was begun under the shah, it was never completed due to Iraqi bombing of the facility and the German government's subsequent intervention to prevent work being resumed.[47] In 1990 and 1992, the German government refused German firms permission to transfer $300 million worth of equipment to Iran. On the second occasion, the denial was justified on the grounds that Iran was an area of tension and the equipment was dual-use.[48] This led the Iranians to criticize Germany for failing to allow Iran to import materials and equipment to complete the plant, as it was legitimately permitted to do as a party to the Nuclear Non-Proliferation Treaty.[49] Subsequently, the German government forbade Siemens from exporting 450 megatons of uranium hexafluoride belonging to Iran, intended as feedstock for the initial cores of the two reactors that were begun at Bushehr.[50]

In 1991, Iran attempted to obtain enriched uranium from France.[51] The Iranians suggested that the deal would help pave the way toward the normalization of relations between the two states, and

---

46. Spector, "Nuclear Proliferation in the Middle East," pp. 187–188.

47. *IAEA Newsbriefs,* Vol. 2, No. 15 (November 25, 1987), cited in *Programme for Promoting Nuclear Non-Proliferation Newsbrief,* No. 1 (March 1988), p. 4.

48. *Programme for Promoting Nuclear Non-Proliferation Newsbrief,* No. 19 (Autumn 1992), p. 11.

49. *Nucleonics Week,* October 25, 1990, cited in *Programme for Promoting Nuclear Non-Proliferation Newsbrief,* No. 12 (Winter 1990/1991), p. 3.

50. *Programme for Promoting Nuclear Non-Proliferation Newsbrief,* No. 33 (First Quarter, 1996), pp. 12–13.

51. David Albright and Mark Hibbs, "Spotlight Shifts to Iran," *Bulletin of the Atomic Scientists,* Vol. 48, No. 2 (March 1992), pp. 9–11.

would also form partial settlement of a financial dispute between the two. France rejected the proposal.[52]

Although there is unanimity between the U.S. and European governments on the issue of Iran's nuclear program, there are disputes over Iranian intentions in the field of CW. Although it had also developed its own CW capability (and there are questions over whether this still exists), it took an active role in efforts to implement the Chemical Weapons Convention (CWC), much to the disquiet of the United States. For example, when the Organization for the Prohibition of Chemical Weapons (OPCW, the institution to implement the CWC) began to look for overseas inspectors, the sixth largest number of applicants came from Iran.[53] In April 1996, Iran hosted a regional training seminar for fifteen Persian Gulf and Central Asian nations on national implementation of the CWC. During the seminar, Iran's ambassador to the United Nations pledged that Iran would "cooperate in every way, on an international and regional level, towards the eradication of all weapons of mass destruction, especially chemical weapons."[54] The United States, however, questions whether Iran is operating in good faith as a member of the CWC. Given the different attitudes of Europe and the United States towards Iran, this question will pose proliferation dilemmas for Transatlantic relations in the future.

U.S.-European Differences

Although there are differences in attitude between the United States and Europe over WMD issues, there are more similarities than differences. The differences that do exist can be accounted for in five main ways.

First, the intelligence resources that the Europeans are able to devote to tracking WMD proliferation in the Middle East are considerably fewer than those employed by the United States. Europe is particularly dependent on the United States for satellite information

---

52. *Programme for Promoting Nuclear Non-Proliferation Newsbrief*, No. 15 (Autumn 1991), p. 4.

53. Comments by OPCW Director of External Relations Sergei Batsanov, "Chemical Weapons Convention Forum," Harvard University, Center for Science and International Affairs, February 8, 1996, cited in *Arms Control Reporter*, April 1996, Section 704.B.605.

54. *Tehran Voice of the Islamic Republic of Iran*, April 23, 1996; in FBIS-NES, April 24, 1996, cited in *Arms Control Reporter*, April 1996, Section 704.B.608.

and signals intelligence (SIGINT). Dependence on U.S. intelligence data generally puts the Europeans in a passive role, as receptors rather than providers of information. For the most part, the Europeans seem to be happy with this division of labor, but the Western European Union (WEU) has taken some initiatives in exploring the use of civilian satellite imagery for purposes of arms control verification. Moreover, the French have launched a satellite that could be similarly used and are interested in launching another, if Germany can be persuaded to share the costs. European dependence on the United States is rather less in terms of human intelligence (HUMINT). However, sometimes when European states have attempted to gather human intelligence, things have gone badly wrong.[55]

Second, there is a difference in context within which WMD proliferation is viewed by the United States and the European states. The United States tends to view the issue in the wider context of global proliferation, and sets the problem states in the Middle East into the same category as "rogue states" such as North Korea. The United States has also consistently had a global thematic approach to the issue of WMD proliferation. Thus the issue is extracted from its regional context, and both the problem and possible solutions and defense policies are decided at an abstract global level. The Clinton administration's counterproliferation policy, for example, is a global approach to WMD, and pays minimal attention to the specific regional context in which the proliferation is occurring.[56] By contrast, the European countries view the issue of WMD primarily in the context of regional

---

55. For example, in the 1980s, the British government allowed a defense firm, Matrix Churchill, to trade with Iraq in order that its directors might gather information on Iraqi WMD programs. Unfortunately the trade continued long after the intelligence source had ceased to be useful. The British Government's intelligence operation backfired in several ways. First, the machine tools provided were found to have been used in manufacturing precision parts for both the nuclear program and the CW program. Second, the operations of Matrix Churchill were exposed by HM Customs and Excise, and charges were brought against the firm's directors. During the trial, the government was shown to have done nothing to prevent its intelligence sources from going to jail, and indeed, four Ministers had signed Public Interest Immunity Certificates designed to deny evidence to the defense, which would have shown that Matrix Churchill was operating with government acquiescence.

56. U.S. Office of the Secretary of Defense, *Proliferation: Threat and Response* (Washington, D.C.: United States Government Printing Office, April 1996); Joseph F. Pilat and Walter L. Kirchner, "The Technological Promise of Counter-

security, and do not extract the question of WMD for special attention. Nevertheless, the European states have agreed to NATO's adoption of a form of counterproliferation.[57] Richard Falkenrath (in Chapter 9 in this volume) perceives this as evidence that Europe has accepted the U.S. judgment of the importance of counterproliferation. However, the European acceptance is grudging, and this should be seen as auguring a war of bureaucratic attrition over its implementation.

Third, there are important differences in the locus for the development of policy on WMD issues between Europe and the United States. Whereas in Europe the presumption is that policies concerning WMD should emanate from the executive, in the United States, policy is also likely to emanate from the legislature.[58] This forces the U.S. administration into an active role either mandated by Congress or designed to preempt congressional policymaking on this issue.

The fourth explanation for differences in approach to WMD proliferation issues relates to the different economic positions of European states and the United States. This raises two issues. The first concerns leverage. European countries have had to adjust to the loss of control over other parts of the world where they once held sway. Their expectations of being able to hold back the diffusion of power are lower. This means that if they wish to contain or roll back proliferation, they must rely on inducements as much as punishments and link the management of this particular question with the management of the multifarious other issues that have acquired local salience. They know that they do not have many cards to play in Middle Eastern politics and do not want to start taking positions that they will find impossible to back up in practice. They do not present themselves as general guarantors of peace and stability to Middle Eastern countries (except perhaps to some Gulf states, but certainly not to the most likely proliferators), and so their leverage is limited.

proliferation," *Washington Quarterly*, Vol. 18, No. 1 (Winter 1995), pp. 145–152; and Harald Müller and Mitchell Reiss, "Counterproliferation: Putting Old Wine in New Bottles," *Washington Quarterly*, Vol. 18, No. 2 (Spring 1995), pp. 143–154.

57. Ashton B. Carter and David Omand, "Countering the Proliferation Risks: Adapting the Alliance to the New Security Environment," *NATO Review*, No. 5 (September 1996), pp. 10–15.

58. Bertrand Goldschmidt, "Proliferation and Non-Proliferation in Western Europe: A Historical Survey," in Harald Müller, ed., *A European Non-Proliferation Policy: Prospects and Problems* (Oxford, U.K.: Clarendon Press, 1987), p. 28.

A second consequence of the economic position of Europe is that the European states both compete and cooperate with each other. Within the European Union they are partners, but in seeking trade abroad, they are often competitors. This means that they are often reluctant to accept export controls (particularly over dual-use technologies and systems) unless there is strong evidence of dangers to security in selling. This accounts for the unwillingness of some states to impose strict export controls on their firms; the aim is to provide as much leeway as possible in order to secure overseas orders. Moreover, the role of the EU in this area is not fully determined and is a source of some disputes.[59] Individual European states are anxious to exploit these disputes out of fear of losing valuable economic revenue to other states. However, differences between U.S. and European approaches to export controls should not be overstated. All the major European states and the United States are, for example, adherents to the Missile Technology Control Regime. There is little friction over this issue. Rather, there are shared U.S. and European concerns about the export activities of states such as Russia, China, North Korea, and about developments in Ukraine.[60]

Finally, differences between Europe and the United States on WMD proliferation are partly attributable to different expectations about the likelihood of force projection into the Middle East. The threat of WMD use against allied forces projected into the Middle East is regarded as the major problem currently faced by the United States. This accounts for the U.S. adoption of counterproliferation, which is designed to enable forces to operate after the failure of nonproliferation policies.[61] The European states, by contrast, have traditionally had a much lower expectation of being involved in power projection into the region and therefore place less emphasis on this issue. However, there are signs that changes in European defense policies mean that the divide between the Transatlantic allies is diminishing; the change is not a consequence of U.S. pressure. Rather,

---

59. Paul Cornish, *The Arms Trade And Europe* (London: Royal Institute of International Affairs and Pinter, 1995).

60. Philip Finnegan, *Defense News*, February 5–11, 1996, cited in *Arms Control Reporter*, June 1996, Section 706.B.199; *Jane's Defence Weekly*, May 1, 1996; *Seoul Yonhap*, May 3, 1996, in FBIS-EAS, May 3, 1996, cited in *Arms Control Reporter*, July 1996, Section 706.B.201; and Bill Gertz, *Washington Times*, June 10, 1996, cited in *Arms Control Reporter*, July 1996, Section 706.B.203.

61. Pilat and Kirchner, "The Technological Promise of Counterproliferation," pp. 145–152.

the attitudes of France and Britain toward force projection into the region are shifting, following arms sales agreements between the two states and Middle Eastern clients, principally the United Arab Emirates. These agreements include defense cooperation, joint exercises, and promises to come to the aid of the country should it be attacked. The French have signed an unprecedented agreement to place forces under UAE command in such an emergency.[62] These agreements suggest that the threat of WMD use against forces projected into the Middle East is soon to achieve a new salience for Britain and France.

Policy Recommendations

Four changes in current Translatlantic policies on WMD are discussed here: a re-focusing of export control efforts; provision of a multilateral forum where WMD issues can be discussed; the monitoring of "deception technologies"; and a division of labor within the Transatlantic alliance that would allow the United States and European states to play to their individual strengths.

EXPORT CONTROLS

A major problem inhibiting attempts to tighten up export controls is the desperation of both commercial enterprises and governments to make sales in a competitive market. In such a situation, as David Kay has noted, "the operating rule of the commercial world is 'don't ask, just sell'."[63] Kay highlights another important problem with attempting to constrain WMD programs through tighter export controls: increasing amounts of exports are dual-use. It is important to note that attempts to control WMD proliferation in the Middle East through supply-side manipulation are increasingly being undermined by the consequences of the globalization process and the prevailing free-trade philosophy. The development of a global economy means that the number of routes by which goods can reach a destination are endless. Moreover, the deregulation of economic activity which has accompanied the move to a free-trade system means that it is increasingly difficult to track flows of goods, services, and money.

---

62. Giovanni de Briganti, "France, UAE Solidify Relationship in Arms Sales, Defense," *Defense News*, Vol. 10, No. 18 (May 8–14, 1995), p. 29.

63. David Kay, "Denial and Deception Practices of WMD Proliferators: Iraq and Beyond," *Washington Quarterly*, Vol. 18, No. 1 (Winter 1995), p. 309.

Although still tougher export controls over sensitive dual-use items may be desirable, these could be difficult to achieve short of another crisis spurring action. Furthermore, in terms of finished weapons as well as critical technology, the Europeans are not the major problem. More troubling are the actions of North Korea, Libya, and also China. The latter consistently promises export restraint while continuing to supply nuclear technologies and ballistic missiles to the region.[64]

A precondition for the further tightening of controls over dual-use exports appears to be a shared identification of the problem. This is currently lacking. Thus there have been disputes among the members of the Wassenaar Arrangement (the follow-on regime to CoCom, the Cold War–era Coordinating Committee on East-West Trade, which was intended to manage and control dual-use technologies and conventional weapons exports) over the way in which Iran should be treated. As has been shown in preceding chapters, the European states do not regard the threat from Iran in quite the same light as does the United States. In negotiations over the Wassenaar Arrangement, the major tensions thus far seem to have been between Russia and the United States over the Russian export relationship with Iran. It may be, however, that this has provided a useful shield to hide tensions between the United States and Europe on the question of Iran.

Given that attempts to strengthen alliance export controls will be contested, attention should be focused on export control problems. The most useful future direction for export controls is to extend them to other supplier and potential supplier states. For this to be achieved, a forum has to be found to spread the word about the problems posed by WMD.

PROVIDE A FORUM FOR DISCUSSING WMD ISSUES

It might be possible to re-institute a modified version of the P5 talks, excluding the contentious issue of conventional arms sales and concentrating on WMD. This would provide a forum in which the United States and Europe could work together to modify the behavior of other key supplier states such as China and Russia. More useful would be a forum that brought the allies into contact with potential dual-use supplier states. It would therefore be desirable to quickly bring the Wassenaar Arrangement into force, even if agreement is

---

64. *SIPRI Yearbook 1992*, p. 98.

imperfect, so that the regime can begin the work on WMD issues and particularly the thorny problem of controls over dual-use systems and technologies. This would also begin the process of embedding and institutionalizing the norm of strict export controls. Given the wider membership of the Wassenaar Arrangement, which includes states from the former Soviet Union and East Central Europe, the forum should be regarded as an opportunity to head off problems before they arise. In the future, these states could become important sources of dual-use WMD systems and technologies. By wrapping these states into a regime such as Wassenaar (and possibly also using the Organization for Security and Cooperation in Europe [OSCE] in the same manner) the way in which they conduct exports can be influenced positively to avoid problems in the future.

Bringing Wassenaar into force would have another important advantage: it would provide a forum in which information could be shared about the cumulation of dual-use goods going to key states. The case of Iraq showed that it gained a lot of advantage from the lack of any central tracking of its purchases, so each dual-use acquisition was judged only in the light of that particular purchase, rather than it being known that this was one of many such procurements. The wide membership of the Wassenaar Arrangement makes such a project of information exchange (even if only retrospectively) a potentially valuable tool in the fight against WMD proliferation in the Middle East. It would also facilitate better management of exports if the Wassenaar states were to agree upon a common end-use certificate and devote more resources to the customs checks on such certificates and the cargoes they accompany.

MONITOR DECEPTION TECHNOLOGIES

One type of exports that should be monitored closely—if not actually controlled—is the technologies that could assist in a deception effort to hide the development of WMD. Among the technologies of relevance are pollution control technologies, electronic emission control systems, and data encryption systems. As David Kay has pointed out, these types of technologies are increasingly becoming available on the civil market and could greatly aid a state intent on hiding its WMD program.[65] The Europeans and Americans should work together to ensure that the spread of such technologies is monitored

---

65. Kay, "Denial and Deception," p. 321.

by organizations such as the Wassenaar Arrangement, Nuclear Suppliers Group, and IAEA.

PLAY TO OUR STRENGTHS

A likely irritant in future Transatlantic relations is the U.S. desire to see European states play a more active role in WMD issues. Although there are some areas where European governments may be toughening their stance (such as force projection and attitudes to ballistic missile defense), I agree with Richard Falkenrath that generally the European states have little inclination to greater activism. However, rather than viewing these differences of approach within the alliance as a problem, as Falkenrath does, they should be viewed as an opportunity. By allowing each side of the partnership to play to its strengths, it should be possible to pursue a "good cop–bad cop" policy that keeps open lines of communication with problem states (providing an all-important safety valve) but applies pressure in a more effective manner by using a range of tools. Rather than viewing divergent approaches as a problem, it may be that a twin-track strategy can be employed to the advantage of all.

Chapter 11

Military Force Projection

Richard L. Kugler

This chapter examines how the United States and its European allies plan to project military power into the Persian Gulf and Greater Middle East. In particular, it examines prospects for increasing the European contribution to this critical strategic mission. The analysis offers an American point of view, but does so in an objective manner that evaluates the policy options fairly. It addresses the political basics, but it also pays attention to the all-important military details, which will affect Transatlantic cooperation in this complex arena.[1]

This chapter puts forth the thesis that the current situation is unsatisfactory and cannot endure, but it can be changed for the better. The United States cannot continue being the primary—nearly exclusive—defender of Western interests in the Persian Gulf and Middle East. For powerful reasons that apply on both sides of the Atlantic, a greater European contribution is needed. Accordingly, this chapter develops a new strategic model of "shared responsibility" for allocating military roles and missions to the United States and Europe in more co-equal ways. If adopted, this model would replace the current "quasi-unilateral" model that assigns the bulk of the load to the United States.

The potential benefits of this model are huge, but can it be brought to life? Contrary to widespread impressions that the difficulties are

---

1. For related analyses, see David C. Gompert and F. Stephen Larrabee, *America and Europe: A Partnership For a New Era* (London: Cambridge University Press, 1997); David C. Gompert and Richard L. Kugler, "Rebuilding the Team: How to Get Allies to Do More in Defense of Common Interests," RAND Issue Paper, Santa Monica, Calif., September 1996; and Ronald D. Asmus, Robert D. Blackwill, and F. Stephen Larrabee, "Can NATO Survive?" *Washington Quarterly*, Vol. 19, No. 2 (Spring 1996).

too large to be overcome, this historic departure is feasible in the coming years. It will not be easy, nor will it be accomplished overnight. It will require a demanding menu of steps: new Transatlantic political collaboration, new European defense programs, and new operational plans for guiding the ways in which U.S. and European forces work together in the region. Provided the necessary political willpower is generated and the effort is carried out wisely, however, a different and better future can be created. The alliance's own history provides ample reason to judge that the presence of barriers need not freeze the North Atlantic Treaty Organization (NATO) into immobility. The alliance won the Cold War because it was able to surmount barriers like these on many occasions. The skeptics are already being proven wrong in a different arena: NATO is reforming its command structure, operating in Bosnia, and preparing to enlarge eastward. It can handle planning for the Persian Gulf and the Middle East if its members want it to do so.

The key issue is: how can this demanding change be accomplished? This chapter begins by providing a road map for overcoming the inevitable difficulties by confronting them head-on and by shaping effective approaches for orchestrating a favorable outcome. Next, it examines the multiple reasons why pursuing greater U.S.-European collaboration makes success a feasible proposition. It then crafts an illustrative European defense improvement program, one that seems both adequate and achievable. Next, it develops a political approach for mobilizing the Europeans to respond and for using NATO to get the job done. Finally, it develops a military approach for ensuring that once European forces are prepared for projection missions, they can operate effectively with U.S. forces in the Gulf and other areas. Throughout, it argues that a combination of effort and skill can make shared responsibility happen because there is a world of difference between a hard task and an impossible task.

This chapter does not pretend to offer a blueprint for resolving current tensions in U.S. and European diplomacy across the Greater Middle East. What it offers instead is a bold strategic departure in defense affairs so that the deeper, more threatening dangers facing the Transatlantic alliance can be overcome. If they are to pursue this departure, the United States and Europe will need to draw closer in their daily diplomacy, something they should be doing anyway. In essence, the emerging situation calls for a better overall Western strategy, one that includes both a common diplomacy and greater cooperation in defense planning. The purpose of this chapter is to examine how the second half of such a strategy can be assembled in ways that transform difficulty into success.

Putting This Chapter in Perspective

Transatlantic defense cooperation in the Persian Gulf and Middle East may be the next big item on the Western alliance's agenda, perhaps equaling or even surpassing NATO enlargement in importance. It is an issue that should not be shirked. Accordingly, this chapter is aimed at audiences in both the United States and Europe. Oddly, the United States is not yet demanding greater military help from Europe. During the Cold War it complained loudly about burden-sharing, when the problem was less serious than it is today. It needs to speak out, for this is the only way to get Europe's attention. The Europeans should listen, not only to safeguard the alliance, but also to protect their own interests. They cannot afford to be militarily weak in the Persian Gulf forever, or to allow the United States to become disillusioned with them.

This chapter has a different tone than François Heisbourg's insightful chapter (Chapter 12 in this volume). Whereas this chapter addresses European military requirements to be fulfilled, Heisbourg focuses more on the political barriers to meeting them. Yet both chapters agree on the issue's importance. Their conclusions about the future military agenda are similar. This chapter calls for eight European divisions for Middle East and Gulf missions. Heisbourg concludes that four divisions may be forthcoming, and their top priority would be defense of the Gulf. Perhaps Heisbourg overstates the barriers: they are real, yet they plausibly can be overcome if Europe wakes up to its own strategic vulnerability. This chapter therefore recommends a visible policy effort to accomplish its goals, one that is different from the less ambitious, more evolutionary approach favored by Heisbourg. But even if Heisbourg is right, a 50 percent solution is not bad—much better than a 0 percent solution. Together, the two chapters provide hope that Americans and Europeans can find common ground on this issue.

This chapter disagrees with arguments that rule out military improvements because the Middle East political situation is allegedly too delicate for a stronger assertion of Western (i.e., U.S. and European) power. It acknowledges that Western diplomacy should be sensitive to how friends and adversaries will react, but not at the cost of leaving both the Persian Gulf oilfields and the Transatlantic alliance vulnerable to a great catastrophe. This chapter also disagrees with the "good cop–bad cop" metaphor: that the Europeans should be the good or nice cop in the Middle East, and the Americans, the bad or tough cop. Even this metaphor acknowledges that it takes two cops to enforce the law, and they must act as a team. The bad cop must be sensitive to the crook's rights or else the crook will never come clean. The good cop must be willing to draw his gun if necessary, or the crook will shoot the bad cop and get away. If both cops work together, they stand a good chance of preventing crimes, and solving those that occur.

Can the United States and Europe work together in this way? In particular, can they resolve their diplomatic quarrels so that they can cooperate on defense affairs? The task may be hard, but it can be eased if priorities are kept in mind. Diplomacy should serve grand strategy, not the other way around. Basic U.S. and European interests in this region are compatible. The task is not to make their foreign policies identical, but instead to make them similar enough so that a common military strategy becomes possible. In situations like this, the normal answer is a compromise, one that leaves both sides satisfied. In fact, compromise can lead to a better policy; neither side has a lock hold on truth. Provided both sides get their strategic bearings straight, the door to the shared responsibility model can be opened in ways that produce big security payoffs and make diplomatic cooperation easier.

Why Is Greater U.S.-European Collaboration Desirable?

Why is a greater European contribution to Persian Gulf and Middle East military missions desirable? The simple answer is that the United States badly needs more European help, and that for its own good, Europe is best advised to give it. If they develop the capacity to collaborate better, they will both gain big, enduring strategic benefits. They will reduce the risks that the alliance could fall apart due to disputes about the Greater Middle East. Moreover, they will enhance stability, security, deterrence, and defense across the entire region, especially in the Persian Gulf. Because these benefits are so attractive, they make an effort to build better European capabilities a viable proposition, provided it is handled skillfully.

HISTORY'S LEGACY

A more detailed analysis of the numerous reasons to launch this effort can best begin by recalling history's legacy. History is the source of the current anomalous situation, in which the European allies play only a minor supporting role in this region even though they have major interests at stake and the resources to do a good deal more if they were to reconfigure their force postures. This history supports the conclusion that a different pattern is possible if an attempt is made to break with a past that is no longer a reliable guide to the future.

During the Cold War's early years, the European allies—mainly Britain and France—were heavily involved in this region in a manner that reflected their colonial heritage. The result was a series of stressful political clashes between them and the United States, which was starting to put its own diplomatic imprint on the region with post-colonial policies in mind. As a result, the Suez crisis of 1956 and France's involvement in the Algerian war inflicted major damage on NATO's cohesion. Afterward, Britain and France largely withdrew from the region and refocused their defense strategies on Europe. The United States was left responsible for filling the resulting vacuum. Its own capability for Gulf operations was weak, but the Vietnam War and other preoccupations prevented any immediate improvements. By the mid-1970s, the West's growing dependence upon Gulf oil was making the region a vital interest in its strategic calculus, but still nothing was done.

At the time, Washington relied on Iran to act as a pro-Western surrogate in the Gulf. But when the shah fell in the late 1970s and the Soviet Union invaded Afghanistan, it became worried about a potential Soviet invasion aimed at seizing the vital Gulf oil fields and about local instability. As a result, the United States made a profound change in its global military strategy, which heretofore had focused on Europe and Asia. The new strategy called for building a strong capability to defend the Gulf, not by stationing large U.S. forces there in peacetime, but by rapidly projecting them from the continental United States (CONUS) in an emergency. As a consequence, the Pentagon created a new Central Command (CENTCOM) for Gulf missions and funded expensive mobility programs so that a large force could be deployed quickly.

Some thought was given to asking the European allies to contribute, but the idea was rejected. One reason was that the United States wanted to be free from having to coordinate its plans with European allies that might have different priorities in mind. Another reason was the need to concentrate allied forces on defending Western Europe, which was menaced by the Warsaw Pact. The United States therefore proposed that as sizable U.S. forces in

CONUS were diverted away from European reinforcement missions toward the Gulf, the NATO allies would strengthen their forces in Europe in order to compensate for the diversion. When the allies agreed, a *de facto* division of labor emerged. The Europeans took no steps to strengthen their quite modest forces for projection operations. The United States sought to use European bases and NATO logistics support in helping deploy U.S. forces to the Gulf. But this aside, Persian Gulf security became mostly an American show.

The agreed-upon division of labor was first put to the test when naval ships were sent to keep the Gulf sea-lanes open during the Iran-Iraq war. Although the British and other Europeans contributed, the U.S. Navy led the way. When the Gulf War occurred in 1990–91, the United States sent a huge force of over 600,000 troops. Most NATO allies agreed to help, but they lacked the capacity to send large forces. The British and French sent a division apiece, plus aircraft and ships. Several other European allies made token contributions, all of which were helpful. For its part, Germany sent no forces but it did make a large financial contribution. Nonetheless, the Western portion of the Desert Storm force was 85 percent American and only 15 percent European. A similar pattern has prevailed in the various peace support missions and crisis deployments launched since then.

What exists today is a strategic model of national military roles and missions that has evolved in response to historical circumstances but is now deeply ingrained. It will remain alive unless it is consciously changed because it has acquired considerable bureaucratic momentum on both sides of the Atlantic. In contrast to NATO's emphasis on multilateralism and major allied responsibilities in Europe, this model calls upon the United States to manage the Gulf's peacetime affairs mostly by itself. When a military operation must be launched—small or large—U.S. forces typically provide about 80–90 percent of the total, and the Europeans only 10–20 percent. Moreover, the Europeans are not formally obligated to make even these contributions. Rather than make force commitments in advance, they participate in each operation on an *ad hoc* basis, for the particular crisis at hand, without regard to any wider application.

Because the United States lacks confidence in future allied contributions, it forges its Gulf defense plans on the premise that its forces must be large enough to meet military requirements almost alone. It welcomes European allies when they choose to participate, but it does not count on them. As a result, the demanding Gulf contingency has become the basis for justifying and consuming fully one-half of the U.S. military posture. Indeed, U.S. forces stationed in Europe evidently find their war-fighting rationale in this contingency. For its part, NATO prepares no combined plans and programs for Persian Gulf operations by either the integrated command or by a unified European coalition outside the control of SACEUR (Supreme Allied Commander, Europe) and SACLANT (Supreme Allied Commander, Atlantic). The European countries are left free to prepare for these operations on their own, according to their individual predilections.

REASONS FOR A NEW MODEL

Now that the Cold War threat to Europe has ended, the current model of quasi-unilateral U.S. responsibility seems miscast. The Europeans arguably have equivalent or even greater interests at stake in the Persian Gulf and Middle East than does the United States; they are located closer, and together their defense spending is about two-thirds that of the Department of Defense's budget. Yet they do not contribute to Gulf security in commensurate ways. To be sure, some analysts are content with the status quo. They argue that the current model seems to be working, so why modify a satisfactory thing? They also judge that a major change would be too hard, too costly, and too risky. In my view, they underestimate the dangers posed by the future, and they fail to grasp the compelling reasons for a new model.

The first reason for a new model is political. If the United States is going to remain present in Europe, it has a legitimate right to expect a Transatlantic alliance that assists it in the dangerous Persian Gulf. The Europeans have strong reasons to respond: to keep on the good side of the Americans and to better protect their own interests. Moreover, a new model of shared responsibility might pave the way toward greater diplomatic unity between the Americans and Europeans. With more European allies by its side, the United States might be more willing to listen to European views on regional diplomacy. It might also be less worried that any steps to soften its stance toward adversaries could weaken its ability to defend the Persian Gulf if war breaks out. Because of their more serious military role, the Europeans might be less preoccupied with their commercial interests and less inclined to criticize the Americans for being too focused on military affairs. Greater U.S.-European unity, in turn, might increase both partners' diplomatic influence in the region. At a minimum, adversaries there would be less able to play divide-and-conquer.

A new model based on larger European contributions would also promote fairer burden-sharing and thereby reduce a grave risk to the alliance. During the Cold War, the current model seemed fair because Western Europe was equally as endangered as the Gulf. But that situation has now changed. Although the Gulf remains unstable, Europe is at peace. Eventually the American people will tire of carrying endless Gulf burdens while the Europeans defend borders that are no longer threatened. U.S. troops might start withdrawing from Europe, and American support for European goals on the continent might diminish.

This could happen even in peacetime. Something considerably worse could happen if another big Gulf war occurs, and it proves messy in ways that produce heavy casualties. If almost all of these casualties are American, the inevitable consequence will be outrage, all the more because of the widely held belief that Europe needs Gulf oil at least as much as the United States. Doubtless the Europeans would argue that the technicalities of the oil market and overall burden-sharing excuse them from putting their soldiers at risk in the Gulf. But these arguments might matter for little in the United States when American blood has been spilled. The Transatlantic alliance easily could fall apart because the United States might wash its hands of its allegedly free-riding European allies.

Other considerations also argue for a new model. Any future Gulf intervention will require a strong multinational coalition of Western powers. At a minimum, U.S. forces will require overflight rights in Europe and help in sailing U.S. transport ships through the Mediterranean. But this is not enough. The United States will be unable to act decisively if it does not enjoy Europe's broader support and active involvement. Although an *ad hoc* coalition that provided this support was hastily assembled during the Gulf War, the worrisome fact is that deterrence had failed because Iraq evidently doubted the ability of the United States and the Europeans to respond together. Although the conditions then were uniquely favorable to political collaboration as the Western powers scrambled to respond, they might not be so lucky next time. Prior agreement on U.S.-European cooperation can cement the coalition in place before a future event, thereby enhancing prospects for preventing a crisis from occurring and for reacting effectively if war does break out.

Moreover, the United States might find itself in need of greater European contributions for military reasons. The current U.S. posture may be adequate for handling two concurrent "major regional conflicts" (MRCs) in Korea and the Gulf, but it has no surplus assets. If this posture is reduced due to budgetary shortfalls and modernization needs, it might no longer be adequate. Even if it is not reduced, growing military needs in Asia and elsewhere could drain U.S. forces away from the Gulf. An equal concern is that the Pentagon is likely to begin re-engineering its force structure in the coming years, and this step could render some of its forces unready at any single moment. The combination of force cuts, other theaters, and re-engineering could compound the effect.[2]

Even if the current U.S. posture for the Gulf—about 6–7 divisions, 10 fighter wings, and 5 carriers—remains intact, the region's military requirements might grow in future years. The current Iraqi threat to the Gulf oil fields is modest, but future adversaries may be better-armed, and there may be several of them. U.S. forces will become stronger as the "Revolution in Military Affairs" (RMA) provides better C4/ISR systems and smart munitions.[3] Yet these technologies will not be a cure-all. They should not lead to the illusion of permanent, unchallengeable U.S. superiority regardless of how a war takes place. Adversaries may develop asymmetric strategies, better air defenses, accurate offensive missiles, and weapons of mass destruction. In addition, U.S. and allied forces might not have months to deploy and weeks to conduct air bombardment before launching ground operations. These factors could make the next Gulf war a difficult affair, one that stretches U.S. capabilities.

In addition, another Gulf war is not the only contingency worth worrying about. Much depends upon political trends that are hard to forecast, but the future could witness an upsurge of Western military operations not only in the Persian Gulf, but across the Greater Middle East as well. The ongoing stabilization operations directed at Iraq may be the forerunner of multiple peace support missions and crisis interventions in the Mediterranean, North Africa, Sub-Saharan Africa, and the vast zone covering the Middle East and Southwest Asia. If so, U.S. forces will be run ragged trying to handle these missions while staying prepared for a major war. For this reason alone, additional European force contributions could be not only desirable, but mandatory.

---

2. For analysis of future directions in the U.S. defense posture and strategy, see Paul K. Davis, David C. Gompert, and Richard L. Kugler, "Adaptiveness in National Defense: The Basis of a New Framework," RAND Issue Paper, Santa Monica, Calif., August 1996.

3. "C4/ISR" means command, control, communications, computers, intelligence, surveillance, and reconnaissance.

Components of a New Model of U.S.-European Cooperation

Today the Europeans possess only modest military capabilities for projection missions, and although some are upgrading their forces for operations around Europe, they have little taste for greater responsibilities in the Persian Gulf and the Middle East. But this situation is a product of past strategic choices and an existing policy mindset. It can be made to change as the future unfolds: not overnight, but gradually over the passage of a few years. After all, many of these countries operated large forces in far-flung places in earlier decades. Nearly all possess the wealth and technology to become better at power projection if the commitment is made. As the threat of major war in Europe continues to fade, they will become more free to assist the United States in defending Western interests in other theaters. If the United States finds itself facing growing military requirements with diminishing forces, it will have a powerful incentive to welcome them.

A new model would not replace U.S. forces with European forces in some wholesale way. Rather, it would add European forces to a still-large U.S. contribution, thereby forging a more equal balance of assets and responsibilities. This new model would have three features. First, it would replace *ad hoc* practices with formal European commitments so that the European countries know what is required of them, and the United States can be confident that these commitments will be forthcoming at the moment of truth. Second, it would employ NATO to help orchestrate the European preparedness effort, but without formally assigning all Persian Gulf and Middle East missions to the integrated command. Third, it would elevate European contributions from today's level of 10–20 percent of the total to a higher level of 30–50 percent. For example, the Europeans might plan to provide one-third of the forces needed for a major Gulf war, and one-half of the forces needed for lesser missions.

This model is not the only new approach that could be contemplated, but it is the one that makes best sense. One alternative would be an even starker geographic division of labor. In it, the NATO allies would assume full responsibility for Europe, and U.S. forces would withdraw from Europe in order to take even greater responsibility for the Persian Gulf and Middle East. Another alternative would be the polar opposite: the NATO integrated command would assume responsibility for the region in such total ways that CENTCOM would be disestablished and U.S. forces would play a minority role.

However, neither of these alternatives makes sense from the American perspective. Whereas the former would erode U.S. influence in Europe to an unhealthy degree, the latter would have an equivalent effect in the Gulf. Neither alternative, moreover, would serve Europe's interests. The former would deprive Europe of the United States' stabilizing influence, and the latter would hand the Europeans and NATO more responsibility in the Persian Gulf and Middle East than they can bear. The shared responsibility model steers a sound middle course between these two extremes in ways that aspire to leave Europe with undiminished stability and the Persian Gulf and Middle East with fairer burden-sharing and greater security than now.

What target should be set for improving European projection forces? The target should meet future military requirements, and it should be achievable. That is, it should generate enough forces to gain the benefits of the shared responsibility model, yet not so many that Europe's political circuits are overloaded. These two criteria imply a posture that is real, not symbolic, but still moderate in size.

An ideal but flexible target would call for a European posture similar in size to the current U.S. force for the Gulf. It would include 7–8 divisions, 400–500 combat aircraft, and 40–50 ships. This posture, however, would be configured somewhat differently than U.S. forces. Whereas about one-half of it would be prepared for major combat operations, the other half would be designed for less-demanding peace support missions and crisis interventions. It thus would provide a flexible portfolio of assets that could be employed in a wide spectrum of military contingencies. It might take the form of a NATO "Combined Joint Task Force" (CJTF) that would be planned by the NATO integrated command but operated outside NATO in some cases. Regardless of the command arrangements, its key characteristic is that it would be militarily capable of performing diverse missions in peace, crisis, and war. Unlike the situation today, it would possess the readiness, logistics, and mobility assets needed to operate in the Persian Gulf and the Middle East promptly and effectively.

What Are the Prospects for Increasing European Capabilities?

Can a European projection force of this size and capability be built in ways that bring the shared responsibility model to life? The answer is yes, if a strong effort is launched and carried out effectively. By getting serious about the enterprise and acting skillfully, the stage can be set for the Europeans not only to endorse the idea but also to take the necessary concrete steps.

Big doses of effort and skill are needed because the distance to be covered is large. The Europeans are still so locked into fading NATO border defense missions that they would be hard-pressed to project even one-fourth of the required forces in a timely fashion. In absence of U.S. military support, moreover, even these forces could not readily work together in carrying out combined operations, or in sustaining themselves for a significant period against serious opposition. If a more effective posture is to be assembled, it will require a major improvement upon what the Europeans can provide today.[4]

Because the United States is the alliance's leader, it must play an active role in urging a reform effort of this magnitude. Yet it is the Europeans who will have to do most of the reforming. Although some Europeans are beginning to see the need for such an effort, many argue that it is beyond the pale: that Europe is too inward-looking to help defend the Gulf. To Americans who expect better of the Europeans, this argument comes across as self-serving and self-defeating. After all, the United States has weighty domestic problems of its own, but they do not prevent it from defending its overseas interests or protecting its allies. Throughout the Cold War, the Europeans often cited their domestic inhibitions. Yet when their safety was threatened, they responded on countless occasions with defense efforts that may not have been perfect, but at least were adequate. Today they are far more wealthy and better united than in previous decades. In other areas, they are pursuing ambitious strategic innovations: building the EU and enlarging NATO. They are quite capable of responding in the Persian Gulf if they take stock of their own self-interests, mobilize their willpower, and spend the necessary political capital. The reason that a consensus does not exist today is that, apart from French President Jacques Chirac, nobody has tried to build it.

Provided a consensus is built, the centerpiece of a European power projection effort must be NATO, not the European Union (EU) or the Western European Union (WEU), and not the individual European countries acting on their own. NATO is the only institution capable of forging military cooperation between the United States and Europe, fashioning bold departures, and achieving widespread success with limited funds. Pursuit of a new model would necessitate a major

---

4. For more analysis, see Richard L. Kugler, *U.S.–West European Cooperation in Out-of-Area Operations* (Santa Monica, Calif.: RAND, 1994).

change in NATO's strategic concept and associated defense plans. This does not mean that NATO itself would conduct every military operation. For example, NATO might perform some Middle East missions, delegate others to a CJTF, and merely help deploy European forces to the Gulf, where they would be integrated into CENTCOM. But this model does mean that NATO would organize the force-preparedness effort in ways that transform separate national efforts into a collective response. As a practical matter, NATO would become a multi-theater alliance. It would remain primarily focused on Europe, but it would acquire a major contributing role in the Persian Gulf and Middle East as well.

MOBILIZING EUROPE'S SUPPORT

Success requires that European governments make a firm political commitment to the enterprise. Within each participating country, a new foreign policy and defense consensus in favor of greater power projection will be needed, as well as a willingness to work closely with alliance partners. Few countries are enthusiastic, but they have ample reasons for thinking differently about the future. One reason is to keep on friendly terms with the United States so that it does not abandon Europe and NATO in frustration over unfair burdens and free riders. A second reason is to protect their own interests, especially their access to oil that is vital to their economies. A third reason is to promote stability in a heavily populated, unstable region that lies almost next door to Europe. A fourth reason is the growing risk that military threats, including weapons of mass destruction, might arise from the Middle East and become aimed at Europe. A fourth reason is to backstop the United States in case it gets so tied down in other theaters that it cannot handle the Persian Gulf and the Middle East alone. A fifth reason is to enhance Gulf security so that U.S. forces stationed in Europe can perform their NATO missions with lessened concern about being deployed to the Gulf at a moment's notice. Provided the Europeans choose to think clearly about the strategic basics, these reasons are ample to justify an innovative approach aimed at remedying their current deficiencies.

Britain and France are the countries that most likely would respond favorably provided their own interests are respected. Germany might be the most likely to balk. Other countries with distant-area horizons such as Belgium, the Netherlands, Italy, and Spain could be expected to fall into the middle, suspended between interest and doubt. The final result would likely be driven by a collective dynamic, and by the degree to which the United States exerts leadership on behalf of the departure. Consequently, an alliance-wide consensus would not be easy to build, but with so much at stake, it might be feasible.

A consensus-building effort could begin with U.S.-British cooperation; then France could join. The importance of France's support casts a bright spotlight on why the U.S.-French dispute over the Allied Forces Southern Europe (AFSOUTH) command is damaging to both countries and to NATO's emerging strategic agenda. Perhaps a rapprochement can begin with a compromise on AFSOUTH in ways that facilitate U.S.-French cooperation on Mediterranean defense affairs. France's participation would set the stage for Germany to join. For political and military reasons, Germany's participation is critical and will mark the next logical stage in its ongoing strategic transformation into a country that works within NATO to export security outside its borders. With Germany on board, the circle of participants could be steadily widened. Italy and the Low Countries are obvious candidates. The more countries that join the better. Yet the big four are the key.

The argument is often made that due to post–Cold War downsizing, the Europeans do not have the money or the forces to accomplish the task. This argument fades, however, when raw statistics are considered. Together, the European members of NATO are still spending over $160 billion annually on defense. About $40 billion is being spent on acquisition programs. They thus have ample funds for launching projection programs if they are willing to set new priorities. Today they still deploy fully 55 mobilizable divisions, 3,200 combat aircraft, and 300 major ships. A Persian Gulf/Middle East force could be assembled by committing only 10–15 percent of this posture. The remaining forces would be ample for handling European missions.

Moreover, this innovation would not be a leap into a strategic void. The Europeans are already committed to provide about 9 divisions, 600 aircraft, and 40 ships to NATO's Reaction Forces, which are intended for projection missions around Europe's periphery. The task therefore would be one of pursuing a more distant form of power projection, rather than embracing an entirely new mission. Indeed, many countries already possess some projection capabilities even though they would be hard-pressed to fulfill their commitments to NATO's Reaction Force posture. Although most countries would have to upgrade their existing capabilities by a factor of two or three, the total amount is not great when measured in absolute terms. No country would have to commit a full corps or other formations that would total 100,000 troops or more. Indeed, most countries would have to commit only a division or a brigade apiece, along with commensurate air and naval forces: a total of 25,000–50,000 troops. For all of them, this is a manageable proposition.

ENERGIZING NATO

Because of a host of practical complications even if Europe's political support is built, the proposed effort would be complex and taxing in ways requiring NATO to play the role of main orchestrator. One complication is the need for widespread multinational participation, because no single nation could be expected to carry the bulk of the load. Even Britain and France together will not have nearly enough projection forces to meet the entire requirement. A multinational posture could be assembled only if the participating nations agree to cooperate closely so that their efforts are properly coordinated. If they are to cooperate, they will have to reach common agreement on objectives, operational requirements, and military roles and missions: a demanding agenda even when consensus exists on strategic purposes.

A second complication is that the act of preparing for Persian Gulf/Middle East missions cannot be approached in isolation. It would have to be launched even as NATO prepares for other projection missions elsewhere. In the coming years, NATO will be required to develop forces that can help defend its new members in East Central Europe and carry out new missions. It is also likely to face the prospect of carrying out peace support missions. The combined effect could be a major shift of NATO military strategy away from the current emphasis on main defense missions toward power projection. Whereas today less than one-half of the Allied Forces Central Command's (AFCENT) active forces are earmarked for projection missions, tomorrow virtually all of them might have to be allocated, thereby transforming AFCENT into a reservoir for power projection rather than NATO's premier border defense force.

A third complication is that the Europeans would have to pursue defense programs that, for them, are new. The United States has lengthy experience in handling the programmatic complexities of major power projection missions, but for the most part, the Europeans do not. Even if the United States provides the necessary strategic airlift and C^4/ISR assets, the Europeans would need to make many changes. They would have to alter their personnel policies so that the soldiers assigned to projection forces can be legally sent abroad. They would have to develop new training regimens, new doctrines, and new procedures. They would have to develop new operational plans (OPlans) that are configured to project large forces across long distances. They would need to upgrade their communications systems, improve their logistics support assets, assemble sealift transports, procure some new equipment, reconfigure some weapons, buy the necessary supplies, prepare facilities for onloading and offloading, and pre-position some matériel abroad. Even as they pursue these measures within their own postures, they would have to pursue multinational integration with the forces of other countries in such areas as sealift, logistics, and air defense. Individually these steps are manageable, but together they create an enterprise that takes years to work out, one that would bring about major changes in every country's ways of doing military business.

The fourth complication is that of funding. Provided the necessary programs are spread out over a period of years, the act of preparing for projection missions would cost only about $4–5 billion per year. In political terms, this expense is readily affordable because it amounts only to 2–3 percent of Europe's annual defense spending. However, unless defense budgets are raised, an unlikely event, the required funds could be generated only by accepting cutbacks elsewhere. Even today, European generals complain about funding shortages for training, modernization, and logistics support. The act of shifting priorities toward power projection at the expense of further cutbacks in these areas doubtlessly would make many of them complain louder. In all likelihood, properly balanced defense budgets could be maintained only by accepting some safe cuts (e.g., 5–10 percent) in border defense forces.

One of NATO's primary functions is overcoming complications like these. But to be effective, NATO itself must be energized and used wisely. Even if this step is accomplished, progress will be slow because NATO's members have little experience in working with each other outside the alliance's boundaries. Military establishments are complex institutions that cannot be changed overnight. As a result, the effort is likely to take years to accomplish. Yet the U.S. CENTCOM posture took a decade to build, and the results were well worth the effort.

What kind of political strategy within NATO will best produce an effective response? One option is to avoid a big policy debate by quietly trying to encourage European force improvements in evolutionary ways, out of the limelight. This strategy might minimize controversy in the short term, but its effects would be modest, and eventually they would attract public attention. A second strategy is to employ some already-accepted contingency as a vehicle to develop European forces that, with modest adjustments, could also be used in the Gulf. The most likely contingency is defense of Turkey. This strategy might work, but only if the Europeans become animated by the prospect of defending Turkey. A third strategy is to provoke a policy debate and to use it as a vehicle to mobilize support for building a Gulf capability. The choice is the alliance's to make, but NATO's history suggests that if the goal is a decisive response, the third strategy is normally best.

Regardless of the strategy, success will not be achievable if only rhetorical commitments are made. These commitments must be backed up by the determination to work hard on the thorny military details. The key is to use NATO's planning mechanisms, which themselves will have to be transformed so that they can handle major power projection missions not only outside the alliance's borders, but outside Europe as well. If NATO's mechanisms are used, effective coalition planning can unfold. NATO's military commanders and civilian leaders can identify force requirements, create force goals, determine resource guidance, and establish program priorities. Then, the participating nations can forge country plans that will be evaluated by NATO officials in the context of multinational requirements and choreographed in the proper ways.

What the situation requires is creation of a visionary NATO program—similar to the Long Term Defense Plan (LTDP) and Conventional Defense Initiative (CDI) of the Cold War—that aims at enhancing European power projection capabilities for multiple new missions.[5] Designing and carrying this out will require hard work. If this coalition planning is pursued, however, the outcome can be a slow but steady progress toward European forces that truly can project military power into the Persian Gulf and Middle East as well as East Central Europe. Not everyone will agree with this guarded yet optimistic forecast. But it is given credibility by NATO's own history of often stressful and imperfect innovations that, when the dust settled, proved to be strategic successes.

What will happen if the effort fails? The answer is that degree matters. A wholesale failure would greatly damage NATO, but this is

---

5. "LTDP" refers to the Carter administration's Long Term Defense Plan; "CDI" refers to the Reagan administration's Conventional Defense Initiative. For analysis, see Richard L. Kugler, *Commitment to Purpose: How Alliance Partnership Won the Cold War* (Santa Monica, Calif.: RAND, 1994).

unlikely to happen. NATO defense efforts seldom fail totally. Even the disappointments yield something. The most probable failure scenario is a partial response. But if Heisbourg is correct in saying that the traffic will bear a four-division response, this result will be a success in relative terms. After all, a half-filled glass would be better than the empty glass of the 1990s.

Can U.S. and European Forces Operate Together Effectively?

The act of creating larger European forces for power projection into the Persian Gulf and the Middle East is the first step toward building a shared responsibility model, but not the only step. An important second step is that of blending greater European contributions with U.S. forces and those of friendly Arab powers so that "operational effectiveness"—the ability to use forces effectively to achieve key political-military objectives—is also enhanced. Success in this critical arena is not a foregone conclusion. More is not always better: adding additional forces to the total posture does not automatically translate into higher operational effectiveness. Indeed, the opposite can be the case if the consequence is reduced political cohesion and a diminished capacity to carry out military deployments and campaign plans in an efficient, decisive manner. Because significant operational problems are likely to arise if more European forces are introduced into the equation, these problems must be faced squarely. Experience shows they can be solved, but only through combined planning that is driven by political wisdom and military professionalism, and that pays careful attention to ensuring that European forces can be deployed and employed sensibly in a Gulf crisis.

WHY MULTINATIONAL OPERATIONS ARE HARD

An analysis of operational effectiveness must begin by recognizing the vast military differences between Europe and the Persian Gulf/Middle East. In Europe today, NATO focuses mostly on preserving stability, integrating new partners and members, and carrying out peace support missions and minor crisis interventions. With the Cold War over, it no longer has to worry seriously about fighting a major war in Europe anytime soon. The Persian Gulf/Middle East is an entirely different matter. The politics of this region are more turbulent than those of Europe. This region is also laced with multiple dangerous military imbalances, as well as several well-armed potential adversaries willing to fight Western forces if they are perceived as vulnerable due to an uncertain capacity to operate effectively. Some of these adversaries may acquire nuclear weapons and other weapons of mass destruction (WMD), and they may be willing to use them. The principal danger facing Western forces is another big Persian Gulf war, for this is the contingency that could most expose operational problems.

This theater thus demands real military planning focused on actual wars, not just multinational forces that perform mostly political missions or defense plans that are based on the expectation of easily brushing aside incompetent opponents if conflict does break out. The necessity to think seriously about major combat is one reason why U.S. military commanders prefer a force posture that is dominated by American units. U.S. forces typically are better armed and more prepared for war than are the forces of other countries. They are also trained to act cohesively in carrying out a single unified military doctrine. Desert Shield was a success because U.S. forces were allowed to deploy rapidly into the theater unencumbered by constraining alliance politics. Desert Storm was a success partly because it was dominated by U.S. forces that were able to carry out the initial air campaign and the follow-on ground campaign with great effectiveness. Taking into account the constraints that might have arisen, would a more multinational posture, marked by the presence of additional European forces, have been equally effective? Would the Western coalition have won as quickly and decisively, and with so few casualties? Worry about the answer helps to account for the tendency of many U.S. defense planners to view a larger European contribution as a mixed blessing.

Several political complications brought about by greater European participation could erode operational effectiveness if they are not guarded against. One complication is that the United States and its European allies might be pursuing different foreign policy agendas in ways that could influence their capacity to collaborate in carrying out peacetime security operations. Countries do not have to agree on all aspects of diplomacy in order to join together their military forces, but they must be in accord on the strategic basics. Absent this accord, a more assertive Europe could contribute to heightened Transatlantic quarreling about political strategy, resulting in a weakened Western involvement. In addition, a more assertive Europe could alienate some Arab nations, whose cooperation with U.S. forces is equally important if coalition operations are to succeed.

Troubles could also arise when the time comes to use military force. An American fear is that European disagreements with Washington's handling of Iraq and Iran might lead some allies to withhold their forces in event of a crisis or war. Conversely, Europeans might worry about Washington's loyalty to their causes once they become militarily entangled in the Persian Gulf and Middle East. In peace and war, the underlying reality is that combined planning breeds a high degree of interdependence. Reliance on it is safe only when the participants are animated by similar regional stances. Operational effectiveness thus is another reason for building greater U.S.-European diplomatic accord as the shared responsibility model is pursued.

Even when a consensus exists on foreign policy and diplomacy, a second complication can arise: the delicate matter of reaching agreement on command relationships in ways that do not degrade operational effectiveness. An American perspective holds that the current model is advantageous because it allows senior U.S. military officers to dominate the command hierarchy of any Gulf coalition, and therefore to call the military shots. U.S. officers dominated in the Gulf War, and their influence played a major role in shaping the coherent ground, air, and naval campaigns that became Desert Storm. If large European forces are committed to Gulf operations, their presence will justify and necessitate that senior European officers receive commensurately large leadership roles. This especially will be the case if the Europeans arrive as a NATO-sponsored CJTF that allows them to act as a unified bloc.

Regardless of how the Europeans arrive, the result must be a true multinational command structure, in which Americans, Europeans, and Arabs share power and must work by consensus. History shows that this situation can give rise to personal rivalries; moreover, even if harmony prevails, multinational planning can produce incoherent plans. This can be the case because each country brings not only its own political objectives, but also unique attitudes toward military strategy, combat operations, and associated roles and missions. Typically, differences are ironed out by compromise, which might simply reflect the command structure's internal dynamics rather than a unified theory of how to wage war. In essence, too many cooks can spoil the broth, a worry that applies not only to diplomacy, but to military strategy as well.

Even if a coherent strategy and plan are assembled, multinationalism can raise impediments to effective battlefield operations due to differences in the physical composition of the forces themselves. Modern war demands well-coordinated joint operations by ground, air, and naval components that work well together. The three U.S. services themselves encounter troubles in working together, while also striving to use their own assets in effective ways. These troubles could grow as the degree of multinational participation increases. Although U.S. and European forces have worked hard to achieve compatibility and interoperability, they remain structured somewhat differently, and they therefore operate in dissimilar ways. For example, the United States places greater emphasis on air power than do the Europeans, and its air forces attach greater importance to close air support and battlefield interdiction. Its ground forces are more heavily equipped with artillery, air defense, long-range systems, and logistics assets. Indeed, European forces differ among each other in these and other categories. An additional factor is that, as U.S. forces acquire RMA systems, they will become even more different from European forces, which are not likely to acquire these systems as early or as quickly.

The net effect is that U.S. forces are likely to have different approaches to both defensive and offensive operations than the Europeans. Whereas U.S. forces will employ high-technology systems and assertive operational concepts, most European forces are likely to rely on less sophisticated technology and more conservative concepts, with less emphasis on joint operations, strong logistics systems, high tempo, long-range strikes, and bold maneuvers. These differences are manageable when U.S. forces dominate and allied forces provide only a small portion of the total, as was the case in Desert Storm. But they can be tougher to manage when the contributions are more evenly balanced. If care is not taken, the consequence can be a poorly coordinated operation that erodes military effectiveness; in a demanding war, effectiveness can spell the difference between victory and defeat.

AN APPROACH FOR DEPLOYING AND EMPLOYING FORCES
None of these operational complications rules out the idea of increasing European contributions to security in the Persian Gulf and Middle East. All of them raise problems that are solvable if they are handled carefully. But they raise a cautionary flag that counsels prudence. They also illustrate why wise diplomacy, careful military planning, and combined training will be important if shared responsibility is to be created. After all, force commitments are a means to an end. What

matters is whether they accomplish their strategic goals. The purpose of committing larger European forces to the Persian Gulf and Middle East is to do a better job of protecting Western interests, not to replace the United States or make its life more difficult.

What are the implications for force-sizing, deployment plans, and campaign plans? Perhaps the most important implication is that, until confidence is gained that U.S. and European forces can operate with undiminished effectiveness, their total force commitments should be more than the bare minimum. A margin of safety will be needed. Moreover, U.S. forces should provide the preponderant mass of combat power—perhaps two-thirds of total assets—for waging another Gulf war.

If another Gulf war requires an emergency buildup, quick-reaction U.S. forces should probably deploy first because their mobility assets are better suited to a fast response, and they provide the specialized capabilities—e.g., Patriot missile batteries, interceptors, ground units for screening missions, Aegis cruisers—that are needed to establish secure lines of communication and reception areas. They could be accompanied by some crack European units that fit into the early deployment plan. Following them could come U.S. Air Force reinforcements and Navy carriers, plus the main European forces, which will be suitable for initial defense. Afterward could come heavy U.S. Army units from CONUS, thus providing the strong combat power needed for a counteroffensive. The final stage of deployment would be composed of a theater-wide logistics posture of U.S. and European units with staying power.

In a similar fashion, a coherent theory of battlefield roles and missions, guided by specialization concepts, should animate campaign plans for combat operations. U.S. military forces should perform the missions for which they are best prepared: the high-technology operations and bold maneuvers that are the centerpiece of modern military doctrine. As in the Gulf War, European forces can be employed in a fashion that reflects their specific capabilities and complements U.S. forces. Those forces that have capabilities similar to U.S. forces (e.g., British units) can work directly with American units. Those forces that have different assets (e.g., French forces) can be given supportive missions that take advantage of their capabilities. In this way, a sound combined posture capable of carrying out an effective campaign plan can be assembled. As a consequence, the goals of fair burden-sharing and of military success can both be realized.

Conclusion

Beyond doubt, the idea of increasing European force contributions to Persian Gulf and Middle East missions is a bold strategic departure. So also is the idea of transforming NATO into a multi-theater alliance that looks outside Europe. Those who are relaxed about the future may not see the urgency for this departure, but those who are worried about coming dangers will grasp its importance. The key issue is whether the alliance is to play a serious role in meeting emerging security requirements. Are the United States and Europe to continue working together on truly dangerous problems that are becoming global, or are they to drift apart now that Europe is becoming stable? The answer to this question will determine whether the future is approached in bold ways or not.

If the core problem is to be solved, a new model of shared responsibility will be needed, one that enjoys the support of both the United States and the Europeans. Critics will argue that the difficulties are too hard to overcome. Perhaps so, but effort and skill remain potent weapons for getting the job done. Making intelligent use of NATO is key. This means creating a new and different NATO that can look south even as it moves east. The alliance thus faces a demanding agenda of "double enlargement." The future is uncertain, but the bottom line is that the West will not know what is possible unless it tries to make something better happen. In the final analysis, what other choice does it have?

Chapter 12

The United States, Europe, and Military Force Projection

François Heisbourg

Europphean and American force projection operations in the Middle East are not a novelty: indeed, the U.S. Marines fired their first shots in a foreign intervention on the shores of Tripoli in 1805. Similarly, there is nothing new about the Americans and the Europeans pursuing distinct objectives in such operations: most spectacularly with U.S. opposition against the Suez expedition, an event that remains unpleasantly vivid in French and British memories. Nor have the effects of such differences always remained confined to the specific issue in point: if it remains to be seen to what extent the Gulf War was a "defining moment" of the post–Cold War era, the Suez experience clearly defined British and French defense policies and national strategy for several decades. Britain cast its nuclear lot with the United States in 1958, thus giving their special relationship a new dimension, while France embarked on the road that led it to nuclear independence and withdrawal from an integrated North Atlantic Treaty Organization (NATO).

Given the Middle East's continuing importance to Europe and the United States, the same causes may produce even greater effects on the future of the alliance, in view of the existential challenge that NATO faces after the disappearance of the enemy against which it had been created.

The degree to which alliance partners can agree on prospective and actual military force projection in the Middle East will thus be one of the determinants of NATO's future. But, as in the past, no common objective or specific danger in the Middle East provides a permanent underpinning for a Transatlantic alliance posture in the region. Unlike the Cold War situation, the backdrop of the Soviet threat, which set outer limits to U.S.-European differences on Middle Eastern policy no longer exists: during the Suez crisis, the British and the French had to cease military operations and toe the line of their American security guarantor. Such circumstances no longer prevail.

This chapter is organized as follows. After a broad-brush examination of current force projection objectives and capabilities, the political, military, and strategic trends shaping European force projection are analyzed, including the effects of prospective NATO renovation and enlargement. This will be followed by policy recommendations based on the argument that force projection in the Middle East will remain an area of disagreement between the United States and Europe; that significant practical measures can be taken to mitigate the effects of such disagreements while increasing the effectiveness of specific operations; and that strong attempts to work out ambitious explicit and binding Transatlantic divisions of labor and strategies involving force projection towards the Middle East would not only be in vain, but could prove to be counterproductive to the point of jeopardizing existing Transatlantic cooperation. In this respect, this chapter differs from the more radical, possibly over-ambitious approach adopted by Richard Kugler (Chapter 11).

Objectives and Capabilities

American military objectives for force projection are outlined in the Bottom-Up Review conducted under Les Aspin's stewardship as U.S. Secretary of Defense: the U.S. armed forces should retain, *inter alia,* the capability of waging a war (under U.S. command and control) akin in scale and tempo to the Gulf conflict, while having sufficient force available to simultaneously hold their own in a second major regional conflict.[1] In practice, this entails the existence of both a division-scale rapid reaction force capable of action within a period of days, as well as a much larger expeditionary force comparable to that built up during the five-month period prior to Operation Desert Storm (more than half a million personnel under arms, 1,900 tanks, 300 tanker aircraft servicing more than 1,000 combat aircraft, six aircraft carriers, etc.).[2]

---

1. "Report on the Bottom-Up Review," U.S. Department of Defense, October 1993.

2. "Operation Desert Shield: The Military Build-up," *Strategic Survey 1990–1991* (London: International Institute for Strategic Studies [IISS], 1991), pp. 63–66; and J. McCausland, *The Gulf Conflict: A Military Analysis,* Adelphi Paper No. 282 (London: IISS, 1993).

This further entails a massive air- and sea-lift capability (using both dedicated military means and aircraft and shipping from the civilian sector); pre-positioned equipment, notably in Diego Garcia and Saipan; theater-scale joint command and control structures; global communications and intelligence assets, including a network of space-based communications and information gathering satellites; and, last but not least, the more than 550,000 U.S. soldiers, sailors, Marines, and Air Force personnel deployed during the Gulf War.

In contrast, none of the European countries today has the ambition of conducting a war on a stand-alone basis in the Middle East. In 1970, the United Kingdom dropped its objective of fielding forces capable of acting decisively and on their own east of Suez; in previous years, the British had projected such forces to defeat an attempted coup against King Hussein of Jordan (1958), in Kuwait (against the threat of an Iraqi invasion in 1964), and against anti-government guerrillas in Oman (1969), not to mention the last struggles of decolonization in what became for a time South Yemen. More recently, several European countries have organized their armed forces in order to operate as part of multinational coalitions, be they of a war-making or a peacekeeping nature: Britain, France, Italy, and Spain have kept or set up rapid reaction forces, the largest being the four divisions (French format) of France's Force d'Action Rapide (FAR). These and other countries (Austria, Belgium, Denmark, Finland, the Netherlands, Norway, and Sweden) have also had a policy of preparing for and participating in dedicated UN peacekeeping operations, notably in the Middle East. France and Italy, like the United States, fielded forces in excess of 2,000 soldiers each in the Beirut Multinational Security Force (1982–84); more than 300 allied soldiers were killed as part of that operation. France and the United Kingdom deployed combat forces from the three services during the Gulf War (including some 35,000 British and 15,000 French soldiers), joined by an Italian air force squadron plus naval forces from these and several other European countries (Belgium, Denmark, Greece, the Netherlands, Norway, Poland, and Spain). Several European states participated in Operation Provide Comfort in Kurdistan.

Germany, which had previously been totally absent from military conflicts, prepared politically and militarily for some participation in both peacekeeping, for the first time in Somalia in 1992–93, and coercive operations, as in the air operation Deliberate Force in Bosnia in August–September 1995. In the Middle East, Germany had a modest presence, mainly with military transport, in the relief operations in

Kurdistan in 1991, and in the logistical support of the United Nations Special Commission's (UNSCOM) activities in Iraq. Germany is currently setting up crisis reaction forces (KRK, or *Krisenreaktionskräfte*) whose two largely professional divisions could eventually be part of coalition operations in the Middle East.

European capabilities are in keeping with their Middle East force projection ambitions: participation in coalition operations, yes; exercising leadership in a coalition or operating on a stand-alone basis, no. This lack of ambition stands in contrast to European objectives towards other theaters of operations. Thus, France has demonstrated its readiness and ability to conduct stand-alone operations within the African states with which France has defense agreements (with an upper limit of around 5,000 troops, reached with great logistical difficulty in Chad in 1984). Forceful operations were conducted in the Comoros in 1995 and in the Central African Republic in 1996. The United Kingdom, for its part, proceeded with the daring reconquest of the Falklands in 1982.

Collectively, European airlift capabilities are approximately an order of magnitude smaller than those of the United States (see Table 1); furthermore, these capabilities are not pooled between European countries, which further reduces Europe's overall ability to engage in significant force projection. European reliance on foreign (notably U.S. but also Russian and Ukrainian) airlift was the norm in the Gulf War, and in Rwanda in 1994.

No European country has the ability to orchestrate inter-service, multinational, theater-scale military operations. Only the United States, notably its Central Command (CENTCOM), and NATO are capable of commanding and controlling the engagement of such forces, as in the Gulf or during the coercive phase of operations in Bosnia. France alone in continental Europe has a permanent capability to orchestrate national inter-service force projection operations, as a consequence of its experience with small but complex expeditions in Africa and, more recently, the Gulf War.

European strategic communications—the United Kingdom's Skynet communications satellite network; France's Syracuse; the military channel of Spain's Hispasat, etc.—are sufficient for participation in coalition operations but not in keeping with a broader role. Strategic reconnaissance has made a major step forward with the entry into service in 1995 of the *Helios IA* surveillance satellite, which provides France, Italy, and Spain with direct access to their own "overhead" data. Even if U.S. investment in this field remains vastly greater than Europe's, for force projection purposes the minimum capability necessary to avoid utter dependence on U.S. (or other) resources in this area may be within Europe's grasp. However, European states have yet to develop the type of all-sources "data fusion" that characterizes U.S. theater commands.

European human resources and military hardware are not, in themselves, lacking. Collectively, the members of the Western European Union (WEU), have standing military forces of around 2.3 million (compared to some 1.5 million for the United States), along with 3,500 combat aircraft and 9,700 main battle tanks.[3] However, with the exception of forces earmarked for NATO, these numbers cannot be considered as a whole from a military planning perspective. Furthermore, most European countries still have conscript forces, which are not politically or operationally ideal for force projection purposes. Things are changing in this area: the United Kingdom (since 1963), Luxembourg (since 1966), Belgium (since 1994), and the Netherlands (since 1996) have all-volunteer forces, and both France and Spain will go professional by 2002. Given the increasing problems encountered by Germany and Italy in managing conscription in a post–Cold War situation, it is doubtful that the status quo can survive much longer there either.

POLITICAL FORCES

The Middle East has not always been at the center of U.S. defense and military policy; it was not until 1979–80, with the Iranian revolution and the Soviet invasion of Afghanistan, that the United States declared the Gulf to be an area of vital interest, and that specific military measures were taken to give U.S. forces the ability to project themselves effectively in that area. In previous years, the region was no doubt central to U.S. security concerns, be they economic (oil), political (Israel), or security-related (the competition with the Soviet Union), but it had remained peripheral in military terms: the Sixth Fleet was able to operate in the Mediterranean and the Seventh Fleet extended its reach into the Indian Ocean. But it took the U.S. build-up of Diego Garcia as a staging and pre-positioning point, the creation of CENTCOM, and the conclusion of military cooperation agreements in the Gulf to give the United States a true military force projection capability in the Middle East during the eighties. This has further

---

3. Data derived from *The Military Balance 1996–1997* (London: IISS, 1996).

Table 1. American and European MFP Capabilities: Selected Quantitative Elements of Comparison.

United States		Members of the WEU[a]		
Airlift				
U.S.A.F. transport		**Long-range transport**		
C-17	27	DC-8, B-707,		
C-5	126	A-310, Tristar,		
C-141	217	VC-10	47	(including 27 tanker-transports: excluding CRAF-type aircraft)
Navy and U.S. Marines transport				
DC-9	10	C-130:	129	(including 5 tankers)
C-130	174	C-160 Transall	227	(including 14 tankers)
Dedicated tankers		**Dedicated tankers**	20	
KC-135	549			
KC-10	59			
CRAF (long range)	418			

Military Space-Based Systems[b]

Early Warning Satellites: 3+1 D.S.B.

Optical Reconnaissance Satellites		**Optical Reconnaissance Satellites**	
KH-11	3?	*Helios-I*	1
KH-12 IKON	1		
ARP-731	1		

Radar Satellites

Lacrosse	1
OSUS Clusters (Ocean Surveillance)	4

Elint/Comint Satellites

Chalet (Vortex)	2
Magnum	2
Jumpseat	2

Navigation and Ranging Satellites

Navstar (Global Positioning System) Includes Nuclear Detonation Detection Sensors	24

Table 1. *continued* **American and European MFP Capabilities: Selected Quantitative Elements of Comparison.**

United States		Members of the WEU	
Naval Power Projection			
Catapult-Launch Aircraft Carriers	12	Catapult-Launch Aircraft Carriers	2
Assault Carriers/Landing Ships	11	Assault Carriers	5
Naval and USMC Combat Aircraft (F.14, F.18, A-6, AV-8B)	est. 1500	Naval Combat Aircraft	est. 220
Landing Platform/ Ship-dock	26	Landing Platform/ Ship-dock	12
Military Sealift[c]			
Operating Vessels	21		
Afloat Pre-positioned ships	34		
Standby Sealift Ships	7		
Ready Reserve Ships	92		
Principal Foreign-Based Forces[d]			
In Germany	75,000	In Germany (U.K., F, B, NL)	48,100
In Japan	44,600	In Bosnia	20,300
In Korea	35,900	In Cyprus	4,200
Vth Fleet (on average one carrier group)		In Djibouti	3,900
VIth Fleet	16,500	Total French Forces Deployed[e]	
VIIth Fleet	19,500[f]	Outside metro. France	52,500
Kuwait	1 Army Brigade	Outside NATO	37,500
Total Europe	127,100	Total UK Forces Deployed[g]	
Total East Asia	96,800[h]	Outside of UK	48,300
		Outside NATO	19,500

SOURCE: *The Military Balance 1966–97* (London: IISS, 1996).

a. The ten full members of the Western European Union are: Belgium, France, Germany, Greece, Italy, Luxembourg, the Netherlands, Portugal, Spain, and the United Kingdom.

b. Does not include dedicated military communication satellites (in service in France, the United Kingdom, and the United States).

c. Active, standby, and ready.

d. U.S. figures exclude on-going operations (e.g., IFOR, Southern Watch).

e. Including on-going operations.

f. Home port in Hawaii.

g. Excluding on-going operations.

h. Excluding Seventh Fleet.

been fleshed out by the permanent stationing of forces in Kuwait and Saudi Arabia since the Gulf War.

The U.S. military commitment in the region thus has a relatively recent past, and although it has a robust present, its future is not pre-ordained. In addition, it is the result of a purely American set of decisions: the United States has for somewhat less than two decades considered the Gulf area to be of vital American interest in military terms. This reminder serves a dual purpose. First, from a European standpoint, the primacy of a military (notably military force projection) response to challenges emanating from, or concerning, the Middle East is not self-evident: economic, political, and diplomatic engagement can be of greater relevance. That the United States currently attributes to it such a primacy is an undeniable, but historically recent and potentially reversible fact. Second, although there have been common threats posed by the Soviet Union to Europe and America alike, and although America and Europe are bound by common values as well as by a defense pact (NATO), European and American objectives in the Middle East are not permanently tied together; there is no consensus on a permanent and common set of interests, aims, and policies regarding the Middle East. Reversing the Iraqi invasion of Kuwait, dealing with subsequent effects in Kurdistan, and seizing the opportunity of drawing Iraq's biological, chemical, and nuclear fangs were important occurrences, but they did not necessarily imply a broad and lasting common vision of regional challenges. Furthermore, many European states consider other parts of the Arab world—notably the Maghreb—as being at least as important to their national interest as the Gulf.

The prospects for U.S.-European cooperation in the Middle East thus hinge on the degree of Transatlantic and intra-European convergence or divergence on a number of issues. The relationship with Iran, the largest regional power, is one major area of difference. The European Union's "critical dialogue" has stood in stark contrast to the U.S. policy of freezing out Iran. U.S. political and economic relations with Iran lie substantially below the level that the United States entertained with Stalin's Soviet Union and are similar to those with pre-1970 communist China; even Cuba has a large U.S. interest section in Havana and charter flights to Miami. Such a divergence concerning a key player in the Gulf's balance of power makes it difficult to lay the foundations of a common approach relative to force projection operations. Another significant difference is the evaluation of the broader security challenges in the region. Although the

Europeans are just as prone—and possibly even more so, for reasons of proximity—as the Americans to emphasize the combined regional dangers of militant fundamentalism and terrorism (not least in Algeria, a prime French security concern), they do not usually see these as essentially military challenges, nor do the areas concerned necessarily belong to the Middle East in geographical terms. Similarly, the Europeans tend to note that the menace of nuclear proliferation only exceptionally comes in its Iraqi form. In nearly every other recorded case, the proliferation of weapons of mass destruction has been curtailed or rolled back by measures not primarily military in nature, at least in those cases when it was deemed to be dangerous (i.e., excluding Israel's development of nuclear weapons or Saudi Arabia's purchase of forty Chinese CSS-2 intermediate-range missiles).

If, however, the Iraqi exception does demonstrate the need for a military component to nonproliferation policy, it also proves another important point: force projection operations with a direct counterproliferation mission are not sufficient to deal with these military aspects. Only the utter military defeat and partial invasion of Iraq in a war undertaken for a different purpose brought about a situation that made it subsequently possible to deal effectively with the Iraqi weapons of mass destruction (WMD) program. During the Gulf War, the targeting of Iraqi WMD facilities was incomplete, to put it mildly. It is the intrusive work of UNSCOM within Iraq that has done the bulk of the detection and destruction of Iraq's WMD.

In the same way that dedicated force projection was not considered the best way of dealing with North Korea's nuclear program, it is unlikely that military force projection will be the tool of choice to cope with Iranian nuclear ambitions.

Last but not least, a policy of "America says, Europe pays" is unlikely to provide a basis for enhanced U.S.-European military cooperation. As for the Israeli-Arab peace process, the Europeans are invited to stay out of the serious discussion, but their checks are most welcome. As for curbing pariah states, the Europeans are expected to toe the U.S. line, however contrary to international law and practice it may be (e.g., the Helms-Burton legislation and the Iran and Libya Sanctions Act) and however bizarre the U.S. criteria are (putting Cuba in the same basket as Libya and Iran).

In 1996, the United States thought that bombing Iraqi air defense sites and extending the southern air exclusion zone was an appropriate response to the Saddam-Barzani alliance in Kurdistan. The Europeans were expected to support such an awkward syllogism, even though they were informed about it only hours before the fact, although UK and French aircrews were running the same risks as part of the same operations as their American comrades in "Southern Watch" and "Poised Hammer." This is not the stuff of which lasting grand politico-military bargains on force projection can be made.

MILITARY DEVELOPMENTS

If the political backdrop is hardly favorable for greater coordination of U.S. and European force projection in the Middle East, conversely, military developments since the Gulf War offer a number of positive opportunities.

The Gulf War brought home to the Europeans several important lessons. The conflict underscored the need for larger numbers of rapidly deployable and rapidly usable forces than used to be the case. In parallel, the existence of large, non-projectable conscript forces was put in question, notably in France. National inter-service command and control capabilities needed to be expanded, both to conduct larger joint operations and to inter-operate with coalition partners. In France, the Gulf War led to the establishment of an inter-service military staff (EMIA) and the creation of an air-transportable inter-service theater command post (PCIAT). Strategic reconnaissance in its various forms was emphasized, for both crisis prevention and crisis management, for both politico-military decision-making and for operational use by commanders in the field. If the deployment of the *Helios IA* strategic surveillance satellite in 1995 was the result of a pre–Gulf War decision by France, Italy, and Spain, the follow-on program (*Helios II*) was decided after that war, as was the acquisition by France of mobile ground stations enabling deployed forces to access overhead data directly and to factor it into mission planning.

Stand-off capabilities were underscored in view of the requirement to reduce casualties and collateral damage in high-threat operations conducted for strategic, rather than vital, interests. The decisions in 1996 to develop conventional cruise missiles (such as the French SCALP EG, the British Storm Shadow, and the German Taurus) are direct reflections of this new priority.

Increased tactical and battlefield mobility was reconfirmed as a requirement by the Gulf War: the Future Large Aircraft, the Franco-German Tiger combat helicopter, and Britain's and the Netherlands's acquisition of Apache combat helicopters should all contribute towards enhancing European force projection capabilities.

Since the Gulf War, France and the United Kingdom have negotiated bilateral defense agreements with individual Gulf States (Kuwait, Qatar, and the United Arab Emirates).

Post–Cold War budget constraints constitute another determining factor of Europe's military capabilities. Budget cuts do not work in as unambiguous a fashion as is sometimes assumed: although spending cuts clearly do reduce European (and U.S.) ability to expand certain aspects of force projection—most clearly the enormously expensive airlift components—they also have the virtue of forcing a major re-ordering of priorities and a re-shaping of force structures. France's projection capability may well have been damaged, rather than bolstered by the absence of significant budget cuts until 1995: the defense industrial base and the procurement process remained in an unreformed state; Cold War programs continued and received large shares of available spending, crowding out force projection–related programs; a bloated conscript force siphoned off officers, non-commissioned officers, equipment, and Operations and Maintenance (O&M) expenditures, starving the more operational parts of the force structure. Conversely, the United Kingdom may actually have benefited from the fact that real spending cuts began as early as 1985: the reform of the acquisition process ("Best Value for Money"), the slimming down of forces ("Options for Change"), and the improvement of the tooth-to-tail ratio ("Front Line First") come to mind.

Budget cuts are as much an opportunity as a liability. Canceling a major Cold War program or replacing such a program with a less-costly alternative can actually increase the funding available for force projection: an early demise of the S.45 intermediate-range missile or the shorter-range *Hadès* missile, or the acquisition of Super-Puma transport helicopters in lieu of the over-specified NH90, would have released billions of dollars for other purposes in France.

Post–Cold War priorities often come with a comparatively low budget cost. A conventional cruise missile program such as Britain's Storm Shadow costs less than $1 billion over a five-year period; the *Helios II* surveillance satellite program, $2 billion over a seven-year period. This type of spending can be secured through intra-defense budget reshuffling as well as from increases in spending efficiency through reform of the acquisition process.

Such reasoning reaches its limits when it comes to items such as carrier task forces or airlift. The RAND Corporation has estimated that it would cost Europe around $5 billion in capital costs over a five-year period (excluding recurring costs) to acquire the capability to lift a light division along with the means to support the corresponding combat aircraft.[4] All other things remaining equal, this kind of money is not going to become available, either in the form of new funding or as a result of resources released through re-ordering of spending within existing defense budgets. Europe's capability to lift bodies and matériel for force projection is thus not going to increase radically beyond what it is today; this reality will continue to limit the volume of European forces available for projection.

As for carrier task forces, France has been, apart from the United States, the only NATO country to deploy angle-deck, power projection aircraft carriers: the *Clémenceau* and the *Foch*. Budget difficulties have made this a precarious situation: the *Clémenceau* was decommissioned in 1997; the *Charles de Gaulle* nuclear-powered carrier will enter service in 1999 with no sister ship having been firmly scheduled. Even if the construction of a second carrier were undertaken to replace the *Foch*, the unaffordable cost of the in-depth defenses of a carrier task force would—as in the recent past—force the French to avoid exposing their carriers in high-threat environments.

However, Europeanization of defense forces and assets should help improve force projection capabilities. In practice, this means several actual or potential types of initiatives, for example, the creation of integrated military units, first and foremost the Eurocorps, which brings together some 50,000 soldiers, principally from France and Germany, along with Spanish, Belgian, and Luxembourgeois participation. Although much of this Army corps is composed of units optimized for war in Central Europe—not ideal for rapid force projection in the Middle East—the Eurocorps staff has been organizing a force projection capability. Eurocorps was declared operational in December 1995. One of its components, the Franco-German brigade, has been sent to Bosnia as part of the Stabilization Force (SFOR).

Multinational force projection staffs have been set up. The headquarters of the EUROFOR set up in Florence in 1995 is able to control a force of some 10,000 soldiers from rapid deployment units based in France, Italy, Portugal, and Spain; the EUROMARFOR is its air-naval counterpart. Similarly, France and the United Kingdom have set up a Joint Air Group, under a staff located in High Wycombe, England, and a similar initiative is planned in the naval area.

European strategic reconnaissance assets are being produced and

---

4. Project Air Force, *The Independent European Force* (Santa Monica, Calif.: RAND, 1993).

deployed; the *Helios IA* surveillance satellite (lofted in July 1995) provides France, Italy, and Spain with their own military-quality imagery (with France's share some 80 percent of the cost and of the product); the Western European Union, via its image processing center in Torrejòn, Spain, has a degree of access to this resource. *Helios II*, slated for launch in 2001, should considerably expand European capabilities, whether or not Germany joins.

The Western European Union has set up a modest planning staff (the military planning cell) and has experience coordinating European naval forces deployments for escort duty in the Gulf during the late eighties, and subsequently for the implementation of the arms embargo against the former Yugoslavia.

A high degree of commonality characterizes British and French cruise missile programs (Storm Shadow and SCALP EG), with appreciable effects on cost and interoperability.

However, one key area for force projection has remained essentially untouched by this trend of Europeanization: notwithstanding bilateral cooperation between the French and German air transport commands, there are no major pooling arrangements of scarce European airlift capabilities. This is clearly one area in which progress should be made, with a significant strategic and operational return using existing resources.

THE EFFECTS OF NATO RENOVATION AND ENLARGEMENT

NATO renovation offers a major opportunity for improving coordination of force projection. The modernization of a leaner, less territorial, defined command structure and the emphasis on setting up contingency-specific Combined Joint Task Forces (CJTF) should provide clear benefits. More basically, the sea change in NATO's outlook favors such an outcome: whereas during the Cold War, "out of area" was "out of the question," "out of area" contingencies now appear to have become practically the only ones towards which NATO's military machinery can be turned, Bosnia being a case in point.

In addition, France's return to NATO's Military Committee and participation in the debate on NATO's renovation could eliminate one of the essential obstacles to alliance planning and implementation of inter-allied military force projection. Of course, this will only prove to be the case if a lasting compromise is struck concerning NATO's new command structure, notably its southern component (CINCSOUTH); this has been a contentious issue between the United States and some of its European allies, not least the French.

Thus, NATO's renovation is creating an institutional basis for U.S.-European cooperation on force projection. There are also practical steps laid out below which can facilitate the exploitation of this institutional potential. However, although this new basis is a necessary condition, it is not a sufficient one for force projection cooperation: the political and strategic obstacles already alluded to are in no way removed by the simple fact of NATO's change of outlook.

Enlargement of NATO should have relatively limited impact on military force projection in the Middle East. On the positive side of the ledger, modest specialized military resources from Central and Eastern Europe may become somewhat more readily accessible than they are today. Small Czech, Hungarian, and Polish contingents were present in the Gulf and participated in the UN Implementation Forces (IFOR) in Bosnia. Such assets, usable for force projection, will not expand as an automatic result of NATO's enlargement, but their inclusion in NATO's planning process could facilitate their identification and earmarking, and improve their interoperability with other NATO contingents.

Some of these resources may be militarily interesting; and politically, such participation will tend to be useful. Conversely, enlargement could generate some negative effects from the standpoint of force projection, by acting as a distraction from Middle East scenarios. Potential Russian reactions to NATO enlargement—e.g., mischief involving Russian relations with the Baltics and Ukraine—could refocus the defense spending of members (including "old" members) on eastern contingencies. However, it is unlikely that a weak Russia (or any other regional player) will be able and willing to pose a military threat that would call for a major reorientation of financial and military resources toward the East.

None of the prospective new members has had armed forces geared to out-of-Warsaw Pact military operations, so little stands to be lost in terms of force projection, nor should the direct costs of enlargement detract significantly from force projection. The U.S. Department of Defense estimates that from 1997 to 2009, NATO enlargement could generate direct extra costs of $9–12 billion for the old and new members, at an annual rate of $700–$900 million.[5] This represents less than one percent of current defense expenditure in Europe.

---

5. See "Press Release of U.S. Cost Study on NATO Enlargement," U.S. Mission to the North Atlantic Treaty Organization, February 25, 1997. The $9–12 billion figures refer to costs that would not have occurred absent enlargement.

There is one specific area in which enlargement will probably have a negative effect on force projection for the Middle East, and that is NATO infrastructure spending, notably in areas such as air defense, with the Air Command and Control System (ACCS); presumably, the share of expenditure devoted to southern-oriented air defense infrastructure would decline in comparison to what it would have been without enlargement.

STRATEGIC CHOICES

European policies toward military force projection in the Middle East will be largely determined by U.S. strategic choices. The current *de facto* division of labor—the Americans take the lead in military operations, the Europeans provide qualified political support and a minority military contribution—reflects current capabilities; it does not necessarily serve as a guide for future intentions. Notwithstanding allied success in the Gulf War, it is not self-evident that the United States would willingly embark again on a similar venture. If anything, the self-inhibiting emphasis on "zero deaths" may have been reinforced by the unexpectedly benign Gulf War experience.

Indeed, when Saddam Hussein exploited intra-Kurdish feuding in the summer of 1996 to roll back the "safe haven" established after the end of the Gulf War in Northern Iraq, the United States apparently refused to contemplate a remake of "Operation Provide Comfort" with its 30,000 combat troops deployed in Kurdistan in the spring of 1991. Instead, "steel on steel" bombing operations were organized south of Baghdad in unilateral retaliation. Admittedly, it was an election year in the United States, which gave a premium to demonstrating toughness while running minimum risks. However, impunity obtained by cruise missiles is not a substitute for meaningful military engagement of an adversary on his territory.

Technology may emphasize this drift toward risk-adverse arm's-length unilateral projection of fire-power (as distinct from force projection) with U.S.-based strategic bombers, and arsenal ships with home ports in or close to the United States could dispense with in-theater military deployments. Furthermore, the situation in the Middle East may make such a shift appear to be desirable: permanently stationed U.S. forces in the region may contribute to the internal destabilization of the host states, in a manner that does not affect U.S. forces in Europe and East Asia. Removing locally based U.S. forces from the Gulf could, in theory, enhance stability; explicit defense pacts backed up by U.S. forces based elsewhere—notably in

Europe—could be a better solution than the current set-up. In practice, however, a removal of U.S. forces from Saudi Arabia and Kuwait would be interpreted as a sign of disengagement, and would be destabilizing in its own right.

To a degree, the U.S. strategic posture thus combines the disadvantages of aloofness—e.g., the refusal to stop Iraqi forces from entering the former safe haven in Kurdistan—with the potentially destabilizing consequences of troops stationed in nervous Islamic countries. Yet this probably is the best that can be had. An American withdrawal, or a U.S. refusal to engage in a Gulf War or Provide Comfort–type operation, would not lead to the Europeans stepping into America's shoes. Not only are European military capabilities inadequate for taking the lead; but in political terms, the Europeans would not feel compelled to be "more Catholic than the Pope": the Europeans followed the American lead in the Gulf in 1990–91 not only because such a combination would successfully deal with the Iraqi invasion of Kuwait, but also because the U.S.-European alliance depended on such an expression of solidarity, given material expression politically (votes in the United Nations), militarily (British, French, and other forces) and financially ($9 billion from Germany).

Policy Recommendations

During the post–Gulf War period, limited but real practical measures have already been taken by the main European countries for more effective force projection; conversely, political differences between Europe and America concerning the Middle East have certainly not been reduced—the contrary is the case. It is this reality that inspires the following recommendations.

REALIZING EUROPE'S STRATEGIC AND MILITARY POTENTIAL IN THE REGION

A number of new, largely budget-neutral initiatives could be taken by the Europeans to enhance their force projection capability. A Eurocorps-style integrated army corps could be created in the rapid reaction arena. For instance, the first division of the German KRK, the French air mobile division of the FAR, and the United Kingdom's spearhead force could be the heart of such a corps-size intervention force, which would also include the brigade-size assets of EUROFOR. This format would be compatible with other arrangements (Eurocorps, EUROFOR, NATO's Allied Rapid Reaction Corps). Such a "Eurocorps-South" could be double-hatted with NATO, as a southern version of its Allied Rapid Reaction Corps.

At least part of dedicated European air transport could be pooled into a body somewhat akin to NATO's fleet of airborne warning and control aircraft (AWACS), albeit at a lower level of integration. This could include French, British, and German long-range transport aircraft (DC-8, VC-10, A-310, and the like); medium-range Hercules (in service in Britain, Belgium, France, and elsewhere) and Transall (France, Germany), as well as tanker aircraft. In the absence of a crisis involving several European states, each country would continue to use its nationally registered aircraft crewed by its own nationals. In case of a response to a crisis with European (WEU or EU) backing—such as in the Gulf and in Bosnia—the earmarked aircraft would form a single pool. Naturally, greater joint logistics, crew training, and the like could and should be pursued as part of the overall scheme. The pooling agreement could, at least initially, be an initiative of core countries, along the lines of the Eurocorps (France, Germany, Spain, Belgium, Luxembourg). In operational terms, its assets could be put under the control of the CJTF commander responsible for a given crisis. In addition, a European Air Transport Pool could enter into agreements with Russian and Ukrainian companies for access to their heavy airlift assets.

EXPLOITING THE POTENTIAL OF NATO RENOVATION AND ENLARGEMENT
NATO renovation and enlargement is currently in a state of flux, opening significant opportunities for enhancing force projection cooperation.

The CJTF concept is well accepted within NATO, if not always well understood. Combined Joint Task Forces are not simply, or principally, a device whereby the Europeans can draw on NATO assets for European-led operations, even if that is one of their potential effects. However, progress could be hampered by disagreement over the role of NATO's Supreme Allied Commander in Europe (SACEUR), particularly *vis-à-vis* European-led CJTFs. Similarly, downsizing and adapting NATO's cumbersome command structure is a well recognized imperative. But Transatlantic disagreement over the new regional commands, notably concerning the fate of NATO's southern command (CINCSOUTH), could hold up this necessary reordering.

Without substantive agreement on CJTFs and without a refocused command structure, NATO will not realize its potential in the force projection arena, in all probability the only one in which it will have a real military role to play, in the absence of a Central/East European threat.

To achieve a force projection-oriented structure, the following initiatives may be considered in the long term. The first would be to do away with the Major Subordinate Commands (MSCs) or their currently planned successors, the Regional Commands. The move is not as revolutionary as it sounds, even if it would prove traumatic to current and prospective billet-holders and slot-fillers: the MSCs were territorially defined and inward-looking, since they were devoted to the protection of NATO territory and sea-lanes of communication (SLOCs); they were not outward looking and de-territorialized, which is what force projection is (or should be) about. Indeed, IFOR and SFOR make the point: CINCSOUTH may be in charge (although why should an admiral in Naples be responsible for a ground-slogging operation in the Balkan mountains?), but most of the assets come from non-CINCSOUTH forces, with SACEUR acting as the coordinator. Would it not be more appropriate for such contingencies—including force projection operations in the Middle East—to come under the operational control of the relevant CJTF commander?

Second, the division of labor between SACEUR and the Supreme Allied Commander Atlantic (SACLANT) should be redefined. In case of conflict during the Cold War, NATO would have had two broad categories of military missions: actively defending the European theater (under SACEUR) and ensuring naval control of the Atlantic SLOCs (under SACLANT). These missions are not terribly relevant today. Deploying forces to cope with continental contingencies (such as IFOR and SFOR) is one of NATO's current activities. Projecting air and naval forces in a maritime theater, particularly the Mediterranean, is another potential category: this could include such missions as helping evacuate Western nationals from an insurrectional situation in North Africa or responding to rogue state initiatives (as the Americans did against Libya in 1986). Under such a typology, SACEUR would continue to have the first call on current operations in Bosnia; SACLANT would deal with primarily naval and air operations, with the Military Committee and the North Atlantic Council deciding to which category a given contingency belongs. In this configuration, the U.S. Sixth Fleet in its potential NATO role would be earmarked for SACLANT.

Finally, the limited but not insignificant force projection resources of new NATO members should be the object of early and systematic identification and earmarking. They should also be considered as assets that should receive priority treatment in terms of adaptation to NATO standards.

THE ABSENCE OF A COMMON STRATEGY

American attempts to negotiate a grand strategic bargain with Europe concerning the Middle East are doomed to failure. Europeans will refrain from undertaking with the United States the type of "formal commitments" referred to in Richard L. Kugler's chapter in this volume (Chapter 11). Limited exceptions (such as the strictly bilateral agreements between France or the United Kingdom and certain Gulf states) only serve to confirm the rule.

Similarly, the Europeans will not, and should not, accept a pre-determined and permanent (or semi-permanent) share of the military burden in the Middle East, let alone increase it to the levels pre-scribed by Richard Kugler. The disagreements on the long-term policies to be conducted *vis-à-vis* country X, Y, or Z in the region, and the unpredictability of what or who constitutes a common threat make a grand burden-sharing bargain implausible. It should therefore not be attempted. The best that can be achieved is case-by-case consultation and eventual agreement to participate in specific endeavors: Desert Shield, Desert Storm, Provide Comfort, Poised Hammer, Southern Watch, and the like.

An alternative grand bargain, whereby the United States deals mil-itarily with Middle Eastern contingencies and the Europeans with those located in Europe, is even more difficult to contemplate. It is implausible in the face of specific contingencies; for example, one would expect France and Italy to be heavily involved in any military contingency involving the forceful repatriation of their citizens from an insurrection in Tunisia. It is equally difficult to believe that the United States would be less involved than the Europeans in an oper-ation flowing from a security challenge against a country such as, for instance, Poland. Furthermore, such a grand bargain would be destabilizing: withdrawing U.S. forces from Europe would not con-tribute to long-term stability in a Europe which will have become free but which is certainly not whole: no homogeneous security regime encompasses all of the countries of Europe, Russia included. In addi-tion, removing such U.S. assets from Europe would reduce, not improve, America's force projection capability. Finally, assigning to the United States a formal overlordship in a largely unwilling Middle East is not likely to dampen anti-Western passions in the region.

A more modest approach may thus be more fruitful in terms of effective force projection cooperation between the United States and NATO in the Middle East. One strand of such an approach would be to agree to disagree. Americans and Europeans should acknowledge that there is no reason that convergence of Transatlantic interests or policies should exist *vis-à-vis* every Middle Eastern contingency. Procrustean beds will not do anybody any good.

Europeanization would be another component of such a policy. The Europeans should pursue practical endeavors of the sort described above, for their own sake as well as for that of Transatlantic coalition-building; the United States should positively encourage such initiatives, in the same way that the United States, after a period of great reluctance in 1990–91, eventually agreed that ventures such as the Eurocorps were in the general interest. In practice, this would mean, for instance, that the United States would not, as a matter of government policy, attempt to thwart Franco-German plans in the strategic reconnaissance satellite arena. The same applies to the Europeanization of a renovated NATO command structure.

Above and beyond the reforms discussed earlier, Middle East contingencies with a politico-military dimension should be discussed within NATO under the provisions of Article IV.[6] In a sense, this is already done for issues such as proliferation. In order to avoid the appearance of a Western "Crusades" approach to the Islamic world, Article IV consultation on out-of-area issues should not be confined to the Middle East. Thus, all out-of-area contingencies—including Middle Eastern ones—with potential effects on the security of North America and Western Europe should be more systematically addressed at the planning staff level and, to a large extent, independently of the political level. Such planning should be as broad-ranging and apolitical as was similar activity in military staffs in the late nineteenth century before the alliance systems of the time had fallen into place. For its part, the political level of consultation should function when specific circumstances—an actual crisis or threat of crisis—warrant it. *Hors zone* is no longer *hors sujet*, and out of area is no longer out of scope; indeed, it has become the principal topic of NATO planning and action in military terms.

---

6. "The Parties will consult together whenever, in the opinion of any of them, the territorial integrity, political independence or security of any of the Parties is threatened." Article IV of the North Atlantic Treaty, April 4, 1949.

A politically somewhat modest approach combined with practical military measures will not radically transform force projection as it may apply in the Middle East. But it will help improve the political and military capability to field, if need be, effective force projection coalitions. More ambitious attempts may produce the opposite effect, and could furthermore imperil a NATO whose *raison d'être* as a defense organization has been weakened by the end of the Cold War.

Conclusions

Robert D. Blackwill
and Michael Stürmer

There are fundamental reasons why U.S. and European views and policies regarding the Greater Middle East ought to be mutually compatible, complementary, and reinforcing. As this volume makes clear, the Transatlantic community shares three vital supranational interests related to this vast area: ensuring the reliable flow of oil at reasonable prices; slowing the introduction of weapons of mass destruction; and avoiding the spread of Islamic extremism, which would undermine the political stability in the region and seriously threaten the first two interests. Nevertheless, in chapter after chapter of this book we see present and potential policy differences on the two sides of the Atlantic concerning virtually every aspect of Western strategy toward the Greater Middle East.

The reasons for this troubling trend have been enumerated in this volume:

- the end of the Soviet threat has generally loosened Transatlantic solidarity;
- U.S. leadership on many issues, not just the Greater Middle East, is more difficult to sell in Europe today than in the past;
- Europe's effort, led by France and Germany, to develop a common foreign and security policy leads naturally in some cases to neo-Gaullist approaches which seek to enhance Europe's identity by distinguishing it from the United States;
- U.S.-European commercial rivalries are more difficult to manage under present circumstances than during the Cold War, and have a greater potential to damage the overall relationship;
- arms sales to the region evoke particularly ferocious Transatlantic competition; and

- domestic preoccupations on both sides of the Atlantic and weak governments nearly everywhere hinder the development of joint U.S.-European cooperation regarding the region.

The immense region of the Greater Middle East generates so many important and perplexing policy challenges that it is no wonder that America and Europe often disagree on how best to proceed. Whatever public pronouncements are made in West European capitals and in Brussels, the American commitment to Israel is, for familiar reasons, far stronger and deeper than that of Europe. This means that any sustained crisis in the Israeli-Palestinian peace process is likely to generate much more robust criticism of Israel and apologies for the Arabs in Europe than in the United States. In this situation, the Europeans will be tempted because of energy dependence and commercial objectives (and perhaps by the merits of the case) to come down on the side of the Arabs both in the region and at the United Nations. This in turn would create significant strains in the Transatlantic relationship, abetted by the continuing U.S. refusal to allow the Europeans, and especially France, to have any real role in the peace process other than providing a good deal of the money needed.

Iran is another area in which it is unlikely that the United States and Europe will resolve their differences in the near future. Although the American policy of dual containment as applied to Iran is increasingly questioned by U.S. experts outside the government, there is probably too much bad Iranian behavior, too much malignant history between the two countries in the past two decades, and too much bitter passion in U.S. domestic politics and the Congress regarding Iran to expect any major changes in Washington's policy any time soon. As for the Europeans, their policies will be driven primarily by commercial interests and an instinctive aversion to the use of coercive instruments to try to moderate Iran's behavior, but also by doubt as to the long-term viability of dual containment. This approach has gone by the deceptive term "critical dialogue" in Bonn and Brussels, resulting in an inane bilateral colloquy that has unsurprisingly— given its mercantile essence—produced, as made clear by the April 1997 revelations regarding the Iranian government's murderous acts in Germany, no discernible change in Tehran's destabilizing policies in the region and beyond. Thus, here again are basic differences across the Atlantic which fracture the possibility of any joint approach. A further result is congressional legislation (the Iran and Libya Sanctions Act) that would punish European businesses trading with Iran; this presents yet another basis for deterioration of the U.S.-European relationship.

Western policy toward Iraq may also put the Transatlantic relationship under increasing strain. Saddam Hussein's refusal to allow the United Nations full access to his military-industrial complex, and particularly to Iraq's weapons of mass destruction (WMD) facilities, has generated a Transatlantic consensus to continue the tough UN sanctions. This, however, masks another fundamental policy difference between Europe and the United States. Washington's most elemental policy objective *vis-à-vis* Iraq (not expressed in public) is to remove Saddam Hussein from power. Europe, on the other hand, would be satisfied with an improvement in Iraq's cooperation concerning weapons of mass destruction, even if it were Saddam Hussein who made it so; some allies may be willing to lift the UN sanctions for less. Thus far, the Iraqi leader's intransigence has made these differences moot, but that may not remain the case.

The future of Turkey will also pose major challenges to cooperative U.S.-European policies. For the United States, Turkey has become a key regional player in the American effort to keep pressure on Saddam Hussein and is now a pivotal frontline—no longer flank—country in the arc from the Persian Gulf to the Caspian basin. This has led Washington to attempt to manage the Islamist Erbakan government in a way that does not damage the general fabric of U.S.-Turkish relations, while at the same time emphasizing how important the continued secular character of the Turkish state is to the United States. The nations of Western Europe and the European Union (EU) do not appear to view Turkey from this strategic perspective. Instead, EU members make it clear that Turkey has no hope of joining the Union in the next two decades, if ever, and often act as if human rights in Turkey should dominate Western relations with Ankara. Whether these EU policies are caused by economic and ethical reasons or, as the Turks believe, by religious and cultural prejudices, the net effect is to leave relations with Turkey largely up to the United States to manage. Washington regrets what it regards as strategic myopia among its European allies, while the EU contends that the United States willfully ignores the sound judgments in Brussels and European capitals that keep Turkey out of the mainstream of Europe's political and economic life. If Turkey becomes seriously unstable or even hostile to the West, Transatlantic finger-pointing would quickly follow. As for the Caspian basin and Central Asia, commercial rivalries across the Atlantic regarding the development of energy resources could hinder what should be a concerted Western effort to bolster ties to this increasingly important part of the world.

U.S.-European differences regarding the utility of coercive methods and especially the use of military force endure and infect Transatlantic dealings with the Middle East. Although, thanks to American diplomacy, Desert Storm was a timely exception, most European governments instinctively shrink from the notion of military action as a response to virtually any contingency in this region, from the impending or successful acquisition of WMD by a rogue state, to cross-border aggression, to an internal threat to the Saudi monarchy, to a breakdown of civil order in the Maghreb that would endanger Western citizens. If the United States sometimes seems too eager to use military force, the Europeans (except for Britain and sometimes France) appear to believe that to be armed and ready is a provocation in and of itself, and that the decorous civility of EU deliberations can be applied, in a process of reasoning together, to the turbulent and sometimes violent domestic politics and inter-state relations of the Greater Middle East. These primary contrasts in psychological or sociological approaches to military action will be tested by the next politico-military crisis in the region, perhaps the completion of the new Libyan chemical weapons facility.

Here we encounter the division-of-labor issue that was a frequent subject of Transatlantic debate and sometimes acrimony during the Cold War. It seemed to many Americans that the Europeans—and especially the Germans—wished to undertake the more congenial aspects of relations with Moscow and leave the unpleasant and conflictual requirements in Washington's hands. It is easy to imagine a circumstance in which the United States believes confrontation and possibly the use of force is necessary in the Greater Middle East, and the Europeans are persuaded that diplomacy still can produce the desired result, or that military action will simply make the situation worse. If the United States then uses force anyway and numbers of Americans die in the process, and particularly if that action is plausibly also in defense of European vital interests (oil or WMD), one could expect a strongly negative U.S. domestic and congressional reaction against the allies.

Another crucial reason for conflicting U.S.-European approaches regarding the use of force is the widening gap between the military doctrine and capabilities of the United States and those of its European allies. Rapid force projection over long distances has always been a unique U.S. competence. However, the technology-driven revolution in military affairs that is well underway in the U.S. armed forces, as well as the dramatic drop in allied defense spending and military research and development, promise to make joint U.S.-European military operations more difficult to accomplish in the years ahead, while giving the United States an ever-increasing number of unilateral military options. Although Washington would undoubtedly always prefer European political support for any American military operation in the Greater Middle East, the United States may need (or even want) less and less allied participation in such force employment. These diverging secular military trends on the two sides of the Atlantic will thus feed the existing U.S. temptation to consult with the Europeans only after, rather than before, the event, engendering predictable bitterness on the part of West European governments.

A more specific dimension of the issues of coercive methods and the use of force relates to differing U.S.-European approaches to the proliferation of weapons of mass destruction into the region. On this issue, neither side of the Atlantic has an exemplary record in devising coherent strategies to meet the new threats. But West European politicians seem unusually determined to ignore the possibility that within the next ten years, the Greater Middle East might transform the core of European security by generating WMD threats to the European continent itself. This possibility is largely absent from the European debate. The issue of protection against ballistic missile attack also arises in this context, and the United States is gradually developing a bipartisan consensus in support of a vigorous set of U.S. programs to prepare for this emerging regional and eventually intercontinental threat. The allies, in contrast, plead that they have no money for ballistic missile defense; they apparently hope that multilateral diplomacy can solve the problem over the long term. We hope they are right, but we doubt it.

Even with all these present and potential differences between Washington and its European partners regarding the Greater Middle East, one may ask "so what?" What are the regional and geopolitical consequences of these Transatlantic disagreements? How could they affect vital and important U.S. and European national interests in the region and elsewhere?

If the Greater Middle East remains generally tranquil in the next decade, these divergences across the Atlantic will not matter much. However, there is virtually no chance that this area will be stable during the next decade. Threats arise from the domestic fragility of many of the regimes; the endemic instability in Egypt and Algeria; the challenge of political Islam; rivalries among moderate and radical Arab nations; an enduring threat from Iran and perhaps from a revived

Iraq; the continuing struggle between Israel and the Palestinians; the vast oil wealth of the Persian Gulf and Caspian basin; the persisting large-scale conventional arms transfers into the region; any further acquisition of WMD by one or more states in the area; and the uncertain future foreign policy orientation of Russia. All these factors, plus events and variables we cannot foresee, will make the Greater Middle East the most precarious region in the world. This is especially troubling because of the three vital national interests associated with this region that the United States and Western Europe share.

This then raises the question of whether the United States can manage these various challenges more or less on its own, without the assistance of its European allies. The dangers listed above should demonstrate that realistic unilateralist American strategies toward the Greater Middle East do not exist. It is true that Washington could mount the occasional military attack on a new WMD site, and will probably continue to dominate the political side of the Israeli-Palestinian peace process. But beyond that, none of the problems enumerated above can be successfully managed by the United States without the economic and political support of the Europeans. The United States simply does not have the domestic support, political will, financial resources, international influence, or sustained diplomatic excellence to go its own way. Europe is even less prepared to do so. The two sides of the Atlantic partnership will therefore either cooperate closely regarding the challenges of the region in the period ahead, or they will certainly see their respective vital and important national interests damaged over time through U.S.-European bickering, policy paralysis, mixed signals, or conflicting strategies and tactics.

Moreover, serious differences over the Greater Middle East would be likely to infect other dimensions of the Transatlantic relationship, including coping with Russia, buttressing the other newly independent nations of the former Soviet Union and especially Ukraine and oil-rich Central Asia, protecting the Baltic nations, dealing with ethnic and religious conflicts in Europe, opening further the global trading system, ensuring stability in world financial markets, and handling emerging China.

This volume contains many practical recommendations for greater U.S.-European collaboration regarding the Greater Middle East. We close with the eight policy prescriptions that we believe are most crucial to promote Western interests in the region and counter threats to those interests:

- Elevate WMD nonproliferation and counterproliferation efforts, including ballistic missile defense, to the top of the Transatlantic agenda.
- Keep pushing hard on the Arab-Israeli peace process, with the United States in the lead and a supporting role for Europe.
- Maintain the pressure on Iraq at least until Saddam Hussein leaves the scene.
- Offer Iran a comprehensive opening to the West, but only if it first substantially improves its behavior based on agreed Transatlantic criteria, especially with respect to its support for international terrorism.
- Integrate Turkey much more into Western strategic considerations, broadening and deepening Turkey's political and economic relationship with the European Union.
- Intensify Transatlantic political, economic, and security cooperation with the energy-rich nations of the Caspian basin.
- Increase NATO military planning and European power projection capabilities for contingencies in the Greater Middle East.
- Expand Transatlantic economic assistance to the region.

None of these prescriptions will be easy to implement, but a Transatlantic failure to do so will bring Western misfortune in its wake.

Contributors

Robert D. Blackwill teaches foreign and defense policy at Harvard University's Kennedy School of Government, where he is the faculty chairman of the School's Executive Programs for Russian General Officers and for members of the Russian State Duma; of the Executive Program for Senior Chinese Military Officers; and of the Kennedy School/Nina Kung Initiative on U.S.-Chinese Relations. He is the U.S. chairman of the Bertelsmann Group, a forum for U.S.-German-Russian strategic discussions. An adjunct senior fellow at the Council on Foreign Relations in New York, he will chair a task force in 1997–98 for the Council on the future of Transatlantic relations. He serves on the board of *International Security*, on the academic advisory board of the NATO Defense College in Rome, and on the advisory council of the Nixon Center for Peace and Freedom. He is a consultant to the World Bank, the RAND Corporation, and U.S. government agencies. A career diplomat since 1967, he served as Director of West European Affairs on the National Security Council staff; Principal Deputy Assistant Secretary of State for Political-Military Affairs; Principal Deputy Assistant Secretary of State for European Affairs; and U.S. Ambassador and Chief Negotiator at the negotiations with the Warsaw Pact on conventional forces in Europe. He was Special Assistant to President George Bush for European and Soviet Affairs. His most recent books are *Engaging Russia* (Trilateral Commission, 1995) and (with Sergei A. Karaganov) *Damage Limitation or Crisis? Russia and the Outside World* (Brassey's, 1994).

Michael Stürmer read history, political sciences, and philosophy at the Universities of Berlin (FU), London (LSE), and Marburg. Since 1973, he has been a full Professor of Medieval and Modern History at the Friedrich Alexander University in Erlangen-Nürnberg, and is now on long-term leave. Since 1988, he has been Director of the Research Institute for International Affairs (Stiftung Wissenschaft und Politik) in Ebenhausen, Germany. Professor Stürmer has held visiting fellowships or professorships at Harvard University, the Institute for Advanced Studies at Princeton, the Sorbonne, and the University of Toronto. He is a columnist for the *Neue Zürcher Zeitung* and the *Financial Times*, and an adviser to the EU Commission on CFSP, the German Advisory Council, and the J.P. Morgan Bank. He holds the honor of *Officier de la Légion d'honneur*. His recent publications include *Das Ruhelose Reich: Deutschland 1866–1918*, 4th ed. (Severin und Siedler, 1994); *Striking the Balance: Sal. Oppenheim Jr. & Cie., A Family and a Bank* (Weidenfeld and Nicolson, 1994); and *Die Grenzen der Macht: Begegnung der Deutschen mit der Geschichte* (Siedler, 1992).

Richard A. Falkenrath is Executive Director of the Center for Science and International Affairs at the John F. Kennedy School of Government, Harvard University. Prior to his current appointment, Dr. Falkenrath was a Research Fellow in CSIA's International Security Program for two-and-a-half years, as well as a visiting scholar at the German Society for Foreign Affairs in Bonn. He is co-author of *Avoiding Nuclear Anarchy: Containing the Threat of Loose Russian Nuclear Weapons and Fissile Material* (The MIT Press, 1996), as well as the author of *Shaping Europe's Military Order: The Origins and Consequences of the CFE Treaty* (The MIT Press, 1995) and a variety of journal articles on European security, ballistic missile defense, U.S.-Russian arms control, and the U.S.-Russian HEU purchase agreement. Dr. Falkenrath is a consultant to the RAND Corporation, and is also a member of the International Institute for Strategic Studies, the Council on Foreign Relations, the American Economic Association, and the American Council on Germany. He holds a Ph.D. from the Department of War Studies at King's College, London, where he was a British Marshall Scholar, and is a graduate of Occidental College, Los Angeles (*summa cum laude*).

Richard N. Haass is Director of Foreign Policy Studies at the Brookings Institution. He also consults for NBC News, hosts the international affairs forum of *The New York Times* on the Internet, and is a frequent contributor to foreign affairs journals and the op-ed pages of major newspapers. From 1989–1993, he was Special Assistant to President George Bush and Senior Director for Near East and South

Asian Affairs on the staff of the National Security Council. Previously, he served in various posts in the Departments of State and Defense and was a legislative aide in the U.S. Senate. Haass also has been Director of National Security Programs and a Senior Fellow of the Council on Foreign Relations, the Sol M. Linowitz Visiting Professor of International Studies at Hamilton College, a senior associate at the Carnegie Endowment for International Peace, a Lecturer in Public Policy at Harvard University's Kennedy School of Government, and a research associate at the International Institute for Strategic Studies. He has also consulted for numerous government agencies and corporations. A Rhodes Scholar, Haass holds a B.A. degree from Oberlin College and both the Master and Doctor of Philosophy degrees from Oxford University. Dr. Haass is the author of numerous books, including *The Reluctant Sheriff: The United States After the Cold War* (Council on Foreign Relations, 1997) and *Intervention: The Use of American Military Force in the Post–Cold War World* (Carnegie Endowment for International Peace, 1994), which was selected by *Choice* magazine as one of the outstanding academic books of 1995.

François Heisbourg graduated from the Institut d'Etudes Politiques (Sciences-Po) in Paris and from the Ecole Nationale d'Administration (ENA). He became a member of the Foreign Ministry's Policy Planning Staff in charge of nuclear nonproliferation issues from 1978–79; First Secretary at the French Mission to the United Nations in charge of international security issues and outer space affairs from 1979–81; International Security Adviser to the French Minister of Defense, Mr. Charles Hernu, covering the full range of France's security and defense policies from 1981–84; and Vice President of Thomson SA, the French electronics firm, in charge of cooperative ventures with European and U.S. defense industries in the International Affairs Department from 1984–87. He was Director of the International Institute for Strategic Studies (IISS) from 1987–92 and has been a Senior Vice President (Strategic Development) at MATRA Défense since 1992. The author and editor of several books on strategic affairs, he has contributed extensively to the international media and to scholarly journals. Mr. Heisbourg is Chairman of the Executive Committee of the IISS, a Vice Chairman of its Council, and chairs the French Committee of the IISS. He is, *inter alia*, a Member of the Board of the Aspen Institute Berlin; a Fellow of the Royal Society for the Encouragement of Arts, Manufacture and Commerce; and an Adviser to the French Foreign Ministry Policy Planning Staff.

Geoffrey Kemp is the Director of Regional Strategic Programs at the Nixon Center for Peace and Freedom. He received his Ph.D. in Political Science at the Massachusetts Institute of Technology and his M.A. and B.A. degrees from Oxford University. He served in the White House during the first Reagan administration and was Special Assistant to the President for National Security Affairs and Senior Director for Near East and South Asian Affairs on the National Security Council staff. Prior to his current position, he was a Senior Associate at the Carnegie Endowment for International Peace, where he was Director of the Middle East Arms Control Project. From 1970 to 1980, he was on the faculty of the Fletcher School of Law and Diplomacy at Tufts University. He is the author or co-author of several books on the Middle East including *Strategic Geography and the Changing Middle East* and *Point of No Return: The Deadly Struggle for Middle East Peace* (both by the Brookings Institution Press, 1997); *Powder Keg in the Middle East: The Struggle for Gulf Security* (co-editor, Rowman and Littlefield, 1995); *Forever Enemies? American Policy and the Islamic Republic of Iran* (Carnegie Endowment for International Peace, 1994); *India and America After the Cold War* (Carnegie Endowment for International Peace, 1993); and *The Control of the Middle East Arms Race* (Carnegie Endowment for International Peace, 1991).

Heinz Kramer is a Senior Research Analyst in the Research Institute for International Policy and Security at the Research Institute for International Affairs (Stiftung Wissenschaft und Politik) in Ebenhausen, Germany. He is co-editor of *Turkey and the West* (Tauris, 1993) and author of *Die Europäische Gemeinschaft und die Türkei* (Nomos, 1988). As a member of SWP's Research Group on European Affairs, he has published widely on issues such as the European integration process, European-Turkish relations, Turkish foreign relations, EU enlargement, and EU relations with the new Eastern European democracies. He received his doctoral degree from the Faculty of Economics at Saarbrücken University.

Richard L. Kugler has been a Senior Social Scientist at RAND since 1988. Prior to that, he was a Senior Executive in the Office of the Secretary of Defense, where he served from 1975–88, specializing in NATO/Europe and U.S. global defense planning. During 1968–72, he was a U.S. Air Force officer and served in Southeast Asia. He holds a Ph.D. in Political Science from the Massachusetts Institute of Technology, and has been Adjunct Professor of International

Relations at George Washington University. Since joining RAND, he has published eight books on U.S. national security policy, plus articles in *Foreign Affairs, Survival,* and other journals. His current work at RAND focuses on NATO enlargement and reform, the U.S. overseas military presence, and U.S. global military strategy.

F. Stephen Larrabee is a Senior Staff Member at RAND in Washington, D.C. He holds a Ph.D. in Political Science from Columbia University and has taught at Columbia University, Cornell University, New York University, the Paul Nitze School of Advanced International Studies (SAIS), Georgetown University, and the University of Southern California. Before joining RAND, he served as Vice President and Director of Studies of the Institute of East-West Security Studies in New York from 1983–89 and was a distinguished Scholar in Residence at the Institute from 1989–90. From 1978–81 Dr. Larrabee served on the National Security Council staff in the White House as a specialist on Soviet–East European affairs and East-West political-military relations. He is co-editor (with David Gompert) of *America and Europe: A Partnership for a New Era* (Cambridge University Press, 1997), author of *East European Security After the Cold War* (RAND, 1994), editor of *The Volatile Powder Keg: Balkan Security After the Cold War* (American University Press, 1994), co-editor (with Robert Blackwill) of *Conventional Arms Control and East-West Security* (Duke University Press, 1989), and editor of *The Two German States and European Security* (St. Martin's Press, 1989).

Friedemann Müller is a Senior Research Analyst at Germany's Research Institute for International Affairs (Stiftung Wissenschaft und Politik). His research concentrates on the economic development of the East European and post-Soviet space, with a special focus on the energy sector's integration into the world market. His most recent publication is *Rußlands Energiepolitik: Herausforderung für Europa* (Nomos, 1992).

Volker Perthes is a Research Associate and the current head of the Middle East and Mediterranean Program at the Research Institute for International Affairs (Stiftung Wissenschaft und Politik) in Ebenhausen, Germany. He also teaches at the Geschwister Scholl Institute for Political Science of the Ludwig Maximilian University in Munich. From 1991 to 1993, he was an Assistant Professor at the American University in Beirut. He has authored numerous books on the politics and political economy of the Middle East, including *Der Libanon nach dem Bürgerkrieg* (Nomos, 1996), *The Political Economy of Syria under Asad* (Tauris, 1995), and *The Crisis System in the Middle East: The Risks Accompanying the Settlement Process* in Arabic (Centre for Strategic Studies, Research and Documentation). Dr. Perthes received his Ph.D. in Political Science from the University of Duisburg in 1990.

Johannes Reissner has been a Research Fellow on the Middle East at the Research Institute for International Affairs (Stiftung Wissenschaft und Politik) in Ebenhausen, Germany since 1982. His work concentrates mostly on Iran, the Persian Gulf, and Central Asia. Presently, together with Dr. Citha D. Maass (SWP), he is conducting a research project commissioned by the German Ministry of Defense on Afghanistan in a conflicting geostrategic and geoeconomic environment. In 1995, he served as an observer at the OSCE mission in Dushanbe, Tajikistan. Prior to his work with the SWP, Dr. Reissner was a research assistant for the special research project "Tübinger Atlas des Vorderen Orients" (TAVO) of the University of Tübingen, preparing the maps on the history of the Arabian Peninsula in the nineteenth and twentieth centuries. He holds a Ph.D. in Islamic Studies from the Free University of Berlin; the subject of his thesis was the ideology and politics of the Muslim Brethren in Syria. During the seventies he spent several years in Lebanon, Syria, and Saudi Arabia.

Eberhard Rhein was an official with the European Commission from 1961 to 1996. He has spent his career in various positions related to trade, development, and external policy. From 1985 until his retirement in late 1996, he was Director of the Mediterranean and the Middle East Department at the EU Commission. At present, Dr. Rhein is Adviser to the European Policy Centre, a Brussels-based policy think tank on European affairs. He is the author of many articles on European affairs, in particular on European foreign relations. He holds a Ph.D. in Economics from the University of Hamburg.

Robert Satloff is the Executive Director of The Washington Institute for Near East Policy, a public research and educational foundation established in 1985 to promote informed debate on U.S. policy in the Middle East. A member of the Institute staff since 1985, he has written widely on Palestinian and Jordanian affairs and the political repercussions of Islamic politics on regional stability. He is the author and editor of a number of important works, including *Troubles on the East Bank: Challenges to the Domestic Stability of Jordan* (Praeger, 1996); *From Abdullah to Hussein: Jordan in Transition* (Oxford University Press, 1994); and *The Politics of Change in the Middle East* (Westview, 1993). In addition, he has written two Policy Paper monographs published by the Institute: *"They Cannot Stop Our Tongues": Islamic Activism in Jordan* and *Army and Politics in Mubarak's Egypt.* A professional lecturer at Johns Hopkins' School of Advanced and International Studies (SAIS), Dr. Satloff received his doctorate in Oriental Studies (modern Middle Eastern history) from St. Antony's College, Oxford University.

Joanna Spear is a Lecturer in Proliferation in the Department of War Studies at King's College, London. She was previously Director of the Graduate Program in International Studies at the University of Sheffield. Dr. Spear spent two years as a Post-Doctoral Research Fellow at the Center for Science and International Affairs, Harvard University. She is the author of *Carter and Arms Sales: Implementing the Carter Administration's Conventional Arms Transfer Policy* (Macmillan, 1995), co-editor (with Martin J. Smith) of *The Changing Labour Party* (Routledge, 1992), author of ten chapters in edited volumes, and articles in *Contemporary Security Policy, Harvard International Review*, and *Review of International Studies.* She is currently completing *The Changing Political Economy of the International Arms Trade* (MIT Press, forthcoming).

INDEX

The Robert and Renée Belfer Center for Science and International Affairs

Graham T. Allison, Director
John F. Kennedy School of Government
Harvard University
79 JFK Street, Cambridge MA 02138
(617) 495-1400

The Belfer Center for Science and International Affairs (BCSIA) is the hub of research, teaching, and training in international security affairs, environmental and resource issues, and science and technology policy at Harvard's John F. Kennedy School of Government. The Center's mission is to provide leadership in advancing policy-relevant knowledge about the most important challenges of international security and other critical issues where science, technology, and international affairs intersect.

BCSIA's leadership begins with the recognition of science and technology as driving forces transforming international affairs. The Center integrates insights of social scientists, natural scientists, technologists, and practitioners with experience in government, diplomacy, the military, and business to address these challenges. The Center pursues its mission in four complementary research programs:

- The International Security Program (ISP) addresses the most pressing threats to U.S. national interests and international security.

- The Environment and Natural Resources Program (ENRP) is the locus of Harvard's interdisciplinary research on resource and environmental problems and policy responses.

- The Science, Technology, and Public Policy (STPP) program analyzes ways in which science and technology policy influence international security, resources, environment, and development and such cross-cutting issues as technological innovation and information infrastructure.

- The Strengthening Democratic Institutions (SDI) project catalyzes support for three great transformations in Russia, Ukraine, and the other republics of the former Soviet Union—to sustainable democracies, free market economies, and cooperative international relations.

The heart of the Center is its resident research community of more than one hundred scholars: Harvard faculty, analysts, practitioners, and each year a new, interdisciplinary group of research fellows. BCSIA sponsors frequent seminars, workshops, and conferences, many open to the public; maintains a substantial specialized library; and publishes a monograph series and discussion papers. The Center's International Security Program, directed by Steven E. Miller, publishes the CSIA Studies in International Security, and sponsors and edits the quarterly journal *International Security*.

The Center is supported by an endowment established with funds from Robert and Renée Belfer, the Ford Foundation, and Harvard University, by foundation grants, by individual gifts, and by occasional government contracts.